MERMAID MAGIC

Lucy Cavendish and Serene Conneeley

Blessed Bee Publishing

MERMAID MAGIC: Connecting With the Energy of the Ocean
and the Healing Power of Water

First US edition copyright © 2011 Serene Conneeley and Lucy Cavendish

Conneeley, Serene and Cavendish, Lucy
Mermaid Magic: Connecting With the Energy of the Ocean
and the Healing Power of Water
1st edition
ISBN: 978-0-9870505-3-3
        398.364

1. Mermaids.
2. Nature – religious aspects.
3. Spirituality.
4. Folklore and legends.

Published by Blessed Bee
PO Box 449, Newtown, NSW 2042 Australia
Website: www.BlessedBeePublishing.com
Email: SevenSacredSites@yahoo.com.au

Cover image: Jessica Galbreth
Cover design and mermaid illustrations: Daniella Spinetti
Layout: Serene Conneeley

Thank you...

My thanks to the wild oceans of the planet, their inhabitants and magical beings. May we learn to live with you in wisdom and peace. My family, for teaching me love and respect for the oceans and waterways, to swim and surf and know where the rips are. To Mister Love, for the gift of a surfboard six years ago, when I thought I'd forgotten how to ride a wave. To my darling daughter, for the joy and pleasure I receive in sharing the ways of the ocean with you.

Thank you to all the people I interviewed who shared their merwisdoms – much appreciation. A special thank you to my publisher at Blue Angel, Toni Carmine Salerno, for his support with this second Blessed Bee project. Thank you again to Serene – for everything you do. Most of all, I offer my gratitude to the beings of water, for all that they do for this green and blue planet. They inspire the oceanic conservationists and teach us of the blessings of water, the element that sustains life on this amazing planet that we are all so blessed to be living on and sharing with at this time. May we all support her earth and her waters, so our children have a future here, with her.

With love, Lucy xx

Love and gratitude to my precious beloved, for inspiration, encouragement, belief, support and cups of tea, and for mermaiding with me in Hawaii. To my surf-champ dad and ocean-loving mum, for sharing the magic of water with me, and to my sister for laughter, windsurfing, beach camping and dreams of blue lagoons.

Many thanks to the writers, artists, professors, environmentalists and healers I interviewed, for your passion for the marine realm and your generosity in sharing your wisdom. To Lucy for the joy of our second magical adventure, Jessica for the gorgeous cover image, Sabina for the fresh eyes, and lovely Daniella for the beautiful mermaid illustrations, the cover design and immense patience and sweetness.

And to all those embodying the energy of the mermaids and working to save our oceans and waterways, from the scientists and researchers protecting marine species and halting pollution to the environmental groups and activist surfers, and all the individuals who clean up our beaches, protest about oil drilling, sail pirate ships on the high seas to save the whales, devote their whole life to the dolphins or do any of the million other little things that make such a difference... thank you for making the world a better place, and inspiring us all to care more, do more and be more.

With love, Serene xx

Interviews

Contents

The Magic of Mer...

"But what if I'm a mermaid,
with these jeans of his with her name still on it?"
Tori Amos, American singer

Before conscious memory, there was the water. There was the water inside my mother's womb, that I swam in for nearly ten moons, a mermaid in the ocean within my mother. We are born through water, and we enter into a world of air, but I could swim before I can remember, and I learned to stay afloat, to dive and blow bubbles in rock pools, to stare at the light refracting from her surface, to appreciate the stormy blue blacks and the turquoise greens of her moods. I swam as a child in waves right at the liminal place where the land meets the sea, that doorway between the worlds, the gateway between the world of the water and the world of the air.

I spent hours holding my breath beneath the water, opening my short-sighted eyes to her depths, exploring, feeling my way around the rocks near the pools at the shore. I fished with my father off these rocks, was dragged into the ocean more than once, and at seventeen I learned to surf... It demanded courage, and to the waves I was asked to sacrifice pride, time and sometimes flesh! I learned even more deeply of the waves and the tides, the currents and rips and the direction of her winds. I moved from being immersed in the ocean, wanting to breathe under her waters, to riding her surface, feeling her power, and learning so much about her from moving with her, being moved by her.

The ocean is humbling. She teaches you that no matter how much you think you know, there are always surprises. Surfing is humbling. You fall off, are swept under and turned over and over, to rise to your feet and fly on the surface of water, sharing the space with her creatures. And you fall again and again, but as long as you get up, and push yourself to your feet, you are learning. I love being out there early, as the dolphins move past at sunrise over the kelp reefs. I love how light and fast and strong I feel, flying along the face of a wave. I love how each day she changes. Nothing is repeatable in the ocean.

Mermaids are the intermediaries between the human world and the great, deep energies of grandmother ocean. They keep the song of the waters, and they call out to us, to remind us that the great ocean is our true mother and the home of all life.

Within these pages, you'll learn of mermaid magics, songs and stories, legends and spells. You'll discover how to make and create her symbols, and how to work with these, no matter how near or far you are from the call of the sea. You'll come to understand her tides, her relationship with the moon, hear of the sea witches still working their ancient traditions, and you will be taught to draw and create sea runes of authentic magic.

We've included information on divination and identification of seashells, ways to contribute to marine conservation, the messages of sea creatures and traditions from across the world's most amazing and authentic sea cultures. There are techniques and meditations and journey-workings to connect you with mermaids and the energies of the ocean and water from wells, rivers and streams. By connecting with this book, you'll connect to the life force of this incredible element, and you will quench your thirst for the deep knowledge so many of us quest for.

The sea goddess Yemanja is often depicted as a mermaid, a vast, primordial mermaid with a star shining from her head, a mermaid of power who gives birth to the world... Through her we remember that mermaid energy is not simply light, flirtatious and sexual. Mermaid energy symbolises the birth of the world through water. And even though the mermaid's power and energy has been appropriated and diminished, she is growing stronger again.

She returns, the old one who is part human, part ocean creature – and all humans are born of her. Her mirror is the doorway and the entry point to the unseen world. Her tail is the womb from

which we are all born. The salt water is that which we all are suspended in, that which gives life and oxygen to this world of the land. May this book not only help you connect more and more with the mermaid – may it assist us all in falling deeply in love with the waters of this world. For from them, life herself pours forth and blesses this planet.

Oceanic magics and blessings of the waters to us all,

Lucy Cavendish

The Magic of the Ocean...

*"The sea, once it casts its spell,
holds one in its net of wonder forever."*
Jacques Cousteau, French scientist and oceanographer

I've always loved the ocean. Dad was a surfer (and still is), so we were always close to the sea, be it in Sydney's beach suburbs, on the north coast near Byron Bay or in the surf mecca of Margaret River. We lived in a tent by the ocean when I was a baby, and I was bathed in a bucket on the beach. Later, my sister and I loved swimming in the pale green sea, imagining we were Brooke Shields in *Blue Lagoon*, and feeling so dreamy, free and alive. In summer we'd stay in for as long as we could, peering at reefs and pretty fish, at the sunlight streaming through the sparkling surface. In winter we'd brave the icy water, or stand on the shore, jumping over waves, daring each other to run in, shrieking with joy and wonder. We saved whales when they beached nearby, did coastal clean-ups and rallied against over-development, and I never could bring myself to eat fish or any other creature. We spent school holidays camped on a beach, picking up seashells as Dad surfed, delighting in this magical place where sea meets sand meets sky.

When I moved to the city for uni, I still loved the ocean, especially at night, when moonlight makes the foam of the waves phosphorescent, and the twinkling stars provide gentle light to this shadowy realm. Often I'd go to the beach after a night out, alone or with friends, and dive beneath the dark surface, lulled by the sound of the waves, gazing at the stars in the black sky, swept up in the magic of this in-between place, this in-between time. Even in the pool in my pink apartment block, there were moments of magic as I dove to the bottom then slowly spiralled upwards, watching the sunlight pierce the surface of this surreal underwater realm. And there's nothing on earth like watching the sun set into the ocean in the blazing western sky, something I've missed since moving back to the east coast.

I spent months travelling around the coast of Ireland, drinking in the desolate, dramatic sea cliffs and coves, braving the icy seas to swim with a dolphin. I hiked around tiny Scottish islands and stood in awe inside the sea cave at Staffa, where the ocean rushes in and creates the melody that inspired German composer Mendelssohn's *Hebrides Overture*. I explored the black sand beaches of Hawaii, swimming with dolphins, sea turtles and manta rays, floated in warm Pacific Island oceans and wandered rock strewn New Zealand seashores, along with more of Australia's beautiful coast.

The magic of water isn't limited to the sea though, for it exists in the rivers, wells, lakes and springs of the earth too. The healing waters of Chalice Well and Lourdes, the hot mineral springs that emerge along volcanic mountain slopes, the fountains that dot pilgrimage paths like the Camino, all these sources heal, nourish and enliven us. The magic extends to the weather too – the cleansing rain that soothes our soul as well as the parched earth, the energy of storm clouds and torrential downpours. Water makes up at least sixty per cent of our body, and for witches it is the element that is the basis of cleansing, healing and nurturing rituals and spells.

We can't survive without water, yet the rivers and seas are being used and abused, filled with rubbish, its creatures decimated. Several species will become extinct in our lifetime, and many are dying not even to feed people, but as by-catch in unsustainable fishing methods, or to supply aquariums for dolphin shows. But the worst of humanity often inspires the best of it, and I loved interviewing people for this book, finding out about the wonderful campaigns they are involved in, and the simple changes we can all make to create a better world. The image at the end of *The Cove*, of dolphin protector Ric O'Barry standing in a Japanese mall for days on end to send out his message, breaks my heart – while also filling it with gratitude, love and hope. Ric, along with whale crusader Paul Watson, eco warrior and one-time mermaid Daryl Hannah and surfer Dave Rastovich, are just a few of those committed to protecting the ocean and its inhabitants.

Photo: Justin Sayers. Tail: Daniella Spinetti.

And mermaids? I love swimming in the sea, snorkelling with fish and dreaming of an iridescent tail that can swish me away to a world more tranquil than anything on land. I know they were dreamed up in the majesty of humanity's mind, but I love them for bringing beauty and grace to our world, connecting us with the sea, and reminding us of the need to look after this watery realm and all who live in it. Oceans of love,

Serene Conneeley

What Are Mermaids?

"She is mine own,
And I as rich in having such a jewel
As twenty seas, if all their sand were pearl,
The water nectar, and the rocks pure gold."
William Shakespeare, The Two Gentlemen of Verona

"The mermaids are, to me, the deep elemental beings, the wisdom of the sea, the most often unseen ones who cleanse and protect the waterways and their inhabitants. They are no fantasy – they are an elemental force to be reckoned with. We have conjured images of mermaids and beings that most often reflect back to us something of our own wisdoms and prejudices. Unsoulled sirens of the medieval era, heartless vamps in the early 1900s, feisty girl-women in 2000, and finally, now, they are no longer longing for the land – our stories of mermaids are celebrating their true home, their unique abilities, and no longer forcing them to walk, to breathe air, or to fall in love with the men of the land to acquire a human soul. They are Other, and they need not our approval."

Lucy Cavendish

"Mermaids might have been some weird creation from Atlantean times when the culture got a little confused. Or the mermaid might be a representation of human/dolphin/ocean blending, a symbol of the oneness we feel when we slip into the sea... It's different for everyone I guess, and none of us have the right to tell anyone else what to think and feel about our interactions with life. So, whatever a mermaid means to you is whatever it means to you..."

Dave Rastovich, pro surfer and founder of Surfers For Cetaceans

"Humanity has always longed to swim in the sea and fly in the air, and we created mythical creatures that could do this, imbuing them with all the traits we desired – beauty, strength, independence, freedom, flight. Now we've invented ways to breathe underwater like the mermaids, so we've created a new role for them. It doesn't matter that they are simply a beautiful creation of our imagination, because they have power as a symbol. Today they represent a deep connection to our oceans and to marine conservation, and are rallying people to protect our beautiful earth and its waters. Mermaids are returning in new stories, in books, movies, magazines and even TV ad campaigns, re-imagined for a new audience and brought vividly to life. This doesn't make them true (just as vampire legends, the *Twilight* series and the Sookie Stackhouse books don't mean vampires exist), but they are real to us, touching our hearts, sparking our imagination, and connecting us back to the beautiful ocean, to the water that gives us life, and the healing magic of this beautiful, powerful element."

Serene Conneeley

"My first exhibition was called Sirenes, as in the sirens of the sea. To me, mermaids represent feminine power and allure and deception – using their wiles to lure sailors to their certain death upon crashing rocks. I also love the depiction of mermaids and sirens in films, including *O Brother, Where Art Thou?* and even Ben Stiller in *Zoolander*, posing as a merman in his modelling career. The imagery of mermaids is mysterious and alluring, and leaves a lot of room open for fun and play in interpretation."

Skye Andrew, artist

"Mermaids are the mysterious fish people of the sea. The roaring ocean is their home, in the ocean caves they sleep, under the huge waves they play, deep within the ocean darkness is their kingdom, away from human eyes. To me they represent mystery. I think they live on a different plane to us humans, on an ethereal level. I love to walk along the beach with my feet in the sea water, I find it a very releasing experience, especially when contemplating life's ups and downs. I always come home feeling refreshed in mind and body. I try to mentally send the mermaids messages of love, and let them know that I do care for their water home. I also collect rubbish off the beach, and teach my children to do the same."

Voula Par, earth mumma

"To me, mermaids are mythical, magical figures that represent freedom and escape. That's due in part to their ability to swim so gracefully (which I don't have), the fact that the watery world is their oyster (I'm nervous in the ocean, for the aforementioned reason) and also the fact that they're so often represented bare-breasted, which suggests to me a complete lack of self-consciousness (which I'm plagued by). The fact that humans chose to create in their imaginations such a free-spirited figure suggests we have a strong desire to be rid of our earthly chains. Our fascination with mermaids reveals an honest and sincere wish for a better, less regimented life."

Nigel Bartlett, writer

"Mermaids are like unicorns and dragons, and exist in another realm. They are mythical, and are for those who love to dream and dare to hope. I think they are real but of another dimension, and can be visible when they choose to cross the veil, ie in times of trouble to fishermen or drowning folk. I believe they can reach out and connect in some way to female humans who are in essence like merwomen. I've seen them in my mind's eye, but haven't interacted with them. They represent beauty, a yearning feminine sexuality that's out of reach to human males, and are magical. I believe they communicate with King Neptune, and are a balance to his masculine energy."

Karen Wheeler, healer

"I certainly don't see mermaids as ever having been real, instead for me they are an archetypal sea goddess with all the related meanings of the element of water. I also relate them to the temptress, but their energy is sad, hollow and searching. They are untouchable by mere land-dwelling mortals, and to gain a soul they must marry outside their species. So to me the mermaid archetype represents sadness, searching, loneliness and grief."

Angela McDermott, magical woman

"To me, mermaids represent temptation into the deep. They are beautiful, lyrical creatures who tempted people to go with them into the ocean, probably not realising we can't breathe underwater. I think the message of the mermaids is: 'Beware all that seems beautiful, because sometimes it can lead you to your doom.' I believe they are etheric creatures, although there have been sightings and stories of merpeople through the ages, so there may be a kernel of truth."

Andrew Stopps, music teacher

"Mermaids represent the lure to dive deep below the surface of emotions, to explore the dark depths that can be filled with fear but also excitement. The best word for them is temptation. As to whether they're real, I couldn't say for sure, but there are so many parts of the ocean that are unknown. I think they've removed themselves from physical contact and instead communicate through the astral or dream planes. I believe there are people who carry mermaid energy, and when I swim in the ocean I feel the healing energy the water provides."

Brendan Hancock, shamanic witch and crafter

"I love mermaids. I have a painting of one from Hawaii, and I speak to her as I pass by. I don't think mermaids are real, but her image represents a feminine healing energy and a playful free spirit, and wishful thinking about being able to swim under the sea and play with the creatures. And when I run meditation classes, I always get asked to do my Mermaid Going to the Crystal Cave meditation, as people seem to relate to it and find it healing and relaxing."

Sharne Michelle, meditation teacher

"To me, mermaids are the ocean's soul personified. When I was little and wanted to be a mermaid like Ariel, I felt they were in the waves, that they whispered to me between the roars of the waves crashing on the sand, and there was a feeling of completeness that came from being in the water. I'd ask them to create bigger waves so I could ride them to shore, and almost every time I asked, it worked. I believe they are real, but that they exist in a different realm to where we are."

Cynthia Cano, magical traveller

"I love the mermaids. To me they are magical. I love the idea that they could exist, but then logic sets in ☺ I do believe there are what the ancients used to call the sirens, so perhaps they did exist but no longer do? My interest is that they are illustrated so often in old texts and literature – how could they have not been real?"

Vivian Agios, designer

"I believe mermaids exist. I remember past lives as a mermaid, and since I was a child I've always wanted to breathe underwater. To this day I swim like a mermaid, with my ankles together rather than kicking in the traditional way. I believe more and more people are remembering how mermaids once played an important role in their life, or perhaps that they too were once a mermaid or merman."

Trish Anderson-Young, crystal healer

"It would be lovely to think that somewhere in the vastness of the oceans there are mermaids, that these half-women, half-fish creatures exist, but the History Channel had a doco that showed what a real mermaid would look like if it existed. She would not be the beautiful creature we imagine – her human half would have had to adapt to seawater and therefore be bloated, as would her face, and it was proven that hair can't be maintained in seawater, therefore she would be bald. They also showed a rare mammal, the dugong, which is often mistaken for a mermaid. From a distance they have the flowing effect of hair, the long tail and fins near the top of their body that look like arms. Out of water it'd take more imagination to believe it was a mermaid, but if it was swimming away from you in murky water, I could believe it. Then you get into the selkie legends, and it's nice to think that maybe, just maybe... "

Suzanne Adams, fantasy baker

"Mermaids represent the flow of the ocean and the cleansing and healing properties of water. I feel like a mermaid when I'm swimming! They remind me of salty sea dogs, tales of drunken sailors, and the effects of being at sea for weeks and months creating visions from a mixture of loneliness and hope. Mind you, there are some unexplained mermaid tales that could bode true..."

Sabina Collins, writer and musician

"I've always been fascinated by mermaids. I liked the idea that we had some powerful force moving in the sea that was unexplained. I always thought of mermaids as being wondrous, mysterious and free creatures, our more natural and earthed cousins. I like to think they are real as we have no real understanding of the depths and secrets of the darkest parts of the sea. Though I can understand why they keep a low profile – I'd want to protect my privacy too!"

Martine Allars, author of the forthcoming book The Last Mermaid

"I think every little girl's dream is to be a mermaid or to see a mermaid. When I was young I'd go to the beach and cover my legs in the sand. And I love the water. People from different cultures have the same idea of what mermaids are, so that's a cool thing to think about. I'd like to believe, why not? I wanted to do *Aquamarine* as there hadn't been a mermaid story in a while – obviously there's *The Little Mermaid* and *Splash*, and I wanted to do something like that."

Emma Roberts, actress

"To me, mermaids are a representation of that greatest of human traits – imagination. I think we often forget just how marvellous this trait is. Only homo sapiens, with their wild ability to postulate notions of a half-fish body (or a half-horse body, or Spider-powers, or a rubber Batsuit) could dream up something so ridiculously wonderful and magical as a mermaid. It's that same imagination that allows us to dream, to invent, to service myth and science and music and movies and poetry and iPads and Darth Vader and faerytales and magic and wonder... And mermaids."

Justin Sayers, musician

"I think mermaids are beautiful water faery like beings, and there can be both good and evil ones. I think they're real – those myths and legends had to come from somewhere, right? I've loved reading about them. *The Little Mermaid* is such a lovely story, and I think Hans Christian Andersen knew about the world of magic and all its creatures, since he wrote so many wonderful children's stories that have delighted and captured the hearts and minds of children and adults alike for years. I think mermaids can be archetypal too, sea goddesses like Aphrodite and Venus are protectors of the sea, which can also represent that they are protectors of our emotions."

Jessika Larcombe, witch

"When I was young I saw mermaids as faerytale creations, figments of my imagination. Now I believe they exist etherically, but are very real. I've been in the ocean and felt large heavy flapping tails behind me, and something swim under me. I've heard giggles and received beautiful, gentle guidance, and these experiences have seemed real. I believe they are mermaids. They have a friendly, free and wild energy about them. They're like big sisters encouraging me to fulfil my dreams and be my true self, without worrying about what people might think. After a very sad relationship break-up, the mermaids have shown me why I need to be single at this time, and have slowly helped to heal my broken heart, helping me feel stronger and not so afraid to love again. Mermaids seem cheeky and flirty, and have helped me laugh at myself, and to develop socially. Since swimming in the ocean I've become more feminine and sensual. Everyone needs something to believe in. I believe in mermaids, and they haven't let me down yet. How do I know that? Because I'm happy."

Sarah Byrne, teacher and surfer

"Mermaids were a huge part of my childhood imagination – swimming like a mermaid was so peaceful and free. There is something delicious about feeling and moving around, weightless and caressed by water. So for me it was part imagination, part sensory, part activity! They're a beautiful representation of the feminine beauty of ocean creatures, a combination of memories held deep in our DNA and the graceful dugong, so human-like in its mothering. The undine, a water elemental, might also be credited to an underwater creature taking on human form, and it could be the ability to see spirit that exists in the oceanic world as opposed to the earthly plane. So I do think mermaids exist, along with all other keepers and protectors of the magical realms."

Liza Feeney, earth mother and witch

"Most of the wedding ceremonies I conduct are on the beach, which is truly magical. The barefoot bride stands by her groom alongside the waves lapping the shore, and guests are swept away by the romance. The backdrop is the ocean, as vast and deep as the love they share for each other at that moment. The occasional playful dolphin dances through the waves while I welcome the guests, and I like to think that nearby a mermaid is watching and bestowing her blessings on the union too, representing the luscious, all-encompassing and seductive love people experience once in their lifetime."

Anita Revel, civil marriage celebrant

"Mermaids are just a wonderful figment of the imagination – and wishful thinking on the part of ancient mariners who had spent far too long at sea, away from the company of women. It's no surprise the mermaids who feature in sailors' fantasies look like underwater Barbie dolls, with perfect figures, bare breasts and long, flowing hair. But how could such beautiful women reach a vessel in the middle of the ocean, days from land? Why, if they had a dolphin-like tail, gills and the desire to seduce men of course! Which is hilarious considering one theory is that mermaids came about when seafarers saw dugongs – which more closely resemble obese, unattractive peasant women than fantasy babes. Some of the darker Greek myths and classic faerytales involve beautiful mermaids who trick men into joining them in their underwater world, where they can't survive. To me, this darker, evil side of mermaids makes more interesting fiction than the teenage-girl craving for jewel-like scales and super powers."

Elisabeth Knowles, journalist

"I created what I thought was the perfect girl by definition, then assigned a symbol to that girl – and that symbol was a mermaid."

Brian Grazer, producer of Splash

"I didn't want the mermaid, Madison, to be an object. I really wanted her to be a noble character, powerful in her own right, and really worthy of deep love. Daryl was perfect for the mermaid because she had to have a simplicity, but she also had to have a quality that forced your eyes to her. We found with Daryl that she was so capable of swimming beautifully, and holding her breath, and not allowing bubbles to escape, that she could actually exert herself, and hold her breath, and act, for sixty seconds at a time."

Ron Howard, director Splash

"I had been obsessed with the Hans Christian Andersen faerytale *The Little Mermaid* ever since I was a kid. And I fantasised about being one myself – I tied my feet together in the pool and practised swimming like that from a very early age. The best thing about *Splash*'s success was little kids loving it. To this day, when they come up to me, they're like, "Madison!" I've met *hundreds* of kids named Madison, and they all want to go swimming with me. I love that."

Daryl Hannah, Madison in Splash, and environmentalist

"On some level I believe mermaids are real. When I'm near the water I have mermaid dreams and feel their energy. And I've always adored mermaid stories, especially the movie *Splash*, which was such a joyous story for me. So when it came to naming our daughter we wanted a name that was as magical as her coming into the world, as I had a very difficult pregnancy. My husband is a clearance diver in the navy, our son was already a little fish, and we lived on the water. During the pregnancy I knew I wanted to give her a mermaid name, as I felt even more drawn to the energy of the sea. I came up with lots, but my husband didn't like any. Finally I suggested Madison, the mermaid from *Splash*, and he loved it, even though we'd never heard anyone use it as a name. We added an extra D as it looked prettier and more feminine. Our Maddison is now eighteen and there are lots of other Madisons, but at the time I was constantly repeating, spelling and explaining the name to very mixed responses. Now my mermaid is at uni, swims like a fish, loves scuba diving and snorkelling, has crystal blue eyes and is very mermaidy beautiful. We chose the right name!"

Cheralyn Darcey, environmental artist

Jessica's Mermaid Magic

American Jessica Galbreth is an inspiring, magical artist who has long painted mermaids, faeries and other mythological subjects, and she also makes jewellery and altered art pieces. She is now embarking on a new artistic venture, painting angels to add more beauty, hope and peace to the world. Visit Jessica at www.thevintageangel.com.

I consider mermaids to be fantasy creatures, something beautiful from the imaginations of humans, conjured to celebrate our longing for the sea. I think just as all of us have wished to fly with the birds, we've also wished to be able to breathe underwater and swim with the dolphins. I definitely wanted to be a mermaid when I was a kid – I had a special dive with a mermaid "kick" at the end that I was especially proud of. You wouldn't be too impressed with my adult version, but I was pretty swift with my moves as a little one!

I still feel a strong connection to the ocean. There isn't anything quite like the smell of the sea or the sound of rolling waves. To me it celebrates the power and beauty of nature in all its glory.

I've seen manatees swim, and they are amazing! They have such an otherworldly look, so I'm not at all surprised that scientists believe they are the basis of the mermaid myth. As an artist, it's the mermaid's ethereal beauty – the long flowing locks, seashell adornments and the wistful freedom in their eyes – that appeals to me most. My favourite story is Disney's *The Little Mermaid*. I love how Ariel, who lived the life of a mermaid princess that so many of us little girls dreamed of, longed for our human world. It perfectly illustrates our tendency to wish for what we don't have, and reminds us to appreciate the beauty of our own world. It is also a wonderful message of two separate, different worlds merging as one in the name of love.

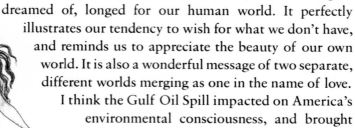

I think the Gulf Oil Spill impacted on America's environmental consciousness, and brought focus to the importance of our oceans. Without them we could not live, and perhaps we needed a reminder. I hope the silver lining will be measures to prevent it happening again.

Daniella's Artistic Magic

Daniella Spinetti is an Australian graphic designer and artist who has designed book covers and created illustrations for *The Book of Faery Magic* and *Seven Sacred Sites*, as well as the beautiful mermaids in this book. She lives in Sydney with her husband, but loves escaping to the warm ocean waters of Hawaii, Thailand and the Greek Islands.

To me, mermaids represent ethereal beauty and tranquillity. All aquatic creatures bring a great deal of calm to my senses. There's also a strong female energy associated with them – my young nieces all want to dress-up as mermaids! And I used to drive my mother mad wanting to be a mermaid when I was young. I'd swim in our pool for hours, refusing to get out, even at meal times. She called me her "water baby" as I spent more time in the water than on dry land!

I have a strong connection to the ocean, and always book holidays to places where I can be near the water. I love waking up and being able to smell the ocean and feel its breeze, even in winter. I've always loved swimming and the feeling of weightlessness in water. When I doodle it's often curvy lines that resemble waves, I'm enthralled by underwater documentaries, and I absolutely love seaweed salad!

As an artist, the fact that mermaids are water creatures gives rise to thoughts of flowing curved lines, soft shading and sea-foam greens and blues. One of my favourite periods in art history is the Pre-Raphaelite movement. John W Waterhouse painted a gorgeous work, *A Mermaid*, that captures the essence of the legend – romantic and serene, with a beautifully haunting undertone.

The stories of mermaids enchanting sailors and luring them to their deaths affected me deeply. I was always so upset by the suggestion that such beautiful creatures (moreover, women) could be responsible for such terrible things. I don't think mermaids are real in a physical sense, but they've pervaded cultures through mythology, and I love that the legends have inspired artists, writers and musicians through the ages, as well as creating a respect for our oceans and all they contain.

Mermaid Timeline

"Down where the mermaids pluck and play,
On their twangling harps in a sea-green day."
Walter de la Mare, English poet

Marvellous Events in Mermaid History

There is a vast uncrossed and uncharted ocean of pre-history in regards to the wonderful mermaid. And while we may know of some landmarks upon the way, there is still so much left to discover. For even in crossing that ocean, we have only just covered her surface. Here, though, are some highlights of the journey into Mermaidia and sea wonders so far!

Lemurian tales and memories offer us visions and past lives as shapeshifting aquatic beings who could move in to and out of the water, become tailed, or breathe air. Latter-day Atlantean memories speak of experiments where Lemurian shapeshifting was attempted to be replicated by making "mermaids". Other Lemurian shapeshifters opted for operations to give them legs, a kind of hobbled foot that is reminiscent of the foot-bound women of China, a practice that only ceased in the 1950s.

Tales of drowned lands, like Kumari Kandam off the southern tip of India, merge with creation stories of aquatic beings such as *Hanuman and the Mermaid*, deities who have resonance in Thailand and Cambodia. The submerged land of Lyonesse, off the west coast of England's Cornwall, and the drowned land of Ys that lies west of France's Brittany, are said to be the homes of beings who transformed into mermaids after their homelands were taken by the sea.

5000BCE: Oannes, the sun god of the ancient Sumerians, was depicted as a human-fish hybrid. He ascended from the ocean each morning and descended into her each evening, and was his sun self in daylight and his aquatic self at night. There are many paintings of Oannes the sea being that remain to this day, including those that cover an entire wall in the Louvre Museum in Paris.

At the same time, Atargatis the merwoman was the goddess of the moon to the Sumerians. She was symbolic of the night, the depths of emotions and sexuality, and the power of the sea. Offerings were made to her by fishermen, and she was depicted with the tail of a sea creature such as a dolphin. She was of the stars and of the sea, and was echoed in later images of the African and Brasilian sea goddess Yemanja, with her star, and Stella Maris, the Christian Virgin of the Sea, as well as the Egyptian goddess Isis, who was also depicted with a star and associated with the sea. Was Atargatis the precursor of the goddess Astarte of the Phoenicians?

2000BCE: Aphrodite, the Greek goddess of love, beauty and sexuality, was born from the sea. Associated with dolphins and shells, she's an aquatic goddess who also roamed the earth, but must return to the sea. She loved the gods Ares and Hephaestus, who both worked with the element of fire. She was the goddess of love, but was also worshipped by sailors wishing for favours of fair winds and great treasures while at sea. Her Roman counterpart, the goddess Venus, shares her oceanic characteristics with her.

500BCE: Salacia, the Roman goddess of the sea, was represented with a dolphin tail. Tales of merfolk, including selkies (seal men and women) and shapeshifted merpeople who walked the land on legs and swam with a tail in the sea, flourished off the coastal kingdoms of modern-day Wales, Scotland, Cornwall and northeast England. In these legends the mermaids are beautiful, and helpful, aiding the village people if they are lost at sea or caught in storms, helping them fish, and being a welcome part of coastal life.

355BCE: Classical Greek philosopher Plato's dialogues, *Timaeus* and *Critias*, were written. They contained the first mention of Atlantis, describing her peak, her virtues and her destruction. The first volume covered speculation on the nature of the physical world and human beings, while the second was a conversation between the philosophers Socrates and Timaeus and the politicians Critias and Hermocrates, in which they discussed the fall of Atlantis as a cautionary tale for the Greece of the day and its growing hubris.

70CE: Roman philosopher Pliny the Elder described in his works the nereids, females who have bodies akin to the fishes, scaled and strange, blue yet beautiful, who swim in the depths of the ocean.

500CE: *The Physiologus*, a spectacular bestiary, was published, attributed to many writers over the years, and translated and added to over the centuries. Within its glorious pages were detailed many mermaid sightings; they were described as having the upper body of a woman and the lower body of a fish, divided at the sacral chakra.

1150: A mermaid was carved in the back of one of the pews in a church in the Cornish village of Zennor, which remains to this day to commemorate the legend of the Mermaid of Zennor. A local man, Matthew Trewella, was a wonderful singer in the church choir, and it's said that the mermaid herself carved the figure into the back of the pew as she sat in her human form, listening to Matthew sing. They fell in love, and he left the world of the air to journey to the sea world, living there to this day with his mermaid love, although they still visit the church and sing to the visitors.

1200s: A sinister propaganda campaign was launched by the Church, and the mermaid began to disassociate from the benevolent being who aided sailors, blessed the fish and cared for the sea. A monk, Bartholomew Angelicus, accused mermaids of stealing and beguiling sailors, enchanting them and dragging them from their ships to drown, which started to be echoed in poetry and art. This led to entries in *Malleus Malleficaram*, the handbook for Inquisitors during the Burning Years, stating that witches could be ducked – and if they didn't drown, it meant they could breathe underwater and were merfolk, and thus were damned. The legend of the heartless sea-female began to take root and grow wildly in the medieval era, where superstitious folk seeking answers for any ailment blamed witches or their oceanic counterpart – mermaids.

1493: The great Italian explorer Christopher Columbus wrote in his sea journal of seeing three mermaids as he sailed through the warm Caribbean waters. "They were not as beautiful as they are painted, although they have a human appearance in the face."

1500s: Artist, inventor and visionary Leonardo da Vinci played around with the idea of flippers for swimming, inspired, some say, after sighting a mermaid. (Swim fins were properly invented in the 1700s by United States Founding Father and scientist Benjamin Franklin, who got the idea from the webbed feet of frogs, and refined by French naval commander Louis de Corlier in the 1930s.)

1515: Sayyida al Hurra, whose name means "noble lady who is free and independent; the woman sovereign who bows to no superior authority" had to flee to Morocco with her family when she was a child to escape the Spanish Inquisition. When her first husband died, she became governor of the northern port city of Tetouan, and turned to piracy to avenge herself on those who had destroyed her childhood. She became a Pirate Queen and controlled the western Mediterranean Sea. When she later married the King of Morocco, she refused to give up her wild seafaring ways, or to have the wedding ceremony in Fez, where he ruled from. So the king moved to be with her, the first time a royal wedding took place away from the capital.

1530: Grace O'Malley, the Pirate Queen of Ireland, was born. After her father's death, Grainne Ni Mhaille led her clan. She invaded England, was the respected adversary of Queen Elizabeth I, and refused to live by the laws of the land that said she could not go to sea or be the chieftain of her people. She lived on the sea all her days, and became a symbol of Irish freedom from English oppression. She was known as the Sea Queen Of Connemara, and commanded three ships and two hundred men from the 1560s to 1603.

1560: Near the island of Mandar, off the west coast of Ceylon (now Sri Lanka), some fishermen claimed to have captured in their nets seven mermaids and mermen. Bosquez, physician to the Viceroy of Goa, performed autopsies on them, which were written up in the official colonial records. He concluded that the internal and external structure of the sea beings resembled that of humans.

1599: A mermaid and her human lover were reported to have been seen embracing at the mouth of the Nile River in Egypt. The encounter was written up in the beguiling *Historia Monstrorum*.

1608: Renowned English explorer Henry Hudson recorded his mermaid sighting near Russia. "It had the tail of a porpoise and was speckled like a macrell," he wrote. "And it was looking earnestly on the men." He described his mermaid as having long black hair, white skin and a woman's breasts.

1614: John Smith, a respected Puritan, said he had seen a mermaid off the coastline of Massachusetts in the US, and was in fear for his soul.

1653: Dutch explorer Hendrick Hamel was shipwrecked off the coast of Korea. He spent ten months there, and wrote in his memoirs of the mermaids he saw, who fed him and the other sailors while they were awaiting rescue.

1718: Off the coast of Borneo, the fourth largest island in the world, a "sea wife" is captured, and held captive in a piteously small tank for observation. She died after several days of this "examination", and, according to her captors, was said to have uttered cries like those of a mouse until her death.

1809: *The Times* in England ran a letter from a schoolmaster who said he'd seen a naked woman sitting on a rock on the Scottish coast, who was plump, full-breasted and green-haired, and that he believed that she was a mermaid because no human woman would swim out that deep through the waves.

1811: A farmer near Kintyre, an island peninsula in western Scotland, reported seeing a mermaid bathing in the ocean, washing her hair then brushing it out in the sunlight as she sat on a rock.

1830: A farm woman in the islands of the Outer Hebrides of Scotland spotted a mermaid in the water, and attempted to capture her by dragging her to shore. The mermaid refused to come to shore willingly, resisted, and was beaten to death by a group of women who attacked her with stones. A local physician and scholar, Alexander Carmichael, conducted the autopsy, describing in great detail the remains of the murdered mermaid.

1837: *The Little Mermaid*, the faerytale by Danish author Hans Christian Andersen, was published. The symbolically loaded story – the mermaid sacrifices her tail for legs and loses her voice, simply to find love with a man who does not return it – ends with the mermaid soulless and turned to sea foam, an echo of the medieval tales where the mermaid is a soulless entity. At this time, scholars of the Christian Church were still debating whether women had souls.

1842: The infamous Feejee Mermaid was placed on display by legendary showman Phineas T Barnum at his American Museum in New York. However it was actually the torso and head of a baby monkey sewn to the back half of a fish and covered in paper-mache. The mummified body of a creature supposedly half-woman and half-fish became a common feature of sideshows of the time.

1857: A sailor reported seeing a mermaid with "full breasts, dark complexion and a comely face" off the coast of Cornwall in England.

1890: Colonial authorities banned female pearl diving in the Torres Strait Islands off the top of Australia, scandalised by this traditional form of pearl harvesting and the nudity of the female divers. Korea and Japan also had a long history of naked women divers, who could have been thought to be mermaids, and represented an unpopular concept of women as independent breadwinners.

1926: American swimmer and Olympic gold medallist Gertrude Ederle became the first woman to swim across the English Channel, also breaking the existing record, held by a man, by nearly two hours despite wild seas. She was dubbed the Queen of the Waves.

1946: Newton Perry, an ex-Navy SEALS trainer, came up with the fantastic concept of having a theme park devoted to mermaids, which he dubbed Weeki Wachee in honour of the nearby spring. The main attraction was an incredible underwater show featuring live mermaids – human women with mermaid tails who free dive and swim with only an air hose, rather than a weighty tank, to survive. This City of Live Mermaids went on to become one of Florida's most famous attractions. Its fortunes fell when Disney World and other theme parks opened up nearby, but it is now enjoying a renaissance, with a new wave of performing mermaids.

1947: On the coast of Scotland's tiny Isle of Muck, part of the Inner Hebrides, an elderly man reported seeing a mermaid sitting on one of his lobster traps brushing her hair.

1971: Starbucks, with its twin-tailed mermaid logo, opened its first store in Seattle. The original mermaid was considered too provocative however, because she was holding her tails apart – supposedly a siren-like invitation for customers to have sex with her – and so the logo was revised, although it remains a mermaid.

1971: Greenpeace was founded to protect the environment and the oceans and other habitats of the world. Years later one of the founders splintered off to form Sea Shepherd, warriors of the sea who put their lives on the line to save all sea creatures.

1976: Jacques Mayol, holder of a dozen world free diving records, became the first person to descend to a hundred metres, and he later broke his own record. During this dive his heartbeat decreased from sixty beats per minute to twenty-seven, an aspect of the mammalian diving reflex of whales, seals and dolphins, and he explored the idea that humans had hidden aquatic potential that could be activated by rigorous training. The movie *The Big Blue* was inspired by his remarkable life and mindset. One of the original Dolphin Children, he believed in the contemporary evolution of Human Dolphinus, and that humans would evolve to live in the ocean. He believed dolphins were his family, and that he was a human dolphin, often speaking of the "dolphin within me".

1982: The Ri was documented in *Cryptozoology*, the journal of the International Society of Cryptozoology (cryptozoology is the search for animals whose existence has not yet been proven, such as the Loch Ness monster). The article, *The Ri – The Unidentified Aquatic Animals of New Ireland* [in Papua New Guinea], said: "An aquatic creature roughly resembling the traditional mermaid and sometimes identified with it, is reportedly known through a variety of encounters with natives of New Ireland. The Ri, as they are called, are frequently sighted by fishermen, occasionally netted or found dead on beaches, and sometimes eaten. Males, females and juveniles are reported... It is unlikely that the animals are dugongs or porpoises, both of which are known to, and readily identified by, the natives." They are described as having human heads and genitalia, a tail and fins...

1997: The birth of Aquatic children – called Dolphin children by some – began, and they added their voices to those of Indigo, Rainbow and Crystal children. Dolphin children have a persistent smile and constant laughter, an insatiable desire to be in or near water, particularly the sea, ocean activism, and a fascination for and belief in mermaids. They represent liberty and freedom of spirit, go their own way, and change the world by being, as Gandhi said, the change they want to see in the world. If they are not taken to or in water they become ill or depressed – they quite literally need the sea.

2002: Unprecedented depths were reached in the free diving world. Cayman Islander Tanya Streeter, nicknamed The Mermaid, reached a depth of a hundred and sixty metres, and stayed underwater for more than three minutes, beating the men's record too.

2004: Following the tragic Boxing Day tsunami of 2004 that devastated vast areas of Thailand and Sri Lanka, there were reports of mermaid corpses being washed up on beaches. The most convincing looking was on the coast at Channai, India, although it was found to have been made from fish and ape parts.

2010, January 3: Scientists found similarities in the brain cortexes of dolphins and humans, and concluded that dolphins are complex and intelligent. They presented a paper saying that it is "morally repugnant" to mistreat them. A month later, Thomas White, professor of ethics at Loyola Marymount University, LA, author of a series of academic studies suggesting dolphins should have rights, declared: "The scientific research suggests that dolphins are 'non-human persons' who qualify for moral standing as individuals."

2010: Human mermaid and oceanic conservationists including Hannah Mermaid and Mermaid Melissa took ocean activism into a new realm. The development of realistic, aesthetically beautiful and lightweight mermaid tails has progressed in leaps and bounds. Mike van Daal, who made Doreen Virtue's mermaid tail, and others have developed this craftsmanship to a new level.

2011, February: Japan called a halt to whaling in the Southern Ocean after the take-it-to-them campaign of Sea Shepherd's eighty-eight volunteers overwhelmed the "scientific research" whaling vessels.

2011, June 18: The Mermaids and Pirates Ball was held in Torpoint, Cornwall, for the first time, as part of the 3 Wishes Faery Fest. Karen Kay, editor of *Mermaids & Mythology* magazine, hosted it. Across the Atlantic Ocean on the same day, the Ninth Annual Mermaid Parade and Ball was held in Coney Island, New York.

2011, August 12 and 13: The World Mermaid Awards and Mermaid Convention were held for the first time. Hosted by Sita Lange and the Maui Mermaids at a Las Vegas hotel, it raised money to save the oceans and maintain water purity. Doreen Virtue's band Obsidian played, and it featured the largest Mermaid Pool Party ever.

Hannah's Real-Life Mermaid Magic

As a child Hannah Fraser wanted to be a mermaid, and she's achieved her dream, transforming into a siren of the deep for TV ads, photo shoots, films and aquarium performances. And it's as a mermaid she's been able to pursue her passion – protecting the ocean and its creatures. A vegetarian yoga practitioner and scuba diver, she recently relocated to Los Angeles to work full-time as a mermaid, after fifteen years in Byron Bay, Australia. Visit her at www.HannahFraser.com.

I've always wanted to be a mermaid. I'd prefer to live in the ocean and just come up for a good dance now and then. I love being weightless, and I feel the most free and expressive underwater. If I can be a visual link to inspire others who have become disconnected from this amazing world, I'll feel I've done something worthwhile.

I made my first tail at age nine, with a plastic tablecloth and pillow stuffing, and I swam in it endlessly until it disintegrated. I was hooked on that feeling, so when I went swimming I'd pretend I had a tail, and I drew pictures of mermaids incessantly. The passion never went away, but it wasn't until I did an underwater modelling job that I realised I could make a new tail and put it to good use. I didn't think at that point it would be a career, it was just my artistic passion.

Being a professional mermaid is a self-created job. It's not easy. It requires graceful movement while holding the breath in a constantly shifting environment, hindered by blurry underwater vision and a costume that binds the legs together. It takes four months of sewing, gluing and constructing to make one of my tails. There's also basic physical preparation, including regular yoga, aerobics, dance and breath practise to help expand the lungs to hold my breath longer – I can hold it two minutes while performing underwater. For photos you must keep the eyes open and the face relaxed while moving slowly enough for the photographer to capture just the right moment – and yes, salt water and chlorine really sting your eyes, especially after six hours in the water! No one can see

clearly underwater, human eyes aren't made that way, but you can learn to be comfortable with it.

I slow my heartbeat by going into a meditative state where I'm not thinking about anything other than where I am, especially if I'm swimming with dangerous wild animals. I need to be aware of them, their movements and how they react to me, so I can adjust what I do to be safe and non-threatening. Swimming with great white sharks was beyond overwhelming! I was so scared I had sweaty palms and nightmares for weeks, and when I did it I was in a fight or flight, moment-of-facing-death experience, but was also very calm, and super conscious of every move the sharks made. I did this for a special on shark intelligence, because sharks always get a really bad rap, and because I wanted to get over my fear of them and show that while they are one of the most effective predators in the world, they are also intelligent sentient beings, not just mindless killing machines ready to gobble the first human that hops in the water with them.

One of the first activism events I did was to defend a water estuary in my town. They wanted to build a four-lane bridge in a sensitive area, so I placed myself in my mermaid tail on the middle of the bridge during a rally in order to stop traffic. The police came, and were at a loss as to how to move a mermaid. It made the front page, and I realised I could make a difference by bringing what I love to a cause. I also worked on a doco for estuaries and wetlands, and protested at Taiji in Japan.

A mermaid is a person who is at one with the ocean, who feels it is "home" in some way. I think there was a dreamtime when mermaids were part of our reality, but we've lost touch with that. I'd like to help awaken people to their personal experience of creative play, where the lines of fantasy and reality blend. Being a mermaid is my life-long expression of joy.

Famous Mermaids

"I'm no ordinary girl,
I'm from the deep blue underworld,
Land or sea, the world's my oyster,
I'm the pearl... No ordinary girl."
Shelley Rosenberg, Australian songwriter, H2O: Just Add Water soundtrack

Sea Sirens in Movies and Literature

Throughout time there have been stories and legends about sea beings, from the Greek and Roman gods of the ocean and the half-woman, half-seal selkies of the remote Celtic isles to the adorable half-mermaid Emily Windsnap in today's best-selling book series. But unlike the faeries, who are fairly universal in look and character all around the world, the mermaids of lore, legend and literature differ from country to country. They can be anything, and do anything, and have any one of a number of creation stories – from the tormented souls of women who have drowned to unions between water deities and mortals to the very foam of the sea itself.

The popular idea of today's mermaid was born from Hans Christian Andersen's faerytale *The Little Mermaid*, about a pretty, sweet natured and kind young sea princess who longs to walk on land and win the heart of a human prince, and sacrifices her tail and her voice (and, some would say, her self-respect) to do so. For his mermaid, the Danish author drew on the water spirits that sixteenth century Swiss physician Paracelsus called undines, who had to marry a mortal to gain a soul. And in turn, Hans's mermaid influenced every writer, artist and movie-maker that came after.

When the film *Splash* was released in 1984, a whole generation of girls wanted to be mermaids, to swim so joyously in the ocean, to be so free and so desirable, and to find such love. Madison became a popular name for girls, and mermaid costumes were the outfit of choice at fancy dress parties. Five years later, Disney gave *The Little Mermaid* a happy ending, enchanting people further with the idea of these beautiful sea beings and the qualities of love they embodied.

But in the Middle Ages mermaids had been depicted as scary, mean-spirited and vain, spending their time brushing their hair on the rocks and delighting in luring men to their doom. They were portrayed as unlucky omens, foretelling storms and disaster – and provoking both – and tormenting sailors with their fate. They were soulless and cruel, and always longing for human qualities and human redemption.

The paintings of the nineteenth century reflected this too, such as the iconic *A Mermaid* and *The Siren*, both by John W Waterhouse, *The Land Baby* by John Collier and *The Fisherman and the Syren* by Frederic Leighton, which show lots of hair combing, gazing at their own reflections and dragging their lovers under the waves to a watery grave. Modern artists have added goddess elements to this traditional image, making their mermaids stronger, more independent and far more sensual and intriguing.

In legends they were treated more kindly. In Irish tales Li Ban was an Otherworldly woman, depicted first as a sea bird, then a deity. She was later Christianised, becoming a mortal woman transformed into a mermaid in a flood, who emerged three hundred years later as a baptised saint. In Scottish legend the mermaids are called ceasgs, which translates as maid of the wave, magical half-woman, half-salmon creatures, the latter symbolising wisdom.

In the stories of China, the tears of their beautiful mermaids turned into pearls, and they were said to spend their time working for humans – although they were less friendly to those who sought to catch them, singing them into a coma! There are also Native American legends of a golden tailed merman who guided starving tribes across the ocean to new lands when ice covered their home. And when William Shakespeare wrote about a mermaid in *A Midsummer Night's Dream*, she was a force of feminine power, calming angry seas and charming stars from the night sky.

There is no singular idea of what a mermaid is. Sometimes they are portrayed as water sprites and nymphs, sometimes they are sea goddesses, and sometimes they are seals who come ashore and drop their skins to emerge as women. In European countries they are the restless ghosts of drowned women. The sirens of Homer's *The Odyssey* were half-woman, half-bird, not fish-women at all, and in the Americas their "mermaid" was a selfish girl who was transformed into a sea goddess when her father tossed her overboard to drown.

Mermaids are whatever we want them to be, and that is part of their charm – we can imbue them with any qualities or powers. Today they are rising up from the sea again to recapture our imagination, prettier and kinder than many from the past, stronger and more powerful, and with a great passion for marine conservation. They are feisty eco warriors like the Venice mermaids of Michelle Lovric's beautiful books, who are saving a city from itself; the graceful, more confident and secret half of Liz Kessler's Emily Windsnap; the sassy schoolgirls who put friendship before boys in *H2O: Just Add Water*; and objects of sensual, sexual beauty in ads hawking everything from bleach and breath mints to martinis, Coors beer, 7Up and Evian water. Most importantly, they are also real-life sea beings like Hannah Mermaid, an environmental activist fighting to protect the ocean and its creatures by embodying this most beautiful of legends.

The Little Mermaid

The classic faerytale *The Little Mermaid*, written by Danish author Hans Christian Andersen and first published in 1837, is an epic story of love, hope and sacrifice, with a dark sadness to it. The power of the mermaids in this story is that they live to three hundred years old, something humans would no doubt covet in their quest for immortality. But when they die they simply turn into sea foam, whereas human beings, we are told, have a soul that lives eternally.

The Little Mermaid of the title is the youngest of the widowed Sea King's six daughters, and the only one to fall in love with the human world, which "appeared to her far larger and more beautiful than her own", and a young prince in particular. When a huge storm sinks his ship she saves him from drowning, and begins to pine for his love, and an immortal soul. The prince however has no idea she exists, so she goes to the Sea Witch to make a devilish bargain. She will have legs, and the chance to meet the prince, but in return she must give up her beautiful voice (and tongue) to the witch, and accept that every step she takes will cause agonising pain, and she can never be a mermaid again. She sacrifices her family, her home under the sea and her own identity and longevity, knowing that if she fails to win the prince's love, and he marries another, she will dissolve into sea foam and disappear forever.

Of course, despite the Little Mermaid's beauty and grace, the prince falls in love with the girl he can talk to, who he thinks saved him from the shipwreck, and the lovelorn mermaid knows she will die at dawn on the morning after his wedding. Her siblings visit the Sea Witch and sacrifice their beautiful hair in order to save their sister – they give her a knife, and if she plunges it into the prince's heart before morning, she will return to her mermaid life.

She cannot kill the man she loves though, and so, resigned to death, she dives gracefully overboard to become part of the waves – at which point she finds herself floating upwards, transformed into a spirit of the air and told that while she does not have an immortal soul, she may one day obtain one through doing good deeds. This ending was added later however – originally she simply dissolved into foam, her sacrifice all for nothing. This Little Mermaid has been depicted artistically in many different forms in a range of beautifully illustrated books, from a dark and lovely mermaid to a sweeter blonde sea being, as well as on stage and in several films.

Ariel

Disney turned *The Little Mermaid* faerytale into an animated film in 1989, transforming it into a kid-friendly musical full of comedic characters, larger-than-life villains and vibrant song and dance routines, with a far more happy-ever-after ending. It charmed a generation of young girls who wanted to be just like sassy and sweet sixteen-year-old mermaid Ariel, who spends her days swimming around the sea with her best friend Flounder, a talking fish, collecting human artefacts which she stores in a secret grotto, and chatting to Scuttle the seagull, who regales her with hilariously wrong information about the human race.

Her father King Triton – a merman who wields a magical trident, the source of his power, and views man as nothing more than a predator – forbids her to go back to the surface. But Ariel sneaks out one night and sees Prince Eric partying on his ship, and is instantly smitten. When a sudden storm hits and he almost drowns, Ariel saves him, but swims away before he can see her.

Totally lovesick, she makes a pact with Ursula the sea witch – she'll be transformed into a human for three days, in which time she must receive true love's kiss from Eric. If she fails, she will be Ursula's.

Like the original faerytale, Ariel pays dearly – in exchange for legs, she must give her voice to Ursula, who removes it magically and stores it in a nautilus shell. Flounder takes Ariel to the surface before she drowns and lays her on a beach, where she is found by Prince Eric. After many mishaps and misadventures, a grand sacrifice from King Triton and an evil plot by Ursula to gain his trident and rule the underwater kingdom, it all ends well. Eric saves the king's life, and he in turn transforms Ariel into a human, so she can wed her true love and become one of the ten Disney Princesses.

In 1991 a TV series began, also called *The Little Mermaid*, which chronicled Ariel's life before she met Prince Eric, and involved lots of adventures with Flounder, Sebastian the crab and her six older sisters (Disney gave her an extra sibling). In 2000 the direct-to-video movie sequel *The Little Mermaid II: Return to the Sea* was released, in which Ariel and Eric have a daughter named Melody. When Melody's life is threatened by Ursula's sister Morgana, Ariel must return to her mermaid form to save her. And in 2008, the direct-to-DVD prequel *The Little Mermaid: Ariel's Beginning* came out, which showed Ariel and her sisters as children, living happily with their father King Triton (here referred to as the son of Poseidon) and their mother Queen Athena, and the events that unfolded after Athena was killed by pirates, which explains Triton's hatred of humanity.

This Little Mermaid is sweet and pretty, with a beautiful voice, long red hair, vivid blue eyes, a purple shell bikini top and an iridescent green tail. The animators based her on a combination of model Sherri Stoner and actress Alyssa Milano...

Phoebe from Charmed

When Alyssa Milano was sixteen and starring in *Who's the Boss?*, she was the inspiration for Disney's mermaid Ariel. Years later, while playing Phoebe in *Charmed*, she portrayed a mermaid inspired by the film in season five's double-episode opener *A Witch's Tail*.

The innocent in this story is Mylie, a mermaid who's fallen in love with a mortal and made a pact with the evil Sea Hag. She is given legs and thirty days as a woman, in which time her boyfriend must tell her he loves her. If he does, she'll become mortal – if he doesn't, Mylie must surrender her mermaid immortality (and her life) to the hag, who sucks it out from the chest into a nautilus shell.

There are a few *Splash* moments as raindrops start to reveal some of her scales, a hairdryer is used to retain her legs, and she's placed in a bathtub so she won't dry out. Eventually the Sea Hag tracks Mylie down to Halliwell Manor and abducts her. When the three sisters cast a spell to find her it has an unexpected consequence – Phoebe is transformed into a mermaid. She finds the Sea Hag's grotto and calls for Leo and the girls. They save their innocent, but Phoebe, broken-hearted over the end of her marriage to Cole, loves the new freedom that being a mermaid represents, and refuses to leave the sea, preferring to swim away from her problems. She tells her sisters she's staying in the ocean, and that "it's everything that Mylie said it was – it's complete freedom!" To which Mylie sadly replies: "The call of the sea. It'll turn her heart cold if she lets it..."

The Little Mermaid

In 1987, Faerie Tale Theatre released a live-action telemovie version of *The Little Mermaid*, starring Pam Dawber of *Mork & Mindy* fame as the young mermaid, and Helen Mirren as her beautiful and sweet-natured royal love rival. The concept was dreamed up by actress-turned-producer Shelley Duvall, who gathered many big stars together to bring twenty-six of the world's most loved faerytales to life. This one is very sweet, maintaining the sadness of the original story with a sense of love and sacrifice. The special effects are hilarious, as we are so used to the marvels of *Harry Potter* and *Avatar*, but it is wonderful to see Helen Mirren, along with Karen Black as the Sea Witch and Brian Dennehy as King Neptune, acting the story out. The whole series is now available on DVD.

Madison

The beautiful, vulnerable yet wonderfully free spirited mermaid Madison in the 1984 film *Splash* inspired a longing in millions of girls to take to the ocean and swim away to a magical new life under the sea, especially if you could take your mortal love with you.

Daryl Hannah depicted Madison perfectly, as the strong yet gentle mermaid longing for love but not willing to sacrifice herself for it, and she became the modern image of a mermaid.

As the movie begins, a young boy on a seaside holiday with his parents sees something in the water and jumps in, even though he can't swim. A young girl grasps his hand and keeps him afloat, and the two form a deep connection before he is plucked from the water and taken back home to New York. Although the boy, Allen, dismisses the glimpse of her tail as a hallucination, as an adult he subconsciously sabotages all his relationships because he longs to re-experience what he felt as a child. After another break-up, he returns to the ocean and falls overboard, and is again saved by Madison, who has always yearned for him too. This time she has his wallet, so she goes to New York to find him, arriving at Liberty Island naked and promptly being arrested for indecent exposure.

Although the scene was deleted, Madison saw a sea hag and struck a Faustian bargain, so she knows she only has six days on land before she must return to the ocean forever, and she must wet her tail every day. In this story, a mermaid's tail will transform into legs if dried out, which allows her to come ashore, but will quickly return if she is splashed with water, which leads to many funny moments. When she first speaks it is a strange series of clicks and whistles like a dolphin, but she learns to speak English by watching TV for a day. She can also grant Allen the power to breathe underwater while he is with her – but if he takes the plunge, he can never return to land.

"I had been obsessed with the Hans Christian Andersen faerytale *The Little Mermaid* ever since I was a kid," says Daryl, who did all her own swimming scenes. "And I'd fantasised about being one myself since I was little – I tied my feet together in the pool and practised swimming like that from a very early age."

Director Ron Howard had planned to hire a body double for the underwater scenes, until he realised Daryl could do the mermaid swim better than anyone they auditioned, hold her breath for longer and look more natural doing it. The tail was fully functional – when she had it on the camera crew and safety team couldn't keep up with her, although once in the tail she couldn't get out, and she had to be hoisted out of the water and lie on the deck during lunchbreaks.

After *Splash* Daryl continued acting, but she considers her most important role that of environmental crusader. Meanwhile Madison has lived on in a whole generation of girls who were given that name. In the movie she picks her name from the closest street sign – Madison Avenue – and Allen tells her it's not a real name, which it wasn't then. But its popularity skyrocketed, and that, along with the poster of Daryl in her fish tail, came to embody the energy of the mermaid.

Rikki, Cleo, Emma and Bella

In the fun, magical TV series *H2O: Just Add Water*, three teenage girls get stranded on a mysterious island, and while they are exploring they fall through a tunnel in a dormant volcano into a cavern. The only way out is through the pool that leads out to the reef. As they nervously jump into the water, the full moon shines down, bathing the pool, and the girls, in golden, sparkling light.

The next day, one by one, they realise they are now mermaids, and that exposure to even a splash of water or a drop of rain will transform their legs into tails – not the most convenient thing for Emma, the school swim star, Cleo, who works part-time at a marine park, or Rikki, the new girl who already felt like an outsider. They also discover they have a mermaid power – Emma can freeze water, Cleo can mould it into shapes, control its direction and increase its volume, and Rikki can boil water or anything containing water.

They use their powers for good, saving sea turtles, helping a sick dolphin and teaching bullies a lesson or two, but their powers also cause them grief, and there are lots of comical moments when they try to explain away their sudden change. Together they forge a close friendship to protect their secret and help each other when they encounter problems, such as a spilled drink at a sleepover, a marine biologist who gets a bit too close to their secret or the town bad boy who is determined to find out what's going on.

The swimming scenes are beautiful, when the three girls revel in their mermaidenry, the wise old crone they encounter provides wisdom and depth, and their close tie to the moon and its phases and magic is intriguing. In the third series Bella, an Irish mermaid, joins the cast, bringing more strands of legend to the show.

H2O: Just Add Water incorporates mermaid lore, marine conservation and real friendship – a bit like *Charmed*, without the boy obsessions and revealing outfits. It screens in more than a hundred and thirty countries and has an audience of over two hundred million, spreading the magic of mermaids around the world.

Aquamarine

The sweet mermaid film *Aquamarine*, released in 2006 and based loosely on the novel by Alice Hoffman, combines elements of mermaid legend with a coming of age story, a wonderful friendship and a beautiful and unexpected ending. Two teenage girls, Claire, played by Emma Roberts, and Hailey, played by teen singer JoJo, are spending their last summer together before Hailey has to leave Florida for Australia, where her marine biologist mum has scored the job of her dreams. On one of their last nights together they find a mermaid in the pool at the local beach club. Aquamarine has been washed ashore during a freak storm, created by her all-powerful merfather because she refused an arranged marriage to a selfish, spoiled merman. Her father believes that love is a myth, but he gives her three days to prove it exists – if she fails, she must return to the sea and get married to the man he has chosen.

Aquamarine enlists Hailey and Claire's help to find true love, promising them a wish if all goes to plan and she can convince the local beach babe to love her within the allotted time. Of course in faerytales and Disney movies love at first sight is entirely possible, and even expected, but this movie is far more realistic, with a beautiful twist at the end. Aquamarine has several mermaid powers. She can assume human form on land – providing she doesn't get wet – but as soon as the sun sets she transforms back into her mermaid self, making it hard to date! She can also create small waves and weather patterns, although not the huge storms her dad can stir up, she can ring people from her sea home using a giant conch shell, and she has the power to grant wishes to any human who helps her.

The Mermaids of Venice

In the enchanting book *The Undrowned Child*, a haunting faerytale is interwoven with the true history of Venice. The heroines are a school of mermaids who live in a gilded cavern beneath the city, wisely ruled by their beautiful queen Lussa and her bravest warrior Chissa. These "lovely creatures" are the secret guardians of the islands. In 1310, when the traitor Bajamonte Tiepolo tried to destroy Venice and kill the Doge, the mermaids were instrumental in his downfall. When an entire family was drowning, it was the mermaids who rescued the baby of the title and got her safely out of Venice so she could survive to fulfil the prophecy. It is they who have kept the ancient Creature beneath the lagoon asleep for a thousand years with the power of their singing. And now that it has awoken – partly due to the environmental devastation wreaked by humans and partly due to the restless spirit of Tiepolo, who is working baddened magic in order to sink Venice forever – it is up to them to save their city once more.

These mermaids are strong, wise and independent. Author Michelle Lovric says: "My mermaids have a serious job to do – to save Venice from a vile enemy. They were never going to be girlie types who sat around combing their hair." For this reason she has given them fierce, rough-as-guts language to suit their mission, learned from the sailors and pirates who visited Venice over the centuries. "What a drivelswigger! Drags on like a sea-cow's saliva!" says one. "My gib was atwitch, I might of knowed it. Human childer smell most peculiar, I do declare freely," warns another. "And now dey have crippen up upon us, bless my owld soul!"

The sailors who taught the mermaids Humantongue also introduced them to Eastern spices. They make their own medicines, such as fermented chilli jelly, and create dishes like curried lagoon samphire, char-crusted sea-gherkin and seaweed-cocoa with cayenne pepper – all vegetarian, of course, for how can they eat their fellow sea creatures? They scry the future in an upturned turtle shell, have the power to change people's minds, which is how they averted the disaster of 1310, they run a printing press to influence the population and discredit the evil taking over, and Lussa can communicate with Teodora, the child of the prophecy, through a magical book.

Teodora, who is most impressed that the mermaids are so unlike the stereotypical vain and lazy creatures she has read about in faerytales, has a few powers herself. She is a vedeparole, who can see spoken words written upon the air, by which she can learn much about who utters them, and a lettrice-del-cuore, who can read people's hearts just by touching their chest. She can also slip "between the linings", becoming invisible to adults, so she can carry out the mermaids' mission and help them to save Venice.

And in the wonderful sequel *The Mourning Emporium*, Teodora and her friend Renzo must join forces with the London mermaids, staunch two-tailed melusines who have their own quirks and powers, to restore the balance of good and evil in their city.

Michelle's Venetian Mermaid Magic

Michelle Lovric is a novelist, journalist and anthologist, as well as a history buff and avid researcher, and the author of the lushly passionate and beautifully poetic books *Carnevale*, *The Floating Book*, *The Remedy* and *The Book of Human Skin*, as well as the young adult mermaid novels *The Undrowned Child* and its entrancing sequel *The Mourning Emporium*. Born and raised in the ocean city of Sydney, Australia, Michelle now splits her time between an apartment overlooking London's River Thames and a flat on Venice's Grand Canal, places that seep through into her work, weaving colour, history and the magic of water into her enchanting tales. Visit her at www.MichelleLovric.com.

Teo noted with approval that these mermaids showed no sign at all of sitting around gazing at themselves in mirrors like the mermaids in children's stories. Instead they were all busy with a complicated, highly technical task… The mermaids were printing…

The Undrowned Child

For me, the Venetian mermaids in *The Undrowned Child* and *The Mourning Emporium* represent the citizens of Venice in a metaphorical way. They are practically invisible – it requires a leap of the imagination to see them. And this is how it is with the modern Venetians, practically buried under the mass of tourism. There are fewer than sixty thousand Venetians left, compared with twenty million visitors annually. What to do? Live a secret life "between the linings" – that's the Venetian solution. The real Venetians have an earthy sense of humour and they love tasty, spicy food. Some of them are also warriors, battling to save their city from the forces of greed, from pollution and from crimes of taste (like the huge advertising billboards that deface the town these days). For Venice isn't dead and she isn't drowning. To some extent the real Venice is just hiding, something one senses rather than glimpses.

The lips of all the mermaids were a most exquisite moist red, and completely smooth, just like coral. The mermaids' sea-green eyes slanted slightly upwards, fringed by luxuriant lashes. When they looked down, their eyelids resembled white cowrie shells. Their long hair was fluffy and tousled. None looked more than sixteen... Renzo gaped at the lovely creatures with a mixture of fear and admiration.

The Undrowned Child

My London mermaids are effete, languid creatures addicted to patent nostrums for ladies, such as Charles Forde's Bile Beans for Biliousness or Dr Blaud's Capsules, which, according to the manufacturer, produce "pure, rich blood without any disagreeable effects and are recommended by the medical faculty as the best remedy for bloodlessness". But they eventually remember their warrior function, and their archery skills, and help to save their city.

Each writer will create his or her own mermaid, who fulfils a necessary symbolic function. That's one of the beauties of a mythical species – the sheer imaginative utility. I don't think any of us are striving towards a composite, or an ideal. That would be a waste of mermaid. Of course, when you write for children or young adults, you have to think about the role models you are creating. I wasn't enthusiastic about the trope of a long-haired beauty who sits about combing her hair and singing songs to seduce men. Who must lose her voice if she wants to marry a human man – no! I wanted to write post-feminist mermaids: active, eloquent and passionate, as well as greedy. So I gave my Venetian mermaids fairly foul tongues and a rich sense of humour. For how else could mermaids learn to talk Humantongue except by eavesdropping on sailors and pirates? That's why they don't talk like Jane Austen.

The Starbucks Mermaid

Millions of people around the world see a mermaid on a daily basis, hidden in plain sight as part of the Starbucks Coffee logo. Described by the company as a "twin-tailed siren", and by the United States Patent and Trademark Office as "the design of a siren (a two-tailed mermaid) wearing a crown", it's believed to have been co-opted by the company to align with the seductive, impossible to resist song of the siren, and thus imply the irresistibility of their beverages.

The original 1970s logo was brown, and was copied from a fifteenth century illustration of a bare-breasted, two-tailed melusine wearing a crown – although the gap between her two tails was closed to lessen the sexual connotation, and she had a much friendlier face. Despite the changes, blogger Michael Krakovskiy described the logo as "a family-unfriendly image of a fish-woman spreading her tails."

In the mid-eighties, when the company expanded, a more stylised version of the logo was created by designer Doug Fast in order to reproduce more easily on their cups. The logo changed from brown to green, but it was still the full siren, although her hair became longer and thicker to cover her breasts, and her two tails were more abstract. In 1992, Doug says, he enlarged the siren "to eliminate the spread, so-called suggestive, tails," and that's the version we see today, with the mermaid cropped so only the top of her tails are seen. Now a new variant that appears in some stores has her as a single-tailed mermaid.

The company is named in part after Starbuck, Captain Ahab's first mate in the novel *Moby Dick*, which the founders thought evoked the romance of the high seas, the seafaring tradition of the early coffee traders, and the seductive powers of the siren. They have also taken on board the eco warrior nature of the mermaid. In Seattle, the home of Starbucks, the company collaborated with the council to implement a comprehensive recycling and composting program, which led to a new law requiring all single-use food service packaging at restaurants and grocery stores to be recyclable or compostable. Starbucks stores got in early, and the company plans to roll the program out internationally by 2015. They are also committed to ethically sourcing and roasting their coffee beans, employ a director of environmental impact, and are on track to reducing their water consumption by twenty-five per cent, using at least fifty per cent renewable electricity, and boosting the use of reusable cups and other methods of reducing their carbon footprint.

Syrena and Tamara

In the fourth *Pirates of the Caribbean* blockbuster, *On Stranger Tides*, Captain Jack Sparrow and his motley crew encounter some of the devilish mermaids of legend when they set out to find the elusive fountain of youth which they're protecting. French actress Astrid Berges-Frisbey plays Syrena, with Aussie Gemma Ward as beautiful but deadly Tamara, Queen of the Mermaids. "Tamara is the typical siren," Gemma says. "And what I found interesting about the mermaids in this movie is that the producers stayed true to mermaid mythology. The original story of *The Little Mermaid* was very gruesome – a lot of the old faerytales are."

Actor Geoffrey Rush admits he only signed on to reprise his role as Captain Barbossa because the mermaids brought a new angle to the franchise. "I thought they'd done everything you could do, but I hadn't thought about mermaids. The mermaids are fantastic, because they are beautiful creatures of the sea that lure the sailors in, and then they suddenly turn into piranhas. They just tear ships apart and they're feral. It's very exciting," he says.

Dora the Mermaid

Preschool favourite Dora the Explorer spends time as a mermaid in the movie *Dora Saves the Mermaid Kingdom*, which has a sweet, gentle environmental message. The adventure begins on Clean Up the Beach Day, when Dora and her monkey Boots are picking up rubbish at their local beach. They come across a clam who tells them that an evil octopus, who sails around the oceans gleefully dumping garbage everywhere, is threatening the survival of the water and all its creatures, including the mermaids. Their princess Mariana had a magic crown that allowed her to wish the garbage away and keep the ocean safe, but it has disappeared, and now the whales can't see where they're going, the fish are struggling to survive, the merfolk are getting sick, and their beautiful underwater kingdom is about to disappear forever under an avalanche of trash.

Dora finds the crown washed up on the beach, but it takes a lot of work to get it back to Mariana. She has to count her way across Seashell Bridge, work out how to get around Pirate Island, save a whale from crashing, call on her wildlife adventuring cousin Diego and some dolphins he knows to get across the sea, and then become a mermaid herself in order to wish the rubbish away and save the day. And she still doesn't have enough magic to clear away all the garbage, so she has to call on all the sea creatures to help with the clean-up. In the end she restores the crown to Mariana, converts the octopus, having seen the error of his ways, into a keen recycler, and receives a special thank you necklace so that she can visit the mermaid kingdom whenever she wants to.

The Mermaid Queen

In the kids book *Little Miss Trouble and the Mermaid*, Little Miss Trouble goes to Seatown for a holiday, and gets up to her usual tricks – causing trouble. She splashes one friend and blames another, which leaves Little Miss Splendid sprayed with icy water. She kicks sand all over Mr Strong but says it was Mr Sneeze, which sees him buried in sand up to his nose. She's having the time of her life, causing trouble for everyone else – until a mermaid takes her down to the bottom of the sea for a meeting with the Mermaid Queen.

This beautiful but fiery Mermaid Queen, angry that her visitor has been causing so much trouble on the beach that she rules over, reveals that she has the power to teach her a lesson. Written and illustrated by Adam Hargreaves, based on the famous Mr Men and Little Miss books created by his father Roger, it's one of a new series that introduces magical elements to these classic tales, such as *Little Miss Naughty and the Good Fairy*, *Little Miss Sunshine and the Wicked Witch*, *Little Miss Shy and the Fairy Godmother* and *Little Miss Lucky and the Naughty Pixies*.

Syrenka

In Poland, the coat of arms of the capital city of Warsaw is a syrenka, which translates as "little mermaid", a blonde warrior woman with a fish tail and a sword, shield and crown, identified as Melusina. According to legend, it was this mermaid that led Duke Boleslaw II of Masovia to a small fishing village and instructed him to build there the city of Warsaw at the end of the thirteenth century. And the mermaid remains Warsaw's symbol today, with many statues of them throughout the city. Another version of the story says the mermaid swam to Warsaw from the Baltic Sea because she loved the Griffin, the ancient defender of the city, and that when he was killed in battle defending Warsaw against the invading Swedes, she became defender of the city to avenge his death.

Another Polish legend claims that two of Greek sea god Triton's daughters set off on an adventure through the oceans. When they got to what is now the port city of Copenhagen, the capital of Denmark, one of them stayed there, and is today immortalised in the mermaid statue in the harbour (although this actually celebrates the Danish faerytale *The Little Mermaid*), while the other is said to have swum on until she reached the mouth of the Vistula River, which she travelled along until she came to Warsaw, where she stayed, and was much admired for her beauty and pretty voice.

Selkies, Merrows and Mermaids

JK Rowling created a type of merfolk in the Harry Potter books, although they are far less beautiful than the usual mer depictions – with fishy eyes, strange shark-like teeth, grey skin, skull-like faces and wild green hair. She calls them selkies, and they live in the lake at Hogwarts and speak a language known as Mermish, which can only be understood by non-merpeople when it is heard underwater.

They appear in *The Half-Blood Prince*, but are central to the story in *Harry Potter and the Goblet of Fire*, when one of the clues in the Triwizard Tournament is an egg that emits a loud screech when opened. After much puzzlement, the contestants finally realise that the sound is Mermish, and must be listened to underwater for the clue to be understood. For the task it speaks of, someone precious to each of the four champions is tied up in the middle of the lake, deep under the water, and guarded by merpeople, and must be saved from drowning within the allotted time.

The merpeople are incredibly fierce looking, threatening the contestants with tridents and trying to scare them off. They become enraged when Harry tries to rescue two of the hostages, and hinder his rise to the surface – although they later tell Dumbledore, one of the few wizards able to speak Mermish, that Harry was very brave.

In the Harry Potter universe there are a few different types of merpeople – the selkies of Scotland and the merrows of Ireland, as well as the beautiful sirens, who are more like the mermaids we know, and are depicted in a pretty stained glass window in the bathroom where Harry takes his egg. All these sea creatures are a separate species, not a mix of human and fish, although nasty Dolores Umbridge wants them rounded up and tagged because she hates half-breeds so much – a powerful allegory of modern issues.

The Selkie

Selkies are portrayed in a lovelier, more traditional light in the 1994 movie *The Secret of Roan Inish*. At its heart is a mysterious selkie woman, who is seldom seen on screen but whose presence is always felt. The idea of her is woven into the fabric of the film's tiny coastal fishing community, and while most of the villagers consider her a figure of legend, to one family she is very real. While she is not strictly a mermaid, selkies are mythical sea beings often linked to the former, seals that can shed their skin at will and become a woman, even passing for a time in the mortal world and able to marry human men.

Ten-year-old Fiona learns of the selkie when she is sent to the village after the death of her mother, to live with her grandparents. Their cottage overlooks the island rumoured to be the abode of the selkies, where the family once lived and where Fiona's brother went missing years before. The family's secrets are revealed to Fiona by her cousin Tadhg, who is one of the "dark ones", dark of hair and eye like her brother was, and somehow touched by magic, and she becomes determined to discover the truth about her brother's disappearance. After she learns that one of her ancestors captured a selkie and made her his wife, then has a strange communication with a seal, she is powerfully drawn to Roan Inish – Seal Island – and the derelict old family home. She spends all her time there, exploring and restoring the old cottage, and becomes convinced that her brother is still alive and living with the Seal People.

The selkie is portrayed by Susan Lynch, the real-life sister of John Lynch who plays Tadhg, and she brings a haunting depth to the part of this creature who drifts between two identities, seal and human – never half and half like a mermaid, but living between two worlds while never fully of either one. The legend of the selkie is common to many of the old coastal communities of the British Isles, where seals were plentiful and myth and magic were commonplace. The movie was set along the rugged coastline of Donegal in northwest Ireland, although the book it is based on, *Secret of the Ron Mor Skerry* by Rosalie Fry, was set in Scotland.

The Seal People

In Juliet Marillier's enchanting book *Wolfskin*, set in the Light Isles of Orkney, off the north coast of Scotland, the legend of the selkie is also brought to life. These magical sea beings are members of the Seal Tribe, who dwell in the ocean and along the shores of a tiny nearby island, a place of disappearances, strange lights, mists and shadows. They are an ancient, elusive and deeply dangerous race, regarded with much respect as well as with wariness by the people of the Isles – but not by the Norse invaders who threaten the traditional way of life. After a tragic, treacherous event, Nessa, princess and priestess of the Isles and keeper of the mysteries, must call on the Seal Tribe for help, something that is only ever considered in a time of greatest need, such can be the consequences of awakening their strange power, for in this story they are depicted as more dangerous and cruel-hearted than in some retellings, ancient and Other, and far removed from mankind and human emotions.

Nessa sheds seven tears into the sea to summon them, and five selkies respond – women yet not women, fragile and wild sea creatures, with eyes all liquid darkness and their voices made of notes, not words. They help her to make a magical ritual object that chills her with its ingredients, its purpose and its incredible power, and honour her with a precious gift, never given lightly.

Juliet also included the selkies in the sequel to *Wolfskin*, the wonderful *Fox Mask*, in the character of Watcher, who is a descendant of a selkie mother and a human father. And in *Child of the Prophecy*, part of her beautiful Sevenwaters Trilogy, the faeries turn Darragh into a selkie in order to save him.

Local Hero

This touching 1983 movie, set in a small fishing village in Scotland and full of huge open skies and wonderful expanses of brooding ocean, is about the clash between a small coastal community and big business, in this case an American oil company that wants to buy the entire town and the surrounding properties to make way for a huge refinery. An uptight, materialistic executive is flown to the village to get to know the locals in order to convince them to sell – but instead he makes friends with the eccentric villagers, coming to love the relaxed seaside lifestyle, beginning to see the magic in the night sky and the beauty in a seashell, and falling under the spell of beautiful but mysterious marine researcher Marina, who has webbed toes and seems more at home in the water than on land, leading him to suspect she is a mermaid.

Australia's Mermaid

Annette Kellerman was an Australian swimmer who was nicknamed The Mermaid, and credited with inventing synchronised swimming after she performed a water ballet in a glass tank in New York in 1907. A weakness in her legs as a child required her to wear steel braces, and she started swim classes in an attempt to strengthen them. She soon broke several state swim records, and went on to give swimming exhibitions and perform in a mermaid act at an aquarium. At the time women were expected to wear dresses over pantaloons to swim, which Annette refused to do – she advocated for the right of women to swim in more suitable attire, and was arrested on a US beach for wearing a one-piece swimsuit she had designed, which later led to her creating her own swimwear range.

While based in America, Annette began acting, and she was the first woman to film a nude scene (must have been all that mermaid energy giving her the confidence!), in the movie *A Daughter of the Gods*. She also starred in *The Mermaid*, *Venus of the South Seas* and other aquatic-themed films, in which she did all her own stunts and created her own tails, the latter inspiring the mermaid costumes at Florida's Weeki Wachee Springs, as well as the designers for the movie *Splash*. The story of her life was celebrated in the film *Million Dollar Mermaid*, and she was the subject of a documentary called *The Original Mermaid* and a book called *Mermaid Queen: The Spectacular True Story Of Annette Kellerman, Who Swam Her Way To Fame, Fortune & Swimsuit History*.

The American Mermaid

Esther Williams played Aussie mermaid Annette Kellerman in the 1952 Hollywood film *Million Dollar Mermaid*, and that became her nickname – she said Clark Gable was the first to call her a mermaid, and everyone else followed. Esther began her career as a swimmer. She broke many Californian records, and was tipped to win gold at the 1940 Olympics, until they were cancelled due to the outbreak of World War II. Instead she took a job at Billy Rose's Aquacade, performing alongside Olympic swimmer and *Tarzan* star Johnny Weissmuller. While there she caught the eye of Hollywood scouts, and she was quickly signed by movie studio MGM. She starred in several aquamusicals, films featuring lots of diving and synchronised swimming, before breaking into the mainstream. She retired from

Hollywood in the 1960s, and relaunched herself as a businesswoman and the face of a swimwear range and a brand of swimming pools. She also made instructional swimming videos for kids and commentated on the synchronised swimming at later Olympics.

Mermaids

This Australian telemovie was made in 2003, and centres on three mermaid sisters who are estranged because of their lifestyle choices. Diana, the eldest, still lives in the sea, while Venus and June have chosen to make their life on land, as these mermaids, like Madison in *Splash*, have a tail when they are wet, but legs when they are dry. When their father is murdered by an unscrupulous fisherman, they band together to avenge his death, and get to know each other all over again. They each have a magical ability related to their Roman goddess name – Diana has super strength, Venus can hypnotise men to obey her and move objects with her mind, and June, who just wants to be loved a la Ariel, can communicate with sea creatures.

Aquaman

This comic book character debuted in 1941 in the stories of other superheroes, but he eventually got his own titles, became a founding member of the Justice League of America, and has carried over into TV, including his own series and appearances in *Smallville*, as well as movies and video games. He is known as the king of Atlantis and ruler of the ocean, and his villain-fighting powers include super strength, super speed, invulnerability, the ability to stay underwater indefinitely (he sometimes has gills), and the power to communicate with sea creatures using telepathy – although in early versions he spoke to them in their own language. He can also exist on land, although he needs to stay well hydrated, of course!

In one of his origin stories, he is a human whose father was a famous underwater explorer who discovered the sunken kingdom of Atlantis, and locked himself in its library to study all their secrets, eventually discovering how humans could live under the sea, drawing oxygen from the water and gaining super powers. In a reworked origin story arc in 1989, he is born to Queen Atlanna and the wizard Atlan in the Atlantean city of Poseidonis, but is abandoned on the seashore because of his blond hair, and raised by a lighthouse keeper, growing up to fight villains as Aquaman.

Man from Atlantis

This character appeared in four sci-fi telemovies in 1977, followed by a thirteen episode TV series. Patrick Duffy played the lead, a man suffering from amnesia who is nursed back to health by a pretty doctor, and is given the name Mark Harris. Soon his superpowers are revealed – including superhuman strength and the ability to breathe underwater and withstand extreme depth pressures. He is soon recruited by a government agency, the Foundation For Oceanic Research, which explores the depths of the ocean in a submarine called the Cetacean, named for the whales, dolphins and porpoises. Mark is believed to be the only survivor of the lost civilisation of Atlantis, and has to help protect humanity from nasty villains. This was the first American TV series to be shown in China, in 1980, and Marvel also made it into a comic.

Musical Mermaid Muses

Mermaids have also inspired musicians, weaving their way into music such as nineteenth century German composer Felix Mendelssohn's *The Fair Melusina* overture and his contemporary Richard Wagner's *Der Ring des Nibelungen*, which speaks of the Rhine River mermaids known as loreleis, while Taiwanese composer Fan-Long Ko wrote of the sirens of old in his *The Weeping Mermaid* score.

Mermaids and other magical beings also inspired the new album *Enchanted*, by *Mermaids & Mythology* magazine editor and singer Karen Kay and her musician partner Michael Tingle, especially the beautiful song *Oceanik Magick* (you can find out more about their music at www.faeriemusic.com). English band The Waterboys also wrote about mermaids, a singer/songwriter who calls herself Ocean released an album, *Mermaid Music*, that includes the track *Siren Song*, there is an Atlanta beach-pop band called Mermaids, and French jazz and soul singer Sarah Khider recorded the beautiful *Mermaid Song*, which was also used in a Chivas Regal ad.

"The moon is fully risen, and shines over the sea,
As you glide in my vision, the time is standing still...
In the garden of the sea, I see you looking over,
With my wistful melody, you leap into the water,
This is the mermaid song, The singing of my sisters..."
Sarah Khider and Chito, Mermaid Song

Another gorgeous song is *Black Mermaid* by Canadian singer/ songwriter Esthero, which is as much about the siren within as any external sea being. She has written for and collaborated with Kanye West, the Black Eyed Peas, Nelly Furtado and many more, as well as making her own albums, and will soon release her new one, *Everything is Expensive*, which includes the heartbreakingly beautiful *Black Mermaid*. Visit her at www.facebook.com/esthero.

Emily Windsnap

English author Liz Kessler has created a wonderful heroine in twelve-year-old Emily, who lives on a boat by the sea with her mum, but has never been in the water. A bit of an outsider and loner, her discovery during swimming lessons at school that she is half mermaid is a shock, and also makes her feel more like a freak than ever. But as she comes to terms with her big secret, and starts to work out why her mum remembers nothing about her father, and just who the sinister lighthouse keeper is, a whole host of adventures unfold, and she learns a lot about herself as well as her family.

Emily has the ability to turn into a mermaid when she is submerged in water. A few sprinkles of rain don't affect her, which is convenient, and it takes a few minutes in water for the fusing together of her legs process to begin, which avoids any of the walking past a sprinkler/ being thrown in a pool/getting caught in the rain/a boat splashing water as it goes by scenarios that plague the mermaids from *Splash* and *H2O: Just Add Water*, all of which is certainly a plus when living on a boat at the seaside! And her legs return fairly quickly from their tail form after she gets out of the water, which avoids many problems.

Being half-human also gives her the power to walk on land, which the merfolk she meets can't do. In fact many of her greatest strengths come from her humanity rather than her mer powers, although these qualities are only revealed to her when she integrates this new aspect of her self – they are qualities she's always had, but wasn't aware of.

The mermaid community in Emily's universe is ruled by King Neptune, a tough and quick-to-convict ruler, and there are many strands of mermaid folklore woven into the story. But at the heart of it this is a very human story, with Emily's quest to find her father and the blossoming friendship she discovers with fellow twelve-year-old Shona easy to relate to – the fact that they both have tails is interesting to her, but not key to her feelings for them.

Liz's Mythical Mermaid Magic

Children's author Liz Kessler was living on a houseboat on a canal when she started writing the beautiful Emily Windsnap books, about a young girl who discovers that she's half-mermaid. Liz has now settled in magical Cornwall, on the southwest tip of England, where she loves walking along the windswept beaches, surfing in the wild seas and writing about mermaids. She has always been fascinated by the ocean and the mysteries of the deep – while in her magical Philippa Fisher series she explores faery lore and the enchantment of the English countryside and its stone circles. Visit her and find out more at www.LizKessler.co.uk.

I first discovered mermaids while I was living on a narrowboat on the Macclesfield Canal just outside Manchester. I had an idea for a poem about a girl who lived on a boat with her mum. The girl had a secret, which was that when she went into water she became a mermaid. I was persuaded to turn the poem into a novel, and *The Tail of Emily Windsnap* was born!

Funnily enough, I've never been hugely into mermaids of popular legend. My mermaids tend to be ordinary children, like contemporary children today. They just happen to be able to live underwater as well! My favourite mermaid? Emily Windsnap ☺

To research the series, I spent a lot of time by the sea, and watched lots of programs like *The Blue Planet*. For *Emily Windsnap and the Monster from the Deep*, which is set in the Bermuda Triangle, I went to Bermuda. I went out snorkelling every day, then sat on the beach with my notebook, writing about what I'd seen. There's a lot in that book that is absolutely from there – the fish, and the sand, and the sea. And for the third book, *The Castle in the Mist*, I spent a couple of weeks at St Michael's Mount in Cornwall, which inspired the story.

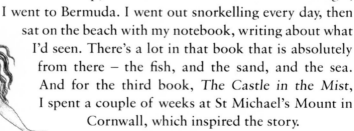

What I like most about mermaids, apart from the fact that they are totally cool because they can live both on land and in the sea, is the fact that they are mythical and magical – and

to me they represent the possibilities that lie all around us, if we only open our minds enough to believe that they might really exist.

Emily is an ordinary, contemporary girl, with the ordinary concerns and worries of a young girl today. When she finds out that she becomes a mermaid in water, her life completely changes and a whole new world opens up to her, not just physically, but in all sorts of other ways too. She's quite adventurous, and likes a challenge – and she can't help getting herself into trouble because of this. She is fiercely loyal to those she loves, and she isn't afraid to stand up and say what she thinks. She's pretty cool!

I think that mermaids could exist, and may exist, and while no one can prove that they do, no one can prove that they don't either. And that is what I love so much about them.

The ocean forms over three quarters of our planet, so I find it hard to imagine that anyone *doesn't* feel a deep connection to it. And because my books are set in and near the sea, being near the sea inspires me. Living by the water for me is *hugely* important! Not just for my writing, but if it doesn't sound too precious to say it, I feel that I need it for my spirit too. Now that I live in Cornwall, I can't imagine ever not living by the sea again. The thought of it makes me feel claustrophobic – I think perhaps I'm a little tiny part mermaid myself.

Our lives today are so full of all sorts of materialistic things, and it's very easy for us to lose track of things like looking after our planet, our seas, our fellow life. These things are all massively important. I don't really bring these issues into my books, because I'm always nervous of sounding too preachy, but it is important to me. And like lots of us, I'm guilty of not doing enough to protect our planet and our seas. We should all do much more, or we will lose them.

How to See Mermaids

"I started early, took my dog,
And visited the Sea.
The mermaids in the basement
Came out to look at me…"
Emily Dickinson, American poet

Connecting With the Sea Beings

Just as in poet Emily Dickinson's chant-like words, the best way to connect with mermaids is to start out early and go to the sea. For some of us, this is as easy as breathing. I love our mother the ocean, and feel only half alive when I'm away from it for a sustained period. I get into water often, and have done some foolhardy things. A friend used to be convinced that it's my incredibly poor eyesight that makes me go for huge waves when I'm surfing, and I have been injured quite seriously several times while catching waves. But I hunger for it. And I know that I should, I must, be able to breathe underwater. I love the underwater world, but I do not like masks and tanks, which one day I may learn to overcome. S-l-o-w-l-y!

I love the mermaids, whose song I have heard, whose notes I have sung back in my attempt to let them know I love them, and wish to be with them. I have seen them, and they are all so unique, as diverse as the creatures of the great mother ocean herself. Twin-tailed, selkie-sleek, dolphin-enchanting, nautilus-feelers – mer creatures are complex and very different to the beings of land. They live within a different element. They need not "breathe" as we do. They experience weightlessness. And if they are cast ashore the weight of gravity and air can crush them alive. These magical creatures with the head and torso of a man or woman and the body and tail of a fish, live within the waters of this world, and so there may be many more of them than there are land creatures and elementals – there is, after all, so much more sea than land on this planet.

They are champions of sexuality and freedom, allure and power. They protect travellers and guide mariners across oceans. They cleanse from us the toxins and diseases of flesh, clearing us and freeing us. They can predict storms and future events, and some can even grant wishes to humans who encounter them. They are great teachers of wisdom and knowledge, and they can also replenish our physical energy, as well as refreshing and renewing our spirits. They are associated with the goddesses Yemanja and Aphrodite, Mother Mary, Mary Magdalene, Neptune, prostitution, virginity, irresistible desire, and the yearning for a love so great that we transform our very physical selves.

They are also so very stolen. We have taken from them again and again, working with their image in books and movies, which no matter how diluted carry the cleansing sting of saltwater wisdom.

As a child, I would swim with my legs tied together, always wishing to transform one day beneath the waters. I held my breath. I opened my eyes. I imagined my hair was alive. I wished more than anything to live within the water, to be supported and held by the ocean, the womb of the world. The freedom, the beauty and the wild innocence is so very beguiling.

Some of us with open hearts, who have that sea blood within our veins, have seen mermaids with our eyes wide open. At the same time, another may be staring in the same place and see nothing at all, nothing but the sparkling deep blue, whereas I see the selkie woman bobbing above the water, her tail slapping the surface as if to invite me to enter and dance in the waters with her.

But we can all see these creatures of sea and land with our spirit eye, our third eye as it is often called. Quite often we cannot see certain energies because our brain protects us from seeing that which the mind has been trained to believe does not exist.

One way to see them is to gather pieces of driftwood at a liminal time. Find ones beyond the shoreline that have had much time to dry in the sun. Burn the wood upon the beach, and sing songs – just make them up – around this driftwood fire. The mermaids will come closer, to see who it is that calls, and you too will be able to see more brightly, more powerfully, with your spirit eye.

They interact with us on an energetic level, using our auric field to manifest "physically" – but only when they choose to, and only when we are ready to have the experience. And a mermaid may appear to one soul and seem beautiful, wild, inspiring, while another, who is fearful and has unresolved hate of the feminine within them, will see a predatory siren out to steal the breath that flows from their lips.

If you truly wish to see mermaids, you must see them with your heart, with your untrained mer senses. They are rarely seen with the eyes. When you call the mer to come to you, know they do not have human values. They are Other, and this is their wisdom. Establish trust by making an offering of time, energy or physical work to the ocean and its inhabitants. Work with the mer for the greater good – for the betterment of all, especially the sea peoples.

After all, we are kin, the merfolk and we landfolk. The kinship between humans and merbeings is folklore to some, imagination to others, and a tradition that is prevalent for coastal peoples all over the planet. Some families in Scotland and Ireland still claim descent from mermaids. Families of the Orkney Isles with a genetic trait of slightly webbed hands claim it is due to an ancestor who fled from her unhappy marriage into the arms of a handsome selkie man, whose loyalty and love allowed her to live between the sea and the land. The Native American tribe called Penobscot also claims descent from a mermaid. Others believe the mermaid or merman is our original Lemurian and later Atlantean form, when we were both water and land creatures, able to breathe and live in both elements with ease.

The Power of Mer : Their Healing Gifts to Humans

We can communicate with the merworld easily, beautifully and safely, and they can teach us about different forms of communication and enable us to develop telepathic skills. There are some ways to make the meetings more likely – follow these steps and incorporate the merfolk into your magic, and you will more easily connect with their energy to work on healing the many issues they can help with.

Work with west: The traditional direction associated with the mermaid is west, and her colours are those of the ocean – blues, greens and even the shades of sunset. Of course, if you live on the east coast this will shift, and her direction will become east. The direction to call to merbeings is wherever the water lies.

Work with mirrors: Water is a mirror, thus the mermaid offers us a way to see ourselves. Her magical mirror is a powerful scrying tool for us to work with to look deep within our own depths and darknesses, surface and light.

Explore liminal times and tidal surges: The times of day you are most likely to encounter them are the liminal times – dawn, dusk, sunrise and sunset, and at tide-turn and moon cycle points like dark moon, full moon, new moon and first quarter.

Heal your sensuality: Merfolk work with our fertility in a healing manner, and they can assist women with menstrual and fertility issues, and men with their potency and desire!

Eat the mer way: Working with mermaid magic can also naturally begin to reshape your diet. You may begin to easefully introduce natural sea vegetables, fish and seafood, and to incorporate the omega 3 fatty acids present in so much seafood, particularly salmon, into your body. Omega 3 assists people with dietary problems, is anti-carcinogenic, improves skin tone, colour and collagen quantity and quality, and stabilises brain chemistry.

Increase playtime: The mermaids also suggest that we swim more, play more and have sea salt baths, which help to clear our auric body of any negativity and stale, old energy and beliefs we may be holding on to, especially regarding sexuality and issues of who we are within our various relationships.

Learn saltwater wisdom: The salt water aspect of the mermaid is extremely important to her magic. Water is the element that symbolises cleansing, purification and the quenching of thirst, but salt water is a variation on this element. Its qualities are to draw out impurities, flavour our lives, harmonise us and create the mineral richness that is the bedrock of fertility. Blood, in our wombs and at menstruation, is salty. Seawater also enables us to float – it is more buoyant than fresh water and more difficult to move through. It is more complex, more cleansing and sometimes stronger than fresh water. We can't drink it, so there is an element of mistrust from many humans in regards to salt water, although it sustains the life of so many other creatures, and offers we humans so very much in the form of nourishment. This lack of clarity does not make the mermaids' element deceptive, rather it makes us question what we assume to be true, and to taste before we drink deeply. Water also represents the unconscious, our urges, desires, instincts and psychic abilities. Salt water symbolises these abilities taken to a very high vibratory degree.

Enjoy beauty rituals and adornment: The tools the mermaid has been gifted with also perfectly illustrate her gifts to us. Her comb represents the precious and sacred nature of caring for our own physical selves. In acknowledging that our bodies deserve time and reverence, there is a ritualistic element to all beauty routines that can be lifted out of the mundane and commercial world and into the sacred, making of our bodies an honoured temple which we love and respect and demonstrate gratitude for. By honouring it, we honour most deeply the god and the goddess and the spark of life itself.

Develop independence: The mermaid reminds us how to maintain who we are within intimate relationships. Her unabashed beauty, sexuality and unselfconscious allure show us we are desirable and powerful simply for being alive. Conversely, if we feel repelled or fearful of the mermaid who is happy in her skin, it is indicative that we have a wounded aspect to our sexuality. If we feel affinity only with the mermaid who gives up her self to be joined with a lover, we should examine just how much of ourselves we change to be with a partner. This mermaid syndrome extends to those who change their appearance, interests or religion to be with a lover. The mermaid's presence in our lives requires that we become closer to who we truly are, and honour our own truths instead of adopting and adapting to another's, sacrificing who we are in order to be with another – who may not require that we change at all!

Revel in femininity and mutability: The mermaid also suggests to us that we need to see the strength in femininity and in being overtly female. For men, this can mean experimenting with being submissive, passive and more feeling, and offering an openness from time to time. For women who have been unsure about how to be feminine and open, the mermaid can show us how to be magnetic, attractive and powerful, yet all without force.

The Mermaid Connection Meditation

Find yourself a comfortable place. Light a driftwood fire if you are so lucky as to have a fireplace, scatter some shells about you, put on music like Debussy's *La Mer*. Be comfortable, neither too warm nor too cold, and turn off phones and anything that may interrupt this time of communication and going deep with the merfolk. You can either read this and feel it, record it for your own self, or have a friend read it to you, then you read it to them. However you work with these words, they will take you deep into the liminal world of Mer, and introduce you to aspects of self that are the mermaid's buried treasure – *your* sunken treasures...

You stand on the shore. A long golden shore, deserted, with only the deep blue sea before you, glittering deeply, prisms of light shining into your eyes, and yet there is no harsh glare nor pain from the sun. It is dawn, and the colours of the sky reflect each of your own energy's colours. And you stare out at the horizon, and you begin to see a form upon the water.

A woman, dancing upon the waves. With her are sea creatures of all kinds, dolphins laughing and playing with her, surfing along her silver and gold form, deep-sea animals moving beneath, and the eight-legged ones, and the fish, skimming the surface and leaping into the light, and whales behind her, singing the song of the deep.

And this woman dances towards you, and you move forward slowly to greet her, your feet lapped by the cool, salty waters of the womb of the world, the great ocean, the womb that is your home, and you stretch out one hand towards her, and she reaches you. She takes your hands and, laughing, smiles into your eyes with a force of love, and beauty, and delight, and sheer joy. She is the ocean's goddess, she who crosses the boundaries of elements, and she is beautiful, as are you. She is Aphrodite, and you stand on the sacred shores of Ancient Cyprus, and will join her now in her sacred temple.

She moves towards you, and takes a deep breath. From her you hear no words, but the message is clear. She breathes this breath deep into your solar plexus, and you feel the woundings of this area, the place where you have held your fear of beauty and womanly power, move and shift. She takes another deep breath, and breathes into your spirit eye, and you can feel a stirring, and a breathing, from that place. Her hand holding yours, you move forward into the vivid blue waters of this ancient sea, and go deeper, and deeper, and deeper... and you finally go beneath the waves.

As you go beneath the waves you realise you are still breathing, but from a place you have not breathed before, not this lifetime, from between your eyes. Your spirit eye has opened up and is breathing, slower than your land breath. You gaze down at your body, and see it is transforming. It may take the shape of a fish, a beautiful tropical fish with patterns and colours never seen above on the dry land. You may be a nautilus-tailed one, or you may have the tail of a dolphin. See your body changing, and know you are returning to your true form, that of the ocean, and it was in this form your own female ancestors first came forth from the oceans, and walked upon the land. And when they did so, something was left behind... a certain freedom, to be completely at one with the womb, the water, the element that rules emotions and love, your psyche and the great flow of all life.

Aphrodite, whose form is also fluid, shifting, changing, takes you beneath to the great underwater caverns, and in this place lies a temple, in no state of ruin. Simple, silver, shining, it lies beneath the waves, intact and precious and protected. And you go with her to this temple, and she takes you to a golden room, shining with the light streaming through the water's blues and greens and greys, and in this place live the mermaids, and the men of the waters, who all greet you as one of their own. They are all beautiful.

Slowly, one of the young men swims towards you with a mirror, a large mirror into which you gaze, and through the waters you see the truths of the beliefs you have held about your own self, form and light.

"You are beautiful," they tell you. "Love this self and form." And you see the forms of the self, and the true form of your soul, the shining form of beauty, its radiant light streaming forth and through all matter, and you see now the difference it has made in this world, that your form and face is beautiful, has power, is strong and delightful. You see the face of a parent gazing at you in wonder, that one so beautiful could have come forth into this world, and you now know that this truth happens every time a soul is born into this world.

You see the face of lovers, who have adored you and your form, and you now believe their love. You see your own face, and you marvel that you could ever have been critical of this loveliness and this beauty. And in this underwater world, where your form is different, you understand that you were born beautiful, will leave this world beautiful, and that beauty is the truth of who you are.

You take one last look into the magical mirror, and you understand the purpose for this visit. Aphrodite comes to you, and smiles, and takes your hand one more time, and together you swim to the shore. Your fins and breathing hole slowly morph back into the forms of an earth dweller, and yet you know you have not left the sea behind, because you carry her and her treasures within you. And this form you are now in, you were once inside your mother's womb. And this salty world is one you are aligned with in deeper ways than you have ever known before.

Your legs move forward under the water, feet moving gently on the sand, and Aphrodite moves to the shore with you one more time. She stands with you, looks out to sea, then turns to you, and breathes again into your third eye area, and breathes one more time into your solar plexus, and places one warm hand on your womb, and you feel your sacral area stirring to full and beautiful life.

Slowly she moves away, singing and sending waves of love to you. The dolphins move with her, all the creatures of the sea accompany her, and you are alone once more upon the shore.

You look down, and before you there is a gift from Aphrodite and the people of Mer. You bend down and take it, and promise now to remember the truth.

You are beauty incarnate in form.

You were born beautiful.

You will leave this world beautiful.

And you are beautiful now...

And know that this is the whole of the truth, and cannot be changed, despite the illusions of the earthly world.

Know this, and love who you are in form, and judge it not. Beauty in truth cannot be judged. It is beyond such human scruples and divisions. And slowly breathing in this truth, say: "I am beauty. I am love. I am joy. I am radiant. I am mer-born." And return...

The Song of the Mermaids

"Maid-of-the-Wave, oh! Listen to our singing;
The white moon is winging its way o'er the sea.
Maid-of-the-Wave, the white moon is shining,
And we are all pining, sweet sister, for thee.
Maid-of-the-Wave, would thou wert near us!
Come now to cheer us. Oh, hear us! Oh, hear us."
Traditional folk song of the British Isles

Singing the Mermaids to You

Song is life itself. Our voice carries the breath, and song carries the pure note of the spirit, a message from the soul, uniting the outer world with all that dwells within us. Song carries story, tale and meaning, and notes that can literally part the walls between worlds, and heal broken hearts and torn spirits.

All elementals wish for you to free your voice, to sing your song and make a sound that will contribute to the energy of the world – but none want you to sing more than the beautiful mermaids! Mermaids and music go together. They are said to sing while combing their long, living hair on the rocks, and they croon to the ocean a song of love and tenderness. Their song connects you to the ebb and flow of the sea and her tides, the moon, and to your body and its rhythms too. The song they sing is life-giving, and creates energetic nourishment. When you sing your song, you will be nourishing the world – no matter what you may have been told about your voice!

Singing is an instinctual trait for humans, we communicate so much via our voice. We have lost track in many ways of the magic of the voice today, given we communicate so much via the screen and the words we write upon it – but there is a song in sound and in words. Notes correspond to energies, and to the world around us. By singing to the sea and the creatures of the sea as the mermaids do, we begin to sing a part of ourselves back to life.

And the song is the spell and the enactment.

Musical-enchanted encounters are many in the legends of the mermaids and fae. And Pan, the great god of music that weaves a spell, is the herald of the New Time, of the space between the worlds in which all can be revealed, when we understand that we are only seeing such a small part of the whole with our human self.

No people on the planet, no culture, has ever been without song, language and dance – and these things are banned again and again when it comes time to rob us of our magic. There were various bans on women's voices being heard by the Abrahamic religions. Men in some Jewish sects are still forbidden to hear the singing of women. And it was not until 1955 that a papal edict lifted a ban on women singing during Mass. Pope Pius XII gave the cautious go-ahead for female singers – with the proviso that they stay far from the altar! (Sadly, once women were permitted into Catholic church choirs, men left them in droves. They are now the ones whose voices are rarely heard. Why men found the prospect of singing with women so unappealing is something of a mystery.)

Some say that the way the worlds are opened and we enter the realms of the fae or the mermaids is by song – that sounds hold the key to openings where we transcend and move through realities. Many faerytales and legends speak of a lost song, note or chord, which if restored can take us to Faery and bring us home again. Sometimes it is played on a harp made from whalebone, so the sea once again has the sound that can unpeel the veil, and let us see within the realms that swirl around us, invisible as radio frequencies, but as able to be tuned in to if we find the right note to sing.

The nereids protected sailors, but it was said that their enchanting song was sacred to Poseidon, and so he alone could hear them. However the walls of coral gave way, and let their song leak out and pour forth into the world, carried on waves, reaching the shore. Oceans carry these healing songs, these notes, tones and vibrations, which become healing white noise that can place us in a tranquil, happy state effortlessly, no matter what is taking place in our lives.

A mermaid's song is as powerful as her other totems, the mirror, shell, hair and comb. Her very name means "sea virgin", and so there is a strong correlation to the Mary archetype in Christianity, and, according to some scholars, to the Magdalene bloodline.

To medieval Christians, and coastal dwellers of the sea kingdoms of the Celts, the mermaid linked passion and destruction. The fear of the mermaid's song is reflected in the Church laws that, in 578CE, banned women from singing in church. This was challenged in 754, but upheld. No women were to sing in God's house. These laws held far into the twentieth century, and led to the castration of young men throughout the eighteenth and nineteenth centuries – the castrati were adolescent men with beautiful voices who were castrated so they could maintain the notes. Somehow, the sound of the voice of a castrated young man, barely out of childhood, was considered less offensive to God than the sound of a woman's voice.

The tainted sexual beliefs of the medieval era led to a hatred of the body, of sexuality, and a demonisation of women – and of anything that could lure men to give in to their bodies and their passions. Love making was not seen as a sacrament, but as a sin.

The mermaid, with her song drawing men to their sensual selves, encouraging them to dive into the primordial mother and sea, could not be stifled – but her song could be said, again and again, to be evil and harmful. A beautiful tale by Oscar Wilde, called *The Fisherman and His Soul*, has bone-chilling passages that speak of this mistrust and hatred of the body, this mistrust and hatred of women, this mistrust and hatred of the sea and the voice of women.

"The love of the body is vile, and vile and evil are the pagan things God suffers to wander through His world. Accursed be the fauns of the woodland, and accursed be the singers of the sea!" the priest tells the fisherman, who wants to give up his soul to live with his true love, a mermaid. "I have heard them at night-time, and they have sought to lure me from my beads. They tap at the window and laugh. They whisper into my ears the tale of their perilous joys. They tempt me with temptations, and when I would pray they make mouths at me. They are lost, I tell thee, they are lost."

A woman who sang, and was unwed, was clearly suspect. If she was sexually active, she was ripe for condemnation. Allowing women to sing in church was one of the offences that convicted Paul of Samosata of heresy and had him deposed as bishop in 265CE.

Also in medieval times there flourished the various heresies of the Holy Grail, which became entwined with the tales of the mermaids. Mermaids were used often in heraldry, and were said to be the keepers of the Merovingian bloodline – the bloodline of Mary Magdalene and Christ's children. Many medieval scholars believed Mary to have been from a long line of mermaids, and the symbol of the mermaid as heraldry became shorthand for heretical sympathisers wishing to alert others to their beliefs. If a watermark was a mermaid, you could be sure the users were Gnostics, who believed that Mary had been the loving partner of Christ, and within her was held the sacred blood of the Holy Grail, her womb. Others still believe that she came from the sea. Thus the marriage of the Magdalene and the Christ was the marriage of the sea and the land. Singing, of women, may alert us again to this truth.

The grail holds the sacred blood, but is also the womb, and holds the amniotic fluid of the sea. Thus the Holy Grail is not only women's wombs, it is the sea, and the mistrust we feel about it in comparison with the land. Like the sea, women were said to be mutable, changeable, inconstant, deep, emotional and fertile. So the song of women was mistrusted. It was also said that Saint Patrick not only cast the snakes out of Ireland, but that he turned pagan women into mermaids, and thus they were unsoulled, and never to be trusted. Women's vocality, and the raising of their voices in song, was seen as a progenitor of dangerous heresies, chaos and oblivion. The mermaid though can never die, as she is the life-giving element of water itself, and her song reminds us that we must drink deep from the cauldron of life to truly live.

Singing the Mermaid's Song

When a mermaid sings, she merges the world of the earth with the world of the ocean. The waves of sound are carried on air, and she hears her voice in a completely different way to the manner in which she experiences its sound underwater. When we begin to sing to mermaids – to speak Mer – it may seem strange at first, syllables and words that sound at once weird yet familiar. Mer is the language we all speak in the womb, and it is a song we have sung before we were born, between lives. The sounds are shaped out of the sea's movement itself, and is a lullaby to the waves and tides.

You may have heard the merfolk singing – it sounds very much like a large shell being held to your ear, except that within the whoosh of the white noise of waves breaking upon the shore, you will hear language and melody. This language cannot be said – spoken – it must be shaped with notes. It must be sung!

This song is the one sung in various forms by seals, dolphins, fish and of course whales. It is the song of ancestral memory, and when we sing it, we reawaken to who we truly are. When it is sung, it forms a part of a much larger shape or pattern. All notes make "shapes" – as the tonoscope experiments by scientist Hans Jenny discovered in the 1970s. When we sing Mer, we send shapes into the waters that can be read, just like words, by our mer kinfolk.

Singing with the mermaids is as simple as singing in the shower – who has not done this? – in the bath or by or in a body of water. Of course, singing beneath the water is a wonderful experience too. Whale calls are contained and held in the great currents of the water and sent around the ocean – likewise your song to the mermaids may tap in to one of these underwater tubes and be linked around the entire planet!

There is a wonderful instrument called the gasong, a drum that is vibronic in tone. When played or sung with at a liminal time, at sunset, sunrise or at tide turn, the veils will fall, and you can connect more deeply with the merfolk, and with your own inner merfolk self.

> "Like a man in a dream, for an age it seemed
> I stood as still as a stone,
> While the mermaid sang, and her melody rang,
> like a memory calling me home…"
> The Song of the Mermaid, The Waterboys

There is also a body of beautiful music that evokes the ocean, ranging from traditional sea shanties, sung by sailors for centuries, to modern-day ballads like *Song of the Siren*, written by Tim Buckley and covered by many artists including Sinead O'Connor, This Mortal Coil and Robert Plant, and many more. Oceanic music is usually storytelling – and often carries within it complex and beautiful lyrics of yearning. Wendy Rule created an entire album devoted to the music of the ocean, called *The Lotus Eaters*.

But most heartfelt and powerful of all songs is the one that flows forth on your breath. Allow the words to unfurl. Play.

Simply make sounds. As the beautiful German poet Rainer Maria Rilke writes: "As it happens, the wall between us is very thin. Why couldn't a cry from one of us break it down? It would crumble easily; It would barely make a sound..."

Sing like a wave, like a dolphin, be at one with the song of the tides, of the waves and currents. Some say there are special notes, that when hit at the right octave, allow you to see the merfolk. Whether this is true or not I cannot say. But I have heard the mermaids singing – and while they sang to each other, and not to me, their very blessed song heals, uplifts and enchants. I have seen them singing, and this sight will be one I carry with me to the moment my eyes close for the last time this lifetime.

The Turtle Singers of Kadavu

In Fiji, there is a sacred place called Kadavu, where one of the most beautiful traditions of singing to the creatures of the ocean continues to this day. This is the ritual of calling to the turtles. Within the jagged teeth of the headland's rocks, the women of the village of Namuana cling. They snuggle into small crevices and shallow caves in the cliffs, and begin to chant, over and over, their ancient song. As their voices gather power, giant sea turtles arise to the surface one by one. It is forbidden to take the life of any of these turtles – it is sacred to sing to them, and to have them arise to hear the call.

It is said that if anyone hunts one of these turtles, the creatures will arise and listen no more. This is because the women are said to be able to turn into turtles to escape the men who would harm them or enslave them, and sometimes when the women of this village die, they transform into turtles and revisit the area.

Thus they are singing to their own ancestors, their own womenfolk, and they keep the tradition alive so they too can change and keep the women safe and well. Here is the chant that is sung:

> The women of Namuana are all dressed in mourning,
>   Each carries a sacred club each tattooed in a strange pattern.
>   Do rise to the surface Raudalice, so we may look at you.
>   Do rise to the surface Tinaicoboga, so we may also look at you.

Ella's Deep Mermaid Magic

Ella Risebrow is a faery and mermaid sculptress from the magical town of Byron Bay, Australia, whose works are exhibited and collected worldwide. She also teaches art workshops and does portraits of people as mermaids or other mystical beings. From childhood she has lived close to the ocean and forests, where she experienced prophetic visions and dreams and interpreting them into artworks. She says creativity has always been her expression and main means of existence. Visit Ella at www.EllaRisebrow.com.

I believe in mermaids. Aside from my intuition and knowing, they have appeared to me in my drawings with many signs, symbols and coincidences, showing me that the myths and legends are not fantasy. They are living in the ocean, and have important messages they're revealing for humans. I have also glimpsed them hiding in the coral when I've been snorkelling and diving. They're very well camouflaged and swim away very swiftly and quietly – this is one reason why sightings are so few.

I connect with mermaids within my very soul. Mermaid energy has a particular character of purification, romance, passion, deep emotion, ancient wisdom and love. To be able to see or feel the presence of a mermaid, stillness of the mind is key. One discordant thought and whooosh, they swim off before you can get a glimpse. To connect with their energy, I work with visualisations and meditations in beautiful, colourful underwater gardens. Having your feet in a foot bath of salt water and holding a shell can enhance the meditation. Mermaid gatherings and rituals are wonderful, as are snorkelling, surfing, scuba diving, whale watching, sitting on the beach singing like a siren, and, of course, drinking water. When I'm creating, drawing or doll making, the mermaid energies come through. Filled with awe, I become very emotional and all my walls are washed away, then a calmness ensues and I become one with the mermaid as my hands are guided, gently sculpting or

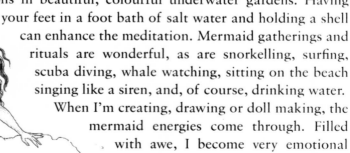

drawing, allowing the merbeing to bridge between the worlds and slowly appear into form so we may see her.

When drawing the energy patterns of the fae, the light streams are a swift upward motion, hence the formation of wings. In contrast, the energy patternings of a mermaid spiral downward, similar to DNA coding and some shell shapes, hence the formation of a tail. Fae invoke the inner child and the inner wild, the instinctive connection and communication with earth. Mermaids evoke the grown-up energy and renewal, and for those who enter these places and are not yet ready, mermaid energy is "deep water". When I make dolls for weddings I am usually led to make mermaids rather than faeries.

Mermaid energy is important because it is refreshing, expansive and liberating – just like a swim in the ocean, the mermaid can replenish and heal us. The ancient stories of mermaids luring men to their death (of self) beneath the ocean is a profound symbolism for abandonment of self into the depths of the soul where a treasure is discovered, transformation takes place and the fearless hero returns purified with renewed life and maturation. The call of the mermaid is very significant right now, with depression being so widespread; her oceanic cleansing can wash away all those stagnant energies and cobwebs. There's a reason ocean rhymes with emotion and that our tears are salty. Also, merfolk cleanse and renew the ocean, so at this time, listening to the call from merfolk for help is very important.

To protect the sea, their home, let's get bombastic about plastic. It is fantastic, but the devastating effect on sea life is drastic. We can recycle, re-use, refuse, and get involved in beach clean-ups. And the more we interact with the sea and her creatures and visit sea rescue places, the more passionate we become about educating ourselves as to what we can do personally.

Sea Witches

"I am the star that rises from the sea,
the twilight sea.
I bring men dreams,
that rule their destiny."
Dion Fortune, The Sea Priestess

Being Drawn to the Magic of the Sea

When we think of witchcraft we might see with our mind's eye a wise woman bent over a cauldron in the midst of a sacred grove. But there are wise women and sage men who stretch their arms out to the sea, and draw the power of the salt, the wind and the waves to them, and raise that power for good. As the world changes once again, and we approach the times when humans must change or be changed, the old gods of the sea and the merfolk and their energies are rising once again – and it is the sea witches, wizards and priestesses who are working with these beings to teach other humans about the magic of the sea, and how she is our mother.

While once sea witches may have attempted to turn winds, call fish to nets and brew strong storms in the ocean's cauldron, today they are just as likely to be raising money for Sea Shepherd, donating their time and resources to ocean conservation, replanting coral reefs, snorkelling, surfing or making powerful wands or talismans from the offerings of our mother the sea.

As we humans continue to create conditions that contribute to elevated sea temperatures and ocean contamination and pollution, the ancient sea mother energies are stirring and being summoned to return and help us. Everyone who is connected to the ocean is feeling this. Even people who live nowhere near the sea are connecting to dolphins, merbeings and oceanic energies.

Being a sea witch today has little to do with controlling the ocean – it has far more to do with raising energy and respect for her, and creating and maintaining a healthy relationship with the creatures of our mother the ocean. Welcome to the powerful and ancient tradition of the sea witches, women and men who worked – and still work – with seafaring communities to engage with the elements in ways that benefit their community.

The Sea : A Special Bond

Stacey Demarco, a respected witch and author from Sydney, Australia, has always lived within sight of the ocean. "My connection to the ocean? It's the wildness. The unknowable. The sheer terror and the deep calm," she says. "The way I can clean myself simply by diving into the salt water. The way I can both live on land and be of the sea as well. I am drawn to the beach especially when it storms. The power of capturing that energy to do spells is incredible.

"I can't actually imagine not doing magical workings by the sea, and certainly also within the water itself. I did this even before I knew I was a 'witch'. Those transitional places – the rock shelves, the sea caves, the sands, the wetlands – are so very powerful in every way. They speak to a very old and core part of myself and also, I think, of most humans," Stacey explains.

"My husband is very much a water man. I believe his link is deeper than mine, although he wouldn't put it in spiritual terms. His connection is so simple – it's just joy. Joy when he enters the water, joy when he surfs, joy when he swims, and the confidence within the water. He has no fear whatsoever!"

For Athene Thompson, a reiki master and aromatherapist from Melbourne, the sea is about cleansing and renewal.

"It happens every time I go near the ocean," she says. "And I don't even have to go in to feel this sense of unity with her. She tells me her stories, she sings, she roars, she nurtures, she listens to me and she can hold any emotion I give to her to be dissolved alongside my soul-secrets, silent prayers and inner visions that I give to her for safe keeping. It is always a fair exchange."

Rowan Darkmoon Dragonstorm is a spiritual writer from Essex, England. For her, the seashore is a sacred space. "The beach for me is nature's ultimate altar – a meeting of the Sea and the Land, a place of transition, a place already between worlds."

Sea witches are the land-dwelling sisters of the mermaids, and work their magics differently. Karen Kay, editor of *Mermaids & Mythology* and *FAE*, lives in Lands End, Cornwall, near the sea kingdom of Lyonesse, often described as the British Atlantis.

"I *have* to be near the sea," Karen says. "I cannot explain why, it's just an instinctive need. I feel more mer than sea witch though. Merbeing feels softer than sea witch, although I'm sure there's an aspect of sea witch within it too. Merbeing feels like a natural connection to the sea energies, while sea witch implies to me more of a power and harnessing of those energies."

It is the harnessing of such powers that has made sea witches famous and feared in seagoing communities like those in Cornwall, in fishing villages along rocky granite coastlines where the energy of millennia of magical practices hovers in the ruins of Tintagel, or is documented in the excellent Museum of Witchcraft in Boscastle. There are some wonderful historic personages, fabled sea witches, whose cunning ways and hard lives have carved their legends into Cornish imaginations, just as King Arthur and Morgan la Fey have.

The Old Ways and Sea Witches

One of the most notorious weather witches of old Cornwall was the fearsome Dolly Pentreath, who lived in the late 1600s. She spoke only Cornish, and never uttered a word of English. She has many nicknames, and is sometimes referred to as the "foul-mouthed fishwife of Mousehole". Dolly made her living selling fish at the marketplace in the village of Mousehole, and selling her own style of astrological readings and magical assistance too! She chronically smoked her pipe, drank bucketloads of beer, saved more than one person's life, flung axes at the local constabulary, who were fearful of her spells and savage, sharp tongue, and cursed and swore with the kind of ferocity and volume usually reserved for the most salty of sailors! She never married, but she gave birth to a son, and Dolly lived, they say, to a hundred and two years old – a very ripe age for a woman who passed from this life in 1777.

When she passed, many believe she took with her the most complete record of the vocabulary of Old Cornish, although that language is being revived and reclaimed today.

This formidable wise woman's plaque reads, in part: *Dolly Pentreath was a fine woman, with a voice you could hear as far away as Newlyn. She had the heart of a lion, and it was said that when a press-gang landed in search of men for the navy, Dolly took up a hatchet and fought them back to their boats, and so cursed them in Old Cornish that the crew never ventured back again. She was artful as well as brave, and saved a man, wanted by the law for a hanging, by hiding him in her chimney. Search they did, and found no man; but Dolly found her tongue, and let them have it; and then she found her thick shoes and let them fly. Then she made for the chopper [an axe], and that cleared the house.*

The Keigwin Arms in Mousehole lays claim to having been Dolly's favourite pub, and the room she frequented is still intact. There you can try your hand at shouting, Dolly-style, out the window to the fishermen coming in with their catches. You might just snare yourself a bargain – something cunning, cuss-mouthed Dolly apparently adored!

Unlike Dolly, about whose face the kindest thing that was ever said was that it was hard, most sea witches are reputed to be beauties. In this tale from old Brittany, the Celtic part of France, the sea witch may be irresistible, but she is never to be trusted.

"It was a palace made of seashells, lovelier than anything you can imagine. A crystal stairway led up to the door, and it was built in such a curious way that at each step you took, the stair sang like a forest bird. All around the palace were immense gardens and lawns of seaweed set with diamonds instead of flowers, and surrounding the gardens was a forest of sea trees.

"Houarn stood in the doorway of the palace, and there in the first room he saw the witch lying on a golden bed. She was dressed in sea-green silk as fine and soft as a wave. Coral ornaments were in her black hair, which fell down to her feet. Her pink and white face was as delicately tinted as the inside of a shell.

"Houarn drew back at the sight of so delightful a being. But the faery rose up smiling and went towards him. Her walk was as lithesome as the sweep of the waves on the rolling sea."

From the Witch of Lok Island, a faerytale from Brittany

Sea witches are often said to be born during storms, cyclones, at sea or with a magical caul over their head. A caul, the remnant of the amniotic membrane which sometimes clings to the head of a newborn infant or covers their face, is said to prevent its bearer from ever drowning. As someone who was born with a caul, and given my love of the ocean, I have had cause many times to be grateful for that blessing.

There is a legend in Cornwall – a place absolutely thriving in its mermaid legends – of the Mermaid of Padstow.

This mermaid would lead the ships up the estuary to safety, guiding them all the way. And then, as the stories so often go, she met a man, and he fell so in love with her that he asked her to be his bride, and come and live with him. She could not live on land, so she refused him, and he felt such pain that he grew violent in his rage and shot her. With her dying breath the keeper of the sailor's safety perished. A great storm blew up from the sea, wrecking boats and shoreline houses, and a great sand bank was created which lies there to this day – known as the Doom Bar.

All along the coastline and islands of the British Isles, on deserted storm-battered beaches and amidst the standing stones of rugged Callanish Island off Scotland's coast, it is easy to imagine a weather witch raising her hands and calling the storms, or asking them to disperse. To do so would take much courage, and the ability to speak clearly and with strength to the elements. Perhaps at these sites on the sacred isles sea witches once stood, and charged their tools, and their hands, with the energy that poured forth from a lightning storm. I have often stood in the sand beneath a stormy sky and raised my witch's knife to charge her with natural, powerful energy, feeling the powers of old.

It is also quite possible to be a powerful practising sea witch and live far from the ocean our mother. Darkrayven Morgaine is a pagan who lives a long way from the beach. That, however, does not stop her incorporating the ocean into her rituals and workings.

"I am definitely a sea witch," she says. "I live far from the ocean, but my soul yearns for it every single day. My ritual robes are decorated with cowrie shells and my altars always have shells on them – an unspoken law almost. I am an air sign and have only lived near the sea for short periods, but I definitely *feel* my power only at the ocean's edge. She is my refuge."

The Power of the Sea Witches

Sea witches are not simply beings of mystic fables, or nasty baddies, as they are cast in tales like *The Little Mermaid*. In my world, the sea witch and the mermaid have a deep and abiding respect for each other. One is a land dweller, the witch, the other is of the sea. But both work with the powers of the ocean – and most often, they work for the good of all.

Sea witches must work with the elements, and so most are not victims of too much vanity! They are unafraid of what keeps most people inside, and they tend to have strong constitutions and steady health, enabling them to withstand temperature extremes and rough conditions. They work with the tides, the winds, the skies and the water, along with the cycles of the moon, and they are never truly in need of a cauldron, as the sea provides the greatest of all witches' tools for these magical practitioners. Even the sand can become a healing surface for those who are awake and aware of the power of the sea.

"I love the sea, but tend to stay on the shore more than in the water," says Natasha Heard, a creator of magical wands and tools, many of which hold mer energy. "I feel there is much magic in the sand, shimmering tiny crystals that cleanse and align my energies as soon as I set foot upon them. My small sea dragon was whispering to me about sandcastles and how we all instinctively create them from our Lemurian and Atlantean memories."

Sea witches often work with objects the merfolk offer – they are the keepers of some of the ocean's powerful energetic tools, which are often gifted to them for their use. They use salt water to clear with, shells to energise and banish, sponges to increase air quality. The coral they protect, and if some comes into their hands they heal it, and use it wisely and well. Driftwood and ropes tied into knots become tools for spells, to bless sailors and ships that go to sea.

Maggie Sinton loves working with driftwood pieces she collects on Western Australian beaches. "I found the most amazing pieces of driftwood in Busselton, and will be making them into sea wands. I love the beach during thunderstorms best – to find a secluded spot where you can strip off and run into the waves, soak in the rain, drown in the thunder and explode in the lightning is divine. Then when you get back to the car you have a good rub down and put on dry clothes – it's pure magic!" she says.

Sea witches do have reputations for being very powerful, and make formidable warriors. Many legends are told of them, from raising storms that drove back the Nazi pilots during the Battle of Britain to raising even more storms to destroy the ships of the Spanish Armada during the reign of Elizabeth I.

Sea Witch Lessons
Times, Tides and Weather Workings

Doing workings at the right time to activate certain energies can make your sea spells very powerful and effective, so consider the direction of the wind, time of tide-turn and moon phase. These energies are there for us – we are part of these cycles and they will impact on us in any case. And it's a good thing to know "which way the wind blows", for practical reasons as well as spiritual, because knowing such things deeply reconnects us to the mother of us all.

If working a spell on the shore, I consider the following:
  ✪ The direction of the wind.
  ✪ The tide times.
  ✪ The sky.
  ✪ The movement of creatures.
  ✪ What the sea offers me in her wisdom – what lies upon her shores can become part of the working.

If a spell or working really needs to be done, I will do it regardless of the timings, but when I can't wait for the ideal conditions, I do attempt to go with the flow of the natural forces as much as possible. Here are some ways to connect with the winds of the four directions, information on tides and their energies, and spells and runes to create your own rituals.

The meaning the wind will have depends very much on where you live – in the northern hemisphere, the north wind is cold and icy, but in Australia, it can be warm and inviting. A wind is northerly if it is *coming* from that direction, not if it is heading in that direction. The old tried and true test of wetting a finger and feeling the direction works every time. Better still, why not become a windvane yourself? Immerse yourself in the water, then feel the air blowing on your skin as you emerge. Feel the direction it is coming from. Magical bliss!

On the east coast of Australia, the ocean is most still just before the north-easterly winds pick up, usually before 10am and after 5pm. And in the afternoons, the southerly winds blow cool air on to the land. Mornings are often the best time for a working, and the liminal times of dawn and dusk, in combination with the liminal doorways of tide-changes and the shoreline itself, offer entrance to other worlds. New and full moons offer other portals, with the new moon being best for beginnings, the dark moon for banishment, and the full moon for stirring great power.

A Sea Witch Knot Spell
Raising and Releasing the Power of Air

Just as sailors are adept at tying intricate knots for different purposes, so too do sea witches know the lore of magical knots – knots to hold the winds, knots to release the winds, and knots to stir up storms. In Boscastle's Museum of Witchcraft in Cornwall there are some old knotted ropes. These authentic pieces of magical history are living remnants of ligature – the art and magic of tying knots to raise and release the energy of air.

Sea witch lore has it that you take a piece of rope from the ship you wish to protect. Then you gather up your intention, draw it to you, feel its power and tie the knot. The energy is then living within the knot, ready to be released when needed. Another intention, another knot. A final intention, another knot. You bind your intent into each knot you create.

Traditionally, sea witches would tie in the power of the wind. When untied at sea, the first knot would release a sweet wind from the southeast – warm and pushing the ship west towards the Sacred Isles. Releasing the second knot would unbind the force of the northerly wind, this time a forceful wind that would speed the ship back to the warm lands of the south. The third knot remained at the discretion of the witch who tied it – it might contain the force of a gale, typhoon or cyclone!

However, not all knot work was for winds – ligature was sometimes used to keep love true while a man was at sea, or to ensure he arrived home well, with all limbs and teeth in place, and with great treasures.

When I have worked with knot magic it has not been so much for weather but for the "winds of change" within my own life. When working with the natural elements, I tend to trust that they know what they are doing – we need to work with a light hand – but I do need assistance. So I tie in energy at the right time – at a new moon or full moon for example – then untie the knot when I need that energy for my altar or spellcasting. This way we honour the natural, and our own timing and needs.

Sea witches would often work with what they found. Shipwrecked wood pieces, shells and stones from the sea, sea creature bones, netting, sea kelps. So it follows that the most powerful ligature rope comes from ships, and is washed up on the shore, streaming with ocean magics. However you work with this ancient art, ligature is a time-honoured, effective form of sea-spell craft, which can help turn the times and tides of our own lives!

... The sea, the sea in
The darkness calls.
The little waves, with
Their soft white hands,
Efface the footprints in the sands,
And the tide rises, the tide falls.
Henry Wadsworth Longfellow, The Tide Rises, The Tide Falls

Lunar and Tidal Magics
Lady Moon and Mother Ocean

The great mother ocean has her tides, her ebbs and flows, her highs and lows, and we on the shore watch in wonder at these each day. But does the bright Lady Moon alone cause these cycles? And what magics can we learn from the tides of the sea?

In the ancient world, there were many peoples. Mountain people who walked with the frost giants for thousands of seasons. Forest people who could move in to and out of the sacred trees, who are now known as dryads and druids. And there were the sea people, who knew the secrets of the tides, the fish, the great cetaceans, and the merpeople.

The sea people watched the ocean, from darkness to brightness to darkness again, and came to know that when the mother of us all breathed in, the tide went out. Infinite treasures were strewn along the shore then, and the ocean would hold the in-breath long enough for us to gather the fish which we would eat, the coral from which came the medicine, the bone from which we would make the harp, and the kelp which we would plough into our fields. Then she breathed out, and the tide came in, in a magical cycle of in and out.

The coming in brought other things too. Waves to ride upon. Hunters, human and oceanic, came closer to the shore. All the time, we would watch the seas, growing more and more aware of their abundance. In her cauldron lived the leaping ones. The small crawling ones. The swimming ones. The clinging ones.

There were periwinkles and gleaming soft-violet sea snails, with their purple medicine and ability to draw out toxins from within our thought fields and from the cells of our brains, the jellyfish that live within our shell-like skulls. There were the sea anemones, the sea stars in the deeper waters, and the great ones like the mulberry plumed kites who swooped down to capture the creatures caught in the tidal slippage.

We watched the storms gather over the oceans, and some took out their small curraghs, canoes or fallen tree friends on the tide from the Blessed Isles, and we began to view the land as the foreign place... And we knew, after watching her for a long time, that the sea mother's tides and cycles were dancing with the sacred moon's waxing and waning. That all in the universe breathed as one. And that thus what was above, was what was below.

And the rituals would be observed and the festivals kept, because that way the mother would breathe in and out more easily – and we would breathe with her, in the way of the cycles of the soul, planet, galaxy, universe. We humans too respond to the moon's tides, to the solar tides, to the galactic tides. The great ocean may respond more readily, but the firm earth also breathes in and out, as do the waters of this beautiful planet.

The tides are also great teachers to we humans. The cycle of the tides are a profound lesson in the inevitable changing of all things, of all environments, sending us the message that there is an ebb and flow to all things, to all natural cycles, and that we flow with them.

Tides and cycles can teach us so much. They are a study of how we must learn to shift our expectations each day – the tides are constant, and yet they are ever changing. Nothing stays exactly the same at the seashore, but the tides get as close to a repeating cycle as is possible once every nineteen years, the time it takes the moon and the sun to do their complete cycle with each other. It is no coincidence that these nineteen-year cycles were the period of study for the druids of the sea kingdoms of Cornwall, Brittany, the Isle of Man, Scotland, Ireland and Wales.

Sea people today observe the tides, the currents, the moon and the winds. They know to fish on a full moon, as the sea creatures are drawn to the light – for three days before, and three days after, the fishing will be good, as the creatures of the dark beneath are drawn to the illumination of the moon.

Ancient peoples would move about the waters with boats lit with sandalwood to draw fish to the surface, imitating the full moon. Today fishermen in the Andaman Sea bless their boats with garlands of flowers and carry lanterns of light in their small vessels as they fish the warm, salty waters of that Asiatic body of water.

It is true, broadly speaking, that the moon's movements produce the movements of the ocean's tides. Tides, when measured, are mathematically harmonic – perfectly spaced and related – in their procession. We could, in effect, find corresponding musical notes to accompany their rising and falling, and thus hear sacred song, the true song of the sea. When I think of this, it inspires me, as mermaids sing, and I often call out to the sea.

I think of the whales, singing their ancestral songs, the great record of the world. Of sailors, wiling away the long nautical miles with sea shanties. The sirens calling Odysseus to the rocks with their beauteous voices. There is a song to the sea, and its keys and notes could be captured and sung by the rising and falling of the waters each day. Each day the mother breathes in, and the mother breathes out. And as she does, the song of the universe is sung.

Our planet has a heartbeat from within, and also responds like a child to a mother to the magnetism of the other heavenly bodies. We are all of us dancing to the rhythms of below and above, in very real ways, each day. These are no fluffy ideas but real geomagnetic forces, forces which create galactic tides that move within us, from high to low, every six hours, four times each day. Even if we were to be in the centre of a desert, the water within our bodies, our womb, our blood, would feel this tug and release, every sundown to sundown.

It is as natural as breathing out and breathing in, and to synch in we need do nothing but live. Yet if we live in partnership with the cycles of lunar-sea, the magic of our lives becomes fuller, deeper, richer, and we live with more ease, flow, courage and gratitude.

We lead, and we yield. We seek, and we retreat. We hunt, and we are hunted. All these things are taught by the simple observation of walking, swimming, dwelling in the oceanic magics.

If you have read *The Book of Faery Magic* or *The Wild Wisdom of the Faery Oracle*, you will know that I share again and again the message of the enchanted liminal spaces. The tideline and the creatures that live right in the in-between are the creatures of true magic – liminal, enchanted in-between beings, who must alter, change and shapeshift each day. If we yield and capitulate at the right times, and then pour ourselves in at the right times, all will be well. This dance is echoed in the varying shapes of the moon as she yields to darkness, then grows in brightness each month, as the women bleed their oceanic bloods each lunar month – thirteen moons.

Time and Tidal Spells and Rituals

Here are some starting points for sea magics to be created in attunement with the sacred ocean and the holy moon. Before gathering any magical tools along the shore, you must make an offering to the sea. We do not take before we give. The ocean provides us all with life on this planet, so let us thank her before collecting her driftwood or her seashells, or casting in our line for fish.

Gathering litter and human debris along the shore is a wonderful offering to the merpeople. My personal creed is that I must collect five pieces of rubbish for any shell I collect, or any violet sea snail shell I give a new home to. I always take a bag with me specifically to collect litter which I dispose of through recycling.

It is no chore, but a joy for me to do this. It lightens me, and makes me happy to be a part of the clearing, the solution. I harbour no feelings of "why should I do this?" I let go and know that there is no reward other than my connection to the merbeings and their home, mother ocean and her cauldron of life deepening, and their trust in me growing. That is well worth it.

Never leave a single thing at the shoreline that does not belong there. It is not right for the water to clear our debris. Throughout the ages we have flung our metals (including coins), our plastics and our other rubbish into lakes, wells, rivers and seas, which contributes to the suffering and choking of creatures such as turtles and pelicans.

One of the most healing acts I have experienced is to bathe in a mermaid's tidal pool. Choose one which is deep enough to immerse yourself in, and be aware that you are entering the home of the sea creatures. Do not be afraid, but be aware of animals such as the blue-ringed octopuses and the spiky sea urchins.

As you bathe in the sacred healing pool, allow it to drain away, at the change of tide, anything that must be left behind in order for you to go forward again, to go to your own personal high tide. The salt water crystals will drag through your auric layer, clearing and cleansing, leaving you feeling light and free, yet very present and clear. The warm waters of the tidal pools make them mermaidenly places of healing, right on the seashore, the amniotic fluid of rebirth that will heal and free you.

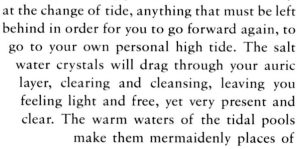

Another powerful ritual is to create a sandcastle, mandala

or sculpture near the tideline to represent whatever you are working on, so shape into the sand – itself an energy field of tiny, sparkling crystals – representations of what you wish to see taken away and cleared. Then wait and watch your sandcastle of release vanish beneath the tide. See and feel the clearing taking place. Then look for an offering from the incoming tide – a shell tumbling in the water, a sea-polished stone, mermaid hair fanning upon the glistening sand. The sea will gift you a sign.

You will achieve wonderful results if you perform this ritual on a receding tide on a waning moon. To make it even more strong and irrevocable, do it as the year turns from light to dark – around Mabon for example, to truly bind this magical act.

Timing and Tidings

A simple guide to moon phases, their timing and their powers is:

☾ New moon: A new lunar cycle begins, so it's time to start your activation of intentions.

◐ Waxing moon: New growth, continued action and results will come about if you work now.

○ Full moon: This is the high tide of power, with an amplifying and creative energy.

☽ Waning moon: The universal energies are withdrawing, with a sucking and pulling impact.

● Dark moon: A time to go within and soul-scry – there will be revelations from within at this time.

The moon's impact is sometimes strongest two days *after* what you can observe with your physical eyes in the night sky. Remember too to have patience – accept that the universal cycles cannot help but answer you at the right time.

It takes at least one full lunar cycle for gentle change to manifest. Two lunar cycles for solidifying the same change. Three for true change. Four for foundational change. Five for life direction change, and so on. For the greatest power, to truly let things go, between nine and thirteen lunar cycles hold the greatest magic, and the cycle holds utter magic at nineteen years.

Yes, from one lunar cycle to nineteen years of thirteen moons, this is a long time in our impatient world. Working with the moon will take energy, time and commitment. You must ask yourself whether you are truly willing to change, if you are truly willing to dance the dance of change with the moon and the ocean.

Of course, if the universal cycles already heard your prayer long before you were born this lifetime, change may be instant. This is the true meaning of divine right timing – the cycles of the universe!

Tides turn generally speaking every six hours. There is a brief pause between tidal shifts. Currents run very strong on the turn of the tide. Do not get caught far out to sea on a small sandlet at turn of tide. Always know the sea movements of where you are working, when the tides will change, where the currents run strong, how often they turn (in some places, tides run slower or faster than the six hour rule of thumb). Ask a local, or check the tides in the newspaper – the fishing section has the lunar cycle and the tidal cycle, which is very handy for magical information.

Generally speaking, there will be two low tides and two high tides each twenty-four-hour period, and one high will have greater impact than the other. Know the shores you are working with – being caught out at sea on rocks with a wild and strong incoming tide is something that is avoidable. If you are concerned you may go into "ritual time" and lose track, be sure to know where a safe place is to work regardless of tidal forces.

Do not be afraid of the sea – but do respect her, and know and learn of her ways. Ask her for information. Watch her. Listen. Give her your time. In return she will grant you wishes, dreams and delight, as well as powerful clearings, visions and connections with all of her creatures, from the smallest one to the larger playful dolphins, the mighty whales and the merpeople.

For the gifts the sea will grant you, you must return the magics. You can do this by literally cleaning the shore when you can, or by making an offering to an organisation that works directly with clearing the seas of human hunters – such as the Sea Shepherd Conservation Society or a local conservation group.

My personal favourite ways to interact with the sea are surfing, clearing the shore of rubbish in simple, low-impact ways, taking little, and working with the oracles of the sea and her merfolk.

May all your interactions with the sea, especially under moonlight, be blessed – and know that every time you bathe within her waters, under her light, you are reborn.

Lunasea

✪ Two daily tides are directly affected by the moon's field of gravity. On earth we have gravity, so too do the moon and the sun.

✪ Both the sun and the moon exert a force on the earth and all its beings, and we respond to all that takes place in this universe.

✪ We notice the water's response to the moon and sun's gravity, but the earth, the mountains and the glaciers feel their magnetism too.

✪ A large ring standing far out from the moon is a sign that a big rain is coming to the seas.

✪ If the ring is off-centre, there will be storms at sea.

✪ A double ring means ice may fall in the sea.

✪ The moon recedes from the earth at about four centimetres a year, meaning our days are growing longer. This process takes millions of years to make a discernible difference, but the subtle shift each year is making some of us who are of the Old Ways feel her loss more, and for others, they feel less and less connected.

✪ The Greek traveller Pytheas sailed to the British Isles in 325BCE and related the large spring tides to the phases of the moon.

✪ There are no words for "time" in Old Gaelic – the only related words are for wind, sea, weather, cycles and moon changes. The word tide comes from the Scots Gaelic.

✪ Seleucus of Seleuca, a city of Babylon, observed the relationship between the moon and the tides in 200BCE.

✪ In 100CE, Chinese philosopher Wang Chong wrote: "The tide's rise and fall follows the moon and varies in magnitude."

✪ The Greek philosopher Philostratus felt that the tides were shaped by the spirit of the moon.

✪ In most places there is a delay between the phases of the moon and the effect on the tide. Spring tides fall two days after the moon phase. This is fascinating to me – does this mean that in real terms we here on earth receive the whole impact of a full moon two days after seeing its light radiating to the earth?

✪ Biological cycles of sea and intertidal creatures – those who live on the liminal shores – and humans occur in multiples of tide-times. Gestation and hatching is timed to the lunar cycle and tidal rhythms perfectly. In women, our menstrual cycle is our inner sea, and matches the lunar tide cycle. This could explain my feeling that many of us were born of the sea, and have shapeshifting qualities lying dormant.

Karen's Merfae Magic

Karen Kay is the editor of *FAE* and *Mermaids & Mythology* magazines. She is creator and director of the 3 Wishes Faery Fest, the Avalon Faery Ball and some exciting new international mermaid events. Karen also writes, sings and performs her own magical music. She lives in Cornwall, in the southwest of England, where the land meets the sea. Visit Karen at www.themermaidmagazine.com.

I haven't seen mermaids with my physical eyes, but I've seen them in my mind's eye, and I also feel their energy strongly. I feel most at home living near the sea, and that's why I love Cornwall. When I first moved here I got very strong visions of mermaids, and I spent weeks drawing them. I don't consider myself an artist, but they seemed to manifest on the paper before my eyes. I remember drawing every single scale on their tails, and there were warrior mermaids with tridents, who did not spend all day looking in the mirror and combing their hair! Sometimes I can feel the mermaids calling to me, and whatever I'm doing I have to stop and go to the seashore.

I feel truly blessed to reside in the wild landscape of Cornwall. I love living near the sea. There are many tails (forgive the pun!) of mermaid sightings and stories on every shore of Cornwall, the most famous one is the Mermaid of Zennor. They say a beautiful Otherworldly woman used to regularly visit a church in the village of Zennor. She'd stand at the back of the church and listen to the beautiful singing of a local man named Matthew Trewella. It is said that one day he looked at her and she smiled at him, and he followed her to a cliff's edge and was never seen again. Many years later, the captain of a ship heard singing. He looked over the side of his ship and saw a beautiful mermaid with long flowing hair. She asked if he would please raise his anchor as it was resting on the door of her house, and she had to get back inside to be with her husband Matthew and their children. This is just one version of the story. There are many other versions, and who knows which one is true, if any?

I believe mermaids can help with emotional issues, and help us come to conclusions by allowing their mer energy to flow around the situation, bringing a crystal-clear, water-like clarity to any situation involving our emotions. They're happy to help us in healing sessions too. I have no set rituals when working with mer energy, every time is unique. I have some tools – shells, holed stones found on a local beach, a mer wand (driftwood in the shape of a wand). They aren't essential, but they help when an instant connection is required. If I'm on the seashore, I start by placing seawater on my third eye while invoking mermaids.

Mer energy can really help with the healing of water, oceans and creatures of the sea. From my connection with merfolk, I know they are very happy that people are remembering them, and are very happy to assist humans in restoring balance to the waters of planet earth, be it the oceans, rivers, lakes, clouds, reservoirs, dams etc.

I always know if someone is a mer person or a fae person, I can see it in their aura and in the way they present themselves in their human form. I feel like I'm a combination of both, a merfae if you like. I feel I've been a mermaid in a past life, perhaps several times. I feel such a strong affinity with the sea, but also a fear – a strange combination! From a very young age it was my mission to have very long hair, perhaps a throwback to when I was a mermaid. I love eating seaweed too, and when I wear shimmering iridescent colours like turquoise, blues, greens and silvers, it transports me back to my life as a mermaid.

Mermaids inspire me to create, and to see the beauty in the world, and to appreciate the oceans, lakes, rivers and streams. They inspire me to value the elixir of life that is water. They inspire me to not use harmful household products like bleach or harsh chemicals, which end up in our water supply and in the ocean, poisoning the fish and the creatures of the sea.

Mermaid Divination

"Divination opens a spiritual window through
which we can see our present situations more clearly,
and peek into possible futures."
Patricia Telesco, American author, priestess and poet

Sea Scrying: Parting the Tides of Time and Working With the Emotion of the Waves

Mermaid divination is a wonderful, powerful, insightful and delightful magical art. Everyone is capable of tuning in to the element of water, and working with her in mystical ways to divine the future, gain clarity in the present and understand the past.

Who has not seen faces in falling waters, forms in waves, white horses on the sea foam? Within the waters, we may see visions of people who will be in our lives, see ourselves as we lived thousands of years ago, and see scenes of great importance in the world. When we allow our vision to see in the waters, we can see right back to the womb, and to the tomb. We can see with and through the emotions, and can grow into balance with them, working with our feelings in respectful, beautiful ways. The insights that follow allow us to understand, plan, evaluate and communicate about what is truly important to our loved ones, our own selves, and to our communities.

In ancient times, the sea was "read" again and again for portents of the future before voyages and to ask for blessings. In this day and age, it is perhaps even more important than ever before to connect to this vast natural source of wisdom. The more we connect, the better we can love and be of service to the ocean, our mother.

While these methods and thoughts may seem strange and mysterious to some, this is simply because we have stopped practising what is so very natural to us! If we practise, we become more and more adept, and we lose any sense of this being weird or odd. It becomes as natural to us as brushing our hair, another magical mermaidenly act!

Scrying is the art of using our actual physical vision to connect with our psychic or inner vision, and involves seeing images in a surface such as a crystal ball. That is what many of us think when we first learn of scrying. However, mermaids scry in bodies of water – all kinds – and this is the original and most natural way to use our Sight and inner vision. For some, the lake was called the dark mirror, for others, the sea was known as the shining cauldron.

It is a practical magical mystery, and is a beautiful, personal way of working with the sea, lakes and sacred bodies of waters – even if the closest we can get is our bathtub or a silver scrying bowl under moonlight. Learning to scry can train us to "see" the patterns that are all around us, and activate our inner vision when we wish to use it. It also teaches us how to turn down this inner vision for when we wish to be fully present with family, friends or simply with ourselves.

The word scry has its roots in the old Anglo Saxon word descry, meaning to reveal or to see. It is also the root of our word describe. When we scry, we are releasing the hold our conscious mind has over our abilities to see, and allowing the waters we are working with to share their wisdoms and insights, even answer our questions. When we scry we work with magical intuition and intention, thus it is a wonderful form of mermaidenly connection that also strengthens and deepens the flow of our natural psychic talents.

How to Sea Scry

Essentially sea scrying relies on the practitioner using a watery surface to gaze upon. What that surface is can vary according to what you prefer, what activates your Sight, and what you have available to you. Many people use a scrying mirror – a mermaid's mirror – a mirror whose glass is either imbued with smoky tones or which has a black backing, making the surface deeper and less reflective. You may wish to find a special mirror for this purpose that has symbols of the sea or shells embedded around the outside.

It is advisable to keep your mermaid scrying mirror for magical use only, as its magic can become strong, and when you wish to use it for everyday activities you could find its psychic purpose makes it difficult to stay in the present moment – even when applying lipstick! Similarly, you may use a kitchen bowl filled with water or scry in the bathtub, however you may not wish to have an impromptu session during normal bath times or while cooking meals, so contemplate using a tool that remains specifically for this magical purpose, to keep your other time free of visions and enhance the clarity of your work.

Water scrying surfaces can include:
○ A silver or black bowl of water.
○ The surface of a lake.
○ The ocean, in which you can read the tides, the waves, the shoreline and the reflections on the surface.
○ A rock pool, a perfect living mermaid scrying mirror.
○ A cauldron brimming with water, which is powerful and practical for the sea witch.

Preparing to Scry

The dark of the moon is a wonderful time for scrying, as your inner vision is at its peak during this beautiful, soft, inward-turning time of mermaid magic, but all phases can be used. The lunar cycle can be worked with thus – dark of the moon for inner knowledge, new moon for how things may transpire, full moon for revelations and waning moon for how best to release. Outdoor night-time scrying is also blissful, and very magical and powerful – and it reconnects us to the priestesses of Avalon and the druids of Britain, who used natural bodies of water such as wells and lakes with which to scry.

Take your scrying bowl. We will use a bowl of water in this example. Space clear the room in which you'll be working. Ensure you are clear, fit and well. If working outside, be sure to be warm enough, and use lantern-style candles so they do not blow out.

Set up your altar simply, with something to represent each of the elements, and light a stick of incense or resin on charcoal, burning bright and safe. On either side of your bowl, light a candle – use beeswax or soy.

Dim the lights, turn off phones and soften external noises with ambient music or the sound of ocean waves, their rhythm leading you into a trance. Lyrics can "feed" the process, so you may wish to avoid this, although some people do prefer to work with music which has this impact as it assists their process.

Take nine deep, slow breaths with your eyes closed, in and out, like the waves and the tides, and gently relax your muscles. Let go of the tension, of the need to hold on to this reality.

With your eyes closed, say: "When I open my eyes, I shall see with my inner vision. I will see into the waters of life and time." Making this statement is a powerful declaration of intent, and the mermaids and sea beings will be sure to assist you.

Open your eyes, and softly gaze upon the surface of your scrying bowl. There is no right or wrong way to scry – simply allow what happens to happen. Sometimes the visions will seem like simple outlines or etchings at first, figures shaping themselves together out of the element you are working with, and then, quite suddenly, the surface may transform into a super-real movie screen on which the images from your inner vision are projected. This can happen with your eyes open, or it can happen within – either way it is an indication that your psychic vision has been switched on.

Some people experience a mist rising, before images begin to slowly appear then move, and others experience almost a complete Otherworld. This may take some time and practise, and finding the element which you are most compatible with.

To complete your scrying ritual, thank the sea beings, the merfolk, and any sea creatures, such as dolphins, turtles, dugongs or whales, for example, who may have come to you. Close your eyes, and again take nine deep breaths. Then run your hand gently over your eyelids. Say: "When I open my eyes I shall see what is there for me to see." Open your eyes. You may like to wave your hand over the bowl three times to disperse the energy.

It is essential to ground after scrying. Have something simple to eat and drink, and place your feet and your palms on the earth to reconnect and ground the watery flow. Drink plenty of water and fresh watery juices. Stay in the flow, yet return to this reality! The reason it is so important to sever the scrying vision is that this inner vision, switched on at all times, can be tiring and burn you out, leading to visions at unexpected moments. It is already likely that, as a psychic and magical person, you may experience these in any case, but it is important that you remain safe and clear when driving, navigating roads, working and doing equally sacred mundane activities – to be clear and present for yourself and for your loved ones. Grounding assists you to be present too, and brings your energy back into the world.

When you are first beginning to scry, only do it for a short period of time each go, and build up from there. Record your visions in your Mermaid Journal or your Book of Shadows. Over time, you will notice your skills blooming and taking shape. Have patience with yourself – we are not all wise mermaids and experienced sea witches at first scrying!

Scrying can be subtle, and it is as much about training yourself to discern these subtle messages as it is about powerful visions. Most of all, it is about cultivating a close and beautiful connection with the mermaids, the sea creatures, the tides and the flows of currents and waves, all of which are the healing, flowing and cleansing qualities of the element of water.

Signs of the Sea

"How could one explain so much with so little?
How could three simple symbols reach out and grab hold of me?
They held rhythm, excitement, spontaneity, and were certainly
part of my inner child – they were pieces of art itself."
Alan Bruce, artist

Oceanic Signs and Symbols

Throughout all cultures, certain signs and symbols have become powerful shorthand for magical powers. Using runes, symbols and other such symbology opens our mind and spirit up to powers and beings, elementals and deities that dwell behind the veil, in the invisible world. Symbols are a kind of universal code – and one we still use every day with logos, insignia and simple street signs, for example. They are also an esoteric key, each symbol a perfect shape to unlock a specific magical door. Some signs and codes have developed exclusively around sea lore – the ones included here could be very useful for your mermaid magics or sea witchery, or even just used as a beautiful symbol to meditate upon and learn more about the deep of the oceans!

Janarric Sea Runes

Along Italy's beautiful coastline live many traditional sea witches. In Raven Grimassi's classic work *Hereditary Witchcraft*, he writes of the Janarric witches who have created a set of symbols to activate and "fire up" their spellworkings, a beautiful visual language that draws exclusively upon the power of the sea. They are similar to runes, although they bear more immediate resemblance to the angelic alphabet developed by Dr John Dee in the sixteenth century.

The Janarric sea runes are simple to recreate, but for them to work, they need to be drawn out in a devotional way. When you do this, the shapes hold real power, and truly communicate their message. Practise drawing them a few times, and see if you relate to the symbol and if it appeals to you. Then, if so, it can be etched into a magical tool, like a necklace, crane bag, athame, cauldron or simply drawn in the sand, as a blessing and way of communicating quickly and powerfully with the beings of the sea.

They can also be tattooed, or etched for a time on to the skin with henna or body paint, to bring about what it is you wish for. They are powerful symbols, the language of the sea gods, and they are to be used wisely and well. However, do not be afraid – we all use symbols, all the time – consider the power of the Coca-Cola logo or the Shell oil company sign. Working with our own symbols is far more powerful and wise than simply drifting in a sea of symbols of capitalism and environmental greed and destruction. Choosing the symbols you surround yourself with will increase the magic in your days, and help you sail the seas of your life with purpose and direction!

Making a Sea Offering With Janarric Runes

Take a lovely shell, quite large, and trace some of the beautiful runes below onto it with your finger. Or you may wish to carve one of these symbols on a shell or piece of driftwood. Though some consider this cruel, it is no more so than drilling a hole to thread a shell on a necklace – and when done with a sense of the sacred, becomes a prayerful act, one which reaches deeply and connects to the divine forces of the seas.

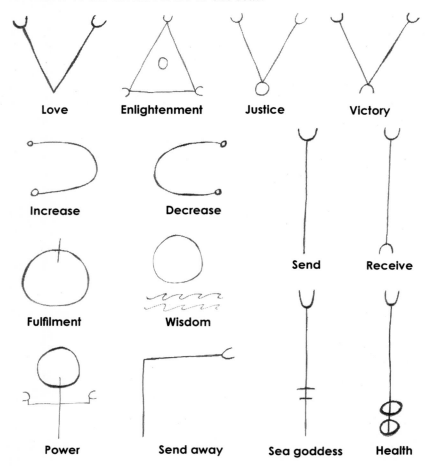

| Love | Enlightenment | Justice | Victory |

| Increase | Decrease | Send | Receive |

| Fulfilment | Wisdom | | |

| Power | Send away | Sea goddess | Health |

Once your rune-shell is ready, gather a flower found growing near the sea, some honey and something precious to you – even a small lock of your hair will help the sea beings know who you are. Take your offering to the ocean's edge at low tide, or as the high tide turns, so you can watch the sea beings take your offering away.

Say three times:
I call to the Mother and the Father of the Sea,
Show me how I can best serve thee.
See this offering, my wish, my vow,
I call upon you both now.
To aid me, help me in my rite,
Yes, lend me your wisdom and your might.
May cycles, tides and moonglow too,
Assist me now in all that I do.

Or simply speak from your heart, which is always a powerful form of magic. It is said though that elemental beings like the mermaids, the fae and those who are of nature love to hear words spoken in rhyme, as the rhythm penetrates the veils and assists the words in reaching the ears of the gods. The symbols also reach far beyond, above and below language and labels, and go directly to the energy of your being, connecting you to the collective unconscious.

Brinrunar Runes

All runes are powerful, as is creating and using your own personal symbol to work with the ocean. But the old Brinrunar runes have years and years of tradition woven into their shapes, and are a sign calling to the ocean. You can work with these runes no matter how far you may be from the shore, in order to bring you back to the energy of the sea, and her cleansing and her power.

The Brinrunar were traditional runes that were carved into ships' prows or into the tackle to keep it and the sailors using it safe and well, protected from storms and able to always find their way. Before you go on any trips, especially over water, you too can use the Brinrunar to protect you. The old gods hear and recognise these letterings, and it makes them pleased indeed to know there are those amongst we modern humans who have not forgotten how to connect and pay tribute to the spirits of the sea.

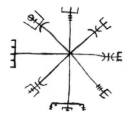

Icelandic singer and seer Bjork has a Brinrunar sea rune as a tattoo on her upper left arm. It is vegvisir, a rune that was drawn on the foreheads of Vikings to guide them through wild seas and bring them home once more, a magical sign to help one find their way through rough weather. Bjork got this tattoo at the age of seventeen. It is a compass, which helps her to know the way, and to always find the right path. It is a powerful rune for voyagers and those who would cross the vast places, travel into the ocean and, symbolically, those who would travel into their own subconscious and live by their own compass. The one who wears this rune, it is said, will never get lost, although to others standing on the shore they may appear to wander.

Here are some Nordic runes, very powerful, spare and clean, which were used in conjunction with sea energy and ocean magics.

Sowilo: This rune means sun, and embodies the energies of the sailor, the traveller and the teacher – sowilo draws to you wise counsel and good governance, inspiration and true teachings. It will bring great blessings if you are to travel, especially over water. Drawing out this rune or working with it magically will recharge, refresh and help you reconnect with flowing, healing energy. It will also help you to move on from stuck situations.

Laguz: This rune is strongly connected to the power of water – all water, including rain, river, lake, well, sea, drinking and life-giving water. It was worked with by sea voyagers to help them get through storms, and the incredible primal power of the ocean when no shore was to be seen. It is associated with emotion, psychic knowledge, intuition, movement and receptivity, and it can also indicate emotions being dominant and perhaps overwhelming. It connects you directly to the Well of Wyrd, the deep nourishing well of life in the Nordic or Asatru traditions, and to Aegir, the sea god of the Norse. Additionally it can assist you in "hiding" or taking something very deep, where it can be protected.

Kenaz: This rune is related to vision, inspiration, revelation, knowledge and creativity. It indicates change, and the cleansing power of the ocean to wash away stagnant thoughts or situations, and prepare for something new. It also holds the mer energy of sensuality, passion and love, and changing for the better.

Celtic Love Knot: The Celtic knots so beloved in artworks, and which can be found on rings, spoons and monuments in the Celtic sea kingdoms, have their origin as sea ropes. There is a Celtic knot called the sailor's knot, made of two intertwined ropes looping together, becoming one, with no beginning and no end, which became known over time as the Celtic Lover's Knot. It symbolises ecstatic union, coming together and perfect marriage. Celtic sailors wove these for their sweethearts while at sea.

The Sea Labyrinths of the Northern Lands

In Cornwall, in a small town to the north of Tintagel, you will find something marvellous if you ask the locals for directions, and walk over a ruined mill and search along the sea cliffs, for into the rocks here are carved two Cretan labyrinths. Both are small, and no one truly knows how they came to be here, or why they are here. But they have been dated to 4000BCE – and they point to the fact that labyrinths are a sacred and vital part of oceanic magics.

Labyrinths are winding, weaving places. To enter a labyrinth is to enter another world. To trace one with your fingertip, or to walk one physically, is to still, focus and draw into oneself powerful energies. Labyrinths can be used for meditation, as a spiritual process to let go of and leave behind that which must be banished, or walked to manifest something new, or to understand oneself with far greater depth. They can also be used to weather witch, as the sailors of old are said to have done.

In old Nordic sea villages, like Landsort on the small Swedish island of Oja, there exist the remains of ancient sea labyrinths down by the shoreline. At Kuggoren, an ancient sea town on the Swedish coast, there is a stone labyrinth that is square and solid in shape.

These labyrinths are found mostly along coastlines, and in both Finland and Sweden they were walked by shamans and sailors to protect the community against the very real, very cruel hazards of a life at sea and by the sea, to ensure the nets were always full of fish to feed their people, that sailors were safe at sea, and to save their towns from the cruel and tearing sea storms that could wreak havoc in such places. These labyrinths were also walked to prevent the arrival of sailors from other lands who would seek to lay claim to their ways, their women and their towns.

There is also evidence that shepherds built stone labyrinths in the fields of the European countryside, to protect against predators, as they believed that the labyrinth would draw a wolf or fox into its confines and confuse them, sending them away without harming their sheep. A spell was walked into a labyrinth, and thus its energy remained for whoever walked the path in times to come. In Glastonbury, England, there is a labyrinth on the slopes of the Tor which has been walked for centuries, and is still walked today, that also holds the magic of all those who have passed along it.

Historian JA Udde, from Haparanda in northern Sweden, relies on oral history to trace the evidence of the use of labyrinths by Nordic magical folk. He says there are labyrinths that were built into the islands of the cold North Sea to calm strong winds. The locals believed that the winds would enter the labyrinth, and be slowed by having to enter or leave a town that way. Similarly, these magical paths were thought to be able to draw fish into the nets of sailors.

It was thought that if a labyrinth had seven levels, it had to be walked by the sea wizard seven times, in and out, to awaken its deep magic. People in the towns would also follow this pattern, to further enhance the magics and add to its power. If a labyrinth had nine levels, it would be walked nine times, and if it had eleven levels, it would be walked eleven times, and so on.

Fisherman Anders Ohman told Udde of his beliefs regarding labyrinths, which had been passed down to him by his own father and his forefathers, who were all fishermen. "If one walked the proper way through the labyrinth, all would go well. But if one walked the wrong way, things would go badly," he explained.

Bo Stjernstrom, another labyrinth researcher, spoke to people in the fishing village of Orno, on the coast of Sweden, who told him that labyrinths were built at the sea's edge, in the tidal zone, to walk to bring luck for fishing. Even in the 1950s, in a small village called Kuggoren, people would walk – and sometimes run – the labyrinth constructed at the sea's edge, to bring luck for an abundance of fish at sea, and to bring all the fishermen home safely.

Sea-Perstitions

Sailors and coastal dwellers had many traditions, laws and superstitions they adhered to in order to guarantee a safe sea voyage, some of which made more sense than others!

❌ Pouring wine on the deck was thought to bring good luck on a long voyage, and ships today are still christened with a bottle of champagne smashed against the prow. A libation to the gods never hurts – even when everyone on deck claims to be Christian!

❌ A naked woman on board was thought to calm the sea, or perhaps this was mere wishful thinking! This is the reason that naked figureheads were carved on the prow of ships. Later however, real-life naked women were considered to be bad luck – one of the many reasons women at sea often cross-dressed.

❌ Black cats were bringers of great good fortune, and were thought to always bring a sailor home safe from a long sea voyage.

❌ It was suggested that sailors avoid people with red hair when going to the ship to begin a journey. Redheads were believed to bring bad luck to a ship – which could be averted if you spoke to the redhead before they spoke to you. This had its genesis in the fact that redheads were feared, especially in the Middle Ages, as witches. Legend has it that all redheads are descended from the Lemurian Prince Idon, whose hair turned red upon reaching Atlantis at sunset.

❌ A silver coin placed under the masthead before setting sail was believed to ensure a successful voyage.

❌ Dolphins swimming with the ship were another sign of good luck. Conversely, killing a dolphin was believed to bring bad luck. Let's keep this tradition going!

❌ It was thought to be unlucky to kill an albatross. Anyone who has studied *The Rime of the Ancient Mariner* will know this!

❌ Cutting your hair or nails at sea was thought to bring bad luck. These were used as offerings to Proserpina, and it was thought that Neptune would become jealous if these offerings were made while in his kingdom. People also feared that a witch would find their hair or nail clippings and be able to use them in spells to control them.

Doreen's Oceanic Magic

American author Doreen Virtue teaches people to communicate with angels. She has a deep connection to the ocean, and dedicates time and money to marine conservation. She has written many inspirational books, including *Healing With the Angels* and *The Lightworker's Way*, and created the beautiful *Magical Mermaids and Dolphins* oracle deck. Doreen is a PADI dive master, and her new joy is swimming in a mermaid tail. She moved from California to the island paradise of Hawaii to swim with wild dolphins and connect with nature. Visit Doreen at www.angeltherapy.com.

Growing up, I was always in a swimming pool or the ocean. I imagined I was a dolphin or a mermaid, and I'd swim with my feet together, with the dolphin undulations. This feeling grew deeper as I got into scuba diving and became a dive master. I moved to Hawaii so I could swim frequently in the warm, clean ocean waters.

The ocean is everything to everyone. It controls the weather and feeds the planet. It's the mother of all physical creation, and in many languages the words Mother and Sea are synonymous. Personally, the ocean is incredibly important to me. I spend as much time in her as I can. I'm actively involved in ocean environmentalism too, including activism to protect sea beings such as sharks, dolphins, whales, turtles, tuna and tropical fish. One reason why I'm a vegan is because I don't want to contribute to the overfishing that has dwindled the fish population and caused bottom trawling to scrape along the sea floors. I contribute a percentage of my income to Oceana, and I'm also a big proponent of Sea Shepherd and their whale protection work.

The simplest thing we can all do to help with marine conservation is to eat no fish. If that's too radical, you can abstain from eating blue fin tuna, which is endangered. Don't wear seashells or coral jewellery, which is taken cruelly from the sea. Don't wear sunscreen when you swim in the ocean, as it contains coral-killing chemicals. And take your trash home when

you go to the beach. Plastic trash is showing up in the ocean at an alarming rate, and sea creatures swallow it and die as a result.

Dolphins are the angels of the sea, who help us to connect with our past. They also bring us the healing rainbow light energy. Dolphins remind us that we can get our responsibilities met while having a lot of fun and being very playful in the process.

The dolphins' aura is rainbow-hued. Our bodies need rainbow light energy for health and energy. Originally we got this energy from being outdoors in full-spectrum sunlight. Then the shifts occurred with smog and the ozone, and humans began living and working indoors with artificial lighting. Now the dolphins are coming closer to humans and bringing the gift of the rainbow lighting. You can meditate upon dolphins and receive this gift.

I definitely feel that mermaids and dolphins are connected. My friend Dana Mermaid and I go out on a boat once or twice a month, put our mermaid tails on, jump in and swim underwater with the dolphins. They seem very intrigued by us and our tails. To me, mermaids represent a return to Atlantis. In Atlantis, dolphins and mermaids co-existed, and so we share a lot of the same histories and life purposes to protect the world's oceans.

Wearing a mermaid tail in water is transformative. It gives you wings and gills. Suddenly you can swim faster and breathe longer underwater. Our tails have built-in monofins, which have two foot pockets like regular flippers, but the fin part's fused together. The monofin compels you to move your feet like a dolphin's or whale's fluke, and causes the natural "dolphin swim" undulation of the stomach and chest. This is a very pleasant, natural and efficient way to swim.

Sea Priestesses

"To stand at the edge of the sea, to sense the ebb and flow of the tides, to feel the breath of a mist moving over a great salt marsh, to watch the flight of shore birds that have swept up and down the surf lines of the continents for untold thousands of years, to see the running of the old eels and the young fish to the sea, is to have knowledge of things that are as nearly eternal as any earthly life can be."
Rachel Carson, American biologist and environmentalist

Maintaining a Connection With the Sea

In order to truly know ourselves, to know our nature, perhaps it is necessary for us to reconnect with the deep ocean. Those who remain unaware of it, unmoved by her ebbs and flows, must remain detached from part of their deepest, most sensual self.

In Dion Fortune's sublime occult novel *The Sea Priestess*, the dull Wilfrid Maxwell is only half alive and painfully aware of it. He goes to the sea seeking respite from his chronic asthma – the man literally cannot breathe. There he meets the enigmatic Vivien Le Fay Morgan and begins, under her instruction, to transform an old ruined sea fort into a temple of Isis. Wilfrid, an archetypal repressed modern man, a model of disconnected masculinity, undergoes an initiation into feminine power. He learns of the moon, the tides, the ancient ways, and of the arts of love and sensuality. He becomes a man, because he discovers the goddess.

"And in those hours while the tide rose, there were delivered to me things whereof but few have dreamed and fewer still have known, and I learnt why Troy was burnt for a woman," he says.

"For this woman was not one woman, but all women; and I who mated with her was not one man, but all men; but these things were part of the lore of the priesthood, and it is not lawful to speak of them." He does not end up with Vivien, but he finally understands that all women are Isis – such is the magic of the sea priestess.

Sea priestesses are those enchanting women who reconnect us with the sea and her magics. They are not only featured in literature and legends, they existed, and exist still in both formal and informal ways. In Finland they are known as volva, a very feminine name, and their fascinating lores are only now beginning to die out. Fortunately, this is not happening without people to rediscover them, relearn and reteach these methods of working with the sea.

There are many indigenous sea priestesses the world over, including the beautiful and revered Bobohizan of Borneo, a land that still maintains much of its tradition and is a fascinating place to visit and experience. When I visited Borneo in 2007 to research the book *The Lost Lands*, I met taxi drivers whose parents were headhunters, and the traditional musical instruments, tattoos, longhouses and ceremonies are still very much alive.

We find references to the sea priestesses in works by historians Geoffrey of Monmouth and the Roman Tacitus, who described the sea priestesses of the British Isles, including those of the blessed Isle of Avalon. While Glastonbury today sits within farmers' fields, in days of old the isle was surrounded by an inland sea.

There are many famous sea priestess and druid communities, including the Isle of Man and perhaps the most revered of all, the Isle of Iona. Iona lies off the west coast of Scotland, isolated and beautiful. It was Christianised in 563CE by Columba, an exiled Irish missionary who was later sainted. His ways were so akin to the druids that his was a peaceful presence, and he communed with the whales and dolphins, dunked himself in the sea at sunrise, and marvelled in his writings at the beauty and wonder of the natural world. He seems less to me a monk and more to me a sea priest, a druid Christ. In fact, sometimes Columba is credited with saying "Christ is my druid," and explaining to the local wise ones that Jesus was a good druid. Iona seems to breed wonders.

Its Gaelic name, Innis-nam Druidbneach, means Island of the Druids. The bones of forty-eight Scottish kings lie in the earth here, and the tiny island is redolent with magic and mystery, a place where faiths intertwine, and turn as one to marvel at the sea and her creatures. Some legends claim that Iona was inhabited by the survivors of the fall of Atlantis, who arrived on Iona's shores fifteen thousand years ago, and that it was home to the northern Hyperboreans before that time. (To find out more about these people, an earth colony and experiment that preceded Lemuria and Atlantis, please refer to *The Lost Lands*.)

Sea Priestesses of Japan

We need not look just to the ancient past, or to the lands of Atlantis or Avalon for the sea priestesses. Perhaps more than any other place on earth today, the memory of the sea priestesses is most strong in the remote southern islands of Okinawa, Japan. To this day there dwells there a powerful group of women, hereditary sea priestesses called noros, whose exclusive function is to commune with the sea gods in ritual, divination and healing and to keep the sacred places, utakis, pure and inviolate. The noros are the priestesses, and the yutas are the mediums who work with the ancestral spirits.

Kudaka Island in Okinawa is one place where the traditions of sea priestesses who are close to the elements and to the birthplace of these run deep and strong. In the year 2000, priestess Hana Nishime knew the secret locations of the sea gods and the nirai-kanai, the legendary realm where all things emerge from the void. Ishiki Beach on Kudaka Island is a sacred place. Visitors who collect coral from there are asked not to time and again by the noros. "Do not take such things home with you. These things the gods placed here. You should not remove them," Hana says.

The noros know the utakis, the sacred places, and they know of the legendary shrine gates through which the gods pass. Called torii, these gates are best left natural, and need no decoration. The noros believe those who are awake will feel their power upon approach, and know what they must do. Some utakis are taboo to men.

Kokan Sasaki, a professor at Komazawa University, is a leading researcher into Japanese shamanism, and attests to the ancient nature of these practices. "If you want to know the roots of ancient Japan, look at the southwestern islands," he says.

Skilled in mediumship, the yutas are often women who have undergone a challenging life experience. Fumiko, a yuta of

Kudaka Island, says yutas fall ill if they do not deliver the messages the gods ask them to send to the people. "Nobody becomes a yuta because they want to," she said in an interview with *The Japan Times* in 2000. "Little by little, things happen that tell you that the gods aren't going to let you live or die, and that they will slowly drive you insane rather than let you go."

Both yutas and noros have come up against great resistance during Japan's long history. In 1673, 1732, 1831 and 1900 both yutas and noros were outlawed, and in 1938, a reward was offered to anyone who turned in women yutas. Despite this, the ceremonies to appoint the noros are still held to this day, although there is a declining number of women who can fulfil the ceremonies and rituals of the past. There are fewer senior noros left to teach their daughters the old ways of the sea priestesses.

Seiko Gigu, an island woman, now carries out the rites of the noros in place of her mother, an elderly noro who is now in a senior citizen's home. "There's so much I don't understand, it's really difficult," Gigu says. "There are not enough people to help – we just have a skeleton of the old rituals," she says.

Some noros feel the rites that are simple and attract tourists will survive, while other more sacred and arcane practices may die out altogether as the generations forget the ways of their ancestors.

But as long as people remember their mother's praying, their daughters will carry on a semblance of the rites of the sea priestesses. One ritual at least is unlikely to die, because it protects the cattle on the island. Making and hanging an akufugeshi, a talisman made of conch, is believed to ward away evil, illness and misfortune. And they still hang outside nearly every door on the islands.

Casting Your Own Sea Priestess Spells

To work in the way inspired by the noro, find a place on a local beach or waterway that feels most sacred to you, and resolve to care for this place, and take nothing from it. Of course you may take from it human garbage, but take nothing the sea gods offer. Let the gods and their offerings lie there, and give thanks for simply seeing and experiencing them – there is no need to "have" them. Or you could make a protective charm from a sea conch, and hang it outside your front door. Like the ancient talismans of the noros, yours too, created with integrity and love, will act as a purification system for any energy entering or departing your home. Cleanse frequently in the sea, and use it well.

If you wish to work the magic of the sea, but live far from her waters, do not be concerned. Instead, make your bathroom the land of the sea, a place of healing and remineralising enrichment for you. Or you can work with a lake, or a bowl of water, or bathe in fresh water and scrub yourself down with sea salt.

Sea Priestess Scrub

In a silver bowl, bless and combine:

✿ One part sea salt, refined. If you have large granules of sea salt, you may wish to use a mortar and pestle so the granules are fine and less harsh on your skin.

✿ One part brown sugar.

✿ One part coconut oil.

✿ A dash of seawater from a sacred place.

✿ Essential oils of neroli, sweet orange, lime – citrus drops, to the count of nine, are best for this blend, to create an uplifting vibration when shedding the skin of the past.

Stir all of this together. I use a seashell to stir with, or simply my hands – it really gets your energy into the blend. I may leave it out to marry, or combine for a night, bathing in the moonlight.

This is a very special blend, because as you are cleansing and moving away energetic and cellular debris, you are simultaneously nourishing your skin, and your skin will be luminous, glowing with health, sweet-smelling and very soft and lovely to the touch.

Light a candle. My preference is nearly always for beeswax with pure wicks. Good beeswax candles ionise the air as they burn, unlike other candles.

They pump the air full of negative ions, which provide us with feel-good energy. Next bring out some sacred seashells, and get into the shower. Before turning on the water, visualise all that no longer serves your mermaid free spirit, your sea priestess self, your sea witch magic, then gently cover your skin with the Sea Priestess Scrub and begin to gently rub, seeing this old skin, this former self, lifting off gently and being removed...

Now turn on the water and see yourself under a beautiful sea waterfall, and this water pouring upon you, cleansing you and freeing you from the toxins of the past, the energy of those experiences, any self-harming thoughts or feelings you may be holding on to, dissolving now all blocks between you and your sensual, mermaidenly self. See all this debris flowing away and down the drain, being transmuted into natural, harmless and healing energy, and returning to the sea without harm, so that it may then return once again as it will, as a part of the great cycle of water.

Seashell Massage

You will need:
⚬ Coconut oil.
⚬ Large smooth cowrie shell.

Rub the oil gently and lovingly into your skin – be generous! Next, take a large smooth cowrie, and run this with some gentle pressure along your limbs. When you find what pressure works best, you can deepen the pressure. You may also wish to use the reverse side of the cowrie, as this gently blades the skin surface, further clearing cells ready for detachment and release.

This little-known art brings great seashell energy right into the skin, deep into your body, energising and healing your physical self, relaxing tension and softening hard knots of muscle held in the neck, limbs, shoulders and back, and allowing these to be more flowing, watery and soft, like the ocean and her beings.

If you have a mermaid friend, you can take turns gifting each other seashell massages – cowrie is a gift from the sea mother Yemanja, and will help you to reclaim and rebirth your mermaidenly self. Every seashell massage is a healing for the sacred feminine, and a way of reconnecting to our oceanic origins.

Michelle's Saltwater Magic

Michelle Pilato is the creator of Soul Indulgence, an online community that brings together inspirational books, meditation CDs, healing wraps, altar cloths, faery wish rings, crystals, psychic readings and more. Over the last few years she's been on her own healing journey to understand her deep pull to the ocean, which she has discovered through an ancestral connection to the Saltwater People of Thursday Island, in Australia's Torres Strait. For thousands of years they have believed the sea is a gift from the creator to be used for sustenance, spirituality, identity and community, and loved and protected in turn. Visit Michelle at www.SoulIndulgence.com.au.

As a child I always believed in mermaids. My sister and I spent many days being mermaids, building caves with sticks we found on the beach across the road from our grandmother's house. We spent a lot of time at various beaches and out on boats during our school holidays. And my mother always said that seeing is not believing, believing is seeing. Although I have not seen a mermaid in the ocean, they have visited me in my dreams for a few years now.

I always had a great connection to the ocean, until I had a scare in my teens – since then, more than twenty years ago, I haven't swum in the sea. But I still hear its call, and get very stressed and restless if I don't visit the ocean at least three or four times a year. I have kept the sea close to me with shells, starfish, pieces of coral and bits of driftwood that I collected when I was a child, along with a picture of a mermaid, on a small altar in my home. And I often have sea salt baths, and tint the water with blue and yellow colouring – these baths calm and protect me from any negativity in my life. They cleanse and heal me with the power of the ocean.

Even though I've stopped swimming, I still hear the call of the sea. And I always go to the beach when I'm stressed, and feel better once I return home. So after many dreams involving underwater adventures, with dolphins, whale sharks and other marine animals, and

diving into caves where I have met mermaids, I went in search of why the sea calls to me so strongly.

I knew that my grandfather was born on Thursday Island in Torres Strait, and that he and his brothers spent most of their days at the beach, barefoot, walking around the tiny island and diving for abalone. He left Thursday Island in 1939 to avoid the war, and moved to Port Douglas in Queensland, where he met my nan, and where my dad was later born.

When we visited him he always took us fishing, and we spent time on boats. He had a lot of knowledge about the sea, and I remember the long days of fishing, and cooking the catch on the beach afterwards. He would tell us about Thursday Island, and we would sing that song *TI My Beautiful Home* by the fire with his family:

"*Old TI my beautiful home, 'tis the place where I was born,*
Where the moon and stars that shine, make me long for home..."

Recently I discovered the story of the Saltwater People, who come from the islands where my grandfather was born, and I felt a real connection. I'm still reading and learning, and my aunties are helping me. I haven't visited Thursday Island yet – my grandfather always wanted to take me there, but he passed away before he could.

I have dreams where I swim down into a cave after diving off the rocks, into the most beautiful turquoise blue water. As I swim, I feel I'm returning home, and a sense of calm comes over me. I meet my mermaid goddess there and she helps me with any concerns I have. She has lovely long dark hair, the most amazing emerald green eyes, and a beautiful tail in tones of gold, blue, green and purple.

I think mermaids represent the wild, untamed energy in women, and are the guardians of the sea. I always feel better when I visit the ocean and call on the mermaids to help with any emotional issues I have. And I'm still doing research on how I can deepen my connection to the sea and maybe one day return for a swim.

Oracles From the Sea Creatures

"I love the dugong because it helped me understand the sacred
feminine and the manifesting power of dreams, song and surrender.
They are the mermaids to me, and the sirens and so many others.
They're up there with the seal for me as a powerful mentor."
Scott Alexander King, author of Animal Dreaming

Receiving Physical Messages

When you have need of wisdom, the mermaids and the sea mother
will always send you the answers to your questions in the form of
living oracles – symbols in flesh – to help guide you on your path,
make daily decisions and assist you in understanding your own
nature. Very often, this sign will come to you in the shape of one of
the ocean's children – a dolphin, a dugong, a shark, a seal...

Sea creatures are powerful and profound messengers from the
sea mother, and they are full of wisdom and assistance for you.
They ask nothing of you in return, but we would all do well to
honour them in small ways each day. This can be as simple as
making an effort to reduce your waste, never leaving rubbish by the
seashore, raising awareness for marine conservation, refusing to
harm creatures and reducing your harmful impact on the oceans.

The sea mother sends to us the mer energies of the deep, and
most people feel a strong connection to a particular sea creature,
no matter where they find themselves living. Even if you are located
many kilometres from the coast, there is often the energy of the
sea. Even the Tibetan glaciers contain ancient sea salts, because the
sea came before the land, and from her depths we have all evolved.

Connecting with sea creatures in the flesh is wonderful and so very emotionally clearing and healing. Even at aquariums, where most of the time the creatures are glassed off from us, we can see them, observe them and connect with them deeply. While I was at Sea World, a theme park on Australia's Gold Coast, for the Animal Dreaming course which I was MCing, I had an interesting encounter with a shark – but one which was not in the water!

We were being taken to the animals first thing in the morning, and two very informative guides had been appointed – one was jocular and very easygoing, the other very strict and very short. When she spoke about the sharks, something she said made my ears prick up. "When sharks are about to attack," she stated, "they exhibit certain behaviours."

As I surf, I thought I would ask whether you could see that behaviour from in the water – helpful for me, and something fascinating to know. She glanced sharply at me.

"Are you a surfer?" she asked. There was an edge to her voice.

"Yes."

"Well, you're in *their* territory," she said in harsh tones. I felt that I had been issued with an order to stay out of the sea.

And this is the essence of shark – being policed, and judged, and ordered, as I felt, is very much an encounter with an authority that has great power, which shark represents. I have been out in the water with dolphins, and my entire being has felt flooded with bliss – no doubt neurotransmitters are stimulated when encountering these beautiful creatures. Even so, there is this sense of the "other". They are not like we humans. We must respect that.

And I have been out in the water with sharks, and my body has been flooded with adrenaline. I turned to the young friend I was surfing with that day, and he nodded, and we simultaneously began paddling for the next wave as fast as we could, to get back to shore.

Shark is like that. Dolphin is different. People smile until their faces hurt when confronted with dolphins who are well and healthy. People with brain injuries report increased cognitive function after interacting with dolphins. I have seen friends weep upon seeing stingrays, as they knew they had ridden them in another form when in Atlantis. I have seen people react with aggression when they see bluebottles lying helpless on the shore. And seahorses leave me flooded with tenderness.

Each sea creature provokes a deep emotional response, and all are messengers for us. Each of us can benefit from tuning in, and going to the ocean, and receiving her messages.

Of course they may not show up physically, such as a dolphin leaping over your surfboard or a sea turtle shuffling out of the water towards you. Therefore, pay attention to the signs all around you. Scott Alexander King always advises people to look at the trucks rolling past with their symbology, the t-shirt someone is wearing, the ads on television featuring creatures. Open up to the messages of the sea creatures – they will reach you, wherever you are.

For some of us, the connection is ancestral and totemic. Laura Bowen is an artist and mother who is descended from the Biripi and Worimi people. In her paintings she has explored the connection to sea turtles in a profound way.

"Sea turtles travel far and see the world. They symbolise travel interstate and overseas. They can live for more than a hundred years, so they also represent the knowledge gained through experience, not only in this life but the information imprinted on us from our ancestors as well," she says.

"Even though they swim far on the ocean's currents and see so much of the world, they instinctively return to the place they were born to lay their eggs, and their children will do the same.

"Sea turtle is associated with the element of water. Water is fluid. It flows and travels, pushing the turtles along on its current. It also corresponds to emotions. In this case it's the emotional attachment we have to home and family. Take heart in knowing that not all choices are ours to make. Sometimes there are energies at work that are greater than us and sometimes it is wise to surrender to their pull," Laura suggests.

Other folk have found their fear of going underwater is alleviated when they connect with dolphin. For Romany witch Maggie Sinton, it is the seahorse that inspires her to keep going under tough conditions. "I love the tough fragility of them, an echo of life really," she says. "But when things appear to be breaking up, their tough streak comes out. It is a creature who cares and shares the workload, very much like my household in many ways."

Jo Greaves, a pagan from Sydney, feels a strong connection to the seals and to their magical form, the selkie. "I have loved many sea creatures for a long time, but my favourite is the seal," she says.

"One came to me in a meditation a few years ago, and still comes to guide me now. Seal reminds me to enjoy myself and find happiness in the simple things in life – like gliding through the water! They are so graceful and beautiful, and even if people think they are ungainly on land, seals show that not all is as it seems as they glide acrobatically through the water.

"The seal also reminds me to listen to my inner voice and trust my instincts. I can sit and watch them for hours on end, and was lucky enough to meet one and pat it at Sea World a couple of years ago. I have also been interested in the folklore surrounding the selkie and have been reading up on that a bit lately," Jo says.

Barbara Beachman, a healer from New South Wales, had an amazing experience with sea turtles and the Hawaiian volcano goddess Pele. "We went to the national park on the Big Island of Hawaii, and oh my word the pull of Pele was so strong," she says. "Never in a million years would I have imagined how strong was her presence. One beach of black sand there is very special. I took heaps of photos of the turtles around the time they lay their eggs. And after Hawaii I realised they are one of my totem animals, representing going with the flow and allowing things to just happen."

Sea Signs: Animal Oracles of the Ocean

Bluebottle: These indicate fear, pain from refusing to do that which you long to do out of fear, staying on the surface in the assumption that it will keep you safe, when in fact going deep will ease the pain and solve the seeming issue or problem.

Blue sea slug: These little ones, glaucus atlanticus, eat the bluebottles, and are the creatures that clean fear away, and represent small steps equalling large achievements, the positive power of small, consistent action and a refusal to be intimidated.

Cungi: A rock-dwelling creature that squirts water at low tide and is soft but tough to the touch, with a meaty inside that's excellent bait for fishing and crabbing. Thus they are able to attract once they reveal their sweetness – and are a message to be tough when necessary, and open and sweet to attract.

Dolphin: These creatures represent play, creativity, deep breathing, third-eye opening, sexuality, freedom, exploration, song, sensuality and dance. Dolphin asks you to rediscover the truth – that your joyful nature and your intelligence are compatible! Dolphins are said by the Dugong people of Africa to hail from Sirius B, and to be our ancestors. We have, they say, evolved from these beings from the first sea, the Milky Way.

Dugong: The mystery, the "other", the unknowable. Shapeshifting, feminine mysteries, sexual power and secret women's business. The yearning to understand and analyse what is not comprehensible with the mind will lead to confusion and mind turmoil. Dugong invites you to accept that some things are not knowable with the mind. Terri Graham, an Australian pagan, says: "There is something very surreal and mysterious about the dugong. Can't quite figure it out, but I always feel weird inside when I see one. Are they in their true form? I'm just not sure."

Fish: All fish speak of transformation – like the brilliant koi that are the last stage before dragon in Japanese lore. Tropical fish represent the fleeting happiness of life, ability to have fun, delight in the moment, bringing together groups of like-minded friends to enjoy each other's company, variety bringing delight and more lessons, the ability to learn without the learning being heavy and cumbersome. Avoid over-intellectualising. Whatever type of fish you observe, consider their behaviour and habits and learn from them.

Gull: Pack mentality, hunger, yearning for freedom, pressure to conform, lack consciousness, poverty consciousness, aggression and a feeling of there never being enough resources. Over-use of voice to say needless things again and again. Repetition in a situation will gain no ground. New strategies are called for.

Jellyfish: Honesty, defence, intentions, internal light, darkness, need to defend, electricity, new power source, light-bulb moments, optimism and hope in tragedy and betrayal. Bluff and threats.

Kite: This small hawk symbolises freedom and flexibility, ability to change direction swiftly and adapt well to new circumstances.

Oystercatcher: This wading bird assists us with finding the right foods to eat and making difficult changes to our diet. It is loyal to its mate and its location – oystercatcher people rarely move far from home. It represents co-operation in relationships, sweet abundance for all, the ability to work hard, raising your voice to be heard, and the need to give clear instructions.

Pelican: Sacred mothering and nurturing of young, mentoring, tendency to separate oneself when dealing with personal darknesses and difficulties, knowing the right place for what must be done, storing abundance for the future, ability to handle challenging times with great dignity and authority. Outcasts often have a pelican moment – they nearly always find their place again, and it is better for being one they have carved out themselves. A tendency to sacrifice oneself for others, and also to give the group more importance than the self. Need for balance.

Penguin: Indicates stoicism in the face of hardship, waiting for the right time, a time of separation in a partnership will bring great rewards, protection and foresight of the future, swift movement emotionally, difficulty translating emotional feelings into actions. Penguins mourn deeply for their chicks, and for each other, so seeing a penguin is a message to observe the rites of passing – whether for a stranger who has touched you, or someone you know or are related to, it is essential to process the grief of losing a loved one.

Sea dragon: Related to seahorses, parent their offspring in much the same way. Have developed extraordinary camouflage, long leafy "limbs" that make them vanish when within the great undersea forests they call home. Like an undersea chameleon, they can change colour to blend in with their surroundings – they are very gentle, and unlike the seahorse, cannot grasp things with their tails. They rely on being unseen, so when a sea dragon enters your life, you're being asked to keep something very quiet – some secrets and aspects of privacy are for people's safety and very survival. Revealing too much at this time could have dangers. They are born completely independent, and must make their way in the world from the moment they are born from their egg, and can pinpoint the exact location of their home. They speak to people who've had very adult responsibilities and situations placed on them from a young age.

Sea eagle: This magnificent being encourages us to take responsibility for the impact of our choices – no excuses for what we do or who we are, regardless of whether it seems "nice" or not to others. Women who connect with sea eagle are being asked to step out of the cliches about being "good" girls, to grow up and acknowledge their inner warrior woman. To dive deep into the self and to find what is needed, and are shown that they are far-sighted and have keen sight, awareness and presentience of their lives. No more excuses. It is time to step up and be your true whole self.

Sea hawk: A messenger from between the worlds, they bring energy from the cauldron of Ceridwen, they speak of readiness to change the journey, death of a situation or stage of life, clear vision for your purpose and remembering the lessons and wisdoms of past experience. Hawk is a great responsibility, for it brings power.

Seahorse: They share parenting and responsibilities, and Lemurian shapeshifters often have seahorse as a totem animal. Indicates stepping outside of gender roles and being imaginative and flexible when it comes to tasks and lessons of parenting. A gentleness, a freedom energy, and an ability to watch, very closely, what is happening and to find a new path through the old ways. Breaking free of conditioning. Pirates believed that seahorses were powerful symbols of protection, and in modern-day Asia, seahorse is considered a powerful potency treatment for men with a lack of sexual desire and stamina. Ability to hold on through chaos.

Seal: Indicates femininity, emotional wisdom, sexual stereotypes, impracticality, the desire to keep and trap what cannot truly be possessed. Seals are the selkies in their "skins", the people of the sea, the islands of the Northern British and Scandinavian lands, where they are called roans. Selkies may be trapped for a time, and give their wild self away, but it is never willingly done. Once they rediscover their true identity they leave. Seals remind you it is better to allow freedom and accept the parameters of relationships.

Sea snake: They live in the tropical waters of the Indian and Pacific Oceans, and have tiny fangs yet are very gentle, and rarely bite except in provocation and self-defence. On land they are cumbersome and hardly able to move, let alone strike, and they are generally brightly, beautifully coloured. They shed their skin up to three times as often as land snakes, rubbing up against a surface like coral and literally unpeeling themselves from their old skin. They do this so frequently as they have many "friends" who live off them – barnacles – so if you have this sea creature come to you in life or vision, you may be being asked to shed some people or situations that are taking too much, giving too little. If you do not shed these, you may be unable to "flow" and could become energetically, and thus physically, drained and tired, and stuck. And sea snakes, like their land brothers, have two penises!

Sea turtle: A sacred, revered creature, considered by many indigenous peoples to be the first of the animals. Messengers of the ocean gods, who could only be killed with great ceremony, most often after the death of a great chieftain or tribal leader in order to secure their safe passage to the Otherworld. This protected them for many thousands of years, until Christianity taught islander people to eat them for food, as they had no soul. They are messengers of travel and great distance, news from afar, and vast journeys. The ancient temples of the Pacific peoples have many sea turtle carvings. They can help journeys to the Otherworld and the land after this life. In the Dreamtime, Budgial the sea turtle represented wisdom and love.

Shark: Authority, the hunt, lawkeeper, enforcer, cleaning up after irresponsibility, sharks can promote fear in people as they are viewed as "trouble". They also clear negative energy from places. They are a sign that what is taking place must be dealt with in a very earnest and serious manner. Not a time for play. Time to do what must be done. There are no half-measures when shark appears.

Stingray: Softness, tenderness, cleansing fear, immense power in gentleness, travel, grace, sensitivity, Atlantis.

Tern: Peaceful group mentality, communal living, agile and quick-thinking solutions to problems facing large groups.

Whales: The keepers of the great treasure-houses of the planet's history, on and off earth. Their song holds the records in which are sung the lines of our ancestry, of the ancients and their teachings, the libraries of healing and information on earth's natural laws, records of your own lifetimes, written and oral histories. They govern protection and the knowledge given to us from the star people. The Minmur of South Australia directly relate them to the Pleiades. Strongly associated with shapeshifters and Lemuria.

Oracles From the Seashells

"Gather a shell from the strewn beach,
And listen at its lips: they sigh
The same desire and mystery,
The echo of the whole sea's speech."
Dante Gabriel Rossetti, The Sea-Limits

The Mer-Magic of Seashells

Each day, if you walk the tideline, you'll find the bounty of the merpeople scattered at your feet. At each low tide, it's possible to walk a length of beach and read from the sea mother herself what is taking place in the world, in your home, and to you personally.

The art of reading seashells, and designating meanings to the kelp and the creatures who live within the magical oceans, is a simple one, which ancient peoples knew much of. We now thoughtlessly walk over shells, and I flinch as I see four-wheel drives crushing them below their heavy wheels, or when people crunch them beneath their feet. They can never leave though, as all will turn to sand and become, in time, shells again.

Seashell divination has a long, secretive history, and is one that is only now being recovered and reinvented. While the ancient cowrie divination art of Cuban Santeria and Haitian Voudou is still very much alive, many of the other ways of our ancestors have disappeared beneath the waves of time. Reading the shells of the sea is an art form in many ancient seafaring cultures. During my research I was delighted and fascinated to see that over and over again the meanings attributed to certain shell forms had acquired the same meanings across cultures. The cowrie is one shell that has a consistent meaning – it was used as currency in many cultures, and also to represent fertility, due to its resemblance to women's genitalia.

Cowrie shells were used in China in 2000BCE, and as recently as 1900CE in the Pacific Islands. Counterfeit cowries were sometimes attempted during trade, so the Chinese introduced metal copies – the character for coin in Chinese script is a cowrie shell. Cowries were traded for gold and ivory in Persia and Egypt, but while the cowrie was universal, the Maldives were the primary supplier, with millions of shells making their way around the planet from there to Africa, China and beyond. They were taken over the Himalayas and through deserts – the value of the sea was recognised as a pure form of energy, which could be traded for foods, cloth, spices and precious metals, and during the eighteenth and nineteenth centuries, for human beings as part of the slave trade.

In the Pacific, the cowrie was so precious that it was forbidden to be worn by any except the chieftains of tribes – and explorers were unsuccessful in trading gold for cowries in the Pacific Islands, as these shells were sacred, and none would part with them.

Cowries were also used in fertility magic. There's evidence they were used in Pompeii in spells, and they've been found in the burial mounds of the ancient peoples of Germany, England, the Orkney Isles, Africa and China, where emperors were buried with nine cowries in their mouth, with which to trade in the afterlife. The higher one's status, the more cowries you took in your mouth to your burial chamber! In Denmark, the Isle of Man and Greece, cowries were placed in the burial mounds along with precious jewellery, swords and ceremonial attire for the afterlife.

People have been working with shell energy in a sacred way for at least fifty thousand years – the earliest evidence of this was found in Africa. During a mining operation, workers found the remains of a child buried so very long ago, before Atlantis fell, and this child was adorned with a seashell pendant, perhaps for protection as they journeyed to the land of their ancestors.

Shells have long captivated people – one example is the Duchess of Portland, Margaret Cavendish (no relation!), who exhausted her massive fortune on a shell collection, amassed by befriending explorers such as James Cook, and Daniel Solander, a conchologist given the task of itemising her astonishing collection in 1768.

Shells have strong protective energies, and very strong love and feminine energies too. It is a rich tradition for the women of Barbados and other Caribbean islands to make sailors Valentine spells cast in shell art, binding their love to them through fair weather and foul – and helping them to avoid sirens of other ports!

People also worked with shells throughout all time – and in contemporary times – to create dyes. Purple moon snails were used to create a very luscious and potent purple dye. However, the stench of boiling and reboiling the shells to extract the vivid purple hue was so strong, and so long-lasting, that the dyers were often hermits, and given special status to compensate for being shunned for their dreadful smell. Many, many shells were used in the creation of this dye – it took up to ten thousand Mediterranean snails to create enough dye to colour a single purple toga, which was the ultimate symbol of wealth and status in Roman society.

There are very strong taboos and laws regarding the way shells can be treated in Melanesia, northeast of Australia, which remains the centre of an island shell trading circle called the Kula Ring. Every shell is considered to have its own story, based both on its shell family and its own personal journey. Not only are shells traded for goods, their stories have value too, and shells with strong stories of protection, for example, are highly sought after. There is a very strict method of trading: Necklaces are traded by travelling in a clockwise direction, and white shell armbands are traded in a counter-clockwise direction. No person can hold a shell for more than ten years – after that it must be passed on, along with all its tales and stories. A famous anthropologist, Bronislaw Malinowski, studied this intricate and very precise system, which is now eroding due to the decimation of indigenous ways in the islands.

Scallop shells are a symbol of the Camino, the pilgrimage path in northern Spain that is completed at the tomb of Saint James in the town of Santiago de Compostela. A preacher and martyr, it is said that after James was murdered he was taken up by angels and placed in a stone boat, where the sea guided his remains to the Iberian Peninsula, and a huge rock covered in shells closed around his body. The shell also represents the different paths of the Camino.

Shells were the instrument used to murder the beautiful pagan philosopher and mathematician Hypatia of Alexandria in 415CE. It is tragic to think that this incredible woman was murdered using the very symbol of femininity, and this cruel killing heralded the beginning of the end of the sacred feminine for many centuries.

However it could never stay down for long. The mermaid and her shells rise again and again, and any ebb is tidal – the tide always turns, and the shell and her keeper, the mermaid, always rise again.

Conchomancy : Pure Energy of the Sea

Reading and working with shells can help you connect directly to mer energies, sea healing and oceanic beings, and help you remember your deep love of the ocean. Just as crystals hold energies and messages, so too do these beautiful living homes and structures of the sea creatures. Each creature resonates with a particular energy, and by connecting with their shell, holding it, feeling its qualities and understanding its connections, you can begin to heal a part of yourself. While we are all perfect and unique expressions of the god and goddess, of nature herself, we are also beautiful works in progress, and messages and healings from the natural world are beautiful, healthful and freely available to all.

Low tide is the most wonderful – and practical – time to search for shells, and a low tide on a new moon will take the waterline even further out, leaving even more of the ocean's treasures available for viewing and respectful collection and admiration.

Shells and Their Energetic Blueprint

Please know that although it is simple to purchase many sea animal and shell parts online or even at markets, to do so is to increase the trade in such goods. If a shell has been mistreated in this way – its occupant killed and discarded – we can help to heal the shell by sending our love. If we do not indulge in purchasing beauty in cruel ways, we increase the love and good fortune in our own life. Too many creatures are sacrificed for us.

When collecting, always be sure that there are no sea creatures still alive in a shell – they are very adept at "hiding". Never take too many, only take a few. And remember the witches' rede – fairly take and fairly give – so always return something to the sea in return for what you have been given.

Abalone: Appearances at present are hiding true beauty – you must find a way to look inside the situation and to see its true beauty. Something precious is out of plain sight – there is safety in keeping a treasure as something that must be searched for, so only the worthy shall know her treasures.

Clam: A clam is a bivalve shell, perfectly mirrored in its other half, so if you find one half of a clam shell, this is a symbol that there has been some kind of separation, and this vacuum must be tended to, and filled mindfully. Ask yourself what has left your life of late. The clam can comfort you while you heal to completion.

Clusterwink: The shell of this small sea snail, which is found clinging in small groups to the side of rocks at the shoreline, has a special feature, bioluminescence – they can send out a "blast" of green light. Bright and sparkling, these creatures use their shell as a reflecting shield to frighten off bird predators, blasting seagulls and oystercatchers with a green ray of light. Not only can they produce this light, they can position their shell to reflect it, making it brighter and scarier for predators. If you collect a clusterwink shell, you are collecting a powerful shield, a way of harmlessly repelling all those who would do you harm. No matter how vulnerable we may seem, like the tiny clusterwink, our very energy can protect, shield and empower us.

Cockle: A sweet and heart-strengthening shell, it offers protection and nurturing in matters to do with love and tender feelings. It helps us find the people we are meant to be with, and to detach from those we are no longer meant to be with. It also reinforces the bonds between friends, lovers, parents and children, and colleagues.

Conch: Infinity, time warps and dimensional slips. Associated with the Hindu god Vishnu, who is said to hold a special conch, Panchajanya, which represents life because it comes out of life-giving waters. These are manifesting shells, expanders of energy, and hold great power to increase whatever is in your life at the time of discovery. However, there are conches that belong to Shiva and to Kali, and can bring banishment and destruction in order to grow anew – they are energy cutting and banishing shells. A conch that has spirals running widdershins (counter-clockwise in the northern hemisphere, clockwise in the south) is a banishing shell, and can work to remove and dissolve or dissipate whatever it is you no longer need. They are associated with the destroyer/rebirth goddess Kali and the god Shiva, are very powerful, and must be treated with respect when used in magic. They are said to create the sound "aum", the first sound, the primordial bringer forth of life, and of death. Conches are associated with spiritual leaders, and are carved into the ancient pyramids of the Maya people, where they are often featured with the puma, who blows the conch shell. Conch is a call to action, and sings the song of the sea. If you raise this sacred sea horn to your lips and blow, you too will summon and stir the energies of the deep – be prepared to awaken lost parts of the self when you work with the energy of the sacred conch! It helps you raise your voice, be heard and speak up at injustice, and summon and attract allies and familiars to you.

Conchomancy: This is the art of divination using seashells. There are many variations, but one of the most influential and renowned is Diloggun, the title given to cowrie divination in the Afro-Caribbean Cuban spirituality of Santeria. The orishas, one of whom is the great primordial sea mother goddess Yemanja, speaks through these cowries in specific formations. It takes many years to master this very exact art. Diloggun divination is conducted by initiates who employ specific and very complex rituals before and during the casting of the cowrie shells.

Cowrie: Abundance, fertility and sacred sex and sexuality are all held in the energy field of this beautiful shell. It is very powerful, and can be used for all women as they move through the cycles from maiden to mother to crone, for menstrual cycle regulation and fertility and protection of children. They also symbolically protect your clan and their stories. Cowries tell the stories of all the sea beings, speaking through their lips to our ears. Cowries are directly associated with the water deity Yemanja, who speaks through the cowrie in divination, fertility rites, and brings forth abundance by offering the cowrie.

Mussel: These bivalve beings are similar to clams in some ways, but their shells are elongated and asymmetrical rather than the more rounded or oval clams. Finding a mussel shell can indicate that you are closing yourself off and isolating yourself from others, so look within to discover why you're shutting others out.

Nautilus: The nautilus shell personifies and embodies the golden ratio, thus it can bring about perfect balance with life's cycles, and is a wonderful shell to work with when change and life's flow seems erratic and too rapid, or stagnant and stuck. It will also help you with your soul's evolution.

Oyster shell: Symbolises the ability to create beauty, to nourish, and to reclaim the ability to provide for oneself and transform any difficulties into objects of great beauty. The oyster must stay in a single position in its lifetime and does not move – so oyster shells remind us of the importance of a place we can call home, and return to, time and again. They also ask us to be still and silent for a time. This may not be a place within the physical world, it may be a place within our own selves that we have created.

Paua shell: Known as treasure-shell (taonga) to the Maori people, the meat of this shellfish was a great delicacy. These shells and shellfish are now protected and can only be brought to the surface by tank-free divers, and licences are hard to come by. The flashing blue-green colours of the paua shell was used specifically for the eyes of the gods in the statues of the Maori people – they depicted the flash and fire of the eyes of the great warriors too. When you wear paua, you are connecting with the eye of the gods – you can truly "see" what is taking place, and have a clear understanding of the history beneath an event. It can also inspire you to stand fast to your principles in difficult circumstances, as this shell represents and grants the courage of the ancient warriors.

Ram's horn shell: These beautiful delicate spiral horns speak of maturity (the larger the spiral, the greater the experience), individuation and masculine endurance. Conversely, due to their fragility, they also speak of the easily wounded masculine ego, and their need to care for their health without fear of being seen as weak. The creature is very rarely seen, as it is a deep-water squid-like being, but the small internal shell is extremely light in weight, very buoyant and strong, so it commonly floats ashore onto beaches all around the world.

Scallop shell: These symbolise beauty, adornment, self-love and looking within and finding much to love. These shells have long been associated with the goddesses Aphrodite and Venus, who are often depicted holding a scallop shell. They are bivalves, so they can assist with finding love and companionship, both for men and for women, as well as allowing us to develop our sensual expression and a healthful sacral chakra. It symbolises the ability to move, dance and have freedom. The name scallop is derived from the Old French escalope, which means shell.

Sea snail, Mediterranean: To overcome issues to do with abundance and self-worth, this shell will assist you in protecting yourself while you grow in abundance and in identity. If this shell comes to you, it is likely you will soon be experiencing more renown and your name will be known by many who you do not know. You must learn to deal with this – and the shell will help you work your way through this situation and retain your privacy.

Sea snail shell, pointed, small: Sea snail shells assist us to draw out worrying thoughts and tiny distractions from the day in order to stay focused, and to attend to many things without losing our insight and broader perspective on the situation.

Sea snail shell, pointed, large: A larger shell magnifies our focus, third-eye insights and development, and is useful for energy healing as well as extractions from the auric field.

Sea snail, violet moon: All sea snails have a drawing, detoxifying energy, and draw forth impurities from your mind. My daughter had a dream that a wonderful healer we know, Natasha Heard, was holding these shells to her ears and drawing forth "bad memories". They indicate it is time to connect with the inner feminine, accept the changes that are coming and know that you are in the process of change and in the midst of a profound cycle. Please see the Lunar and Tidal Magics chapter for more insights, as moon snails carry the energies of both the lunar cycles and the tides.

Gem-mer's Seashell Magic

Australian artistan Gem-mer Sweedman is the creator of Cryshell Magic, a range of magical jewellery that is inspired by the ocean and all its beautiful treasures, combined with crystals from the earth to heal and inspire with mer magic, and connect people with the merfolk. Visit Gem-mer at www.cryshellmagic.com.au.

I've always loved seashells. I recall holidays at the beach as a child, but it wasn't until this year when we moved to the coast that I began to really appreciate their true beauty. I spent more and more time on the beach, looking at and playing with shells, and finally creating with them. I've realised how amazing and powerful they are and how much I love them.

For the merfolk and us on dry land – if we open our hearts to them – seashells are powerful vessels of healing energy, with the ability to clear and cleanse, banish and replace energies. The creatures inside the shells have a purpose in the mer world, for example for healing wounds. I've been working with the merfolk and allowing sea snails to repair my sight through meditation. Shells are carriers of information, of history and time. To the merfolk, and to me, they are powerful tools of healing and ancient knowledge.

It's hard to pick a favourite, because they're all so beautiful, powerful and unique in their own way. I love scallop shells, with their amazing colours and awesome power, but right now heart cockles, clams and ark shells with ancient markings from time and travel are my favourites to create with. They have so much to tell.

Heart cockles are great to start communicating with first – they're simple, full of love, inspiring and very open. I feel that to communicate with shells, you need to be touching them, holding them in your hands, stroking and caressing them. Admire their beauty, where they have come from and what they have been through to get to you. Be grateful for the opportunity, and open your heart to accept the love and knowledge they will share when your mind is still.

For me, shells can carry any type of energy; they're very open, like sponges. Their own little life journeys determine what energies they bring to me. I take each one for what it is, and what they all are is totally unique and individual. That's how it is for me.

People have said that my Cryshell pieces are perfect for clearing energies before and after reiki sessions. Others say that they remind their new guardians of their own mer magic, and help their mer memories and feelings come flooding back.

Mer energies are beautiful, sensual, floaty energies like liquid light. They are full of love and are so watery. There is freedom in mer energies, a sensual freedom to embrace and accept your inner goddess (or god). It is a cleansing energy. The merfolk have so much love and gentleness, they are enveloping, embracing and giving. They have so much knowledge to share for a positive purpose, a positive lifestyle. They also have such inner strength and restraint, are protective and can freely embrace their own warrior strength when needed. They are very gentle in nature, however they have the capacity to go wild, so much respect is needed. All of these qualities and energies are what they offer to us land walkers.

I am a merbeing – a mer-sistar! I connect and converse with the merfolk and play with them at the beach, and connect in my bathroom or with my magical Mer-Cryshells every day. I openly receive the beautiful gifts of seashells and knowledge, and I give the merfolk many thanks and gifts in return. I am energised and inspired by the ocean and her magnificent ways, and long to be beneath her surface with all the beautiful creatures. As I spy her blue-green waters, I take a deep breath and know that I'm home. At times I feel like running to her, especially when I haven't been to her for a few days. And as I get closer, my urge to sprint becomes stronger.

Connecting With Coral

"Corals are living entities – they breathe, reproduce, feed and die.
They represent the entire life cycle, and as such their healing powers
are immense and largely untapped. Just like crystals, I have found
that corals have a vibrational energy that contains much wisdom and
healing when held, infused into an essence or simply meditated near."
Trish Anderson-Young, Australian crystal healer

Poseidon's Castle : Treasure of the Sea

Coral is one of the most beautiful, mysterious creatures on the
planet. The enchanting evidence of a colony of tiny animals, they
develop their intricate underwater towers of red, gold and softest
pinks over thousands of years. Today they are fighting a valiant,
silent battle to survive environmental interference in many forms.

We can all work with the energy of coral every day. It is an
ancient keeper of memories and wisdoms and collective
consciousness, of life itself on this planet. Connecting with this
sacred energy also takes us back to the times before Atlantis, before
even the birth of Lemuria. Coral has been revered for millennia.
It is one of the Buddha's seven sacred treasures (along with gold,
silver, aquamarine, conch shell, emerald and amber), able to restore
tranquillity and serenity in all circumstances.

According to Greek legend, the great and mighty ocean god
Poseidon built his underwater palace out of coral and pearls. And
the husband of Aphrodite, the great scarred metalsmith and
alchemist Hephaestus, first worked with fire, water and coral to
make objects of great beauty and magical power. Greek

philosopher Plato suggested children should wear pieces of coral to ward off illness, and Greek mythology asserts that coral was formed from the blood falling from Medusa's severed head, which is reflected in the Greek name for red coral, gorgeia.

The powerful energy of coral was recognised far beyond Greek shores. The Roman historian Pliny observed that the Gauls (the indigenous tribal peoples of modern-day France) decorated their swords and helmets with coral pieces in order to prevent excessive bleeding during warfare. Sailors believed coral could ease the stormy seas. In Rome, children chewed on pieces of coral when they were teething, and wore talismans of coral to protect them from disease. The Romans also believed coral could ward off sorcery, fires and lightning, and wore it as precious jewellery long before they used pearls. Men in the medieval era who struggled with impotency hoped they'd be lucky enough to be gifted a piece of coral from a sea witch, as it was a known aid to virility. Indeed, Italian men still gift their fiancee with coral – perhaps an echo of this ancient magic, as well as a promise of passionate nights and long good health!

But it is perhaps the very beauty and magic of coral that has now made its future so very fragile. Corals, for their health and flourishing, need clean water, and today more than ever they require active care and awareness. They do not fare well in muddy waters, and their health is directly related to the health of all the oceans.

If you are ever fortunate enough to snorkel where there is living coral, never urinate. That small quantity of nitrogen can kill off entire colonies of coral, as has been done by tourists in countries such as Thailand, the Philippines and Hawaii, where only now the devastating effects of tourists on the reefs are becoming known. Seaweeds, on the other hand, adore urine, so there are colonies of kelps overwhelming the coral colonies, a tragedy which is being combated by the wonderful people who spend their annual holidays establishing coral gardens in very vulnerable areas. Also be careful not to stand on delicate reef systems, especially in clumsy flippers.

Corals are also endangered by the industry that hungers for their beauty. Just like crystal gemstones, coral is routinely harvested using explosives that not only break apart and destroy entire sections of reef, but kill the fish and creatures who live in the coral castles. "They put dynamite and blow them up and get coral and fish," explains environmentalist Harinda Joseph Fernando.

Coral has long been used as a magical talisman to enhance beauty and to ensure protection. It is said that the mermaids shared their precious corals with the seamen they loved, to protect and bless them against sea storms and drowning. But today it is no longer the mermaids choosing – human farmers have depleted the red coral of the Mediterranean to dangerously low levels, and other sources are also under threat. If you do have a piece of this endangered item, please treasure it, respect it, and do something to give back to the coral beings who are now protecting you with their beautiful strong moonblood energy.

Please do know where your coral is coming from. The very best piece is a small piece, washed up on the shore for you. It will carry such strong energy – and is even more precious for knowing the sea offered her to you. There are also many old pieces of vintage coral jewellery, so search in op shops or ask your grandma if she has any coral pieces you can work with, as recycling and reusing what has already been harvested will help prevent further destruction.

Coral planting is now taking place in some very vulnerable places, and many reefs respond and recover well. Coral gardening, an active way of evening out the situation for the corals by removing coral-hungry predators and weeding the kelps that can devastate them, including the crown-of-thorns starfish, is also helping. However it takes many thousands of years for a coral reef such as the Great Barrier Reef to develop, and we are running out of time.

Corals for Conservation (www.coralsforconservation.com) works with fishing communities and the tourism industry to conserve the coral reefs that they – and the oceans of the world – depend on. The program started in Fiji and is spreading outward to other vulnerable sites, so if you feel so moved, you can support their work. Hawaii also has programs of monitoring and educating tourists to protect their beautiful and unique reef systems.

Sacred Coral : A History of This Living Creature

In ancient Mesopotamia, coral was used for warding off evil spirits, was positioned at the entrance of homes to prevent incomers bringing storms and cruelty, disharmony or emotionally destabilising the household. It was said to protect from shipwreck and lightning, and so was often tied to the prow of a seafaring vessel. It can banish nightmares, and bring us through an emotional crisis by guiding us to calmer shores and clearing muddy waters.

As well as being treasured by Buddhists, it is also sacred to Zoroastrians, whose prophet wore coral to protect from the twin evils of ill-wishes and ill-health. And I've recommended working with coral for people with bone issues, as it has high level of calcium and some forms are very hard and strong. It can also increase the health of your bone marrow, and is a boon to women of all ages.

Is it ethical to wear coral, given that it is so endangered? This is something I have thought long on, and there are those who say we should not buy it to adorn ourselves with. Every year coral smugglers take thousands of dollars worth of this precious substance from land to land, and sell the bones of the sea mother, without which she cannot live. So if you do purchase coral, please find out the source of the coral you are using, and be sure to give back to the coral reefs in some form. The mother needs her coral to live – they are often called the canaries of the ocean, as any ill-health in coral comes years before ill-health to all the reef's species.

Each coral family has particular qualities, and each region has an energetic signature that is unique. To tune in to your coral, read the list below, then simply hold your coral in your receiving hand.

Always care for your coral, should you be fortunate enough to have some in your care for a time. You are her keeper and guardian, not her owner, and she requires a gentle touch, as she is a soft and fragile precious being. Never spray it with hairspray (in fact, do not spray your hair with hairspray), do not let synthetic perfumes near her, and wipe her carefully with a moist cloth to clean her. If your coral has been subjected to the cruelty of dyeing, she may bleed the dye when washed. Care for her, and in time she will return to her own natural colour, as you too return to your own natural self.

Coral Types and Their Magical Purposes

Red coral: Prevents bleeding, and is wonderful for the menstrual cycle and for women who are going into their crone years (menopausal). Red coral also heals wounds and makes people strong. It grows very slowly though, perhaps one centimetre a year, and is difficult to harvest without using explosives due to the great depth at which colonies grow, so it is rare and fragile.

Blue coral: This coral can prevent illness and disease developing, and restores balance to the body, soul, emotions and spirit.

Golden coral: This beautiful, rare coral brings abundance and good fortune. If harvested unethically, however, it could have quite the opposite impact! If you do become a keeper of this form of coral, always work with it in a healing way, and know that you must be a guardian to help keep the coral where she belongs – in the seas.

Black coral: This banishes negative energies from your body, in particular bones. It can also assist in banishing disease and aiding people with osteoporosis. Hawaiian black coral is very strong, and contains the energy of the volcano goddess Pele, so it can be called on to light your fire and burn through what must be cleared. It is very rare, and can take more than fifty years to establish, so cherish it.

Angel skin coral: This beautiful soft pink coral can be worked with to prevent and to ease skin conditions such as psoriasis, eczema and sensitive skin and eyes. It also helps with sinus issues, acne and increasing and stabilising liver function.

White coral: This coral symbolises pure rebirth, a time for transformation, allowing yourself to change and develop once again, and love that is unconditional and kind. White coral can also be used to program and store energies.

Underwater Forests and Groves

"I love seaweeds. They are rooted in the ocean bed, yet move gracefully with the movement of the water. So grounded, yet in the flow. When I see them or visualise them I am at once connected and free. They remind me I am of the earth, yet also animated by spirit."
Janelle Woods, Australian writer and women's healthcare worker

A Mermaid's Vegetable Garden

Just as the sacred old growth stands of trees on the land are the dwellings of the myriad beings we call faery, so too the great kelp forests of the underwater worlds are the homes of the mermaids. They are their precious birthing grounds, their underwater hospitals, and they provide shelter from the storms and cyclones that can wreak havoc on the surface far above.

Mermaids and the sea creatures they care for lay down in beds of kelp, soft and velvet smooth, lithe and loving, and they are fed by them, enriched by the nutrients that they hold. Kelp forests are the most beautiful marine environments, interacting perfectly with the structural majesty of the corals. Like undersea forests, they move and sway with the currents, waves, tides and surges. They respond to environmental changes, just as do earth forests, but they have, in most places, avoided decimation. And today they hold minerals and medicines that can heal, and help humanity. They are precious, these forests of the sea, these places where the mermaids dance.

While our ancestors revered the sea forests for their life-enhancing properties, many of us today see seaweed as a nuisance, or something to have fun with. Who has not adorned their head with weed and shouted: "I'm a mermaid!" or encircled their throats with Neptune's pearls, as one bead-like variety of seaweed is called?

Eating seaweed seems strange to many of us, but to people in Japan, Hawaii and many southeast Asian countries it is natural and good, and so very healthful. One day, walking on a beach dear to me, and lamenting the waste of so much kelp rotting – far more than seemed necessary to keep the natural life cycle turning in that area – I was shown images of people eating kelp, using it on their gardens, and working on coral beds to keep the balance intact.

And it does make sense. Eating seaweed and sea vegetables is healthful and natural, and can help us achieve regulated hormonal and thyroid function. They are also a wonderful natural provider of minerals and nutrients for our ever-so-depleted earth soils, and in Scotland, kelp was burned to make the ash that was used to make glass – sea glass, a true mermaid's reflective surface!

Eating sea vegetables is entirely natural. I love eating them, and find them delicious, and so packed with vitamins and minerals. They provide vital energy, and taking them into our body can reinvigorate our tired land senses, and connect us even more deeply to the wonders of the sea. The more we eat, the healthier we grow, and our connection to the sea becomes deeper and stronger too.

Seaweeds such as kombu are a delicious addition to salads and Japanese foods, where it is eaten fresh as sashimi, as a main ingredient in dashi, and as a snack with green tea. Kombu adds protein and minerals, and has the wonderful side effect of reducing flatulence (and yes, that may mean that mermaids do not, indeed!).

If you have ever eaten the mermaidenly delight of sushi, your rice roll will have been wrapped in delicate dried nori, which contains high proportions of iodine, carotene, vitamins A, B and C, as well as significant amounts of calcium and iron.

Kelp, a large brown seaweed, is known as the food tonic of the sea, and contains more than sixty essential vitamins, minerals and trace elements. Kelp, and the laminaria variety in particular, is loaded with iodine, which makes it helpful for those with thyroid issues. The thyroid also powers the throat chakra, so kelp can assist us in finding our true voice – another quality the mermaids teach us.

In 2010, it was discovered that sea kelp contains arginate, a fibre that absorbs fat in the body. This discovery meant that the mermaids' favourite plants were suddenly very desirable for a flourishing weight-loss industry – which will see sea kelps being harvested at a great rate. This shouldn't be an issue though, as rising sea temperatures mean kelps are now overgrowing the delicate coral ecosystems – so harvesting could be useful!

Another vital sea green is spirulina, a microscopic blue-green algae in the shape of a spiral coil, which is harvested from both seawater and fresh water. It's a complete protein, containing all the essential amino acids, and is rich in essential fatty acids, antioxidant vitamins, plus many minerals. In 1974 the United Nations World Food Conference lauded spirulina as the "best food for the future", it is often included in lists of superfoods, and studies show it can lower cholesterol and blood pressure and help arthritis, anaemia, general health issues and energy levels.

As the people of the land grow more and more out of balance, we are turning to the sea to balance our bodies once again. The sea forests are also the keepers of great wisdoms. Kelp teaches us to eat consciously, something many land people have forgotten. The sea sponges teach us to breathe deeply and let the air out again.

The fish, who live simply, and in such beauty, have fed the land peoples for so many years, as well as the creatures who in turn live from them. In the underwater forests there are microsystems, just as there are in the great earthen tree places. There are many species of algae that have yet to be discovered and categorised, and who knows what nutrients and medicines they will hold?

The Benefits of Eating Like a Mermaid

✪ Studies in Japan link eating seaweeds with low rates of breast, colon and lung cancers. Edible brown seaweeds such as kelp boost immune activity and inhibit tumour growth.

✪ Seaweeds are a super-abundant source of iodine, an essential mineral. The one with the greatest amount of iodine is Icelandic kelp, followed by Norwegian. Sargassum and nori contain the least iodine – although they contain many other vital nutrients. If we till the soil with iodine-rich seaweeds, our own plants will up their levels, perhaps compensating for the stripped minerals of the earth.

✪ Seaweeds can make your skin strong, supple and youthful, keep your hair healthy and stimulate hair and nail growth.

✪ They help neutralise heavy-metal pollutants that we take in every day. They are rich in the B vitamins and other nutrients that stabilise nerve function, which help us handle higher loads of stress. Include them in your diet to feel the shift from fatigue to power!

✪ Bladderwrack, despite its scary name, can ease women through menopause by helping to balance wayward hormones.

✪ Sea greens such as Irish moss, kombu, laver, nori, kale, wakame and dulse are all rich in trace minerals that boost immune function, and can help your body metabolise adrenaline and cortisol, and regulate the immune system, making it work more powerfully.

Mermaids please note! The best seaweeds to eat are those found in health food stores or harvested wild yourself from a clean ocean. Do not eat seaweeds that have washed up on the shore. This can be used for fertiliser, but not for consumption.

Kristina's Ocean Magic

Kristina Georges is the director of Samie's Girl Seafoods in Brisbane, Queensland, and feels that for everything she takes from the ocean, she should put something back. She works with the Environmental Protection Agency and fisheries conservation partners to protect marine turtles, and raises funds through SOS – Save our Sea Turtles. Visit her at www.samiesgirl.com.au.

I look at the ocean as the birthplace of life, as mother earth's birthing ground. Just as a child is born with a water sac around it for survival, the ocean unlocks secrets of the past and also holds within it the future. My connection to the sea started when I was a child. Our family weekends were spent at the beaches of Redcliffe, just north of Brisbane, or with Dad taking us out in a dinghy to the islands in Moreton Bay. I grew up with a father who was a fisherman, who then ventured out into a family seafood business, so I have that connection to the sea from my father.

In my business of providing seafood I take from the sea, so I believe I need to give back to the sea. It's like a revolving food chain. As the world is changing, sustainability is becoming key for business, and I think about what I can do for the future of the sea.

I have a project, SOS – Save Our Sea Turtles. I sell environmental bags in my retail store, and all proceeds go to turtle project kits for primary schools. Educating children about the sea and the environment of sea turtles is my passion. I've also sponsored satellite tags for turtles so scientists can study their habitat, and been out in the bay with Professor Limpus, who's been researching sea turtles for forty years, investigating how they migrate, how many eggs they lay, how they nest, where they nest and so on.

Doing these projects for the ocean makes me feel special. To touch a turtle and know I am doing something to help the future is rewarding to my heart. My passion is the sea, my life is the sea. When I look at the ocean, it rejuvenates my blood and clears my mind.

We can all help the ocean by supporting charities that deal with the sea, volunteering with organisations like the Environmental Protection Agency and by knowing that what we throw into our waste at home affects the ocean in some way.

Of all the sea creatures, I feel most connected to sea turtles. They remind me of myself – a sea turtle takes a while to get to its destination, but it always goes back to its home. It has a hard shell of protection, and something that will unlock the past and future of the sea. And the sea turtle is a long survivor, and long-lived. When I touch the turtles and hold the small ones up with great strength, we connect and I feel a knowing that I am a part of a sea.

My strength has always come from my connection to the sea. I believe in magic from the sea. I believe there are kingdoms beneath the sea. I believe in Atlantis. I dream a lot of a magical island where I'm swimming near the rocks, so it's strange that in this life I can't swim. And I believe in mermaids – I am one. I chose the mermaid, as she chose me, for the logo of my business. The mermaid lures humans to the unknown and forbidden. They are beautiful, loving and exotic, and have the power, the magic, of healing the soul.

I also pray to Saint Gerasimos, who is connected to water. He comes from the Greek island of Kefalonia, next to Ithaki, the island my dad is from. Whenever I'm sick I pray to him, and he also protects me every day. I always wear his pendant for strength and protection.

Working With the Ocean

"You cannot discover new oceans
unless you have the courage to lose sight of the shore."
Andre Gide, French author

The Power and Magic of the Seas

The ocean is mutable, a liquid metamorphosis. She has been shifting and changing since the elements themselves emerged from the pre-creation void. From the realm of chaos she flowed, and that inherent ability to transform again and again is one of her most alluring and compelling qualities. Like the lunar cycles, she is constantly inconstant; she can be consistently relied upon to regularly shift and change her mood, colour, force and energy.

For billions of years, the seas have risen, fallen, shifted and moved. Today more than seventy per cent of this planet is water – and ninety-seven per cent of that water is oceanic. The salinity of seawater is between three and four per cent – around thirty-five grams of salt per litre. Our bodies hold almost the same proportion of salt as the sea, when we cry, our tears are the same, as are the womb's amniotic fluids. We are all, no matter how far we are from the sea, born of her, because we have been born from the ocean within our mother.

Life in the oceans is far older than life on the land – thus when we turn to the ocean and its waters for wisdom, we are going very deep into the ancient times of the planet and of our own evolution. We move into the chthonic depths of our emotions, our instincts and our sometime-submerged self when we embrace the wisdom the ocean has to offer.

Here are some ways to understand the ocean you may be living near, or the ones you want to work with. Add this knowledge to your own understanding of different waters, animals and beings – this way, understanding of them deepens and grows.

In truth there is but one ocean, referred to as the World Ocean or Global Ocean, which is an interconnected system of all the earth's marine waters. However it is commonly divided into five principal oceanic areas, divided up in relation to their position around and between the continental land masses. These are the Atlantic, Arctic, Indian, Pacific and Southern Oceans, and in turn these large oceanic waters are interspersed with smaller seas, gulfs and bays.

These five oceans are wild and myriad in their forms and selves, but there is an underlying flavour or quality that stays with them throughout their manifestations across this green and blue planet. The Pacific Ocean will always speak to you of the deepest aspects of your nature, of all that is yet to be discovered, and how you can create jewels out of the chaos of your existence. The Indian Ocean is nearly always sensual in flavour – even at her coldest depth, she is simply refusing to merge, as she does through the rest of her watery realm.

The Pacific Ocean

This ocean is the largest, the oldest and the deepest on the planet. It spreads from the western coast of the Americas to the eastern coast of Japan, China, Russia and Australia, and includes all the Pacific Islands such as Hawaii, Tahiti, Fiji and New Zealand. If you wish to strengthen your contacts with the Lemurian peoples, connect with this deep and beautifully unknown ocean. Also work with the Pacific to connect with the ancestor lines and the untouched parts of yourself. It is for the unknown. It is the deepest ocean, the one that holds the greatest of all the mysteries, and the knowledge of the ages swims in her depths and dwells within her inhabitants.

This magnificent and multi-faceted flow of liquid intelligence covers nearly half the planet, so it is incredibly powerful, and wherever we are, she impacts upon us in some way. This ocean is so large that it could swallow all of the planet's land masses – it is greater in size than all the earth on this planet put together, its depth is higher than the peaks of Everest, and it is speckled with islands of infinite beauty and infinite number.

The Pacific is the home of more than twenty-five thousand islands, more than exists throughout the rest of the world's oceans. It offers life to the greatest number of corals on the planet, and is surrounded by the Ring of Fire, a nearly continuous series of oceanic trenches and active volcanoes around the edges of the ocean, where tectonic plate shifts create a higher incidence of volcanoes and earthquakes than anywhere else.

This ocean is ancient, primordial, life-bringing and easily misunderstood. She is wise, and she is peaceful – and she changes, again and again, as we must too.

Keywords: Ancient, prolific, transformer, immensity.

Work with it to: Get in touch with what is unknown, receive ancient knowledge, change into a deeper, more mature version of the self, expand your self and projects.

The Atlantic Ocean

This ocean swells between the east coast of the Americas and the west coast of Africa and Europe, and has such majesty to it. It is for the knowing of the self – those ancient parts of the self that are just beneath the tideline. It is also an energy that needs replenishing and nurturing, as it has been over-fished and over-hunted for so long. For all that it has been so exploited though, it is the youngest and most enthused of all the seas on the planet.

It is also one of the most diverse, given river waters and melted ices from more than half the world's land masses pour into her waters. It plays host to the mighty waves drawn up by the force of the Roaring Forties winds, which rage across the Southern Ocean between latitudes 40°S and 50°S before pouring into the Atlantic, and is home to the imperilled Gulf Stream, the powerful, warm and swift ocean current that runs up the east coast of the US and Newfoundland before crossing the Atlantic, which warms both the water and the land. It was affected by 2010's Gulf Oil Spill, and has become endangered, its warm current slowing and cooling. In time, we will know what damage has been done.

The Atlantic Ocean plays host to youthful exuberant energy, to the winter storms that raise mountainous waves that devour the shore, and underwater mountain ranges that are twice the size of the Andes. And yet fish some three hundred million years old still inhabit this ocean. Diamonds are mined in Atlantic waters off the coast of the African nation of Namibia, and it contains the energetic nexus that is the Bermuda Triangle, a place where past, present and future are said to converge, resulting in mysterious disappearances, reappearances and bizarre happenings that defy the known laws of nature.

When we tune in to the Atlantic Ocean, we feel the rush of our lifeblood and the roar of energy. We can be buoyed up high, and we can rediscover passions and emotions we thought we were long past. Connecting with the Atlantic is about stamina, and understanding that even youth has its ancient wisdom. It is also wonderful for assisting with young people, or Indigo adults.

Keywords: Youth, vitality, exuberance, passion, rebellion, freedom.

Work with it to: Get in touch with your enthusiasm, grow your motivation, draw and connect with potential friends and mates.

The Arctic Ocean

The Arctic Ocean is located in the northern hemisphere, primarily in the Arctic north pole region, and is the smallest and shallowest of the oceanic divisions. Tuning in to the energy of the Arctic Ocean is to tune in to the celestial realms, the places where the land itself is crystalline, where the sky sways with colours unthought of in our art or imagination.

This extreme ocean is home to the polar bears, the beings who are suffering most as the planet's balance is thrown awry – not by herself, or a natural change, but due to humanity's interference with natural systems. So the Arctic Ocean is the realm of responsibility, intensity and rarity. Seals, polar bears and arctic foxes dwell here, and all keep close to them the secrets of survival. The Arctic is for the preservation of rare species and for the love of creatures such as polar bears, and is a portal to galactic energies.

The smallest of the planet's oceans, it is perhaps the most unoceanic. Much of its water is frozen into the land masses of ice that are necessary for harp seals, polar bears and arctic foxes to continue in their environment (and this ice holds much carbon for us), and if it starts to melt it will prove deadly to these beings, and eventually to the rest of the planet. But there may be hope. Food supply is still high in this region, with more fish feeding off the ice rim than there are anywhere else on the planet. Thus, while this may seem an austere and frozen energy to enter into, it is also extremely abundant when you look, literally, below the surface. And what is on the surface is beyond belief.

Keywords: Stillness, pause, contemplation, open, unique.

Work with it to: Connect with a very still and quiet part of yourself, that can bring forth unique gifts and moments, and to offer yourself more quiet time, a time to listen. To deepen your work with this ocean, simplify and declutter your environment. Wear whites and silvers, and eat very simply for a time to come back to the core of your own self, to a basic yet profound understanding. Make things about what is necessary for life, not what is status-oriented. Keep bare. Welcome a time of pause, before growth begins anew.

The Indian Ocean

Stretching from the west coast of Australia up to the Indian subcontinent and across to the east coast of Africa, this is the warmest ocean in the world, and the most mined. She is about lust, drive, sexuality, greed and balancing desire with sustainability.

This ocean, while warm and comparatively gentle, does not host the variety of sea life that the other more extreme and seemingly harsher oceans do. Her warmth restricts the flourishing of phytoplankton, so she is not as blessed with life. However, she is beautiful, and is known as Ratnakara – a Sanskrit word that translates as the creator of jewels. Indeed, she does provide jewels, in the form of wealth. Her sands are loaded with minerals, so her shores are mined in India, Indonesia, Sri Lanka and Thailand.

This heavy mineral presence also includes offshore deposits of crude oil, so she is mined off the Persian Gulf and Indonesia. Forty per cent of the entire world's oil comes from this ocean, and the fish are thus being depleted at an incredible rate – so fishing is now banned in many areas, except for that done by subsistence peoples.

Beneath these shimmering silken waters lies a sunken continent, Kerguelen, a mysterious realm about which we are only just learning... It is, I feel, a remnant of Lemuria.

Keywords: Ancient, unbridled sensuality, grace, instinct, feminine power, abundance, richness, decoration and adornment.

Work with it to: Create a "look" for yourself and connect with beauty and adornment. This ocean helps you select jewels, pearls and foods that encourage you to see yourself as a rich, sensual being that deserves the luxury of the sensual world. It will also help you understand where you are allowing others to take too freely of your abundant resources – these may need to be protected, and this ocean can help you create healthy barriers and boundaries.

The Southern Ocean

The Southern Ocean, also known as the Antarctic Ocean and the South Polar Ocean, comprises the southernmost stretch of the earth's seas, from latitude 60°S down to Antarctica (although some geographers deny it is a separate body). It has been affected by solar radiation as the ozone hole is situated over it, resulting in DNA mutations in some of her fish and sea creatures. Illegal fishing off the coasts of South America has depleted the stock of Patagonian toothfish, and thousands of seabirds have been injured or killed in this fishing industry. It is also the home of many of the whales, but while there are whaling agreements in place for this ocean, and whaling is prohibited south of latitude 40°S, Japan does not recognise this law. So, although the Southern Ocean is a whale sanctuary, these beings are hunted both outside it, as the whales migrate, and within it, under the guise of "scientific research".

Despite massive mineral, oil and gas fields on its ocean floor, it is forbidden to mine here. It plays host to both a clockwise and an anticlockwise current that circles the globe like an energetic belt, continually transmuting the energies both being sent and being received from and to the planet. The eastward current creates the highest winds known anywhere on earth.

This ocean is rich in fish, krill, seventeen species of penguin, whales, seals and fresh water – many of its icebergs are composed of fresh water rather than salt, which has many scientists excited about it being a possible reservoir of drinking water for humans.

Keywords: Boundaries, thresholds, personal law, sovereignty, personal authority. Transgression and balance, the microcosmic and macrocosmic results to any action. The karmic return of one's action to self, and their wider impact upon the world.

Work with it to: Understand what is okay for you, and what is not, what needs boundaries and protection, and what does not. To understand the long-term impact of your actions, and the ways in which being too "open" has led to some people devaluing what you have to offer. Restrict the offering of your resources to those who treat them with respect and correct intentions. This oceanic energy is also one of bright, swift, very fast inspiration and change.

Everyday Water Magic

Every beach, every pond and every drop of water has its own energy – and perhaps its own caretaker merbeings, including the powerful sea deities. If you wish to work with one of the sea beings, remember to work with integrity. Make an offering. Give thanks. Trust. Study and learn. Communicate.

If collecting water for use in spells or workings, such as making a magical vibrational mist, or for banishing, or adding to a mermaid sea-scrub mixture, be sure to gather your water from an area that has as few pollutants as possible. Every kind of water has its own energy, these being, broadly speaking:

☆ Tidal pool water: To help in shifts and transitions.
☆ Deep ocean water: To reveal aspects of self, to bring out the secrets and to know what is mysterious more fully.
☆ Rain water into ocean: Purifying, cleansing.
☆ River running into the ocean: To understand what you must change, and know the many aspects of who you are.
☆ Lake behind ocean: Manifesting and gathering harvest and abundance.
☆ Dew on coastal trees: Rebirth, growth in a new direction, beauty and fulfilment.

Jasmine's Sea-Green Magic

American artist Jasmine Becket-Griffith is a painter of fabulous mermaids and sea creatures, available in prints and *The Oracle of Shadows & Light*. Her work combines wide-eyed whimsy with a darker aesthetic. Elements of gothic fantasy, faeries, the beauty of nature, the supernatural, historical references and many cultural influences appear in her artwork. She lives in Celebration, Florida, with her husband/assistant Matt and their cats Mama Wolf and Tigrillo. View Jasmine's online gallery at www.strangeling.com.

I love how changeable the ocean is. I have seen crystal-clear, swimming-pool-like coves turn into hurricane nightmares in the space of a day! It is so mercurial, showing such extremes. I think a lot of people forget that our earth mostly consists of the ocean, with bits of land popping up here and there. Visually it appeals to me because it's always changing – the waves are ever-moving, and the colour and mood changes so much throughout the day. Colour choice is always a challenging and fun aspect when painting the sea, since water is both transparent and reflective. It's easy to think the ocean is blue, but in reality it's a prism of colour, and it is consistently affected by the clouds above and the creatures below.

The ocean makes me very aware of nature. It also makes me feel very small, in a humbling and introspective way. On a practical level, it affects things like the weather and winds, and that keeps everybody on their toes. And on a psychological level, I like being on the edge or precipice of the "surface" – as if living on the end of the earth makes me part of both worlds.

One of my favourite things to do when I'm by the ocean is to walk along the shore and simply see what washes up. I also really enjoy walking along rocky shores where the water is collected in tide pools. I love all of the tidal critters – their lives seem so different than mine.

I spent my first twenty years in Kansas City, Missouri – pretty darned landlocked! But my family made several road trips to the ocean when I was a kid that left a tremendous impression on me – so much so that one of the first things I did as an adult was move to Florida!

Typically I'm very controlled with my painting, I paint very "tightly", but when painting something like the sea, or showing rays of light reflecting through water, or the gentle waving of kelp below the waves, I really have to get out of my usual restrictive movements and bring a more leisurely feel to my brushstrokes. I sometimes paint water with my left hand (even though I'm right-handed) because I think it's controlled a bit by a different part of my brain. I also use more actual water in my paint when painting water – I'll sometimes use just a few drops of acrylic paint suspended in several drops of water to give a very transparent appearance.

Mermaids are a wonderful subject as you can really have fun with the figure. Where does the tail start? Does she have fins? Are her hands webbed? Are those seashells like a bikini top or do they just sorta grow there? Do mermaids have bellybuttons? Do they hatch from eggs? The possibilities are endless! And thematically there are so many directions to go. The enormous natural world of the ocean environment is a treasure trove of inspiration – all the beautiful plants and animals already extant can be a part of the mermaid's world – and then the speculation and addition of fantastical mermaid culture and magic provides so many creative options!

I first remember painting some mermaids when I was five, with watercolours in kindergarten. I really started getting into it more when I was nine or ten – when Disney's *The Little Mermaid* came out! Prior to that I mostly read about mermaids in mythology books. I was often bored by "real world" stress and going to school every day. I had a lot of health problems growing up, and I think mermaids represented a sort of escapism for me. My love for mermaids continued to grow certainly from that point. And when I was a teenager one of the first presents I gave my boyfriend (now my husband) was a self-portrait of me as a mermaid!

I strongly feel that mermaids should not be limited only to the ocean – like the Sewer Mermaid in the *Oracle of Shadows & Light*. I am a

proponent of fresh water mermaids, brackish mermaids, tiny wiggly little puddle mermaids, night-time swimming pool mermaids. Just like any other species, I'm sure that mermaids would have to figure out a way to co-exist with various modern technological inventions and invasive humans.

Nearly every civilisation with a connection to the sea has some sort of mermaid or water nymph, and it is interesting to me to see the differences and similarities. Mermaids pop up everywhere.

I love visiting Mexico – there is a folklore character, La Sirena, who is depicted in a popular card game, whose imagery appears in a lot of Mexican folk art. After getting back from the Yucatan once I painted my La Sirena piece – it combined the Mexican mermaid character with a Dia de Los Muertos (Day of the Dead) theme.

In Paris I saw a recurring mermaid theme in paintings from the Louvre, and also in a lot of Rococo decoration and architecture in the city. The word Rococo is a combination of the French words rocaille, stone, and coquilles, meaning shell, and of course when I think of stones and shells I think of mermaids. Soon after I painted Mermaid in Rococo, a mermaid with an elaborate Rococo-era hairstyle and swirling golden gilding on her tail.

In Japan and China I make a point of visiting the beautiful formal gardens that have amazing koi ponds. It's so tranquil to watch the colourful koi fishes darting in and out from underneath the lotus blossoms – this has inspired several paintings featuring mermaids with koi-like tails, with attendant koi fish, surrounded by lilypads.

I've never seen a mermaid, but I'm always on the lookout! The ocean is unfathomably large, and vastly unexplored. Nearly every expedition to unchartered areas bears the discovery of new species. Heck, if we only recently discovered the giant squids, I'm sure some dainty mermaids could be hiding down there too!

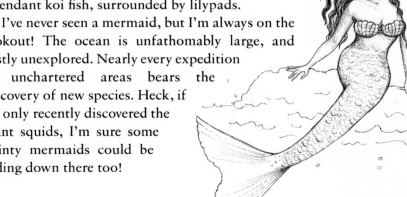

Lost Lands of the Mer

"Knowing her fate, Atlantis sent out ships to all corners of the earth.
On board were the twelve – the poet, the physician, the farmer, the
scientist, the magician and the other so-called gods of our legends.
Though gods they were, and as the elders of our time choose
to remain blind, let us rejoice and let us sing,
and dance and ring in the new. Hail Atlantis."

Donovan, Scottish singer

Lyonesse/Lethowstow

If you stand at the very edge of the earth in England, and gaze out
through the salt spray to the fabled West, you may hear the tolling
of bells beneath the waves. If you do, the Lost Land of Lyonesse is
calling to you, and her merfolk have marvellous qualities and
messages for you. Lyonesse is said to lie in the waters between
Land's End in Cornwall and the Isles of Scilly, a sprinkle of
Mediterranean-style islands that lie forty-five kilometres to the
west of the Cornish peninsula. These waters are warm, and
beautiful, and home to a drowned land.

Lyonesse's capital, the City of Lions, is said to be marked by the
Seven Stones, a series of rocks, each with a name such as the Armed
Knight, that mark the position of this vast and legendary city
beneath the waves. The City of Lions was the home of the churches,
and bells rang out each day from a hundred and forty towers. Today,
those bells still ring – but were they churches as we know them, and
are the bells perhaps the voices of the past reaching up to the world
of air so we can hear them once again?

The people of Lyonesse were said to be shown how to transform, and those who agreed to transform to mer, form a curious type of merfolk. To this day, all along this watery path lie massive underwater kelp forests, and those who see the mermaids of Lyonesse say they speak and call with an ancient tongue, and tone – one note – much like the sound of the legendary bells. They are said to have greenish skin, from living in the underwater forests and groves, and long golden hair, and they are Celtic in appearance.

These mer help us retain our ancestral connection to the Celts and the pre-Celtic indigenous peoples of Britain. They know their own stories and tales of what happened in the lands of air, and they are able to assist us with connecting to the sacred old ways of Avalon and other Celtic lands that are lost in time, yet so alive in people's hearts. These mer are often single tailed, and on many occasions have harps made from whalebone that has washed up upon the shore. They adore music, and bring lovers together across the miles. They assist with soulmates, and can draw you closer to the one you love, though you may doubt you will ever meet them.

There is a special landmark, St Michael's Mount, a tiny island off the coast of Penzance in Cornwall, which is connected to the mainland by a rocky causeway at low tide, but accessible only by boat at high tide. There is a beautiful old castle and church atop its hill, and it is a great vantage point for sea kingdom watchers.

The Lost Land of Lyonesse is located along the Michael and Mary leylines that run through the sacred sites of England, including St Michael's Mount, Glastonbury and Avebury. Also known as Dragon or Serpent lines, the energy here is emotional, intuitive, watery and receptive. One cannot walk the leys here, as you can on the land, but you can travel it by ferry from Penzance. Collecting water here can assist you in connecting strongly with the powers of the Dragon line – the land dragons at that point become sea snakes, and continue their journey around the blue green planet.

Ys

Once, a long time ago, Brittany was called Amorica – it was re-named Brittany by the Romans, long after the Celts had carved their influence into the long lines of rocks and standing stones that mark the dramatic coastline of the Lost Land of Ys.

Gradlon, legend says, was the fifth century chieftain of Amorica. He married a beautiful pagan woman, but had himself converted to Christianity under the guidance of the priest (and later saint) Guenole. Their daughter Dahut followed the Old Ways, and for her, Gradlon created a spectacular and most enchanting city, called Ys, also known as Is, Ker-Is and Ker-Ys. With trade between the lands of Persia and the Mediterranean common at this time, the city was multicultural, exotic and extremely bohemian. There was no guilt, but instead great love, and the Old Ways were practised.

There were walls built all around this fabulous city to hold back the tide, and the key to the gate that let the sea in and out was kept about the throat of Gradlon.

The legend says that Dahut was wicked and depraved – but the legends were written by the monks, and so of course women must be evil, degenerate things. She upheld the Old Ways, worshipped in the sacred sea groves, and wondered whether the sea would be best left to reclaim the land. The monks wrote that Dahut the pagan princess was the lover of the devil himself – interesting, as there is no "devil" in paganism. Perhaps she made love to the nature spirits, or took lovers as she wished, as women of the Old Ways did.

One night Dahut took the key from her father's neck as he lay sleeping, opened the sea lock and allowed the waters to overwhelm the city. Christians say that God was drowning the sinful city – so it is strange then that Dahut herself let the waters in. It seems more likely that this pagan princess was offering to the sea what was hers, and cared little for the city her father had built to glory her.

As the waters rose, Gradlon mounted his white horse to escape with his daughter, but was ordered by God to fling his sinful daughter into the waves, where she was swallowed by the sea and became a mermaid. Or perhaps she begged to be left behind, so she could become her mer self. The only two survivors were the priest who converted the king, and the king – all else were transformed into merfolk, who could shapeshift, strangely enough, into crows.

Today it is said that Dahut can still be seen sitting on the rocks of Douarnenez Bay, on the ragged western coast of Brittany, and that when the tide goes out to its furthest point, the towers of the Lost Land of Ys can still be glimpsed beneath the waves.

There is much to this legend that seems untrue. Perhaps these people were merfolk from the start, forced by the priests to choose land or water, and having to live on the land, in air, permanently – but ultimately wishing to return to the sea.

The mer of this land are all about connecting us to the Old Ways – turning away from what seems like wealth and importance and in some cases "goodness" and instead embracing the elemental side of our nature. Dahut had lovers, and was free, and it was she who reclaimed the key to the sea gates, and allowed the sea – the primordial self – to flow back over the rational, logical, Christianised land, thus returning it to the pagan past. These mer often have split tails – the two-tailed mermaids rarely seen today, which is so they can walk on land or swim in water as they need.

Cantre'r Gwaelod : The Lowland Hundreds

In Wales, there is a Lost Sea Kingdom, a home for merfolk, that is called Cantre'r Gwaelod, in English the Lowland Hundreds. Patrick, that most adversarial of priests to those of the Old Ways, and later the patron saint of Ireland, plays a part in this tale. It is said that he built a causeway extending under the sea in Cardigan Bay on the west coast of Wales, which can be seen at low tide. Named Sarn Badrig, it was to keep out the sea, and of course to keep the land and the mer people separated, and keep them from interbreeding, transforming and loving each other.

Except the sea is more powerful than even a priest's lock. King Gwyddno Garanhir allowed his son, Prince Seithenyn, to care for the keys to the sea gate. In the monks' version he became intoxicated and left it open, and high tide poured in when the tide turned. In the pagan version, he was asked by the sea people to leave the gate open so they could return to their homes and families – so he did. There are massive petrified underwater forests off Wales, said to be the groves of the sea druids, merfolk who keep the Old Ways under the water – metaphorically, in our genetic history or subconscious. If we unblock the boundaries between the logic and the lore, we too can have visions of the sea peoples, and know far more of ourselves.

The merfolk of the Lowland Hundreds are said to be very wise and very beautiful, and they share their knowledge willingly with all those who call to them. They encourage the study of herbal and plant lore, believe that the way we eat changes us, and recommend a vegetarian lifestyle.

Kumari Kandam

The brown skin merfolk of the Lost Land of Kumari Kandam are of Lemurian descent. This paradisical place was part of the vast continent of Lemuria, which ranged across the Pacific Ocean. Off the southern coast of India, below where Sri Lanka currently lies, the Dravidian peoples were of the land and the sea, and these people of Kumari Kandam were the keepers of an ancient book of wisdom, *The Sangam*, which is still revered and respected by today's Tamils. The knowledge in this sacred book was also encoded into Lemurian crystals, and both were housed in temples atop mountains overlooking the sea, and their wisdom was transmitted to everyone without any assistance.

Later however, in Atlantean times, towers were put in, and technologies were developed to amplify the knowledge, and control who was a recipient of the knowledge, and who was not. There were, over time, many more people who did not receive this wisdom. Finally only an elite few were able to receive the knowledge, in concentrated, almost toxic bursts, such was their hunger for power and their ambition to rule.

In Lemurian times, all knowledge was open, none was hidden. But when Atlantis took over this part of the Lemurian lands (Lemurians did not have empires), the knowledge was considered too dangerous, too precious, too empowering to be shared equally, so only the priests and the wise ones were allowed to have access to the books or the crystals and sacred stones that held the knowledge.

Sometime between twelve thousand and fifteen thousand years ago, when Atlantis went under, the kadaktol – the eating of the land – took place. Massive tsunami waves tore inland from the coast, which some say were let loose by the misuse of Atlantean technologies of weather and wind, and the unbalanced bursts of sangam, knowledge, from the sacred crystals and books.

After the tragic Boxing Day tsunami of 2004, which tore the land apart with the sea's power, ancient temples were suddenly visible again. The remains of the City of the Seven Pagodas, famous for its ancient rock hewn temples, monolithic monuments and stone sculptures, were clearly seen at Mahabalipuram, fifty kilometres south of Chennai in the southern Indian state of Tamil Nadu, which have been dated to the Tamil Sangam period of more than two thousand years ago. Their energy was revealed and reignited, some say, so that the energy of Lemuria could begin to diffuse the energy of current-day Atlantean energies that are threatening to repeat the cycle once again.

The folk of these lands shifted into and out of form, and it is said that the Sangam now lies at the bottom of the sea, but that the whales and the shapeshifting gods can read these texts, and the whales sing of them in their songs as they bring the sacred ancient energies around the world.

The merfolk of these lands have the knowledge of the Sangam – natural law, literature and sacred truth in story and song. They share this knowledge with the whales, and they in turn share this knowledge with the other creatures of the sea. We, when we connect with the energy of whale and sea, connect with this ancient Lemurian knowledge too.

Sundaland

Beneath the waves, in the ocean between Malaysia and the amazing country of Borneo, lies a Lost Land called Sundaland. Thought by some scholars to be a remnant of Atlantis, it actually seems more likely that it is a part of the original Lemuria, and was converted to Atlantean ways by colonists from that empire around twenty-five thousand years ago.

Sundalanders were inventors – sea people who learned the arts of weaving and pottery making, milling, harvesting and growing. They were innovators and agricultural masterminds, and connecting with the deep mer energy of this region gives us a way of connecting deeply to our own inventive spirits.

Sundalanders are also survivors. One of the last remaining slivers of Lemuria was Krakatoa, a volcanic island in the Sunda Strait between Java and Sumatra in Indonesia, which was destroyed by a volcanic eruption in 1883, the most violent volcanic event in history. Sundalanders knew the volatility of their part of what is called the Pacific Ring of Fire, and were able to read the weather and signs of the animals in order to leave before the impact. Westerners who had settled on Krakatoa were not so fortunate, and the eruption killed more than forty thousand people.

Sundaland is said to have been destroyed by a super-volcano thirty thousands years ago. The ancient people of this land were amazing oceanic experts, able to read and ride tides, and some say also to shift into and out of the form of a merperson. They left Lemurian outposts off Madagascar in Africa, and arrived here when parts of the Lemurian continent near Africa began to go down. They drummed, danced and worked with fire in ways that have wonderful connections to African peoples.

They developed giant waterways so they could move around by sea within the land – along the lines of Plato's canals of Atlantis. These were also developed so the merpeople could enter into the land, and so the air people and water people would not be so divided. The seabeds here are also rich in base metals, a quality Plato also described Atlantis as having. Sundaland has been described again and again in ways very much akin to the way Plato described Atlantis. Perhaps they were sister colonies, after the Lemurians were "overtaken".

The merfolk of this region help you alchemise the base metals into precious golds in your life, to know when to grow, when to harvest, and to come up with brilliant solutions to technical challenges. They are extraordinarily intelligent.

Lemuria

Lemuria was a vast continent that existed in the southern hemisphere, in what is now the Pacific Ocean. The Pacific Island chains, including Hawaii, New Zealand and much of Micronesia, are the remnants of this enormous and enormously varied land.

Lemurians shapeshifted into their environment – they were less "dense" than we are in our physical bodies, and although they were more fluid in their physical make-up, they were in love with the physical experience – unlike many people today, who find physicality unspiritual and unappealing! Lemurians had no concept that the physical was in any way "less".

Earth was spirit, spirit was earth, and when we moved into an element, such as the ocean, we merged with it, and transformed. We could shift and change as the situation required, and had a fully alive chakra system than was visible to all – thus all knew of what we were saying, doing and being at any time. Quite often language was unnecessary because of this extreme and very safe empathy.

Lemurian merpeople were shapeshifters, who spent a huge amount of time within the water, feeding from sea kelps that they lived with in great gratitude and empathy. They could sleep within the sea, and often birthed at sea too.

Lemurian cultures varied from place to place. Their appearance, aptitudes and interests changed, but there were commonalities:

☆ Had a living chakra system, including a "living" third eye, with an "eye" like a precious stone or crystal.

☆ Possessed the ability to shapeshift.

☆ They were all water oriented, whereas other civilisations were mountain or sky oriented.

☆ They gave birth at sea.

☆ Had an intimate connection with all that is – the trees, birds, plants. There was not as much separation as there is now.

☆ They were long lived.

☆ Sexual differentiation at what we would think of as adolescence.

☆ They used the minerals of the sea as nutritional supplements.

☆ Possessed the ability to shift gender.

☆ They had patterns on their bodies that shone with light, as a kind of signalling system.

☆ They were highly empathic and telepathic in the early stages, and it was extremely safe to be so in early Lemuria.

☆ Lemurians in the latter stages were very susceptible to what we might describe today as psychic attack.

☆ Remnants of Lemuria exist today in some Aboriginal communities in Australia, those of the saltwater peoples in particular, the Hawaiian peoples and the Polynesian peoples – all those who have legends of whales and dolphins as ancestors.

Many Lemurians shifted permanently into dolphins, whales or merfolk when Lemuria was drowned. Many escaped, as in the tale of Prince Idon, who made it to the colonies of Atlantis with one of many groups of survivors. Many Lemurian survivors have red hair.

Atlantis

We know most of what we think we know about Atlantis through one source, the Classical Greek philosopher Plato. And that source is *not* contemporary. In the fourth century BCE Plato met and worked for a time with an Egyptian priest who shared with him a story his teacher had taught to him – that Egypt was a survivor colony of Ancient Atlantis, a vast empire that was drowned by tsunamis and tidal surges because of their misuse of technology and hubris fifteen thousand years earlier.

Plato's descriptions centre around the town planning of the city of Poseidonisis, the various gods worshipped there, some of whom went on to be worshipped in Egypt and Greece, and the cultural aspects of this perfect place, including their huge armies and navies and a naive, placid populace. It wasn't until much later, through nineteenth century theosophist Madame Blavatsky and twentieth century American medium Edgar Cayce and British occultist Dion Fortune, that further information began to accumulate about the technologies of Atlantis, their misuse and the reasons for its downfall.

Early Atlantis was a peaceful and beautiful place, with solar temples and wonderful energy. Then the Lemurians arrived – some feel this happened after their civilisation was purposefully destroyed by an aggressive and targeted Atlantean campaign to overwhelm these outposts in order to create a homogenous global empire rather than a northern empire. Taking their campaign global was something many Atlanteans were unaware off – they lived such peaceful, idyllic lives, where there seemed to be perfect order and rites and organisation, that it was rarely questioned that perhaps there was a kind of tyranny and monotony to the perfection.

Atlantis received the Lemurian survivors with great generosity. Many were taken into villages along the shoreline, where Atlanteans wondered at the abilities of the Lemurians to shapeshift into other forms according to the environment, with their shining foreheads, their tattoo-like light communication system of symbols on their bodies, and their absolute comfort in physicality.

Atlanteans were very tall, and wore robes that were simple in design and colour coded for their status or place in the culture. They were sexually differentiated at birth, and sexuality was highly ritualised. In some ways the Lemurians seemed to them inspiring and free, in other ways they seemed anarchic and primitive.

For a while though, Atlantis and Lemuria blended – a time I have heard called Atlurian by my guides. Filled with such an astonishing and delightful diversity of people, languages, beings and capabilities, the cities began to evolve. Canals were built deep into the centre of the capital of Poseidonisis so that the merfolk could travel within it, and there was a fascination with all things Lemurian. They became objects of interest, and it became a custom to adopt a Lemurian to learn from. Atlanteans started decorating their third eye region, and wishing that they too could shift their legs to tails simply by entering the deep seas.

But just as Atlanteans were peaceably fascinated with Lemurians, many of the empire's leaders wanted to learn the source of their secrets and mysteries. The priests in their pyramids asked many questions. How was it that they knew what their brothers and sisters were thinking across vast distances? How was it, they wondered, that their bodies lit up with symbols of light, as if their internal organs were lanterns and there were patterns hidden in their skin? How was it they could change and evolve to match their environment with such speed and ease? Why were they so quiet – and why did they never tell the nice untruths that society demanded of the Atlanteans? And why were they all equal? Why did they consider tree and star and animal all to be kin?

Beneath the city, for many years, a series of experiments had been conducted on people, and on creatures, resulting in "monsters". Madame Blavatsky in her writings on Atlantis refers to these beings as "things". Sadly, the Lemurians too were considered a kind of short cut to discovering new ways to create effective slaves, and so there began a series of covert experiments, where third eye stones were removed, and the Lemurians were dissected to search for the origins of their shapeshifting abilities.

Over time, this ability to shapeshift became unfashionable. While in the beginning there had been fascination, the Lemurians soon began to be treated with contempt, and rules were brought in by the pure Atlanteans, that the "impure" Lemurians were to join the slave classes. Many were encouraged to have operations willingly – to create legs for merpeople, to cut part of the spinal column to ensure they stayed in one shape, to have gender distinguished at birth, to avoid uneasiness for the Atlanteans.

The empire's elite effectively began a series of genetic experiments that would result in the DNA of Lemurians and Atlanteans being switched off, limited and compromised, to stop the questioning and the diversity. All the populace was encouraged to have this innoculation, and all were urged to have this operation for their own health and wellbeing – it was a small, very swift injection that effectively switched off the ability of DNA to evolve or switch on quickly and adapt. Some escaped though, refusing the operation, or took to the seas permanently.

Some people today believe that mermaids were an Atlantean experiment gone wrong – a kind of Frankenstein scientific experiment to merge fish and human. But the experiments were on creatures that could shift, and the development of the poor creatures who came to be known as things were a dark and shameful part of Atlantean history.

When Atlantis eventually sank, or, more accurately, was eaten by the cleansing seas, many merpeople chose to go into dolphin, whale or turtle form permanently to remain safe. Some changed to human, and suffered amnesia. Some fled to other areas, to the Lemurian remnants of Micronesia and Hawaii, or Polynesia and parts of what is now called Australia.

They arrived on the back of whales, and with dolphins, and some still retained their abilities to sexualise later in life, to be both man and woman, to communicate with telepathy, and to never lie.

They are many of the most sacred people on the planet today, the indigenous people who have had less interference, and so remain more at peace with their true natures, and with the earth and her magnificent womb, the ocean.

The mer are of Atlantis, and of Lemuria. Many have red hair, and many of the sea gods hail from that time. They can teach us a great deal about the use, and misuse, of power – and about how to make it through the next great earth shift, with what is best about our humanity intact.

Cassandra's Little Mermaid Magic

Cassandra Eason is a cyber witch, druidess, reiki master and Celtic shaman who travels the world teaching and researching. She's the author of more than ninety magical books, including *The New Crystal Bible* and *Becoming Clairvoyant*, and has created a series of *Chronicles of Magick* CDs. She teaches online courses on angels, psychic development, mediumship and ritual for the northern and southern hemispheres. Visit her at www.CassandraEason.com.

Mermaids represent a world between worlds, and from when I was a young child I felt their sorrow, that they were neither completely human nor fully creatures of the sea. I had an illustrated book of Hans Christian Andersen's *The Little Mermaid*, about the young mermaid who fell in love with a prince and sacrificed her lovely voice to a sea witch in return for a pair of legs and the chance to win his heart. When the prince was to marry a human princess instead, the mermaid couldn't return to the sea unless she killed him before the wedding. She refused, and was rewarded for this with the chance of earning a soul by good deeds – but she didn't get the mortal happiness and love she craved.

I identified with the Little Mermaid through to my teenage years because I was a very clever child from a poor home who won a scholarship to a very exclusive school as an experiment. Here I was bullied and made unwelcome even by the teachers, and like the Little Mermaid, I no longer fitted into my old world nor the new.

My favourite mermaid legend I discovered as an adult in Brittany, France, where I spent many months with my children just after I'd trained as a druidess. In Brittany there is a tradition of the Morganas, powerful sea faeries who cause storms and drag sailors to their deaths beneath the waves – in an unsuccessful attempt, it is said, to satisfy their own passions, because the sailors they captured could not breathe beneath the water.

The Morgana legends first appeared at the time Brittany was Christianised, in the fifth century, when the druidesses, pagan priestesses and noblewomen who would not convert to the new religion were drowned for their disobedience. The first Morgan was Dahut, daughter of Gradlon, the King of Cornouaille who created Ys, a beautiful city in Finisterre on the northwest coast of Brittany. The city was built below sea level, with walls to keep back the water. A dyke was opened to allow the fishing boats to leave and enter.

Dahut probably continued to worship the pagan deities as a druidess herself, and so was in constant conflict with Corentin, the bishop of Quimper. According to the local stories still told in this area, where I carried out a great deal of research into faery legends, Dahut was accused of bringing disrepute to the city with her unbridled passions and, it is claimed, caused the destruction of the city by handing the keys to the dyke to her lover the devil. He flooded the town, and the waves drowned all the citizens except for Gradlon, Corentin and Dahut, who clung to the back of her father's horse. But the bishop told Gradlon to cast his wicked daughter into the sea or he too would be drowned, so Gradlon pushed his daughter into the water, leaving her to perish. Dahut did not die, it is said, but was transformed into the vengeful Marie Morgana. The other Morganas were other drowned pagan priestesses.

Other versions of the tale assign the role of the condemning cleric to Saint Guenole, who was the first missionary to the area. This is obviously a Christianised version of an account of an actual town with poor sea defences that was submerged. The coast is rocky and treacherous, and the area is often shrouded in mist. Locals say they can hear the bells of the city beneath the waves, and fishermen out early still claim to see the Morganas sitting on the rocks combing their hair and waiting to lure boats onto the rocks and claim their lovers.

The Morganas are probably named after Morgan la Fey, the sorceress half-sister of King Arthur, who was associated with Brittany as one of the mythical Ladies of the Lake, and also falsely accused of treachery as she followed the old religion.

To me mermaids, like mermen, are pure elementals, representing the power of

the sea in all her moods, playful and coquettish, admiring themselves and combing their hair in their pearl mirrors, sometimes sullen as the grey water, refusing to interact with humans, a reminder that they are of themselves, a force of nature.

We create stories about them to reassure ourselves that they are somehow like us, and to explain a power of the untamed waters, beautiful and dreadful, healing but also sometimes indifferent to the plight of sailors. For mother sea drowns not out of anger but because she can at her fiercest be too overwhelming for people in even the strongest ships.

I work with mermaid energies by making offerings, different according to the waters: in the Indian or Pacific Oceans small pearls, in the Atlantic or Baltic, offerings of bone or shell. I call them on the outgoing tide to carry away sickness, sorrow and what is no longer needed, and cast my tribute on the seventh incoming wave as I wade out. I wait to see what offerings the sea women return for mine, a beautiful shell, a piece of driftwood. Holding it, I close my eyes and hear the mer messages in the resounding foam.

I write on the shore, below the tideline, and dance a circle of sand, allowing the mermaids to take the wish I have written with driftwood over and over again in the centre, as the tide washes over my footstep circle. And in moonlight I dance a spiral labyrinth in the waters and cast six black stones to take away injustice and six white ones straight after, calling on the mermaids to send resolution without harm.

Always I use their power in a way I can understand within my reality, for mermaids may in fact be beyond definition, outside control of human attempts to give stable form. The price mermaids pay for power, magic and the freedom of the ocean is to not belong when darkness comes and humans close the curtains. I understand that, for I also am in my soul outside the magic circle of life looking in. I am the mermaid.

What's Your Mermaid Archetype?

Mermaids have embodied many different things through the ages, from the powerful, nurturing and sensual mother goddesses to the self-sacrificing Little Mermaid, who gave up her tail and her voice for the love of a man. In earlier times, mermaids were credited with guiding humans lost at sea and sharing their wisdom with them, but later they were transformed into a more sinister form of womanhood, cruel temptresses who manipulated men into falling under their spell. They have changed in tone as society has, from the portent of stormy seas coastal villagers thought they were, to the Christian influence of the Middle Ages that turned them into soulless seducers and bad influences who needed to be punished. Other legends tell of women bound to their husbands and trapped into marriage against their will, reflecting a time of arranged matches and the stereotype of the "good wife", or those who must keep their deepest self a secret from their beloved. So what does our longing to be a mermaiden say about us, and can we work with their energies to empower ourselves and learn to love more deeply?

Atargatis : The First Mermaid

"The most common way people give up their power
is by thinking they don't have any."
Alice Walker, American writer

The first mermaid traces her roots back thousands of years to Ancient Sumeria and the lands now known as the Middle East. There are several versions of her story however, as evidence of her presence survives only in rare fragments, broken statues and second-hand accounts written millennia later by historians trying to understand the past, and a culture and people so foreign to them.

In some, Atargatis was a young priestess in the Mediterranean seaport of Ascalon, who had dedicated her life, and virginity, to the great mother goddess Astarte. One day as she was washing the temple robes down on the shoreline, a sailor returning from months at sea found her and forced himself upon her. Devastated at the sacrilege, she killed him with her bow and arrow. Later she discovered she was pregnant, and when her time came she climbed the nearby cliffs, gave birth to a daughter she wrapped carefully and placed securely, then flung herself into the ocean below. As she sank beneath the waves, the goddess she had served cleansed her of grief and shame and transformed her into a half-woman, half-fish sea goddess.

Others claim that Atargatis herself was the great mother goddess of these ancient lands, whose symbol was a fish as it represented her fertility and life-giving powers, thus explaining the fish tail on one of her statues. Her worship later spread to other Mediterranean countries, including Greece, where she was known as Derceto and regarded as a form of Aphrodite, their goddess of love who was said to have been born from the foam of the ocean waves.

In the first century BCE, Greek historian Diodorus, citing earlier sources, wrote that the goddess Atargatis had become smitten with a mortal youth and fallen pregnant to him. So mortified by this was she, so he claimed, that once she gave birth to her daughter she flung herself into a lake, where her body was transformed into that of a fish, while her head and torso remained female.

Two centuries later, Assyrian writer Lucian of Samosata visited the holy city of Ascalon and wrote about its goddess, who was associated with rivers and springs as well as with animals. He called her Hera, although it is thought he was referring to Atargatis. Back then gods and goddesses were often merged with other deities and adopted by new peoples when a country was invaded or tribes and communities travelled to distant lands. He wrote of a statue of her flanked by doves, and another with fish eyes and a fish headdress.

Today Atargatis is described as the first mermaid, but there are other deities who have also embodied this mermaid energy over time, and been thought to manifest in mermaid form.

Yemanja, the mother goddess of many Afro-American religions, is considered the queen of the ocean and the mother of all life. Her name is a contraction of the African words "yeye emo eja", which translate as "Mother whose children are like fish". In Brasilian Candomble she is depicted as a mermaid, and offerings to her include mirrors, combs, jewellery, flowers and shells. She is the patron deity of fishermen and shipwreck survivors, the spirit of moonlight and the principle of all creation. In Cuban Santeria and Haitian Voudou she is the mother of all living things, the owner of all the waters, the essence of motherhood and the protector of children.

In Africa and the Caribbean islands, Yemanja merges with Mami Wata, a mermaid goddess with healing powers. She is depicted as a fish or a serpent from the waist down, or as an inhumanly beautiful human woman, and she carries combs, mirrors and watches, which have become popular offerings to her. There are legends of her taking her followers to her underwater realm while they are swimming or boating, from where they return with new spiritual wisdom.

In Greek legend and modern paganism, Aphrodite was the goddess of the ocean and of love, and was born from the sea foam. Less romantically it is said that this foam was the result of the titan Cronus severing his father the sky god Uranus's genitals and throwing them in the sea. According to seventh century BCE Greek poet Hesiod, in his genealogical work *Theogony*, the genitals "were carried over the sea a long time, and white foam arose from the immortal flesh; with it a girl grew" – the girl who became Aphrodite.

Her Roman equivalent is Venus, who had similar oceanic attributes and was portrayed standing in a giant scallop shell in the fifteenth century painting The Birth of Venus by Sandro Botticelli. She was also known as Venus Anadyomene – Venus Rising From the Sea – and echoed the Greek legend that she was born a woman, not a baby who had to grow to adulthood, from out of the ocean.

Perhaps because so much of Greece is surrounded by sea, they had many deities of the waters, including the goddesses Amphitrite, Leucothea and Alcyone and the gods Poseidon, Oceanus and Nereus, along with the fifty sea nymphs known as nereids, who helped sailors survive storms, and the many known as oceanides, who were each the patron spirit of a spring, river, sea, lake or pond.

In Hawaii, Namakaokahai was the goddess of the sea, associated with the element of water. She fought with her younger sister Pele, who had seduced her husband (how mermaidenly of her!), and their battle is still played out today in the fiery explosion that occurs when the lava of Pele's volcano rushes down into Namakaokahai's ocean, a collision between the two primal forces of fire and water.

In Egypt, Hathor was a protector goddess who ruled love, joy and music and was associated with the Nile and thus fertility, and had a mother aspect like other water goddesses. In South America, the Inkan ocean goddess was Mama Cocha, the sea mother, who ruled over fishing and provided food and nourishment for her people. Ixchel was the Mayan goddess of the waters, while the Aztecs had many, including Chalchiuhtlicue the goddess of running water and Atlacamani the goddess of oceanic storms.

Connecting with her archetype: Throughout most world cultures, the mother goddess who brings forth all life is linked to the sea, just as we come forth from the sea of our mother's womb. The sea, and women, bring forth life, and fish represent fertility – thus the mermaid who combines both worlds and qualities became representative of the nurturing mother archetype and a symbol of the divine feminine, which you can tap in to when you need to nurture or be nurtured.

Mermaids and goddesses are objects of desire and creators of life, filled with potential, possibility and passion, and sensuality as well as a mothering instinct. This energy can be invoked to help you see yourself more clearly, to meet the goddess within you, and to connect with your secret self so you can bring out all your qualities of nurturing and love, and your power to breathe new life into the world – whether this be literal, or the new life of a relationship, magical project or business plan. The mermaids who embody the energy of the goddess remind you to see the beauty and strength you have within you, your own goddess glow that shines from within if only you will acknowledge it, believe in it and celebrate it.

Melusine : The Secretive Mermaid

"You never lose by loving. You always lose by holding back."
Barbara DeAngelis, American relationships expert

Melusine, also known as Melusina, is a mermaid of European folklore. Sometimes she is half-woman, half-snake, a "double-tailed serpent, odious and winged, horrifying and terrible," in other stories she is a tragic mermaid. King Richard, known as Richard the Lionheart, claimed he was descended from the magical

Melusine. German writer and philosopher Johann Wolfgang von Goethe drew on her story in *Die Neue Melusine*, and composer Felix Mendelssohn wrote *The Fair Melusina*. A melusine is part of the Booker-winning novel *Possession*, by English author AS Byatt, the mermaids from London in the magical story *The Mourning Emporium* by Michelle Lovric are staunch two-tailed melusines, and American singer Tori Amos wrote about these mystical beings in *Dolphin Song* (and also has songs called *Merman* and *Siren*).

The legend of the melusine was popular in the Middle Ages. In France it was said that a recently widowed king fell in love with a faery woman, Pressina, who agreed to marry him on the proviso that he not interrupt her in her private chambers. When she gave birth to three daughters however, he was so overcome with excitement that he burst in, unthinking, on his family. Pressina left, taking their daughters – Palatina, Meliora and Melusina – with her. When the girls grew up and discovered they were princesses who could have been living in a castle rather than the wilderness, Melusina decided to punish her father for all she had lost. When her mother discovered the plot she cursed her daughter, declaring that once a week Melusina would transform into a mermaid, and that if she wanted to marry she must extract a promise of privacy every Saturday in order to bathe her tail. She did fall in love, and marry and have children, and for years her husband allowed her a day away every week without question. But finally, poisoned by mistrust thanks to the suspicion of others, he followed her and saw her tail. He loved her anyway – but she left in that instant, angry that he'd broken his word.

A variation of this tale is set in Britain, and is about a Scottish king who meets the beautiful fae woman Pressyne in a magical forest. They married on the condition that he never enter her private chamber while she was giving birth or bathing their children, and he agreed. She had triplets – Palatyne, Melior and Melusine – but when her husband rushed in to see them, she whisked them off to the Isle of Avalon, never to return. When these sisters grew up, rich in the magic of Avalon, they captured their father and locked him deep within a mountain as punishment. When Pressyne found out, she cursed her daughters to become half-serpents every Saturday.

Melusine went to France, where she met Raymond of Poitou. They fell in love, married and had children. He broke his word and discovered her secret, which didn't bother him at all, and she forgave him for prying. They continued living happily until the day he called her a serpent during an argument in front of the court – she changed into a dragon and flew away. In another retelling her husband knew her secret but never mentioned it, until one child after another was born deformed. When one of their sons attacked a monastery and killed all the monks, he screamed at his wife that it was the fault of her monstrous self, and she, devastated that he knew her secret, left forever. Sir Walter Scott told a similar melusine tale in his nineteenth century book *Minstrelsy of the Scottish Border*.

In Luxembourg, Melusina was said to be the wife of a count, who she wed on the condition that she have one day and one night of privacy a month. They were happily married for years, until his curiosity got the better of him and he followed her to her chambers beneath the castle, spied through the keyhole, and saw her fish tail in the bath. When she realised he had betrayed his promise, she leaped out the window into the Alzette River, where she lived as a mermaid for the rest of her days (or, in other variations, sank into the ground, surfacing every seven years with a small key, in the hope that someone would release her from the curse).

In German legend, Melusina appears as a beautiful maiden living alone in a forest castle, who dazzled a lost knight with her hospitality, beauty and conversation. He proposed to her, and she agreed, if he would allow her to spend Fridays alone, without interruption. They lived joyously together for a long time, having many beautiful children, and trusting and loving each other completely. But a visitor to the castle introduced doubt into the knight's mind by questioning his wife's fidelity. So he searched for her, and finally found her swimming in a pool beneath the castle. As soon as their eyes met, she disappeared, never to return again.

The melusine legend can be read in two ways. One, that the husband didn't trust his wife enough and deserved to lose her – and much is made of her righteous indignation that he "spied" on her to discover her secret. But there is another perspective – that she did not trust him enough to reveal her true self to him, and the end of the marriage, which hurt him as much as it hurt her, was due to her stubbornness in keeping her secret, and that it was she who did not love him enough to share her whole self.

For the melusine represents secrecy, privacy, and being unwilling to share your deepest, darkest secret. Too afraid to show your inner self to your loved one, scared perhaps that they will reject you. The moral of the story is, in part, that love and happiness can only be achieved when each person has a little time to themselves, in order to maintain their identity, and that you must be allowed – and allow in turn – freedom and a little solitude. Yet equally it is that you must have the courage to be yourself with your partner. Mistrust and possessiveness are fatal to a loving relationship, but creating jealousy through your actions is just as harmful – can anyone blame the husband for wondering what his wife got up to every single Saturday?

Connecting with her archetype: For many women (and men), it can feel that there is no time for yourself, and no identity that is yours alone. Everyone needs time away from the partnership, to nurture their talents and continue to develop as an individual – and give their loved ones time for themselves without feeling threatened by it, or suspecting that they just want to get away from you. You also need to trust your beloved, and be open to sharing every part of your self, especially if it impacts on the relationship. Melusina wouldn't share her true self with her husband who loved her dearly. He didn't respect her privacy, granted – but she didn't trust him with her very self.

This archetype is a little like a tarot card that can be read with a reversed meaning if displayed upside down, because on the one hand you deserve to have your privacy respected, but just as valid is the lesson about trusting that your partner will love you no matter what, because in most of the retellings, the husband is not alarmed by Melusine's tail and loves her anyway, despite her supposed flaw. Sometimes we are so good at hating an aspect of ourselves that we obsess over it until it becomes huge and unforgivable in our mind, and we imagine it will be a dealbreaker in a relationship.

But even a secret as big as a tail becomes smaller in the scheme of your whole personality and past, and will more often than not be accepted and even embraced, if you can bring yourself to share it, and trust your beloved enough to tell them. Happy union is achieved when there is respect and trust – yet Melusine does not trust her husband with her secret, and does not trust that he loves her for her true self and not just the person she presents herself as. You need to be with someone who loves you for who you are – if they don't accept you, tail and all, they don't deserve to be with you, and you should wait for someone better. But if you don't even give them the chance to love all of you, and keep a huge part of your life a secret, then perhaps *they* deserve someone better...

Sirens: The Mermaids of Seduction and Temptation

"A mermaid found a swimming lad, picked him for her own.
Pressed her body to his body, laughed; and plunging down,
Forgot in cruel happiness, that even lovers drown."
William Butler Yeats, A Young Man and Old

Another mermaid archetype is the siren, the beautiful woman who sits on a rock at sea or along a river and entrances sailors, seducing them, drawing them and their boats to them with a promise of love. These are the mermaids celebrated in the poetry of the Romantic era, and they are echoed in different legends from around the world.

Very well known are the loreleis, European water elementals who have their origins in the German sprites who lived in the Rhine River, and sat on cliffs singing haunting melodies that drove sailors to distraction – and straight onto the rocks to their death. Also known as sirens, and the basis for many mermaid tales, these beautiful nymphs are considered protectors as well as harbingers of death, and it's believed by some that if approached in a respectful manner, they might help humans rather than harming them.

In the Celtic-influenced region of Brittany in western France are the korrigans, a group of beautiful white-clad faery women who are elementals of both water and earth. They live in sacred springs, forest rivers and water fountains, and are associated with the druidesses of the area. According to some they have a reputation for trickery, leading travellers astray when the mood takes them. Others believe they are the spirits of former druidesses, cursed by the early Church and condemned to haunt the waters forever.

Fossegrims are the Scandinavian water faeries that live in lakes and streams, waterfalls and fjords, who are made up partly of water. They can shapeshift into handsome young men who lure women with their beauty and sweet songs, then drown them, much like the female sea sirens, while others scream a warning at dangerous stretches of water to prevent accidents. Tales abound of fossegrims who married mortal women, but they waste away if they have to move too far from their watery home, and most unions end in separation when the merbeing goes back to his water source.

Similar stories abound in Russia of the rusalkas, beautiful female nature spirits associated with both water and earth, who take their power from water. They love to dance in the moonlight, and often entice young men or children to join their revelry. They're attributed with healing powers, and they bless the land with fertility and protection, and aid nearby human communities. In return people leave ribbons tied in birch trees and small offerings. Rusalkas are said to be able to shapeshift from their invisible form into young, innocent women or older warrior queens, but if they move away from their watery home their power diminishes. They are thought to be the spirit of women who drowned or died badly – those who were burned at the stake or murdered by lovers, or who pined away from unrequited love or drowned themselves in despair.

In Slavic legend the rusalkas are the spirits of young women who drowned, fated to remain near the waterway where they died and haunt it until their death is avenged. They wear white, and are wild, free and independent, with their long hair down and out, untamed and unbound to signify their new freedom and their mermaidenly qualities. They're said to transform into women to come ashore, dancing all night and seducing men, then slipping back into the water with a lover and drowning him in their watery realm.

Originally sirens weren't mermaids at all, but half-bird women – sometimes depicted as a bird with a woman's face, or a woman with a bird's head, or the body of a woman with the feet and wings of a bird. (Clearly mermaids made more sense!) In Greek mythology the sirens were half-bird, half-woman, and it was only much later that they were transformed into mermaids. They were most commonly portrayed as dangerous bird-women, who seduced sailors with their enchanting music and voices and lured them to their rocky island so their ships would wreck and all onboard would drown. In *The Odyssey*, Homer's epic eighth century BCE work, he described two sirens, and said that the hero, Odysseus (known as Ulysses in Roman versions of the myth), wanted so badly to hear their song that he ordered his sailors to tie him to the mast of the ship, and not release him no matter how hard he begged them, and to stuff their own ears with beeswax to avoid being tempted by the siren song. According to Roman poet Ovid, the sirens had been companions to the young goddess Persephone, who were then given wings to search for her when she was abducted.

Later they transformed into half-fish women (possibly because the Greek word for wing and fin is the same, pteron), yet they kept their dangerous quality, and were believed to lure men to their death with their beauty and their song. In the late 1400s, Italian artist, inventor and scientist Leonardo da Vinci wrote of them: "The siren sings so sweetly that she lulls the mariners to sleep; then she climbs upon the ships and kills the sleeping mariners." In the 1800s, English writer Walter Perry described them thus: "Their song, though irresistibly sweet, was no less sad than sweet, and lapped both body and soul in a fatal lethargy, the forerunner of death and corruption."

At the start of the 1900s, English classical scholar and expert on Greek mythology Jane Harrison wrote: "Sirens are mantic creatures like the Sphinx with whom they have much in common, knowing both the past and the future. Their song takes effect at midday, in a windless calm. The end of that song is death." In modern times, there is a *Simpsons* episode where Selma and Patty play the sirens who lure Homer as Odysseus and his crew to the Island of Sirens with a haunting melody and the promise of hot sex – although once the sailors see them they quickly head off in another direction.

Connecting with her archetype: Sirens symbolise temptation and sensual delights, and in their positive aspect this energy can bring fun, joy and love to your life. But there can also be a lack of caring, and even a streak of cruelty, within this vibration, and channelling the baser aspects of the siren can rebound badly. Using your sexuality to control or manipulate anyone is unhealthy for them as well as for you, and can lead to emptiness and a spiral of self-loathing. The siren reminds you to be confident within yourself and proud of your body, but to know always that it, and you, are sacred. That love and relationships are wonderful, but that you should not sell yourself short or do anything you feel uncomfortable with, or think you have to parade around half naked or have sex you don't want to have just to be liked.

The right partner will love you for who you are, and will not need to be titillated into being interested. But acting in this way can backfire, and the wrong person may respond to your signals, someone who will not respect you or treat you with the honour that is your birthright. Nor should you tease or torment people by leading them on when you have no intention of following through, or be surprised if people think badly of you if you act in a way that is contrary to the truth of who you are. (This is not to say that sexuality is bad – *au contraire, mon cheri* – but it should be on your terms, and for your reasons, and not to make someone like you or to try to tempt them away from someone else.)

If you interact with people with integrity, honesty and respect, those qualities will be returned to you, but you must develop and exude self-love and self-respect if you want to channel the positive energies of the siren and not the less savoury aspects. The term "siren song" refers to a temptation that is hard to resist but which, if heeded, will cause pain, regret or sadness, and the sacrifice of all you hold dear – in Odysseus's case, his wife, for others it may be self-respect or personal safety – usually for an offer that sounded better than it really is. You connect with the power of the siren when you emulate her self-confidence, self-love and self-respect, not the lower energies of temptress and harlot cast on her by the Church. So let your inner light shine, feel the sensuality and love you embody, and hold out for the one who appreciates you just the way you are, and sees the sacred within you.

The Little Mermaid: The One Who Sacrifices Herself

"Don't compromise yourself. You are all you've got."
Janis Joplin, American singer and songwriter

In many ways the siren and the Little Mermaid are complete opposites, one giving up everything for a man, the other taking everything from him. Yet the energy of both, when it is out of balance, can lead to a lack of self-esteem and self-love, and a need for nurturing and self-discovery, and a reconnection with the power and beauty of your inner mermaiden.

The Little Mermaid has a "grass is always greener" mentality, in love with humans and wishing desperately to swap her tail for legs and what she believes is a better life. She doesn't appreciate the love her family has for her, or see the beauty of what she already has. How many of us long, even for a moment, to be a mermaid princess, at one with the ocean and its creatures, living a life of total freedom and beauty beneath the waves? Yet she sacrifices her family, her friends, her tail (the symbol of freedom) and her voice (the symbol of everything she is and stands for), for the chance to be with a man she barely knows, suffering unimaginable pain in the process, and the possibility that she will be left with nothing, disappearing forever if she doesn't win his heart – a metaphor for our invisibility perhaps, if we give up ourselves for a partner.

Today, in a world where women have more equality than ever before, and are stronger and more sure of their rights, it would seem that this sweet and self-sacrificing mermaid would have no meaning. Yet this archetype remains important, for there are still many people who, either consciously or not, embody this energy, who give up their job, their friends, their religion, their family or their voice, in order to please a partner. This is not a criticism – I'm sure we've all done it at some point, to some degree – but an acknowledgement and a reminder, so hopefully we can learn from it and never do it again.

Connecting with her archetype: Compromising in a relationship is healthy and necessary. Stubbornly refusing to make any concessions, being unwilling to give way or concede any point of view, spells doom, for part of being in love is wanting to make your partner happy, and working together to find the best way to build a shared life where both of you are equally fulfilled. It's about being stronger together than individually, and supporting each other and being supported in turn. For those who refuse to even consider any other ways or opinions, who won't budge an inch because they perceive it as a sign of weakness, the Little Mermaid can be a gentle nudge to realise that sometimes compromise is a manifestation of quiet strength, not weakness, and can bring you far more than you ever imagined.

But letting go of something for the greater good or to gain something even better is very different to giving in or giving up your true self. Sacrificing your own happiness for someone else's will never be fulfilling for you, leading to resentment and pain, and won't make the object of your affection that happy in the long run either. Think of how many people – men and women – end up leaving the partner who caters to their every whim for someone who challenges them, excites them and even disagrees with them.

The Little Mermaid, whose sacrifice was all for nothing because giving up herself left her insipid and uninteresting, overlooked by the prince in favour of the woman who could engage him in conversation and show her own personality, is a reminder that you are more wonderful and more loveable when you are truly yourself.

You are too important, too beautiful in your individuality and inner strength, to give up your self to please someone else. Don't give up your life for anyone, no matter how much you feel that you love them, because changing yourself – be it swapping a tail for legs or giving up your political ideals for an opposing ideology or sacrificing your friends – in order to impress someone is never worth it. You will slowly lose your self-respect and self-identity, and start doubting yourself, hiding your light and radiance away until you are a pale shadow of your true self. If someone does not love you for who and what you are, move on. Find someone who sees your inner beauty and encourages you to shine as brightly as you can, who will encourage you to be more than you already are, not less.

Sedna : The Selfish Mermaid

"Once mermaids mocked your ships,
With wet and scarlet lips, and fish-dark difficult hips…
Then undines danced with sirens on the shore,
From his cloudy stall, you heard the kraken call,
And, mad with twisting flame, the firedrake roar."
Kenneth Slessor, Australian poet

Sedna is a sea goddess of the Inuit and other peoples of the ice and snow, renowned throughout the Arctic region and considered a mermaid, a beautiful but quick-to-anger water being who is half-woman, half-fish. She is also known as Satsuma Arnaa (mother of the deep) and Arnapkapfaaluk (big bad woman).

Her creation story is definitely one of the strangest of all. According to legend, Sedna was a beautiful but spoiled young woman, who lived with her parents (or, in some versions, just her father) in comfort, and turned down every suitor who asked for her hand in marriage, preferring to keep her luxurious lifestyle where she didn't have to work or look after a husband. Finally a handsome, wealthy looking man arrived, and swept her off her feet. He promised her riches, happiness and a life free of drudgery, and she proudly set off for his homeland with him. But when they got to his windswept and desolate island home, he transformed into a crow, and cackled with delight as Sedna began to weep. Instead of the life of queenly pleasure she'd anticipated, she lived in a cold, tattered tent, ate nothing but raw fish, and cried all day and night in misery.

When her father came to visit, she poured out her woes and begged him to take her home. Angry at his daughter's treatment, he killed the crow and sailed off with Sedna in his kayak – but the crow's bird friends discovered his body and followed, seeking vengeance. They descended on the boat, whipping up the ocean into a whirlpool, and the terrified father threw his daughter overboard in an attempt to appease the crows. Arms reached up to drag her under, and she clung desperately to the side of the boat, begging her father to save her. Not willing to die for his selfish daughter, he cut off her fingers with his hunting knife, and she was swept beneath the sea.

Her severed fingers became the dolphins, whales, seals and walruses, and as she hit the bottom of the ocean her legs turned into a fish tail. She became known as the great mother of the ocean, the protector of its creatures, and the goddess from whom all life flows. It is she who bestows blessings on her people, it is said, with plentiful fish and other creatures. And when fishing lines are empty and harpoons miss their mark, it is believed that Sedna has grown angry, and must be appeased. A shaman journeys down to her at these times to comb her hair, and thus soothe her fury, since she has no fingers to do this mermaidenly job herself. Once calm, she releases the animals to fill her people's fishing nets. She is considered a vengeful and mercurial goddess, and fishermen and hunters make sacrifices and offerings to her in the hope that she will reward them with abundance.

There are several variations of the Sedna legend and creation story, but they all involve a selfish young woman who refuses to marry any of the men her parents present to her, who ends up with a birdman – sometimes a crow, sometimes a raven – and is later thrown overboard by her father in an effort to appease the vengeful birds, who then chops off her fingers (with a knife, or an axe, or by smashing the sea-frozen digits with a hammer so that they snap off), to prevent her from reboarding the vessel. In one story she refuses to wed any of the suitors her father introduces her to, and marries a dog just to spite him, enraging him into taking her out to sea and throwing her overboard. There are echoes of this tale in the story of the Lost City of Ys, where the king, Gradlon, had to sacrifice his selfish daughter Dahut to the rising waters in order to save himself from the restless ocean.

Connecting with her archetype: The Sedna legend has always struck me as a very strange story, where a selfish, spoiled and thoughtless young woman is rewarded by becoming a goddess – and a petulant, grumpy one at that. It is hard to feel sympathy for someone who was so callous to her family, who thought herself so much better than every suitor who approached her. Yet she didn't deserve to be tricked into an awful marriage or treated so badly by her husband, nor to be sacrificed to the sea. Her father is also an unsympathetic man – he goes to rescue his daughter, feels remorse that she is so unhappy and kills the birdman to free her, but as soon as his life is threatened he quickly throws her overboard to save his own skin. It's no wonder that Sedna is so full of resentment, at her husband for making her miserable, and at her father for letting her die. Only now, in her solitude on the sea floor, with all the creatures of the ocean to commune with, has she finally found happiness.

Sedna reminds people to look below the shallowness of appearance, to get to know someone properly before being whisked off to faraway lands, or giving up your home or your job. She turns down some wonderful men in favour of someone seemingly wealthy and pleasing to the eye, and pays a huge price for her superficiality.

The Selkie : Trapped Between Two Parallel Lives

"When fate hands you a lemon, make lemonade."
Dale Carnegie, American writer and self-improvement guru

The selkie of the Celtic Isles is sister to the mermaid, but is one of two things – sometimes woman, sometimes seal – rather than a being who is half and half. She is never the two at once, although a small part of the consciousness of each remains whatever her form. This water being is graceful, slow and gentle, deep thinking and soulful, with the pain of her capture clear in her huge dark eyes. This is the saddest of all the mermaid stories, for it is all about capture and control, of being wrenched from their oceanic existence and trapped in the world of man against their will.

According to legend, to capture a selkie you must surprise her when she has stepped ashore and cast off her seal skin to dance on the sand, and steal this vital part of her, keeping it locked away and hidden forever. If a person can do this, the selkie will be under their control, and must do whatever is asked, which is usually marriage and a life in the fishing village by the sea where the man resides.

If she is caught, the selkie's fatalistic outlook means she will be a good wife and mother, dutiful and kind, and there are occasional stories of the selkie falling in love with her captor, having children and carving out a reasonably happy life on land. But always a part of her yearns for the sea, and remains oblivious to the worries and joys of humanity, and disinterested in interacting with the wider community. She may even be considered haughty, so unconcerned about socialising is she, and so unwilling to give up the hope of returning to her real home, and her seal husband and their family.

The selkie, once captured, is powerless, and part of her remains painfully aware that she is a captive – as does her husband, who guards her skin carefully, fearful that if given the choice his wife will choose the sea. The man who has her skin controls her, as he possesses the thing that symbolises her freedom and true nature. It seems strange to me that a man would want to trap a woman so, keeping her with him against her will, knowing she was not in love with him, even if she grows to like him, and aware that a part of her true self is missing, lost to memories of the sea and her life there with her seal kindred, who are still dancing beneath the waves, graceful and free.

In Scotland and Ireland there are many a tale of a young man who has come across a group of dancing seal women, and quickly stolen a skin, ignoring the tearful pleas of the young seal woman who is left alone on the beach as her sisters slip back into their skins and into the water, who has married her and started a family. Often it is one of the children who stumbles upon the hidden seal skin and shows it to their mother, not knowing what it is, and thus allowing her to return at last to her ocean family.

Many Celtic people claim descent from these people of the sea, and are believed to be immune to drowning as a result. These families also hold the seal as sacred, refusing to hunt it for food, in much the same way Australian Aboriginal people do not hunt their totem animal, which has proved to be of huge benefit to the environment.

In the myths and legends of Scandinavia, it is said that on January six, Twelfth Night, the selkies come ashore and slip out of their seal skins, keen, for a moment or two, to feel the earth beneath their feet, to dance upon the beach under the moonlight, and that if you can steal one of the skins and hide it from her, you can make her your wife. And an Icelandic legend recounts how a selkie was captured and taken as a human wife, and had seven children with her human husband – and yet while she loved them, she pined too for her seven seal children and her seal spouse.

But, like most of the stories, eventually an unknowing son or daughter stumbles across the carefully hidden seal skin – sometimes it is in a locked chest, sometimes buried beneath a bale of hay or corn – and, curious, shows it to their mother. She, rapturous with delight, grabs it from them and runs down to the ocean, barely stopping to say goodbye. At this moment the grieving and sense of loss is reversed, and the man who kept the woman pining for her old ocean life is left to mourn the loss of his beloved, and the children too feel the disappearance of their mother deeply.

It's also said that if a selkie discovers her hidden skin and escapes back to the sea, she will keep a watchful eye over her human family, helping her human husband catch fish even as she remains with her seal love in the sea, and coming back sometimes to play with her human children. There are also stories of seal men coming ashore and having children with human women, but they do not stay with them, and are not bound to because these relationships are mutual. They return to the ocean straightaway, and often come back a year later to take the child to live with them beneath the waves, a wrench for the human mother, who has lost her seal love and now her baby.

The beautiful film *The Secret of Roan Inish* explores the selkie myth and the yearning of the seal woman to return to the sea, and the sadness of those left behind on the shore when she does. The power object – in this case her seal skin – is also echoed in other sea being stories, such as the film *Mermaids* starring Erika Heynatz, where one mermaid is enslaved by an unscrupulous man who has her object of power, and thus has control over her.

Connecting with her archetype: The selkie symbolises a fatalism that breaks the heart, as well as a silent, Otherworldly and mysterious power within, which lets her survive in a situation so foreign to her. Most importantly, she is the opposite of the Little Mermaid, content with her life and what she has, and not seeking outside validation or trying to be something she is not. She loves the sea, and her seal life.

When she is captured and made to live on land as part of a new family though, she makes the best of the situation, which is a positive quality we could probably all use a little of now and then. Yet she always maintains the hope of being released to go back to her family under the waves, a sense of hope that can inspire us all, and the knowledge that all things are possible.

The undercurrent of this legend is about control, and there are many different ways to control someone, from the threat of violence and emotional blackmail to being so nice that they feel obligated to do what you want. Be sure that you never pressure anyone into doing something they don't want to do, even if you think it's for their own good, and be strong enough to resist any pressure on you. This is your life, and you must follow your dreams and create the life you want. There are parallels in the selkie archetype with the old-fashioned notion of arranged marriages, where the woman (or girl) was given to a man as his bride, and expected to fulfil her wifely duties and obligations without complaint, and without any say over her own life – when matrimony meant giving over your will to your husband. Today though women control their own lives and fates, they hold their own metaphorical seal skin, and if they marry they do it for love, not duty. Be sure to value and give thanks for the blessings of choice that you have, and use them wisely and well.

Eco Warrior Mermaid

"For in the end we will conserve only what we love. We will love only what we understand. We will understand only what we are taught."
Baba Dioum, Senegalese environmentalist

Today, mermaids have been reimagined again, as beautiful sea beings we can connect with for healing, love and transformation, as manifestations of the ocean goddess and the magic of water, and as eco warriors who are inspiring a new wave of environmental consciousness and a generation of activists determined to protect the oceanic realm and all the creatures that live beneath the waves.

Connecting with her archetype: You can evoke and channel this energy by doing something, no matter how small, to help the earth and the oceans. Go to the beach and drink in the beauty of sun, sand, sea and sky, and meditate on what would best suit you, or flip to the Marine Conservation chapter for some more ideas...

Connecting With Your Inner Mermaid

*"I must be a mermaid, Rango.
I have no fear of depths and a great fear of shallow living."*
Anais Nin, *The Four-Chambered Heart*

How To Tap In To Your Own Magical Self

Mermaids have been weaving their long, wild hair around our hearts and filling us with a love of the ocean and the cool, cleansing power of its waters for hundreds of years. They are the stuff of dreams and legends, their beauty inspiring incredible artworks, their mystery intriguing writers and poets, and their friendship with fellow sea creatures encouraging a protectiveness in us of their watery realm.

Mermaids embody the principles of feminine strength and independence, of beauty on your own terms, and womanly power and mystique. They have a complex, mercurial nature that is rooted in freedom as well as wisdom, and symbolise sensuality and self-assurance. Some see them as vain and superficial, or tragic and self-sacrificing, but to others they display a beauty that comes from within, from being true to yourself and expressing the beauty of your heart. They can be seen as a manifestation of the mystery of the ocean, the unknowable depths of its waters, as well as the mystery and wonder of the subconscious mind.

Whether you believe mermaids exist or are simply a wonderful figment of the imagination, connecting with the archetypal energy of the sea maiden can help you get in touch with the untamed and uninhibited free spirit that lies deep within you. This is the part of you that is a brave warrior priestess, controlling your own destiny and living your life deeply and fully, with courage and passion, and the sense of joy that comes with knowing you are fulfilling all the promise and potential within you.

Ponder what it is about this siren of the sea that most inspires, fascinates and intrigues you. What does she symbolise to you, how does she make you feel, and which personality traits of hers do you most admire? It might be her freedom to swim off on her own at any moment, or her ability to enchant and intrigue all those who meet her. Perhaps it's her sense of independence and solitude, or her deep connection to the ocean.

To me, mermaids seem unafraid to dive deeply into life, to plunge into the sea of the subconscious and explore the swirl of emotions. They bring fears up to the surface to frolic in the calm waters of the seashore and dissolve in the sunshine. They dance on the waves, ride the thrashing stormy swells with ease, and shoot down into the dark of the deepest sea to expose and heal their fears. They are graceful and in touch with their physicality, at one with their body, vibrantly aware of it and connected with it, and comfortable in their skin (and scales!). These sea beings are confident, assured and truly alive. They swim through the waters – of the ocean and of life – full of grace and gratitude, ease and feminine power.

In many stories mermaids are associated with treasure, but tapping in to your own magical self is not about material gain – rather it is about finding the treasure within your own self. Channelling mermaid energy can give you a new appreciation of your self and your sensuality, and singing your siren's song can help you hear the voice inside, connect with your intuition and knowingness, and start trusting the gut feelings you have always had, but too easily managed to ignore.

To begin, spend some time on your own. Every mermaid loves – and needs – to spend time alone, so give yourself the precious gift of time and space. Rather than fearing those times when you're left to your own devices, embrace your inner mermaid and draw strength from the solitude, luxuriating in the freedom you have to do, and be, exactly what you want, and allowing it to recharge and energise you. When you spend all your time with other people, it's easy to slip into patterns of acting as you imagine they expect you to – supportive friend, loving partner, efficient co-worker, well-behaved child, busy parent – and putting your desires last.

Part of the allure of the mermaid is that she lives on her own terms, and does what she wants to do. Taking time out for yourself can help you remember who you are, and what you want. It's not about becoming selfish or oblivious to other people, just ensuring that there is balance in how you treat yourself compared to others. You might want to curl up on the couch with a book, go for a walk through the park or along the beach, have a bubble bath, gaze out the window and daydream, create something crafty or whip up a meal – whatever it is, allow yourself the luxury of spending time alone, and begin to value yourself as a companion.

Your Mermaidenly Journal of Treasures

To start communicating with your inner mermaid, create your own mermaid journal to record all your discoveries as you dive into the deep, emotion-filled waters of your own subconscious and begin charting your own course. You can fill it with beautiful art, favourite quotes and random thoughts, transcribe your meditations and your dreams, write out your explorations and answers to the exercises in this book and notes on things you want to investigate further, draw pictures to express yourself, and record your magical rituals and the conversations you have with your mermaiden self.

You could buy a pretty journal, or get a huge blank notebook and design the cover yourself, decorating it with shells, pictures of the ocean, your own paintings of mermaids or little silver sea siren charms. Or you may want to use a lever arch folder so you can add pages when you want to and move them around, or a wooden treasure box you can fill not only with your written words, but things you find, like seashells, precious stones, crystals, mermaid statues or jewellery, and things you make – paintings, cassette recordings, craft projects.

My mermaid journal was a gift from my beloved, covered in black velvet and emblazoned with a beautiful mermaid painting by Jessica Galbreth (who painted our cover mermaid). It's filled with notes, quotes, symbols and sketches I would never show anyone, but which have meaning to me and help me unlock some of my thoughts, ideas, ideals and issues.

Don't worry about spoiling a pretty book with your scrawl or saving it for something special – you are special, and now is the time to begin. Having something beautiful to write in will inspire you, encourage you to engage with it more often, and reinforce that your time is sacred, and getting to know yourself is to be treasured.

Once you've chosen your journal, consecrate it in a way that has meaning for you. You might want to take it to the beach, sprinkle it with sand, leave it on your altar for a day or two, pass it through some cleansing incense smoke or place it under your pillow for a night – listen to the singing of your heart to know what will have the most significance for you.

When you're ready, imagine yourself as a beautiful creature of the deep. What do you look like? What qualities do you have? Which of these echo your self as you are now, and which are traits you admire and aspire to emulate?

Get out some pencils or paints and draw a mermaid. Don't worry about how "good" or "bad" you think you are at this – it's not about being perfect, it's about expressing a feeling, revealing what it is that mermaids mean to you, and the qualities that you most want to embody. If the idea of sketching it yourself is too stressful, find an image of a mermaid you are powerfully drawn to – you can buy inexpensive prints from many beautiful fantasy artists, or find a picture of real-life mermaids like Hannah Mermaid and Mermaid Dana, or actresses such as Daryl Hannah in the movie *Splash* or Phoebe Tonkin and Cariba Heine in TV's sweet series *H2O: Just Add Water*, or a pretty greeting card or art book.

Meditate on the picture, or simply call an image to your mind of yourself with a beautiful tail and long hair, sitting on a rock, lolling in the shallows or diving deep within the ocean. Swim in the wild waters of your imagination, visualising yourself as you play in the ocean waves. Feel the soft, nurturing quality of the water as it caresses your skin and sweeps your hair gently back from your face. Sense the bubbles of air fizzing against you. Float on your back, gently held by the buoyant water, and feel yourself supported, and your worries washed softly away, as the ocean waves cleanse and reinvigorate you, leaving you weightless and dreamy.

Feel yourself letting go of stress, unclenching the muscles of your physical body as you relax your grip on the worries in your mind. Breathe slowly and joyously, smiling at the beauty of the sunshine, the day, the world. Listen for the sound of voices on the wind, from a mermaid or from your own heart, and trust them. Write it all down in your journal, and allow yourself to return to this daydream whenever you can so you can further communicate with your mermaid self.

If there's a specific issue you're trying to deal with, connect to your mermaid self and listen to the answers. You might want to try an active imagination exercise, where you bring the issue to mind and begin a dialogue, not consciously controlling what is said, but letting your mind wander where it will and conversing with the "mermaid you" and simply observing where it goes and what tangents you end up discussing. Or send a telepathic message to this inner you and have a conversation, perhaps speaking out loud and recording it on a dictaphone.

Alternatively you could jot down a question about a situation you're facing with the hand you write with, then start answering it with your other hand. When you can finally decipher the scrawl, you'll discover some incredible pieces of wisdom you weren't conscious of knowing, but which were within you all along. Using your non-dominant hand connects you with a different part of the brain and helps you access the subconscious, so you'll learn a lot about why you act the way you do, what you really feel about various issues, and any fears, self-limiting thoughts and strengths you may not have been aware of. It's all about unlocking the energy, power and knowledge you already possess, and going deep within to discover what you already know.

Dive Into Your Dreams

You can also submerge yourself in the watery realm of your night-time dreamscapes. Dreaming is like submerging yourself in the ocean, diving into the swirling waters of your subconscious, and the symbols and messages in your dreams can help you know yourself better. Not all dreams are significant – sometimes they're just a cleaning out and releasing of the mundane stuff that clutters your mind, which your brain doesn't need to hold on to and store.

But some dreams will have meaning – and you are the best person to interpret this, not a dream guru or magazine columnist who's never met you. A book of symbols can help you begin, but it's more effective if you create your own dictionary of symbols. A mermaid for instance means very different things to different people – to some she might be a warning or omen, as she was to sailors in days gone by, to others she's a figure of beauty and sensuality, to others still she could be a symbol that they're sacrificing too much.

You might want to only record the dreams that seem significant and remain vivid throughout the following day, or you may prefer to train yourself to recall them all, writing them down as soon as you wake up each morning and seeking out meaning in the threads you can weave between them. This will also make it easier to determine which ones are significant and which are just byproducts of your brain processes, and improve your dream retention.

It can also be interesting to journal about what the ocean means to you. It is so much a part of our planet, and even those who live far from the sea know its pull from books, movies and poetry, or stories handed down through the generations. Its waves can represent the waves of life, the ebb and flow of our fortunes, the swells that can pull the rug out from under us, interspersed between the ease of calm waters and the soothing buoyancy of a smooth summer sea.

Does the ocean bring back happy memories of family holidays, of warm summers and ice-cream, or of being sticky and sunburnt and scared? If you've been caught in a rip or know someone who was injured at sea it could represent fear rather than freedom, and being unfamiliar with the water can also create apprehension. I was caught in a rip a few times as a kid, which was scary, but I was rescued each time, and it didn't dent my confidence, probably because we grew up near the beach and Dad was so confident in the water. I took it as a learning experience, knowing that the flow of the water was an important lesson, like understanding the flow of life – anticipating the unseen dangers, and attuning yourself to your environment and your surroundings, being aware of undercurrents in the sea and in relationships. Learning the consequences of the currents in the water, and of your actions.

Sarah's Surfing Magic

Sarah Byrne is an early childhood teacher who loves working with the younger people of this world. She loves their honesty, curiosity and eagerness to learn. In her spare time, learning to surf has become much more than a sport or a hobby to Sarah – it's a metaphysical adventure into the ocean, a way to embrace her sensuality, overcome fears and delve into the depths of her soul.

I feel I was guided to start surfing. I swam competitively for years, and for a few years after that I couldn't go near the water. I think I was burnt out by the pressure of winning, and training five hours a day had erased the magic. Then last year, I started seeing pictures of people surfing, and they seemed so happy, so free, so light! I was also presented with the saying: "Only a surfer knows the feeling," over and over. I was stuck in a rut, searching for something, so I went on a journey to discover this feeling, a feeling I longed for, the feeling that helped me to rediscover my self again. I went surfing!

Surfing has taught me so much in such a short time, and I'm so thankful that at times I cry tears of gratitude. Surfing and life share such parallels in lessons to be learned. I can see why I was guided to learn about surfing – to learn about myself and life. I've learned to believe in myself more. I've learned the importance of balance, both on a surfboard and in life. I've learned to let go and trust in the *process* of learning to surf more than aiming to be good, just as I've learned to let go and trust the process of life more than worrying about where I'll end up. I'm learning to be patient, and that the only way I can fail, at surfing and in life, is to give up. Just as I feel the ocean breathing when I'm drifting on my board, I've learned to breathe and stay calm. I'm learning to love and trust again. Most of all, I've learned how truly magical the ocean and my life can be if I keep an open mind and an open heart. And I know there's more to discover, and I'm so excited to find out what it is.

Surfing has given me a new appreciation of the ocean, and life. Since I've

been surfing, it's like the ocean has been teaching me about life through metaphor. When I first began I was in a dark place. The day I started to wake up, I was out on my board, drifting, and worrying, wondering how I could escape my troubles. Then a voice in my mind said: "This is life, you are alive, it may be hard at times, but it's better than not being here at all." I don't know if I just thought it, but it seemed too positive for where I was at the time. So I thanked the voice as if it was someone swimming next to me.

Another day there was a wave coming, bigger than the waves I'd usually be game enough to catch. I battled internally, wondering what to do. The voice told me: "Just ride the wave, don't let fear hold you back, face it." I knew something was guiding me, because I thought, "Oh well, if I break my neck at least I don't have to go to work," so I wasn't in a place to be giving myself uplifting advice.

So I paddled with everything I had in me, not just energy, but fear, anger, even love and hope. I wanted to make it work, not just the surfing, but my life. I was incredibly focused on where I would put my hands on the board, where I would stand. I got up, I put my arms out for balance, and I rode my first real wave. The speed, the feeling of the wave turning under me, the sun, the thrill, it was golden. From that day on, my life has changed. I've always loved the ocean, but suddenly I felt like I belonged to the ocean. I felt loved. I felt free. I felt safe.

For me, I need to be in the water. I just feel more fulfilled in the water. I feel more whole and healed. I used to wear a wetsuit, but I stopped as I noticed the difference when my skin wasn't covered by the water. I feel that being in the water, swimming underwater, being taken in by her rhythm, is a truly freeing, magical experience. It's definitely beauty to the senses.

Start Manifesting Your Heart's Desire

If you feel the siren's call but need a little direction, write a list in your mermaid journal, beginning "I would love to…" Include the big dreams, the small dreams, the long-held desires, the secret wishes and the recent whims – write down everything you can think of that will make your heart sing.

Then go over each one, and think about what's stopping you. A girl I know says it has always been her life's dream to swim with dolphins, yet she lives just an hour from where a group takes swimmers out to do just that. So what's stopping her? And what is stopping you? Is it the idea of the dream, and the anticipation of doing it "one day", that you like best? (Which is fine, it's always nice to have something to look forward to!) Are you worried that the reality of it won't be quite as good as the way you imagine it, so you put it off so it always remains golden?

Look over your list and work out which one will be the easiest to make happen. *And do it.* I always feel such a sense of accomplishment and confidence when I complete something, and that feeling can carry over into my next, perhaps bigger, task. Often the only obstacle to achieving something is our own mindset, our misperceptions and our own – often unfounded – fears. So if your big dream seems hard, make a small one come true first, then tap in to that energy to work on the main one.

Then read over the list again and choose the one that is most important and means the most to you. Write down all the so-called reasons that are stopping you from making it happen, and go over each one. You should be able to break each one down until there are no more excuses, because if it's your dream, nothing should be able to stop you. Any obstacles are just things to find a way over, or to encourage new ideas and strategies, or refocus you in a new direction.

If you really want to do something, you'll find a way to do it. And if you don't, you'll find an excuse.

Be honest with yourself when looking at your reasons. If the main impediment is that you don't have time or can't be bothered, be open to a new dream. There's always time, it's just a matter of prioritising – sacrificing some TV time, or nights out. Of course there's always the possibility that you just don't want to do it badly enough, and that's fine. We grow up, we change, we learn new things and experience different situations, and it's perfectly understandable that sometimes our dreams will change. If this is the case, that's great – you can cross it off your list and redirect your energy to something you really do want to make happen.

Or are you waiting for the right time? The perfect conditions? Someone else to give you a jump start? The time will never be truly "right", and the conditions will never be "perfect", and it's nobody else's responsibility but your own. Making a dream come true involves working with what you have, and doing it anyway.

Now break your goal down into smaller, more easily achievable and less daunting tasks. If you want to write a book, sit down right now and write out a plot outline, a list of chapter headings or some notes. If you do something to further your dream every day, it will eventually happen. Ticking something off each day, no matter how small that thing is, will also inspire you to continue.

If you want to travel, go to a travel agent or look online to find out how much it will cost to go where you want to go and what time of year is better suited to you. Start a scrapbook, adding photos and articles about the place, fun facts, places you'd like to stay, things you want to see and do there. Find out what season it will be when you want to go, and how they celebrate the turning points of the earth there. Add rituals, festivals and events you want to be part of. Make it real to you. If their main language is different to yours, start learning a few words a day – you'll be amazed how quickly you can form sentences if you stick at it. Open a bank account and set up a ten dollar a week (or more if you can) direct deposit. You won't miss ten dollars, but it will add up over time, and as you see the total growing, it will inspire you to save even more.

If you want to get fit, start walking for fifteen minutes every day, join a netball team or put on a CD and dance around the room. The secret, if you can call it that, to achieving anything is to break it down into a series of small but doable things. Writing a book, climbing a mountain, saving for your dream holiday, learning a language or getting a qualification might seem overwhelming and almost impossible to achieve – but writing a page a day is not hard. Walking for ten minutes is nothing. Sacrificing a few coffees a week is easy. Booking a guitar lesson can be done in an instant.

Work out what the first step you need to take is – and do it now. No excuses. And do something else tomorrow, and the next day.

Keep a record of everything you do over the next few weeks, by writing it on a calendar square each day, having a manifestation board you can add a gold star or a faery sticker to for every step further you take, having a computer spreadsheet to plot it on or listing it in your mermaid journal. It's not important how you do it, just that you do it. Not only will it be bringing you closer to your goal, it will also spur you on as you see how much you've already done. My motto? Don't look at how far you have to go, look at how far you've already come – and celebrate that success.

After a month, look back at your list and assess what you've achieved. Can you continue going forward in the way you have been, or do you need to go off on a tangent? Sometimes getting to where you want to go requires a few detours, and the confidence to take an unknown path. As you progress, you may also find new or better ways to achieve your dream. Be a bit flexible, and stay open to new opportunities or new ways of doing things.

Most of all, be prepared to work really hard. There's no easy way, no short cut, no magic trick. Don't kid yourself with: "If it's meant to be it will happen." It will happen if you make it happen. It's up to you. No one else can do it for you. But if it's a burning desire, you owe it to yourself to make it happen, or exhaust yourself trying. Your mermaid self is yearning to succeed, so harness her wild ocean energy and get started!

Need some inspiration? My sweet friend Stephanie made her short film, and had it selected for a film festival, through pure drive, ambition, dedication and passion. She worked her butt off. She wrote, directed, and learned to shoot. She did work experience at places that would teach her what she needed to know. She set up a fund where friends could invest in the film (and get a credit at the end), so she could buy the equipment she needed. Don't be scared to ask for support, feedback, advice, introductions, criticism. People want you to achieve your dream, and will help you make it come true, because enthusiasm is catching. Passion for your project encourages other people to fight to complete theirs, and your success will inspire others to believe they can get there too.

Lucy and I have no special powers, but we've worked ridiculously hard for years and years, and are determined to make our dreams come true. It's not easy. And it's not always fun. We have to work to pay the rent while writing our books, which can be hard to juggle.

Often we have to sacrifice paying work so we can write, which leaves us broke, or sacrifice our writing time in order to pay the bills. There are times we forego socialising with our friends or our family, ban ourselves from reading books for fun, and force ourselves to stay at the computer until we collapse.

Sometimes we hate writing, or we get bored. There are things that happen that discourage us or depress us. We've been bitterly disappointed and let down by colleagues. We're both pretty good at procrastinating too (hello Facebook friends!), and we have moments when we want to throw our hands in the air and stop, or break down in tears and give up. Sometimes it all seems too hard. But we're also absolutely committed to meeting our deadlines, and not letting each other – or ourselves – down, and we're prepared to work day and night to get it done. We encourage each other to keep going, share our frustrations and vent about how we've been unfairly treated, then turn it into a source of amusement and further drive. Mostly, we just keep working, plodding along when it seems inspiration has deserted us, knowing that if we keep writing, keep researching, keep editing, it will eventually return.

People are often disappointed to hear that the major factor in achieving a dream, be it writing a book, learning to surf or finding a new job, is plain old-fashioned hard work. "Genius is one per cent inspiration and ninety-nine per cent perspiration," said American inventor Thomas Edison. "We often miss opportunity because it is dressed in overalls and looks like work." He's right.

Connecting with your inner mermaid and fulfilling all the potential within you is also about confidence and state of mind. Remaining positive and looking for the good in each situation, learning from and letting go of perceived failures, and trying again. And again. And again. So many people expect achievements to come easy, and give up the minute it seems like hard work. Or they come to an obstacle or disappointment and decide that it's a sign, and there's no point going on. But you can transform setbacks into challenges and grow from each one, strengthening your resolve and getting closer and closer to your goal with each new experience. Following your dreams, and making them come true, involves dedication, passion, resourcefulness, the occasional sacrifice and the ability to work really hard. Don't be scared though – it's all worth it in the end!

Mermaid Moon Magic

Another way to activate your watery muse is to connect with the moon phases and the tides. Download a tide chart for your area from the Net, or find one in your local paper, and spend time at the beach watching the difference. Even if you live far from the sea, chart the ebb and flow of your emotions and see how it corresponds to the tidal system. Determine whether the time of day, the phase of the moon or your sleep patterns influence your mood. If you feel sluggish or a little down in the morning, do something active when you wake up, even if it's just a few yoga stretches, a brisk walk around the block or ten minutes of hula hooping. If you feel sad or lethargic every afternoon, nip out for a brisk walk around the block instead of making another coffee. Sometimes even getting up to walk to the printer can wake you up a little.

Learn about the weather too – how high and low pressure systems influence weather patterns and swells, as well as your mood. Don't buy into the claims of some mermaidenly schools of thought, that insist they can teach you to create rain from thin air, send hurricanes off course and avert floods, droughts or tsunamis. How arrogant to assume we can control the forces of nature, or that we should. And who has the gall to think they should decide where to divert a hurricane from, and who it should be inflicted on instead? And if it *is* true that they can, what do they have against Haiti, Japan, New Zealand and Australia?

Mermaidenry is a personal journey, and the magic you weave is to create a happier, more confident and productive life for you. It's not up to us to influence anyone else, inflict our will on others, decide who should be flooded and who should be spared, or to assume to know what is best for anyone other than ourselves. Instead of worrying about how to control the elements, become conscious of the moods of our planet and align yourself with its energies, so you can live in balance with the earth and the sea, feel the swelling tides within you, and become attuned to the universal whole we're all part of.

Begin to understand the seasons, in their traditional and symbolic sense, as well as how they unfold where you live. Chart the rhythms of the rain and the sun, the moon phases and the tides for a year and a day, and work out how you feel in different weather and different seasons. How do heat and cold affect you? Are you more comfortable when it's hot and dry, or do you come alive during the rainy season? Do you yearn for the summer sun to warm your bones, the crispness of autumn to energise you, the chill of winter to brace you for what is ahead, the vibrancy of spring to help you germinate your own ideas? When you become one with the cycle of the ever changing rhythms of the planet, you can reach your full potential, working with the energies rather than against, and giving yourself the best chance to get ahead.

And then you will start to hear your inner voice, the call of the siren within, which is to remind you to be all you can be, and do all that you want to do. It will gently encourage (or forcefully push) you to make your dreams come true. And if you continue ignoring it, don't be surprised if you finally feel a scream welling up within you, demanding to know what it is that is stopping you from achieving your dreams.

You can also embody the mermaid physically. Long hair has always been an important part of mermaid symbology, adding to the sense of freedom, wildness and untamed spirit attributed to them. Let your hair be wild for a while. It doesn't matter how long or short it is, just let it down, unconstrained and free, and allow that feeling to seep into your psyche. Drape yourself in pearls, slip into a sea-green silk shirt, slink into a turquoise sequinned skirt, or simply tie a sarong around your waist and walk barefoot along the sand, the riverbank or a city street.

Dive Right In

Another way to connect with your inner mermaid is to submerge yourself in her realm. Physically dive into the ocean, a river or a pool, feeling the water swirl around you and washing away stress. Swimming in the ocean is such a beautiful, cleansing thing to do, physically and emotionally. Being underwater is so dreamy too, so surreal and Otherworldly. It really is another realm beneath the surface, a green, sparkling, soft and gentle world. Time seems to slow down, distractions fade, sight is lessened and sound is muffled. Many people who are clumsy on land (like me!) find a new grace in the water, a feeling of connection and of being in your element.

Clasp your hands over your head, arms outstretched, and try to swim like a mermaid, in one fluid motion, body rippling and undulating, feeling the smoothness and ease of the movement. (Admittedly this takes a while to get down, and be careful in a shallow pool – I scraped and cut my fingers along the bottom, not realising the strength of my mermaid propulsion!). When I was little I used to go to the beach or race down the hill to the river to swim all the time, and now, years later, I still feel such a sense of freedom and joy when I swim, whether it's in a lap pool or the ocean.

Recently I rediscovered the joys of snorkelling too. Floating on the green surface as I peered down into a world of enchantment was so beautiful, and as I swam around with a school of brightly coloured fish, or dived down to the sandy bottom to get closer to a starfish or sea urchin, I felt such a sense of peace, so connected with the ocean and all its creatures. The cool water and the beauty of this undersea world soothed my mind and mood, and opened my heart. I felt graceful and languid like a mermaid, my hair floating and dancing around me, all movement so slight and easy, as I became immersed in this wondrous, light-filled and transformational realm. Even sitting on the seashore, watching the waves come in, hearing the ebb and flow of the tides and feeling the sunshine on your face or the raw power of stormy seas and salty air, can connect you to your watery muse.

It can also be fun to create a magical ocean altar, where you can connect with the energy of the mermaids and the sea, and more deeply to your own intuition. It will become a place where you can sit in quiet reflection, perform rituals, spellwork and divination, and communicate with the beings of the sea, real or imagined. You can set up a permanent altar, or it can be a moving celebration of your magic, ready to be assembled wherever you are, indoors or outdoors. Start with something to represent the four elements – a candle for fire, incense for air, a crystal for earth and a chalice for water – then add pieces that have meaning for you. Seashells you collect at the beach, a painting of a mermaid or a silver charm, a dolphin sculpture, a dish of seawater, a pearl – whatever symbolises the sea to you will help you create this sacred space and begin your ocean magic.

Bathing Magic For Your Inner Mermaid

"The bathtub evokes those moments when you're in the ocean, standing in the water up to your hipbones, hair falling around your shoulders, an oyster shell in your hand. Who could doubt that you're standing on true fins? The magic of mermaidenry lies in fleeting moments of inbetween – between towel and bath water, sand and sea."
Amanda Adams, American author

The Tub : Your Own Deep Sea

You can also evoke the physicality of your inner mermaiden in the bath. Fill it with foaming bubbles and lean your feet up against the end of the tub, imagining your tail submerged beneath the sea foam, and feeling the warm, comforting water swirl around you, supporting you, holding you, nourishing you. As all the stress and strain drains from your body, the healing salts and minerals soak in and the heat warms you through, it's easy to drift away into an altered state of consciousness and access the merbeing within.

Adding essential oils can help you float away into a different state of mind too. French mermaid Melusina was reputed to bathe in warm water scented with bergamot and wild rose, and aromatherapy can be very healing physically, emotionally and spiritually. Whether you burn the oils while you bathe or add them to the bath water, you can invoke any mood you want, from the calmest seas – try lavender, chamomile or vanilla – to the most bracing, icy swells – try rosemary, sweet orange, ginger or citrus. Add the oils to half a tablespoon of a carrier oil such as sweet almond, avocado, grapeseed or jojoba, and pour that into the warm bath just before you get in, to ensure the essential oils don't evaporate in the heat. The healing powers of these oils will be absorbed into the skin as well as inhaled.

A saltwater bath can be a powerful cleansing and detoxification process, your at-home version of a dive into the depths of the ocean, which is especially wonderful when you're preparing for magical mermaid rituals, as it washes away old energy and attunes you to the energy of the sea. Physically it also helps to detoxify the body, drawing out impurities, aiding skin conditions such as psoriasis and opening the pores and plumping the skin a little, which softens it and creates a healthy glow. Salt also makes the water more buoyant, which is why high concentrations are used in flotation therapy. A saltwater soak is good for the skin, as it contains many minerals and nutrients that can be easily absorbed.

Salts are used in many exfoliators, face and body scrubs and beauty products, including the sea salt scrub, marine mask and honey and seaweed moisturiser set I started using recently, which transports me straight to the seaside the moment I taste the salt, or breathe in the sweet scent of the ocean fragrance.

Seaweeds, known as the vegetables of the ocean, are the active ingredient in many high end face creams, due to their power of oxygenation, which nourishes and revitalises the skin. They are rich in skincare vitamins including retinol (vitamin A) and vitamins E and K, which are fat soluble, making them more easily absorbed within a carrier oil, as well as the water soluble C and B group vitamins, sixty vital trace elements and twelve essential minerals, so they're great to eat, and to add to your beauty products.

If you're creating your own body scrubs and bath salts, use a finer grained salt for the former, so it is gentle as well as more effective, and a coarser grained one for bath salts, so they dissolve more slowly in the tub. There are many different kinds of salts you can use for bathing and beauty products, which all have varied chemical make-ups, with different minerals and trace elements present, and thus different therapeutic benefits.

Sea salt is extracted from the ocean by evaporating the surrounding seawater, and comes in many forms, from the heavily processed table salt you sprinkle on your food to organic sea salt crystals that are better for you, both in your food and in your bath water.

Table salt is more than ninety-seven per cent sodium chloride, with the rest comprised of chemicals such as moisture absorbents, anti-caking agents and other additives. It's dried at more than 650°C (1200°F), which alters the natural chemical structure of the salt and strips it of its therapeutic benefits, leaving an unnatural chemical form of salt that strips water from your cells as the body tries to neutralise it, and is void of the vital trace minerals of natural salts.

Coarse organic sea salt crystals differ from manufactured table salt because they still have the extra minerals, including sulphate, magnesium, calcium, bicarbonate and bromide, within it, and it comes from unpolluted water sources and is often harvested and dried by hand, rather than by chemical extraction, with wooden tools because metal can taint it. So organic sea salt crystals are healthy to use in food – and some natural salt in the diet is essential for good health – and also make a good base for body scrubs, bath salts and other beauty products.

Physically, pure organic sea salt regulates and lowers blood pressure, minimises irregular heartbeats, acts as a natural antihistamine, clears sinus passageways and cleanses lungs of mucous, improves muscle strength, maintains the correct balance of electrolytes in the body and regulates blood sugar levels. It has antiseptic properties too, so gargling salt water is good for sore throats, mouth irritations and ulcers.

Dead Sea salts are harvested from the Dead Sea (funnily enough), located between Jordan and Israel, which is six times saltier than the ocean and is the world's richest source of natural salts. It has such a high concentration of dissolved minerals that the water is incredibly dense – people can't sink in it, or even swim very well, instead just bobbing or floating on the surface. Its thirty-five therapeutic minerals include zinc, calcium, potassium, bromine, sulphur and iodine, and it is only ten per cent sodium, as opposed to the ninety per cent that table salt has.

Soaking in the Dead Sea, or in a bath with its salts added, is wonderful for the skin and is also renowned for relieving the pain of arthritis and rheumatism, headaches and muscle and joint pain,  as well as treating insomnia and other sleep disorders, reducing water retention, increasing circulation and decreasing heart rate, easing anxiety and, apparently, even minimising cellulite. It also nourishes and softens the skin, cleanses and detoxifies, and soothes rashes, psoriasis, eczema, acne and many allergic reactions, hence its use in many beauty and bath products.

Himalayan salts are harvested from ancient seabeds in the isolated, pollution-free Himalaya Mountains, and are the most pure salt form in the world. They contain eighty-four essential minerals, including magnesium, calcium, iron and potassium. This makes them a healthy alternative to normal table salt for adding to food, as well as a super ingredient in bath and beauty products and in atmosphere re-charging salt lamps, which increase the negative ions in your home by up to three hundred per cent, boosting mood and neutralising pathogens and toxins, which is especially helpful for asthma and allergy sufferers, as well as everyday computer users who are exposed to electromagnetic frequencies.

Himalayan salts are a pretty pinky-red colour, due to the presence of the mineral-rich pink algae in the waters they're harvested from. These salts are mined by hand from pollution-free areas, and hand-washed for added purity, so it is salt in its most natural form, with all its vibrational energy intact.

These salts are known as white gold because of their purity and value, and are believed to contain all the natural elements in the same form as the elements in the human body – the same elements found in the original primal sea. In a bath, Himalayan salts cleanse and detoxify the skin, leaving it smoother, softer and cleaner, and are very healing for dry skin, psoriasis and acne.

They soothe insect bites and heal blisters – a paste made from the salts dissolved in warm water then cooled is effective, or simply have a salt bath – and have brought relief to many suffering from arthritis, joint pain and insomnia. They also ensure a healthy pH balance in your cells, particularly brain cells, ease and prevent muscle cramps, increase bone strength, boost sinus and respiratory health and regulate water content in the body. Your skin continues to absorb the minerals for up to three hours after your bath, so for best results don't shower before drying off.

One of the most popular and easy-to-find bath salts is Epsom salt, magnesium chloride, which is a naturally occurring mineral found in seawater, geothermal mineral springs, lakes and rocks. It can also be manufactured, so look for natural Epsom salts, which dissolve more quickly, are more bio-available for absorption through the skin, and don't have chemical additives.

Epsom salts are wonderful for the skin, making it softer and clearer, soothing itches and reducing the sting and swelling of bites. It's also great for aching muscles, migraines, regulating the activity of more than three hundred enzymes, lowering blood pressure and hypertension, easing sprains, muscle soreness and joint pain, helping muscles and nerves function properly, making insulin more effective, reducing inflammation and muscle cramps and easing stress and insomnia. It can also soothe cranky children and improve sleep cycles – Epsom salts are a key ingredient in gripe water.

According to Dr Natasha Campbell-McBride, founder of the Cambridge Nutrition Clinic in England, magnesium is a crucial mineral, and one that many people lack. And she says this easily corrected deficiency is the cause of more than ninety per cent of hypertension cases. "Magnesium is one of the most precious minerals in the body, but magnesium deficiency is widespread because we eat too many processed carbohydrates," she says. "The magnesium and sulphates in Epsom salt help detoxify the body. Adding half a cup of Epsom salt to a bath and soaking every other day for thirty minutes is very effective."

"Living without adequate levels of magnesium is like trying to operate a machine with the power off, and like a machine, it's likely to malfunction," agrees Dr Christiane Northrup, an ob/gyn and author of Women's Bodies, Women's Wisdom. "Magnesium is essential for the functioning of more than three hundred different enzymes in the body, particularly those that produce, transport, store and utilise energy, and controls adrenal stress hormones, helps maintain normal brain function, blood pressure, vascular tone and blood flow, and can prevent premature labour."

Magnesium-rich foods should be eaten, and supplements can be consumed, but this vital mineral is effectively absorbed by the skin, so a warm bath is also a great, relaxing way to up your levels. Just add a cup of Epsom salts and soak away your aches, pains and worries. Three times a week is recommended for optimum health.

Magnesium can also be used in the garden, encouraging extra growth and plant health, as it helps seeds germinate, makes plants grow bushier and produce more flowers, increases chlorophyll production and improves phosphorus and nitrogen uptake.

Baking soda, sodium bicarbonate, is another salt that can be used in bathing. It is found in many natural mineral springs, and neutralises acidity. Also known as baking soda, bread soda, cooking soda and bicarbonate of soda, it is an ingredient in cooking, where it makes dough rise, and has been used as a cleaning agent since the time of the Egyptians. It is used as an antacid to treat indigestion and heartburn, as well as to ease stomach pains and gas, and in gripe water for infants with teething pain, colic, gastrointestinal discomfort or reflux. Sodium bicarbonate is also used to soothe burns and scalding and prevent blistering or scarring, to relieve insect bites and to soften skin. Its particles are fine in texture, which makes it a gentle yet effective exfoliant to remove dead skin cells and boost health, and it's an ingredient in toothpastes, shampoos and deodorants, as well as in many cleaning products.

Boron is another natural salt. Also known as sodium borate, it's a mineral that helps build strong bones, treat osteoarthritis and improve muscle coordination. It's used in detergents, cosmetics and spa products, and as an anti-fungal compound and an insecticide.

When making your own bath products and beauty treats, there are a variety of salts to choose from, so experiment with Epsom, Dead Sea, Himalayan, baking soda and sea salts to see what works best for you, or you can use a mix of a few of them.

Mermaid Bath Salts

To prepare for a mermaid ritual or to strengthen your connection with the sea beings, create your own blend of bath salts then soak in a magical bath, breathing in your oceanic connection. Here is how to create a beautiful, natural and simple bath salt mixture.

- ☆ 3 parts Epsom salts.
- ☆ 2 parts baking soda.
- ☆ 1 part sea salt crystals.
- ☆ 1 part dried seaweed (or, if that seems too weird, use dried lavender or chamomile flowers).

Place all the ingredients in a large glass bowl and gently combine. Store in a pretty glass jar with a few seashells in it, or attach them to a ribbon around the top. Add four tablespoons to your bath as the tub is filling and drift away in mermaid daydreams.

★ If you're low on ingredients, mix 2 cups of Epsom salts with 1 cup of coarse sea salts, add several drops of essential oils and mix well. Leave them out to dry for a few hours, then pour into glass jars to store. You can add a few drops of blue or green food colouring with the essential oils to make it look more oceanic.

★ You can also mix together 1 part Epsom salts and 1 part baking soda with a few drops of essential oils, depending on what you have in your cupboard right now.

★ And if it's time you're low on, simply mix a handful of Epsom salts with a little water until it becomes creamy and turns into a smooth paste, and rub it all over your body before getting in the bath or shower. Rub the mixture into your skin as you bathe and you'll soon notice softer, smoother skin. Or you can wait until after your bath or shower, and massage a handful of Epsom salts over your wet skin – you can leave it on to absorb into the skin.

Simple Sea Salt Body Scrub

☆ ½ cup sea salts (or Himalayan, Dead Sea or Epsom).
☆ ¼ cup carrier oil such as coconut, jojoba or sweet almond oil.
☆ A few drops of your favourite essential oils (optional).

Place the salt into a glass bowl and stir in the carrier oil with a wooden spoon. Blend well, until it's thick but not too hard. If it gets too hard, you can add a splash of water or an extra teaspoon of oil, and if it's too soft keep mixing, and add a little more salt if necessary. You want it to be a bit coarse, so it exfoliates well, and sticks to the skin rather than running off. When you are happy with the consistency, add the essential oils (if you want to) – five drops should be fine. Mix well, and it's ready to go – rub it into the skin before showering, then rinse it off once you're under the water. For a scrub suitable for the face, use a finer grain of salt and perhaps skip the essential oils, as they could irritate the delicate skin of your face.

Sea Tea Bags

You can also make a cute tea bag to go into your bath – which I love the idea of because I love tea!

- ☆ ½ cup coarse organic sea salts – or Dead Sea or Himalayan.
- ☆ ½ cup dried flowers – chamomile is nice, or lavender, or rose, or whatever you prefer.
- ☆ Your favourite essential oil – I love bergamot, for that heady Earl Grey scent, but sweet orange oil is also lovely, and lavender is calming. You can use one, or a few, depending on which flowers you choose and what mood you want your bath to transport you to.
- ☆ Little organza bags or pieces of muslin.

Pour the salts into a glass bowl, add around ten drops of essential oil and mix well. Allow to dry, then stir in the dried flowers and spoon the mixture into the organza bags. When you have a bath, place one of the sea bags in the water, and the salts will slowly dissolve, giving you the benefit of the minerals within them, and the healing power of the essential oils and herbal flowers.

Excellent Exfoliators

- ☆ 2 cups Epsom salts.
- ☆ ¼ cup petroleum jelly.
- ☆ A few drops of your favourite essential oil (lavender is gentle and soothing).

Combine ingredients well, then apply the mixture to your body, concentrating on dry skin patches and rough bits, like your elbows and heels, and gently massage to exfoliate.

- ☆ ½ teaspoon Epsom salts.
- ☆ A dollop of your usual cleansing cream.

To create a gentle but exfoliating deep-pore facial cleanse, add the salts to your cleanser, mix well then massage it onto your face and neck, before rinsing off with cool water and gently patting dry.

Trish's Bathing Magic

Trish Anderson-Young is the founder of The Mermaid's Garden, which offers fragrant sea salt infusions, essential oil blends and vibrational essences. She works with Australian bush flower essences as well as her own range, is a reiki practitioner and crystal healer, and loves the ocean. Visit Trish at www.mermaidsgarden.com.

I was very blessed to grow up on the northern beaches of Sydney, with Long Reef Aquatic Reserve like a backyard to explore. I spent hours there, collecting shells, playing in rock pools and interacting with the starfish, sea urchins, crabs and fish. Over the decades, I've witnessed the reef go from bountiful to desolate and back to bountiful again. The thing that sticks in my mind is the fragility of life on the reef, and this got me thinking of the fragility of all life on this planet.

The ocean provides a home to some of the most incredible creatures on the planet, and also represents the hidden aspects of our emotions and provides a mirror to our soul. Through observing and connecting to the ebb and flow of the tides, the effect of storms upon oceans, the floods and tsunamis and the regenerative forces of natural springs, we can gain insight as to how our own emotions function.

Sea salt baths let me reconnect with the ocean from the comfort of home, and provide deep cleansing of the physical and emotional body. When you bathe in sea salt you feel lighter, restoring serenity to your soul. When I created a range of bath salt infusions, I felt it was important to combine the healing properties of both Himalayan and Australian salts. Himalayan salt is the purest form of salt on the planet, free from air-borne and water-borne pollutants. It is easily absorbed into the skin, helping to detox stress from the body and replenish necessary minerals. I also use Australian sea salts for balance. Energetically, Himalayan salt carries the vibrations of ancient times and represents darkness, while Australian sun-dried sea salt contains the energetic resonance of sunlight and the fire element, creating a balance between night and day as well as ancient and new.

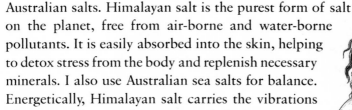

Crystal Magic For Your Inner Mermaid

"There are seven mermaid princesses and seven pearls.
The reason I sing is to convey my love. The reason the pearl sparkles
is to brighten the sea. And so I can never forget the sound of the
waves or the warmth of the sea. Sea! You are our greatest treasure."
Mermaid Melody Pichi Pichi Pitch, Japanese manga

Channelling the Power of Sea Gems

Another way to connect with your inner mermaiden is to start working with oceanic crystals and precious gems. Mermaids have long been associated with pearls, corals and other sparkling treasures like larimar and peridot, and wearing or creating with these crystals can align you with the energy of the ocean.

Aquamarine The name of this beautiful blue gemstone comes from the Latin aqua meaning water, and mare meaning sea, and it was known to the Romans as water of the sea. Reflecting the beautiful shades and depths of the ocean, it was carried by sailors as a talisman to protect them from drowning, and referred to by them as mermaid's treasure. It symbolises courage and serenity, and increases psychic powers, spiritual harmony and balance. It can calm, relax and soothe stress, align the physical with the spiritual, improve communication and dissolve fear and emotional blocks. At one time goblets were made from aquamarine, as it was believed the crystal's healing power would infuse liquids to soothe sore throats and swollen glands, improve digestion and reduce water retention.

Today aquamarine is used as an elixir and in crystal healings and jewellery for the same purposes, as well as to help conditions related to the kidneys and bladder, as a diuretic to flush out excess fluid, and to maintain balance within the body. It can also help balance the throat chakra and release emotional blocks to communication. Aquamarine, the birthstone for March, has long been considered part of a mermaid's treasure trove, blessed by the sea goddesses and a good luck charm for sailors and all those setting out on a journey, either across the sea, through the outside world or into the inner realms of the mind and emotions.

Moonstone This iridescent, milky crystal looks like a piece of the moon illuminated with rainbows, and holds the energy of the lunar orb and the qualities of the element of water within it. As such, it helps balance the emotions, and can neutralise anger and calm aggressive behaviour, emotional stress and impatience. It enhances intuition and sensitivity, increases psychic visions, and boosts dream awareness and spiritual awakening. In India, moonstones are regarded as dream stones that bring the wearer beautiful night visions.

Moonstone represents new beginnings, and can help shift subconscious thoughts into the conscious mind and manifest thought into action. It balances masculine and feminine energies, and creates deep emotional healing, dissolving blockages and past pain. Physically it brings balance to the body's hormonal and pineal systems, and helps eliminate toxins and soothe the skin and eyes. It works deeply on women's health issues, and in Arabic countries women often wear moonstones sewn into the hem of their clothes as a symbol of fertility.

Moonstone's rainbow effect comes from the spectrum of light it attracts – this play of colour and light, known as adularescence, gives it a mysterious shimmer, so it looks different when it's moved, almost like a holographic effect. A piece of moonstone under the pillow or taken as an elixir has long been used to combat insomnia and prevent sleepwalking, and it's considered a crystal of protection, especially during pregnancy and childbirth, and for travel by sea. It can be used to lift the mood and clear stagnant energy from the body as well as from a room. One of the birthstones for June, it is also associated with planting cycles and with the ocean and its tides.

Peridot This pretty green crystal, known to the Romans as evening emerald and to Hawaiians as Pele's tears, is formed during volcanic eruptions and contains a fiery energy. It's a powerful cleanser and purifier, both physically and emotionally, and helps to release guilt, resentment and negativity and bring peace. In Hawaii there are green sand beaches created from the presence of peridot, which are considered sacred places, and incorporate the energy of the sea as well as this unique shiny crystal, also known as olivine.

You can carry a piece with you to soak up the energy and power that emanates from it, wear it in jewellery, keep a piece under your pillow or create a ritual bath with it to soak up its energies. The birthstone for August, it has long been thought to ward off evil spirits, and physically it is a powerful tonic, releasing toxins, cleansing the body and purifying the mind, and helping you to let go of old baggage, the past and people that cause you pain. It motivates growth and change, sharpens the mind and boosts awareness and confidence.

"All art is autobiographical.
The pearl is the oyster's autobiography."
Federico Fellini, Italian film director

Pearl These beautiful iridescent gems are deeply connected to the sea through their creation – they are produced within the soft tissue of a living shelled mollusc in reaction to an irritant such as sand or a parasite – and have long been considered the jewel of choice for mermaids. Grown within the ocean (as well as in freshwater rivers and lakes), they help people attune to the ebb and flow of life, and find balance and calm. They represent purity, innocence and integrity, and can be used to sharpen your focus, concentration and clarity, as well as assisting meditation and embodying serenity, tranquillity and wisdom.

They are aligned with the power of the sea and the magic of the moon, which makes them effective at balancing emotions, diminishing stress and soothing hurt, while physically they're said to increase fertility, ease childbirth, boost immunity and relieve digestive disorders. Traditionally they have been used by divers as a talisman to prevent shark attacks, and by women as a symbol of beauty, refinement and grace. Like a mermaid's enchanted looking glass, pearls act as a mirror through which people can see their true self, as well as how they are perceived by others, and can improve confidence and self-worth. They symbolise purity of heart, and help connect people to the simple truths of their life. The process of a pearl, beginning as a grain of sand and developing, over time, into something precious and of great value, also symbolises the immense potential that each of us holds deep within, which can be nurtured and developed into whatever we want to become.

Known as the stone of sincerity, the pearl is one of the birthstones for June, as well as the gemstone of thirtieth wedding anniversaries, and encapsulates love, purity and joy. As with all sea treasures, be sure to choose ethically grown and harvested pearls. The freshwater cultured pearls used in the jewellery sold on the Hunger Site for instance are produced in pearl farms from large clams that live up to seven years. Pearl sacs are harvested every two years without killing the clams.

Mother of pearl This beautiful iridescent shell lining emits the gentle healing power of the ocean, and is calming, soothing and relaxing. Linked to the moon and the sea, mother of pearl boosts intuition and psychic powers, calms fears, and brings clarity to a situation, shifting confusion and creating harmony. It relieves stress, nurtures and heals the soul, and helps people express themselves, their love and their deepest emotions. It attunes people to the energy of the divine feminine, and creates a feeling of being nurtured, mothered and supported emotionally. Mother of pearl, sourced from the shells of pearl oysters, freshwater pearl mussels and abalone, reflects light like a rainbow, and brings colour and energy to your life.

Physically it is part of the creation of pearls, which links it to sweetness and innocence, and it purifies the environment, transmutes lower energies into a more loving vibration and protects against negativity. It's thought to improve high blood pressure, dizziness, vision and wound healing, and has been crushed up and used in cosmetics to soften the skin, as well as in old healing remedies. One of the treasures of the sea, mother of pearl has been used as a talisman to bring wealth and prosperity, and in the creation of jewellery, craft and religious icons for a long time.

Ocean jasper This recently discovered, strangely beautiful crystal is found at just one remote place on the Madagascar coast, and can only be mined – by hand – at low tide, for at other times it hides away beneath the swirling ocean waters. Its appearance is a swirl of different colours, blues and greens with splashes of pink, red, black, white and gold, which can appear in tiny bubbles, larger orbs, wavy lines and other wild patterns. It is aligned with the element of water physically, being located on the edge of the ocean, as well as emotionally, being a powerful agent of change and release.

Ocean jasper helps bring unresolved, long-buried emotions to the surface, where they can be examined in the warm light of day and revealed as less important than you'd believed. It then helps wash away the impact of these emotions, and nurtures you into a gentle healing space, much like a calm sea after a storm. Ocean jasper is a stone of joy, helping release negativity and stress, and radiates positive energy, promoting relaxation, positive self-image and self-expression, and a focus on the positive aspects of your life. It encourages the release of limiting thought patterns and stuck emotions that can manifest as physical symptoms, and is used to balance the glandular, endocrine and thyroid systems, soothe digestive issues and regenerate good health.

Larimar This pale milky crystal displays patterns of blue, blue-green and white that resemble the sea, and invokes a feeling of peace and tranquillity akin to the ocean on a calm day. Formed in basaltic lava, it was discovered in the 1970s, and is found only on the beaches of the Caribbean's Dominican Republic, making it a rare and special gem. The name comes from a combination of Larissa and mar, given to the stone by the man who found it, who named it after his daughter and the Spanish word for sea. Larimar must be mined by hand, as heavy machinery or explosives would destroy it, and the best quality is found more than thirty metres below the earth's surface, making it time consuming (and thus extra precious) to gather, especially given that during the lengthy hurricane season the mine is often closed due to flooding.

Also known as the dolphin stone and the Atlantis stone, larimar is calming and cooling, soothing emotions and helping to release stress and spark clarity. It is associated with the fifth chakra, in the throat area of the body, and is thus linked emotionally to communication, creativity and the power and ability to speak your truth, and physically to throat issues and the immune system. It can help soothe hurt, fear, depression and pain, encourages self-expression, self-acceptance and simplicity, and boosts creativity and passion for your work. It creates harmony and lifts the spirits, and can help you deal with transformation and change. It also supports emotional and physical healing. Through its appearance it is associated with calm skies, a peaceful ocean and the beauty of the earth as seen from space.

Coral This ocean gem is considered by many to be the jewellery of mermaids, and its beautiful, vivid colours have also made it popular with humans, from the Ancient Egyptians to the society ladies of Victorian England. Red-pink coral is the gemstone of thirty-fifth wedding anniversaries and the birthstone of October, while black coral is the state gemstone of Hawaii. Sailors used it as a talisman against bad weather and to ward off hurricanes while at sea, and it was worn by travellers to aid in the safe crossing of rivers and oceans, and for protection from storms (as well as, apparently, curing madness!). Tibetan lamas use coral rosaries, it is one of the seven treasures in Buddhist scriptures, and it was given as a gift to expectant mothers and newborn babies as an amulet of protection. Coral helps restore harmony and calm emotional upsets, increase wisdom and clarity of thought, and bring luck and protection to the home. It increases feelings of peace and stimulates psychic abilities and intuition.

Physically it has been used to treat lung and digestive disorders, arthritis, depression, lethargy, spine, bone and tissue regeneration, to boost blood circulation and heart health and soothe teething in children, and some healers consider it the feminine correspondent to carnelian. Coral comes in many colours – black is associated with male fertility, creativity and physical protection, and guards against misfortune;

pink with female fertility, compassion and love; red and orange with physical healing and vitality; white with nerve health and emotional and psychic development; blue with inner tranquillity; and rare gold coral with health, wellbeing and emotional and physical balance.

Coral is created by tiny marine creatures known as polyps, which have a mouth and tentacles, and eat tiny fish, plankton and algaes. They secrete calcium carbonate, which forms a hard skeleton around them – over time, the tiny skeletons of polyp communities bond together and develop into coral reefs. Most require sunshine to grow, so they're common in shallow tropical waters such as those in Hawaii, Australia and the Mediterranean, although there's also a kind that develops in the colder, deeper waters off Scotland and Alaska.

Coral reefs are rich ecosystems, but today they are threatened by climate change, overfishing, human damage, invasive species and disease, and the harvesting and use of coral is now heavily regulated in many countries to protect this natural resource. Coral combines the energy of the sea from where it comes, and its powers of emotional balancing and calm, with the vitality of the sun that helps it to grow.

Kyanite The blue-green sea colours of this crystal are a reminder of our connection to the whales, dolphins and other creatures of the oceans. It comes in many shades of blue and green, from dark blue through paler blue, turquoise and even a rare lime green. It works holistically, balancing, cleansing and harmonising the energetic field and aligning the chakras. The greener crystals connect especially to the heart chakra and love, from self-love and romantic love to love of the planet, and have a beautiful soft energy, aligned, some say, to the distant dreamy lands of Lemuria, while the bluer stones focus on the throat chakra and communication on all levels, including with your higher self, and give strength and the courage to speak your truth.

It's a great meditation stone, aiding stillness and inspiring tranquillity and inner peace, and a powerful conduit that is attuned to the energies of the ocean and the earth – according to legend, early travellers used it as a compass on land and sea – and it helps foster a strong link to nature. Kyanite is a high vibrational stone, and doesn't need to be cleansed or charged, as it is all contained within itself, a quality that can also help people to become more independent and self-assured, much like a mermaid.

Paua This beautiful shell is from a species of abalone that is only found in the sea around New Zealand – I have a bracelet that was a gift from a friend who lives there. It is similar to mother of pearl but far more colourful, a riot of vibrant iridescent greens and blues, with swirls of pinks, purples, black and even golds and reds running through. Each piece is unique, with different shades and patterns, and the colours change depending on the angle, a result of light being refracted within the crystal layers of its surface.

Traditionally paua was used by Maori peoples to illuminate the eyes of their carvings and as part of ritual tools and spiritual artwork, and it remains a distinctive part of New Zealand jewellery making, sculpture and art today. Spiritually paua is used to increase personal strength and support the wearer through challenges and karmic issues. Physically it helps heal stress by balancing and calming body chemicals and hormones. It is also used as a protective shield and to become less noticeable to others when walking through areas that don't feel safe and in situations where you want to become invisible.

After a dip in stocks from over-harvesting, the paua industry is now managed with a focus on sustainability, with a quota management system and regulations controlling the size of the abalone taken.

Sea glass Many people who live by the ocean are starting to make jewellery from sea glass, which they describe as sea-created gems with no negative impact on the planet, as mining for crystals and harvesting corals can sometimes have. It's a beautiful way to turn trash into treasure – a most mermaidenly thing to do – and transform human garbage into something precious, while cleaning up beaches at the same time. Greenish glass that has been worn smooth by the ocean waves holds the energy of the sea in its construction and colour vibration, and many consider these smooth, frosted and translucent gem-coloured pieces as semiprecious stones.

Searching the shoreline for sea glass is a blend of beachcombing, art and recycling, and it's said that if diamonds are nature's creation improved by man, sea glass is the opposite – man's creation improved by nature. However it's a lengthy process – it takes two decades of weathering for a shard of glass to become a smooth stone. Sea glass pieces could come from an old-fashioned grey-green frosted Coca-Cola bottle, an amber coloured beer bottle, various coloured wine bottles or even an old blue apothecary vial.

Sharne's Crystal Sea Magic

Sharne Michelle is the creator of the Magical Sea Witch, which produces handmade products from the ocean and the earth, including crystal cleansers, smudge sprays, bath salts and magical money bags, as well as sourcing common and unusual crystals. She is a meditation teacher and aromatherapist, and does chakra alignments using crystals and essential oils. She lives by the ocean on the north coast of New South Wales, Australia, gaining strength and peace from the sea. Visit Sharne at www.MagicalSeaWitch.com.

In my early twenties I was diagnosed with chronic fatigue, and while searching for relief I stumbled upon aromatherapy and crystals, and fell in love with the concept of healing with plants and minerals from mother earth. This led to a job with an esoteric store that sold essential oils, crystals and books, and a journey into all things magical. I studied different healing methods and therapies as well as ancient traditions and rituals from around the world, which eventually led me to creating my own healing products and sourcing beautiful, powerful crystals for people.

My first crystal was a piece of jasper that an old opal miner gave me when I was in Coober Pedy in South Australia on a family holiday. I still have it today. I fell in love with the colours and patterns, and was amazed at what mother nature could make.

Now, having worked with crystals for so many years on myself, in the shop and with clients, I've seen how they heal, transform, energise and bring people an amazing sense of peace and magic on their individual journey.

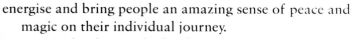

In the shop we had a cleanser so customers could take their new crystal home all clean and energetically sparkling, after having been handled so often in the store. It was also handy because, living in the city, putting crystals out on a full moon to cleanse could be a bit erratic energetically, on top of all the pollution. Over the last ten years I've been experimenting with my own recipe, adding different herbs and essential

oils as my study and knowledge grew. I use crystals in chakra alignments, so I need to cleanse them quickly, thoroughly – and gently – between clients, and the Magical Sea Witch Crystal Cleanser is a wonderful way to do that. It is also blessed during a ritual under a full moon to further enhance its power.

The Smudge Spray came from combining my knowledge of ancient rituals and aromatherapy to help people cleanse spaces where a naked flame or smoke is not possible, like shops, offices and festivals, while travelling and around small children and asthmatics. It's a great alternative to traditional smoking smudge sticks, and you can instantly create a sacred space, change the energy of a room and lift and elevate positive vibrations.

I live near the ocean now, and couldn't bear to be away from it, although I spent the first half of my life terrified by the sea. Seven years ago I went to Hawaii and fell in love with the ocean, her creatures and her power to heal and energise me. It was one of the biggest turning points in my life, and several trips back have just deepened my love. When I came home the first time I knew I'd found a sense of peace I'd never felt before. I went back again, searching for it, but I finally realised that I had to move away from the city and be near the ocean, and lead a more relaxed and magical life every day, to carry that aloha spirit with me wherever I am.

I'm so much more relaxed, centred and grounded now, living by the sea, and I'm more in tune with the daily ebb and flow of mother nature and her cycles. The beach is my own personal grounding, cleansing and healing space, and is a constant source of inspiration and ideas. I can't imagine not being near it now! I love the smell of the ocean – it's like breathing in pure joy. It has an awesome capacity to help us heal and be creative, and we need to honour and respect it, and have gratitude for the blessings the sea brings us.

The Magic of Water

"Throughout the whole of religious tradition, rivers have been gods.
Water has been the soul. And water is the ultimate life. Maybe
that's what we brought out of the African deserts – the notion
that water is life. I think that's a staple, that spring sources and
flowing water are the spirit, are life. The divine influx."
Ted Hughes, British writer and poet laureate

The Nurturing Element

In nature and in western magic and philosophy, earth, air, fire and
water are considered the four elements from which all things are
made, and represent the forces of nature. In the seventh century
BCE, some of the greatest minds of the Classical world wrestled
with the question of what exactly the world and its inhabitants
were made from. First Thales, regarded as one of the Seven Sages
of Greece and the Father of Science, declared that the fundamental
building block of the universe was water.

Later his star pupil Anaximander challenged his view, declaring it
was instead apeiron, a kind of invisible plasma that could morph
into all materials. In turn his successor, sixth century BCE philosopher
Anaximenes, who has a crater on the moon named in his honour,
decided that air was the fundamental element. Later Greek
philosopher Heraclitus, who coined the phrase "nothing endures but
change," refined the idea further, declaring that fire – as the most
changeable element – was the fundamental material of the universe.
Then, as thinking and knowledge continued to progress, Xenophanes
decided that it was earth that was the building block of the universe.

It wasn't until the fifth century BCE that all the singular elemental theories were synthesised into a coherent whole, when philosopher Empedocles argued that all four elements played an equal role, and that earth, air, fire and water – either individually or in combination – make up all matter, and that all matter is comprised of these four "roots". His theory of the four Classical elements was supported by those who followed him, including famed Greek mathematician Plato, who drew on these four elements in his work.

Today ninety-two natural elements are recognised (remember that huge periodic table in chemistry class?), along with a further twenty-six that have been developed in a lab, but Empedocles's original identification of the four basic elements is considered to have foreshadowed recent developments in atomic theory.

These four elements are common to many different cultures, including Hindu, Babylonian and Islamic, who all used earth, air, fire and water to describe physical matter. Fourth century BCE Greek physician Hippocrates, considered the father of Western medicine, used them in describing the make-up and workings of the human body, and early Buddhist writings also drew on these four elements, although they emphasised their sensory aspects rather than the material – earth characterised solidity; water, fluidity; fire, temperature; and air, mobility.

They also correspond to the four scientific forms of matter: earth for solids, water for liquids, air for gases and fire for plasma. (Chinese philosophy differs however, describing the world as being made up of five elements – fire, earth, water, metal and wood.)

Earth, air, fire and water are forces of the physical world, material qualities that also represent emotions, astrological qualities, tarot correspondences and directions. Today magical practitioners incorporate these elements into their rituals in a literal as well as a metaphoric way.

A fifth element, quintessence, from which our word quintessential comes, is also recognised by many traditions. To the Ancient Greeks this fifth element was ether, the pure essence where the gods lived, as opposed to the more physical properties of the four earthly elements. To Hindus it was similar – a contrasting energy of non-matter compared to the physicality of the other four.

In earth-based spiritualities such as paganism, shamanism and druidry, this fifth element is spirit, the element of promise and potential, transcendence and transformation, attributed by some to the god and/or goddess, or the mystical aspect of spiritual belief, and by others to the self within the physical world of the four elements, incorporating will, intent and action.

A pentagram, a five-pointed star, represents the combination of the five elements, while a pentacle – a pentagram enclosed in a circle – indicates that spirit, earth, air, water and fire are all connected, and symbolises the direct and indirect relation of one element to the other. Today it's also a unifying symbol of the pagan community. In many traditions the lower left hand point of the star represents the element of earth, the lower right represents fire, the upper left represents air, the upper right represents water, and the topmost point represents the spirit.

"Physical properties are assigned to the elements: earth is solidity; water cohesion; fire temperature; air motion; space the spatial dimension that accommodates the other four active elements. In addition, the elements are correlated to different emotions, temperaments, directions, colours, tastes, body types, illnesses, thinking styles and character. From the five elements arise the five senses and the five fields of sensual experience; the five negative emotions and the five wisdoms; and the five extensions of the body. They are the five primary pranas or vital energies. They are the constituents of every physical, sensual, mental and spiritual phenomenon."

Tenzin Wangyal Rinpoche, Tibetan teacher

Earth symbolises security, stability, the family and your home. It's about nurturing and being nurtured, the fertility of the land, your body and your dreams, and it helps you create a foundation of safety from which to grow. Embodying practicality, perseverance and steady progress, earth is also associated with grounding and centering, absorbing excess energy so you remain balanced and at peace, and anchoring you in your body and reconnecting you to the physical realm and to the planet.

In the northern hemisphere it is associated with north, while in the south it corresponds to south. Colour correspondences include green and brown, and it's linked by many to the season of autumn. In astrology, the earth signs are Taurus, Virgo and Capricorn, and people born under these signs are believed to be hard working, down to earth, practical, responsible and determined. In tarot, earth is associated with the suit of pentacles (also known as coins or discs), the realm of the home, and health, wealth, work and physicality.

Air symbolises the intellect, communication, knowledge, clarity and truth. It helps you think more clearly, inspires you to dream up new ideas, and fills you with a sense of freedom and joy. Air also represents new beginnings and fresh starts, and reminds you that every day the world is born anew, and that you can be too. It's about moving forward, letting go of regrets and starting again, free of preconceptions and limitations.

Air is often associated with the direction of east, as that is where the sun rises and the new day, and new energy, begins, but this can be transferred if, depending on your location, you have put water in the east. Colour correspondences include yellow and white, and it's linked by many to the season of spring. In astrology, the air signs are Gemini, Libra and Aquarius, and people born under these signs are believed to have strong communication skills, be quick thinking, objective, discerning, full of ideas (if not follow-through) and people-focused. In tarot, air is associated with the suit of swords (also called blades or athames), the realm of the mind, and thoughts, words, challenges and communication.

Fire represents passion, inspiration, decisiveness and intention. It ignites your creativity, sparks your enthusiasm for new projects, and inflames you with the courage to take chances and risk everything to create the life you want. Fire is also associated with purification, for it can burn away bad habits, regret, fear and anger. This element holds the power of transformation within it – if you have the courage to step into its flames and let it consume you.

In the northern hemisphere fire is associated with the south, while in the southern hemisphere it corresponds to the north, as that is where the heat of the equator is. Colour correspondences include red, orange and gold, and it's linked by many to the season of summer. In astrology, the fire signs are Aries, Leo and Sagittarius, and people born under these signs are believed to be action oriented, outgoing, confident, passionate and honest. In tarot, fire is associated with the suit of wands (also called rods or staves), the realm of spirit, and creativity, ambition, action and passion.

▽   **Water** is linked to the emotions, intuition, psychic abilities, dreams and the subconscious. It helps you become attuned to your inner truths and be at peace with your inner feelings, and its gentle fluidity has a nurturing, soothing quality. Water is also associated with cleansing and letting go. It washes away emotional hurts, dissolves pain and anger, soothes your heart and soul, and leaves you feeling cleansed physically, emotionally and spiritually.

Water is often associated with the direction of west, as that is where the sun sets over the ocean, but if you live near a body of water that lies in a different direction, this can be swapped. Colour correspondences include blue and silver, and it's linked by many to the season of winter. In astrology, the water signs are Cancer, Scorpio and Pisces, and people born under these signs are believed to be intuitive, emotional, sensitive, nurturing and sometimes impractical. In tarot, water is associated with the suit of cups (also called chalices or goblets), the realm of the heart, and love, relationships, emotion and empathy.

✡   **Ether or spirit** is a unifying force linked to intent and will, to unification and transformation, and to the sense of potentiality and promise. It is present in the melding of masculine and feminine energies within you and in the merging of the conscious and the unconscious, the physical and the spiritual, the god and the goddess, and the inner and outer worlds. Connecting with this element creates balance and completion within so you can blend your creative, intuitive energy with your powers of logic and reason, and allows you to be all that you can be and achieve everything you dream of. It's also known as akasha, the spiritual power of the universe, and is often associated with the heavens or with deities, but it has its own personal meaning to everyone.

The Healing Power of Water

While no element is more important than another, water is a beautiful one to work with. It can be soothing and nurturing, or fierce and cleansing. Water is linked to harmony, transparency, integration and empathy. It has the power to calm you, bless you and heal you, and it encourages you to trust your own knowing, to merge the wisdom of your heart, soul and mind, and to acknowledge and appreciate your emotions.

The element of water, both physically and spiritually, is associated with cleansing and letting go. Wounds are cleaned with it, sins are absolved by it, and heartache is released through the water of your tears. This element washes away emotional hurts, dissolves pain and anger, soothes your heart and soul, and leaves you feeling cleansed physically, emotionally and spiritually.

Water is present in the lakes, streams and oceans of the planet, in the cooling rains after the heat of summer, in the liquids that nourish and replenish all of life, and in every cell of your body. It makes up the essence of what you are, and it has as many moods as you do – it is a calm sea, a swiftly flowing river, a drop of dew on a flower petal, a tear of laughter or of pain. It shifts and changes as needed, ebbing and flowing like the tides, reflecting the continuing cycles of your life and the changing nature of your emotions.

As the element linked to the emotions, water also encourages you to tune in to what you're feeling and express it, rather than repressing or ignoring the things that matter most to you. As a result, it can be part of powerful rituals to reveal what is most important, and wash away the things you can release.

Water has been essential to all cultures, both physically and spiritually. Early civilisations were based near a river or lake for survival as well as to be part of their magical rituals and observances. To the Egyptians the mighty Nile River was the source of their spiritual sustenance. It was considered the pathway to the afterlife and the boundary between the Land of the Living and the Land of the Dead. It was also their physical life source. The flooding along the banks created the only fertile land in the desert country, while the river provided water, fish and a trade route. They believed the Nile was ruled by Hapy, the god of fertility, and they made elaborate offerings to him to ensure its free flow and the vital annual floods.

You can connect with this element at any water source. Sit on the bank of a river or stream, or on the seashore, and focus on the sounds of the rhythmic flow, lapping or gurgling as it moves. Still your mind, then let it follow the sounds of the water. If you're worried about anything, find a shell, a leaf or a pebble, hold it in your hand and send your thoughts into it. Then throw it in the river or the ocean and watch it float away, taking your troubles with it.

You can also stand outside in the rain, arms outstretched to the sky and face gazing upwards, and let the water wash away any fears, regrets, sadness or painful memories of the past. There's something incredibly liberating about being out in the wildness of a storm and letting the elements wash away all that you want to let go of, but you could also dive into the ocean or a river or soak in a warm scented bath to feel yourself symbolically cleansed and reborn.

Water can help wash away what is no longer necessary and create a fertile base from which to move forward. Get in touch with the things you want to change in your life, whether it's finding a new job, meeting someone, moving house or transforming your spiritual life. You can't achieve your goals until you're certain of what they are. Call on a water goddess, nymph or mermaid to help you, or simply listen to your inner voice and pay attention to the feelings you've long buried to become aware of what you most want.

Scrying, a method of seeing the future by staring at the surface of a body of water and taking note of the images and symbols on it, is also a powerful method of divination and looking within. The priestesses of old gazed into the sacred waters of their healing wells, but it can also be done using a bowl of water, a lake, a crystal ball (as the gypsies so famously do), a piece of black obsidian, a pool of ink or a mirror, which is the method famed seer Nostradamus employed.

To try it, sit by a lake or fill a bowl with water, adding ink if you prefer, light a candle or sit outside under the moonlight, and stare into the water's surface. Clear your mind and focus solely on the water. Take note of any images you see, either there or in your mind's eye, and write them all down so you can analyse and start to interpret them. Scrying requires lots of practise and patience, but can bring intriguing results and inner awareness and growth.

To tap in to the energy of water, you can simply surround yourself with the colour blue, in your clothing, walls or furnishings, the paintings or artworks in your home, or in your garden – plant blue-toned flowers such as bluebells, cornflowers, hyacinths, irises, agapanthus, borage, forget-me-nots, violas, statice, delphinium, bellflowers, gentiana and aristae, or have a bunch of them in a vase.

Sit by a calm lake and stare into its surface, watch a river bubbling over stones, immerse yourself in the ocean or have a long, relaxing bath. Or simply drink a glass of this replenishing, nourishing liquid, and start to feel its power swirling deep within you.

A Meditation to Connect with Water

For a watery meditation session, sit comfortably and start to breathe slowly and calmly. You might like to keep a pen and paper handy to write down anything that comes up for you. And don't be alarmed if you cry, as this is a great way to release old emotional blocks. Often you won't even need to record anything, as this process will naturally release things that are stuck without you needing to be conscious of what to let go of.

Visualise yourself immersed in water of some kind – soaking in a warm scented bath, plunging into the glittering green ocean, swimming across a stream, standing under a misty waterfall, dancing outside in a wild storm or a gentle sun shower. Feel the water on your skin. Sense it soaking into your body, embracing and cleansing your whole being with its nurturing energy.

As you relax further, feel the water washing away any pain, regret, doubt or fear. The lesson of water is of letting go, so relinquish anything that's holding you back from being happy, finding love, or becoming all that you can be. Imagine any negativity being washed away by the water, then see yourself emerging from it refreshed and renewed, shimmering with a new sense of lightness and freedom.

Now go deeper. Picture yourself sitting beside a sacred well, gazing into its surface. Look within its hidden depths, and feel yourself falling gently into your own subconscious. Water symbolises the realms of the imagination, of dreaming, divination and self-discovery, so dive in to your own inner world and connect to your intuition and inner self. You have all the answers inside you, so take notice of the sensations of your body, sense the quiet flickers of intuition you receive, and listen to the inner voice that's trying to communicate with you. If you see images, meditate on them for a moment and consider their meaning for you. If not, simply focus on the lulling sound of the water and its harmonious qualities as it swirls and flows in your mind's eye.

The element of water is about love, trust and compassion, so allow it to provide a safe, nurturing space for you to open up and reveal the secret dreams and desires of your own heart. Take this time to listen to your inner knowing, and start paying attention to the feelings you've long buried.

Sacred Water

Consecrated water is used in many spiritual paths, for many different purposes. It is regular water with salt added to it, and a blessing or invocation said above it. For magical practitioners such water is often used to consecrate the ritual circle and all the tools within it, and to bless those taking part in the ceremony.

In many religions, holy water is water that has been consecrated by a priest or bishop, and it symbolises the water of life. It is used primarily in baptisms, as well as for spiritual cleansing and to bless people, places and objects. Some faiths, such as Catholicism, also use it as a form of protection, to ward off evil and exorcise spirits.

Baptisms, the rituals that signify a person's admission to Christianity, were traditionally conducted through the total immersion of a person in a body of living water, such as a river, lake or ocean. Emersion, the process of emerging from the water after being submerged, was believed to replicate the resurrection of Jesus, and symbolise the death of the old person and the rebirth of the new (hence the term "born again"). While there are some denominations that still carry out adult baptisms in this way, with the individual being forced under the water to signify purification from the sins of the past, today it is more common for it to be carried out with holy water simply sprinkled (aspersion) or poured (affusion) on the head, and it is common for babies to be baptised soon after birth.

This progression from full body immersion in a river to a sprinkling of holy water on the head was in part for convenience – the early church fathers wanted people to be baptised no matter what, and creating holy water helped them in their mission of converting people who lived far from a river or ocean.

The early Christian treatise *The Didache* outlined how a baptism should be performed. "Baptise into the name of the Father, and of the Son, and of the Holy Spirit, in living water. But if you have no living water, baptise into other water [such as a font or tub]; and if you cannot do so in cold water, do so in warm. But if you have neither, pour out water three times upon the head into the name of Father and Son and Holy Spirit."

Some faiths believe that springs, such as the one at Lourdes in France and the one at the monastery of Pochaev Lavra in the Ukraine, provide holy water, although others dispute this, claiming that it is not holy water in the traditional sense as it has not been sanctified by a priest or bishop. Others feel that the presence of the Virgin Mary or Jesus in a vision at the spring is sanctity enough.

Many churches have a font containing holy water at their entrance, in which churchgoers dip their fingers and make the sign of the cross as a reminder of the baptism that cleansed them of sin. In some traditions, holy water cannot be poured down the sink like ordinary water, but must be poured directly into the earth via a separate sink. Blessed salt, sanctified by priests, is sometimes added to holy water, particularly in the Roman Rite of the Catholic Church.

Holy water is also used by some priests to sprinkle, and thus cleanse, the congregation. The liturgy may begin with the rite of blessing and the sprinkling of holy water upon the congregation, which is known as aspersion. A priest uses an aspergillum, such as a brush, branch, a handle with a perforated ball on the end or in some cases a sprig of herbs, to sprinkle the holy water, which is contained in the aspersorium, or holy water container. A priest will also bless objects such as candles and the Palm Sunday palms in this manner.

Aspergillums are also used by some pagans to cleanse their ritual area before a Sabbat ceremony or spellworking, although they use their own blessed water, such as moon charged, crystal infused, fresh spring, river or ocean water.

Full Moon Water

The moon, which is linked to the subconscious, to dreams, desires and secret wishes, and to the dark and beautiful power of the night, is also associated with water. It can help connect you to your shadow self, to the hidden aspects of your psyche, and to the mystical realms of divination and the inner worlds. It is also symbolic of the feminine energy that runs through the universe and within every person, which is calm, receptive, centred, nurturing and spiritual, with a quiet yet intense power.

Charging water with the energy of the moon is a simple way to integrate the two into your life, and your body. Simply leave a glass of water outside under the full moon then drink it the next morning, feeling yourself energised and re-attuned to the soul of nature. You can also leave a bowl or bottle of water out overnight to absorb the moonbeams, and use it in rituals throughout the coming month.

The full moon rises at sunset and sets at sunrise, so this is the most potent night to work with its energies as it will be visible in the sky at this time. The dark and new moons occur during the day, rising at sunrise and setting at sunset, so they aren't in the sky at night, and are barely seen against the light of the sun in the day, although their energies can still be felt. You can also use this moon water in spells and ceremonies, to consecrate ritual tools and purify sacred space, or to water your magical garden.

Crystal Charged Water

Crystals have a strong vibration, which can be transferred into water to drink, added to bathwater for ritual, used to energetically clear a room or purify objects, or as part of a ceremony for healing.

To make your brew, place your chosen crystal in a glass bowl filled with spring water. If the crystal is easily crumbled or reduced to powder, such as selenite or ulexite, place it in a small sealed glass jar or bottle and place that in the water, so it doesn't physically touch the water but its vibrations can still be transferred. You can leave the bowl outside during the day, to receive twelve hours of sunlight, or overnight in the moonlight – your choice of crystal will determine this, as some, like celestite and turquoise, can fade in sunlight – then bottle your water. You can also leave the water covered in a cupboard if you prefer, rather than outside.

Once you're happy that it's ready, pour your brew into small dose bottles – some people like to add one quarter brandy or vodka to three quarters crystal water to preserve it, but this is not essential.

To consume the crystalline energies, add seven drops of your crystal essence to a glass of water morning and night. Or add some to your water bottle and sip it throughout the day, squeeze a few drops under your tongue before meditation, add it to baths to soak up the energy that way, put it in a spray bottle to charge a room with new energy, or use it to clean and charge ritual tools.

Before making your crystal water, and periodically with your other crystals, cleanse the gem physically and etherically. Rinse it under running water to wash away dust and the top layer of stuck energy, then place it in a glass bowl and cover with water. Depending on the type of crystal, you may like to add a tablespoon of sea salt to the water to dispel negative energy, however soft stones such as amber, opal, malachite, jade, freshwater pearls and chrysocolla can be damaged by salt, so don't add it if you're unsure. Leave the bowl outside for a few hours to absorb the energy of the sun and the moon, or longer if you prefer. Then remove the crystal and rinse it under running water to wash away any last energies and the salt.

You can also cleanse crystals by smudging, passing them through the smoke as you burn purifying herbs such as sweetgrass, sage or lavender, or you can leave them in the sunlight for a few hours (as long as they aren't likely to fade), wash them in the ocean or a running river, or infuse them with reiki or reconnective healing energy. (For a list of ocean crystals to work with, see page 200.)

Consecrated Water

There are many other ways to create your own special sacred water, and it can be used in any way you like. Some magical practitioners like to add rose water to their brew, or you can infuse it with a few drops of essential oil, or a sprig of your favourite herb. Some gather the water from a clear running stream or lake, others boil water from the tap and add a dash of salt, or buy spring water from the supermarket. If you can bring fresh seawater back from the beach there's no need to add any salt to preserve it or add the quality of protection to it, and if you have some water from a sacred well, such as Glastonbury's Chalice Well, you can add a few drops to a bottle of normal water to increase its vibration.

Once the water is ready, you can leave it out in the sun or the moonlight, or both, to be charged. You can whisper spells over it, infuse it with white light or reiki, and/or invite in the god and goddess and the energy of the four directions and the four elements to purify your water and fill it with vitality and positivity.

Keep it in a sealed jar in a cool, dark place, and pour any that's left at the end of the month into your garden and make a new batch – you may like to make this part of your regular full or new moon ritual.

Water For Health

"Water symbolises the whole of potentiality;
it is fons et origo, the source of all possible existence."
Mircea Eliade, Romanian philosopher, historian and professor

Water really is the source of life. Our bodies are between sixty and seventy per cent water, and while we can go without food for at least three weeks, more than a few days without water and the body shuts down. Adequate water intake is vital to health and wellbeing – it carries nutrients and oxygen to the cells through the blood, controls the many essential bodily processes, flushes toxins from the organs, aids chemical reactions in the digestive and metabolic systems, lubricates the joints and helps cool the body through perspiration.

"Water is the main means of transport not only for all the materials that are required by the cells, but also for all the cells' waste substances," says Dr Petra Bracht, diet and health expert.

"If the transport network isn't functioning properly because of lack of water, waste isn't taken away but left behind. In medical terminology, this is a 'deposit'. Physicians talk, for example, about the uric acid crystals that trigger a gout attack, and a person is described as 'calcified' when part of their brain has become a salt deposit. Deposits may also collect in the blood vessels over a period of time, until one day they trigger a heart attack, stroke or lung embolism."

A recent study found that even dehydration of as little as one to two per cent of your body weight can reduce your brain's ability to perform at its peak and your body's ability to run at optimum efficiency. A lack of water can lead to headaches, irritation, depression, lack of focus, poor muscle tone, digestive complications, muscle soreness, heartburn, stomach ache, excess body fat and even water retention. According to Kidney Health Australia, symptoms of dehydration include headaches, lethargy, mood changes and slow responses, dry nasal passages, dry or cracked lips, dark-coloured urine, weakness, tiredness, confusion and hallucinations.

And, they explain, if you don't have enough fluid to keep your body hydrated, eventually urination will stop and your kidneys will fail.

The body won't be able to remove toxic waste products, which in extreme cases may result in death.

At birth we are around seventy-eight per cent water, but we slowly dehydrate from there. According to Dr Jeffrey Utz, neuroscientist and paediatrician at America's Allegheny University, our body drops to just sixty-five per cent water within our first year. Adult men are around sixty per cent water and women around fifty-five – some obviously more and some, worryingly, less. The brain and lean muscle tissue is composed of around seventy-five per cent water, the lungs and blood almost ninety per cent, while bone contains twenty-two per cent and body fat ten, so replenishing our water stores is crucial to every bodily process.

Australia's National Health & Medical Research Council recommends a fluid intake of three and a half litres a day for men, with at least two and a half of this coming from liquids – water mostly, but juices, low-fat milk and tea can contribute part of it. The rest can come from food, which has some water content. Fresh fruit and vegies are particularly good, as they have a very high water content (watermelon is around ninety per cent water), and also contain easily absorbable vitamins, minerals and trace elements. For women they recommend almost three litres of water a day, with just over two litres of that coming from water or other fluids, and the rest from food.

America's Mayo Clinic, and most doctors and health professionals, also recommend that we drink around two litres of water a day to replenish what is lost through breathing, sweating, exercise and elimination. The American Institute of Medicine advises that men should drink three litres a day and women two and a half, and a recent dietary report by the US National Research Council recommended almost four litres of water for men and three litres for women. Some naturopaths suggest we drink far more, and many models and actors swear that their huge water intake is the reason they look so good and remain so healthy.

Supermodel Elle Macpherson claims her beauty secret is sunscreen and drinking three litres of water a day. "I have six 500ml bottles that I refill every day. I put them on the kitchen table or my desk and count them down towards the end of the day. It's a good trick, because every time I walk past I can pick up a bottle and drink it as I walk around. I make sure they are gone by the time I go to bed," she says.

"Individual cells of the body are like mini oceans,
being composed primarily of water."
Dr Darren R Weissman, US holistic physician

Certain situations will increase the amount of water you require. Some medications dehydrate you, and additional water is also needed after exercise to replenish what is lost – around two glasses for mild exercise of up to an hour, and more if you exercise over a longer period at a high intensity. Hot or humid weather, indoor heating, high altitudes, pregnancy and nursing as well as illnesses involving fever, vomiting or diarrhoea also increase your water requirements, as do high protein and high fibre diets.

Alcohol and caffeinated beverages such as coffee, tea and cola contain water but are diuretics, causing you to eliminate even more of your water stores. Experts suggest you drink an extra glass of water for every alcoholic or caffeinated beverage you consume. Carbonated drinks contain carbon dioxide, which strips oxygen from the body, so they should also be limited for optimal health.

Some doctors also say proper water intake is a key to weight loss. "By not drinking enough water, many people incur excess body fat, poor muscle tone and size, decreased digestive efficiency and organ function, increased toxicity, joint and muscle soreness and water retention," says US obesity specialist Dr Howard Flaks.

Studies have found that the average person does not drink enough water. And using thirst as a guide won't help, because by the time you feel thirsty, you're already dehydrated. Water can't be stored either, so guzzling down a litre in the morning and thinking that's enough for the day won't work. "Such a large amount can't be used properly and will just pass through the body," says Dr Bracht. "It's far more sensible to sip water throughout the day. This then has enough time to trickle through the blood vessels into the spaces between the cells, and from there into the cells themselves."

It *is* possible to drink too much water, in which case the electrolyte content of the blood is diluted, leading to hyponatremia (low sodium levels in the blood), but this is *very* rare. And while those with severe kidney disease and certain cardiac and respiratory conditions may need to limit their fluids on the advice of their doctors, most people fall into the slightly-to-quite-dehydrated category. So drink up! Your body, mind and spirit will thank you for it.

Water's Healing Power

"Springs and old wells are places of special atmosphere, an interface between the elements of earth and water. The water that comes out of the land has been purified and energised by the earth before it reaches the surface. Its power can be used to bring fertility and healing."
Glennie Kindred, British author, healer and artist

Wells and Springs

Natural springs and wells have long been revered, both for their life-giving water and as a source of spiritual power. In magical traditions they are regarded as places where the veil between the worlds is thin and communication with the gods and goddesses and with other dimensions and realities can be made. They're seen as gateways to the spirit world, and throughout time they have been used to divine the future, cast spells, send messages across vast distances and act as a metaphoric mirror to the soul. In Christian religions they are also special places, rededicated to their saints and a place of pilgrimage and reverence.

They have also been attributed with miraculous healing powers, from the Catholic shrine at Lourdes in France to the magical Chalice Well in Glastonbury, England, which has been an important source of healing and spiritual power for thousands of years.

"Sacred wells and springs form a centre of healing and ritual," says British priestess, teacher and author Cassandra Eason. "They are dedicated to the deities or saints of the religion of the dominant culture, but are still the waters from the Mother's womb. They have attracted worship and been sacred to many religions because of the powerful earth energies that converged at the spot, making Otherworldly connections easier."

In the Americas too, water – known as Life Blood – is revered. According to US shaman and author Steven Farmer: "Springs flow from the ground of Mother Earth and represent her giving, cleansing and purification. For thousands of years there have been reports of miracles occurring as a result of bathing in or partaking of the waters from these natural springs."

Several scientific experiments claim to have discovered that the water from sacred wells is lighter than normal water. And while this effect is not yet understood, pilgrims continue to visit such places for healing and spiritual transformation.

A Sacred Well

The town of Glastonbury, in southwest England, is one of the world's most revered spiritual sites. At its centre is the Tor, a mystical hill that is a repository of much earth energy, and nestled at its base is Chalice Well and its beautiful, peaceful gardens. This is where the druids trained and the Priestesses of Avalon did their seeing, gazing into the sacred wellspring to divine the future, and where they drew the waters to concoct vibrationally charged potions for physical and emotional healing. Today it is still renowned for easing pain, curing illness and treating emotional and spiritual malaise, and people flock here to drink from the sacred Red and White Springs, which have been credited with miracle healings, or submerge themselves in the pool to absorb the vibrational essences, as pilgrims seeking cures did centuries ago.

Miracles of healing attributed to these waters have been documented for centuries. In 1582 John Dee, the Elizabethan mathematician and alchemist, claimed to have found the elixir vitae – the elixir of life and immortality – at the Well. And while he did die, it wasn't until he was in his eighties, a grand old age in those days. In 1750 a man dreamed that if he drank the water every Sunday for seven weeks he would be alleviated of his life-long asthma. He followed his vision and was cured, as were many of the thousands of people who flocked to the town in the hope of their own healing.

Throughout the eighteenth century Glastonbury was a famous spa town, and people would travel great distances to take the waters, drinking from the spring as well as submerging themselves in the Pilgrim's Bath in the gardens near the Well. A pamphlet of the day, called *The Virtues and Efficacies of the Waters of Glastonbury*, records dramatic healings from conditions including rheumatism, deafness, "most difficult and troublesome respiration", ulcers, tuberculosis, paralysis and leprosy. There was also a Pump House in Magdalene Street, opposite the Abbey, an earlier version of current spa resorts, where people went to bathe in and drink of the water that was pumped there from the Well.

Today, modern pilgrims have claimed cures for everything from migraines and kidney disorders to chest infections and depression, but many of the healings seem to be on a more subtle but deeper level. The water is full of iron and other minerals, but that's not the only thing that causes the healings. Instead there is a vibratory force that is released and activated when the spring water comes to the surface from deep within the earth and interacts with the elements of air and light above. This water is also infused with the energy of the leylines that run through the gardens.

Chalice Well is fed by the Red Spring that pours forth from under Chalice Hill, and the water is a constant 11°C (51.8°F). It has a red tint and a metallic taste due to its high iron content, caused by ferrous oxides oxygenating as the water reaches the surface. Nearby is the White Spring, which is fed from a source deep within the Tor. Unlike the iron-rich water of the chalybeate Red Spring, this water is calciferous, with a high calcium carbonate content.

The Red Spring is primarily for physical healing while the White Spring imparts a spiritual quality, so a mix of the two is recommended to create physical and emotional wellbeing. Only a small amount is required – a few drops of each in tap water imparts benefits, and too much can be a little unsettling on the tummy. The two springs also represent the alchemical melding of male and female energies to create wisdom and life force, with the White Spring representing the masculine and the Red or Blood Spring representing the feminine.

Prehistoric tribes drank from the Red Spring at least five

thousand years ago, and the Well has been in constant use since long before the time of Christ. It pumps out more than a hundred thousand litres a day, and has never failed or run dry, even when the country was in drought – there have been times when Chalice Well was the town's only water source.

In addition to drinking from the Well, people use the waters of the Red and White Springs in homeopathic essences, both as a physical treatment and in spiritual rituals as a way to connect with the energies of Glastonbury and Avalon. In the Chalice Well Gardens a healing essence is made from the flowers and buds of the holy thorn tree there, which helps you feel loved, discover your purpose and be supported through transformation. There's also an Essence of Avalon range you can take no matter where you live, which distils the energies of the Well and other Glastonbury sacred sites into vibrational medicines to bring healing and a sense of connection to this powerful place.

You can also meditate on pictures of the Chalice Well Gardens, and let their magic change you. No one really understands how, but just seeing photos of this place has healed people of serious illnesses, without them having to be physically present. There are beautiful images on the website, www.chalicewell.org.uk, and you can also buy paintings, cards, books and jewellery inspired by the Well, the pools and the gardens, as well as exploring the links and finding out more about this sacred place.

A Holy Shrine

The grotto and spring at Lourdes, a small town in southwest France, is a place of Catholic pilgrimage and alleged miracle healings. Located in the foothills of the Pyrenees near the Spanish border and the beginning of the Camino pilgrimage, this shrine is famous for the apparitions of the Virgin Mary that were seen in 1858 by fourteen-year-old peasant girl Bernadette Soubirous. Along the Gave de Pau River that flows through the town is an outcrop of rock called Massabielle, which includes a shallow cave (grotto). It was here, over a period of five months, that Bernadette had eighteen visions of a woman she described as a small young lady, assumed by the townsfolk to be Mother Mary – although neither her sister or the friends or townsfolk who accompanied her ever saw anything.

On one occasion at the grotto Bernadette ate grass she'd picked from the ground, rubbed mud over her face and then swallowed some of it – she explained that the lady told her "to drink of the water of the spring, to wash in it and to eat the herb that grew there," as an act of penance. The next day, according to legend, clear water flowed in the grotto where previously there was mud, and it is this water that is believed to have healing powers. Today the spring can be seen within the grotto, lit from below and protected by a glass screen.

On another occasion Bernadette was instructed: "Please go to the priests and tell them that a chapel is to be built here. Let processions come hither." She passed on the message, and within three years the local priest, Abbe Dominique Peyramale, and his bishop, Monsignor Mascarou Laurence, had bought the land surrounding the grotto and begun work on the first of the churches, which is now known as the Crypt.

Today there are twenty-two separate places of worship, holding services in six official languages, which along with the grotto and the spring, and the taps that dispense the holy water, make up the Sanctuary of Our Lady of Lourdes. Between Easter and All Saints there's a full program of devotional activities, including the instructed processions, Mass, Veneration of the Blessed Sacrament and the Sacrament of Reconciliation. More recently the Water Walk, a series of nine stations each with a small font of Lourdes water, was introduced across the river from the shrine.

There are less services in winter, as there are far less tourists, although the Sanctuary is always open, and while the grounds are closed between midnight and 5am, you can access the grotto twenty-four hours a day through a gate behind the Upper Basilica.

While the basilicas are elaborate and grand – and Lourdes has been dubbed "the Disneyland of the Catholic Church" – the grotto itself remains much as it was, with a statue of Mary for decoration, a plain stone altar for Masses and a stand of candles. There are benches for prayer and contemplation, and a metal box for petitions.

Bernadette's family, who were living in extreme poverty at the time of the visions, became rich as a result, but Bernadette lived a life of misery and ill health (cholera, asthma, bone cancer), swamped by pilgrims and interrogated by members of the Church, and hiding out at a convent five hundred kilometres from her home, where she died aged thirty-five. She was canonised in December

1933, becoming the saint of Lourdes and Nevers and messenger of the Immaculate Conception, which proved true the only personal message she ever received during the apparitions: "I do not promise to make you happy in this life, but in the next." Her Feast Day is celebrated on April sixteen, the date of her death (although she is also celebrated on February eleven and February eighteen), and around two hundred million pilgrims have visited Lourdes since she saw the visions, with the Catholic Church recognising sixty-seven miracle healings. Today, pilgrims both Catholic and spiritual travel to Lourdes, and while the town's population is only fifteen thousand, it hosts five million pilgrims a year. Within France, only Paris has more hotel rooms than this town.

The water from the spring at Lourdes has been tested several times and found to have no special scientific or medical properties (the mayor at the time of the visions had hoped it would have a high mineral content so Lourdes could be developed into a spa town), or any seeming reason for healing, yet there is much anecdotal evidence of it, and the water and the spring remain a symbol of devotion and faith. Pilgrims buy statues and rosary beads containing small vials of the holy water, and fill up jars and bottles from the taps to take home with them, as they do at Chalice Well.

Many also bathe in the water – around three hundred and fifty thousand people a year visit the bathing pools, Piscines in French, to submerge themselves in the waters. Makeshift baths were constructed not long after the original visions.

When French author Emile Zola visited in the 1890s he wrote: "And the water was not exactly inviting. The Grotto Fathers were afraid that the output of the spring would be insufficient, so in those days they had the water in the pools changed just twice a day. As some hundred patients passed through the same water, you can imagine what a horrible slop it was at the end. There was everything in it: threads of blood, sloughed-off skin, scabs, bits of cloth and bandage, an abominable soup of ills... the miracle was that anyone emerged alive from this human slime."

Since then though they have been upgraded, with seventeen separate bath cubicles, and the water in each bath is constantly circulated and purified by irradiation. The water is cold, around 12°C (54°F), and is not heated. Pilgrims immerse themselves for a minute, while prayers are recited around them by other people.

Holy Water

Knock, a small village in the western county of Mayo near Galway, is known as the Irish Lourdes, and is another major Catholic pilgrimage site. Its fame is based on the report of an apparition of the Virgin Mary, Saint Joseph and Saint John the Evangelist, as well as a lamb standing on an altar with a cross behind it that was believed to depict Jesus as the Lamb of God, in the south gable of Knock Parish Church, which occurred in August 1879. Today, statues of the four as they appeared on that night stand in the same spot. The original vision was seen by fifteen people, ranging in age from six to seventy-four, although no message was conveyed.

Ten days after the visions a woman claimed that her daughter Delia Gordon was cured of severe ear problems at the site of the apparition. "I brought Delia to Knock with me to Mass. While we were in the church the pain in her ear attacked her so violently that she began to cry. I brought her out to the gable and bade her to pray. I took the pin of my shawl, picked out a little of the cement from the apparition wall and put it in her ear," she explained. "When I asked her how the pain was, she said: 'Tis gone, Mamma!' And she never had a pain to trouble her since."

Within a year, the parish priest, Archdeacon Bartholomew Cavanagh, claimed there had been three hundred cases in which "persons undergoing some form of bodily suffering, who applied water in which some cement had been dissolved, or had drunk water collected from the ground in front of the gable, were cured, or at least afforded much relief."

As transport around Ireland improved, more and more people visited Knock in search of a cure or to pray at the shrine of Mother Mary. In the 1970s, parish priest Monsignor James Horan began a major rebuilding of the site, with a huge basilica constructed alongside the old church to hold the increasing number of visitors. After the personal pilgrimage of Pope John Paul II in 1979, on the centenary of the apparition, Knock developed into one of the major Marian shrines in the world. Mother Teresa visited in June 1993, and today one and a half million pilgrims visit each year, making it western Ireland's most popular attraction.

In the early days, mortar from the apparition gable was a popular relic, along with water that had been blessed there. Today

it is this holy water that is most valued as a
healing instrument. While there is no spring
like at Lourdes, there's a wall of fountains that
dispense holy water, it is sold in the church shop
and online, and cures are still attributed to its use.

There are many healing wells and springs around the world, which
have been utilised by the indigenous peoples of the land for healing
and divination for thousands of years. They are reputed to be able
to cure ailments ranging from eye problems, infertility, rickets,
digestive problems, skin complaints, gallstones, polio and whooping
cough to lameness, insanity, skin diseases, leprosy and assorted
palsies and agues.

There is a high concentration in Britain, with more than three
thousand wells in Ireland alone, and many of these are accessible
today, and still reputed to have healing powers. In the past they
were attributed to the goddess in her many forms, but later they
were rededicated to a saint or holy woman, and any healing was
credited to God. Chapels were usually constructed nearby, and the
water was used for baptisms. Thus the wells of Bridie, one of the
primary goddesses of the Celtic world, who ruled healing, fertility,
fire and inspiration, were renamed for Saint Brigid, Aine's wells
were taken over by Saint Anne and so on.

This was a common occurrence in the British Isles as Christianity
swept the land, which allowed the old meanings to remain hidden
within the new for those who care to look. During the Reformation,
Protestants dismissed as mere superstition the magical properties
attributed to holy wells by the Catholics, but the stories, and the
belief in their healing power, continues to this day.

In the town of Kildare in Ireland, just fifty kilometres east
of Dublin, the two aspects of Bridie/Brigid are present in
the holy well and perpetual fire at Saint Brigid's Cathedral. In
pre-Christian times, Kildare (from the Gaelic cill dara, meaning
church of the oak) was a shrine to the goddess Bridie, featuring a
healing well that people visited for cures, and a fire temple where
the priestesses of the goddess kept an eternal flame burning as a
symbol of her power. It was a place of pilgrimage, gathering and
reverence, and many pagans still visit the site today to absorb the

old energy. When Christianity was introduced to Ireland in the fifth and sixth centuries, the beloved holy woman Brigid built a monastery on this site and founded an order of nuns, who took over the tending of the perpetual flame. The remains of the fire temple can still be visited today, at the rear of the cathedral that replaced the older building in the thirteenth century.

As for Bridie's Well, since the 1950s there have been two – the original pagan Wayside Well that was later rededicated to the saint and used by Saint Brigid's followers, located near the ruins of the Black Abbey, and the "official" Christian one, larger and more elaborately decorated, in a landscaped grotto nearby. Christian devotion was moved to the latter by the local clergy fifty years ago, ostensibly as it was further from the road and thus safer.

Visitors say you can feel the energy of the goddess as well as the vibration of the saint at both sites, and both have been attributed with healing stories. People still gather water from them in the hope they will be cured of illness – and many leave offerings to the faeries when they do so, adding another layer of magic to the site.

In the tiny English village of Minster, located on the Isle of Sheppey in the Thames Estuary not far from London, there is a holy well that has long been acclaimed for its miracle cures. Dating from at least 1500BCE, it was first a pagan sacred site and place of healing. Later, in the seventh century CE, the widowed queen of Kent founded a nunnery on the site, and used water from the well mixed with herbs to effect "magical cures" for people and animals. She was later canonised for this, becoming Saint Sexburgha, and after she died her daughter and granddaughter continued conducting healings with the well water.

The Abbess's Well of Minster Abbey is now a Scheduled Ancient Monument, and people travel from far and wide to drink the water, which is famous for curing infertility – something the old goddess wells were popular for – as well as blindness, lameness and cancer. Modern-day excavations found a prehistoric bronze statue of the triple goddess in the well, and there have been reports of women with fertility issues becoming pregnant after drinking the water. The land on which it stands is now privately owned, but the water remains free and accessible to the public – visitors are just asked not to throw offerings into the well, in order to keep the water pure.

In the aptly named town of Holywell in northeast Wales lies Saint Winefride's Well, which has been recorded as a healing well since prehistoric times. Known as the Lourdes of Wales, and mentioned as one of the Seven Wonders of Wales in an old poem, the water of the spring forces its way upward through the earth, bubbling into a beautiful pool constructed in the shape of a star. The crystal clear water then flows down into a deep, narrow bath with steps at each end, then continues on to the outdoor bathing pool. People still immerse themselves fully in the (freezing!) water of the pools, as well as drinking the water from a tap next to the spring, in the hope of a cure for everything from skin disorders to broken bones.

According to Christian legend, the spring only burst into being in 660CE, when a local chief beheaded a young noblewoman, Winefride, for choosing a nunnery over his marriage proposal. Healing water is said to have issued forth from where her head fell, then her uncle Bueno reattached her head and brought her back to life – she became an abbess, then after her second and final death she was sainted, as was her uncle.

A shrine was constructed in honour of Winefride in Shrewsbury, England, in the twelfth century, and it and the well both became places of pilgrimage. Richard I visited the well to pray for the success of his crusade, Henry V walked from Shrewsbury to the well as penance in 1416, and it's claimed that in the seventeenth century King James II went there to take the waters with his wife Mary as she hadn't produced an heir to the throne – soon after she became pregnant with their son James III. Today the well is open daily, and pilgrims can bathe in the mornings and afternoons.

Saint Winefride's has an English sister well of the same name, located in the village of Woolston in Shropshire, just across the Welsh border. Long a pagan shrine, it was rededicated to Saint Winefride after her body rested there overnight on its journey from North Wales to Shrewsbury in 1138 – and it is said that the water sprang forth only when her body rested at the site. Pilgrims still come to bathe in the waters, which are renowned for healing bruises, wounds and broken bones, and you can even stay at the Wellhouse now, which has been restored and converted into accommodation (www.landmarktrust.org.uk).

In the region of Brittany in western France, near historic Rennes and not far from the stone alignments of Carnac, lies mythical Broceliande Forest, home to many legends of King Arthur and the Lady of the Lake, aligning it with the energies of Glastonbury as well as Wales. The beautiful forest, filled with lush beeches and oaks up to a thousand years old, is a place of magic and mystery, filled with enchantments and trees that whisper in the wind. Parts of it are said to have been bewitched by Morgaine of the Faeries, particularly the dramatic Val sans Retour (Valley of No Return), where she imprisoned any knights who came by in revenge for her broken heart.

There are several magical locations within the forest, which is called Paimpont on maps, including two sacred water sources. One is the lake called the Mirror of the Faeries, where the Lady of the Lake is believed to reside, the other is Viviane's Fountain of Eternal Youth (Fontaine de Jouvence), which promises immortality to those who drink from it. Traditionally mothers would bring their babies to this spring and dip them in the water, in the hope that they would be blessed by the goddess and the faeries. Later the Church adopted the practice, with parents bringing their babies to the priest, who would sprinkle them with the water in the name of God. Nearby there is also a Fontaine de Barenton, which has a legend attached to it that you can summon rain if you pour some of its water onto the slab in front of it.

There are many sacred springs and water fountains along the Camino pilgrimage path that winds westward through northern Spain. On top of one mountain, between Pamplona and Puente la Reina, is Fuente Reniega, the fountain of renouncement or denial. According to legend the devil, disguised as a fellow walker, tried to tempt a thirsty pilgrim to renounce God, the Virgin Mary and Saint James, patron of the walk, in return for water. When the pilgrim refused, and was close to passing out from thirst, Saint James appeared out of nowhere, took out his scallop shell and dug a hole in the parched earth. A wonderfully clear and refreshing spring gurgled to life, and the saint held his shell full of water to the pilgrim's lips. In other versions of the story he simply guided him to the hidden fountain the devil had offered to show him. Today it is said that every pilgrim should drink from this spring, as its sacred waters will fortify the spirit against the temptation to abandon their pilgrimage if not their god — which crosses some minds at the top of this lofty mountain.

All along the Camino route there are freshwater springs, wells and fountains that provide clean, cold water for sweaty pilgrims, which makes the journey possible. A few days of walking past the fountain of renouncement is Fuente del Vino, the wine fountain, which flows with free wine provided by a local vineyard for pilgrims passing by. It's situated below the twelfth century Cistercian monastery of Irache, and is a highlight for many — thirsty pilgrims consume thirty-five thousand litres of wine a year. It's the site of many funny moments as dedicated walkers take a moment to relax from their gruelling schedule and let their hair down, but given the heat, some pilgrims are more interested in water than wine!

Other Spanish fountains have their own unique legend attached, such as the nineteenth century Fuente de las Canaletas in Barcelona, where drinking the water is said to ensure that you will return to the beautiful old city.

There is a healing spring in Nordenau, a ski resort in Germany a two hour drive east of Dusseldorf. It's located in a cave in a disused slate mine on a property owned by Theo Tommes, who runs the Hotel Tommes. The spring is located at the intersection of three watercourses, and is an earth energy vortex. A laboratory that tested the water claims it is eight per cent lighter than tap water, and it has become known as the German Lourdes. Business has picked up at the hotel, as people flock from around Europe to drink the water, and many have found relief from ailments including high blood pressure, lameness and even blindness.

In Hilo Bay on the Big Island of Hawaii is tiny Coconut Island, known to Hawaiians as Mokuola, which means island of life or healing island. A narrow footbridge extends from beautiful Liliuokalani Garden in Hilo to the island, where people used to flock to drink the water in the sacred spring and touch the ancient healing stone. The Hawaiians believed the spring had curative powers, although it's said the sick had to swim to the island in order to receive a healing. There was a healing temple, or heiau, called Makaoku, and it was also a Pu'uhonua, a place of refuge, which offered absolution and forgiveness to law breakers who could reach its shores. It is a place of great peace and tranquillity, a tiny islet of lava rock, with tropical palm trees waving in the breeze, and sea turtles swimming in the channel between it and the mainland.

Near Cusco in Peru, the waters at Tambo Machay, the Temple of the Water, were used by the Inkas for physical and emotional wellbeing. This was the major complex of baths and fountains for the nobility, and consists of a system of elaborately carved and tiered platforms that channel the water from a holy spring into three waterfalls, which were used to energetically cleanse and purify the royals. Water, known as unu, was a sacred element in Peru, and all the major temples had baths within the grounds so the priests could worship this element, and people would take the waters, either drinking it or bathing in it. These fountains have been pumping water for centuries, and it cascades down through a series of beautiful stone fountains which still work today, energising and refreshing both physically and on a deeper level.

In Brasil, at the Casa de Dom Inacio in the village of Abadiania, John of God does his psychic surgery and healing work. One of his prescriptions is to visit the Sacred Waterfall on his property and submerge yourself in its healing waters. The location of the Casa was chosen because it sits on one of the largest quartz crystal deposits in the world, as quartz amplifies healing vibrations. An underground stream flows through these crystal beds, and is purified and charged with energy before splashing into the waterfall. Surrounded by lush trees, the Sacred Waterfall both cleanses and refreshes for those about to have a healing, and can also continue the healing process – it's said that the entities John of God channels often operate on people here too. It's freezing cold, but so beautiful and healing, a wonderful place to visit in silence, and believed to be a sacred place for direct communication with Spirit.

Water's Healing Power

"Water comes up from the ground, water comes down from the sky.
Water comes into our bodies, water comes out of our bodies.
All life is communicated through water. Nature talks to itself through
the medium of water. We are born of water. We are of water."
Tom Blue Wolf, Native American spiritual guide and artist

Geothermal Mineral Springs

Balneotherapy, from the Latin balneum, meaning bath, is a form of water-based treatment using natural thermal mineral springs to increase wellbeing. It's used to heal illness, boost the immune system, stimulate detoxification, relieve physical stress, boost circulation, aid relaxation and revitalise the body.

In countries such as Japan, where it is known as onsen therapy, and many European nations, bathing regularly in hot mineral springs is an accepted form of healthcare, used to normalise dysfunction, heal disease and maintain health and wellbeing, acting as a preventative as much as a cure. Vichy in France, Baden Baden in Germany, Montecatini in Italy, Karlovy Vary in the Czech Republic, Rotorua in New Zealand and the Blue Lagoon in Iceland have long been visited by people taking advantage of their medicinal waters.

Indigenous peoples in the Americas also have a rich tradition of hot spring therapy, as such places were considered nature's power spots, used for ceremonies and rituals as well as physical healing. Saratoga Hot Springs in New York state, White Sulfur Springs in West Virginia, Glenwood Springs in Colorado and Banff Hot Springs in Canada are just a few recognised for their healing waters.

Charles Davidson, who was so inspired by the Japanese onsen experience that he started Australia's first hot springs spa, Peninsula Hot Springs, says there are around forty natural hot springs in Australia, although some are far out in the wilderness and hard to access. "A natural hot spring, like the one in a muddy river in the Kooma Nation region of southwest Queensland, is as good as it gets," he says. "But there are no toilets, showers, accommodation, massages or any spa-related activities that people like to enjoy."

He also recommends Innot Hot Springs in tropical northern Queensland, where water bubbles from the ground at 78°C (172°F); the crystal-clear Rainbow Springs at Mataranka in the Northern Territory; Tjuwaliyn/Douglas Hot Springs, two hundred kilometres from Darwin, which are cut off during the rainy season and where you may share the pools with crocodiles, flying foxes and bandicoots; Zebedee Hot Springs in Western Australia's stunning Kimberley region; Hastings Caves and Thermal Springs in Tasmania; and the Moree Hot Artesian Pool Complex in northwest New South Wales.

Hot springs are created when rainwater seeps into the earth and is heated far underground then forced back to the surface. The deeper it goes, the hotter it gets, as the centre of the earth is filled with molten liquid rock that reaches temperatures of 6000°C. Volcanic areas such as Hawaii, Japan, Iceland and New Zealand have a large concentration of thermal springs, and in a similar manner, the water at Peninsula Hot Springs is the result of the Selwyn fault line that runs through Victoria's Mornington Peninsula.

"The seismic movement of the fault line generates heat and also encourages the flow of deeper heat from within the earth. The combination of the elevated heat of the earth and the presence of water makes it possible for the hot springs to exist. Water acts as an exchange medium, much like a battery for electrical energy, bringing the heat from the earth to the hot spring pools," Charles says.

"Our water fell as rain ten thousand years ago. It seeped into the earth through faults and fractures, and as it moved underground it was subjected to increased energy from natural geothermal heat, and exposed to gases and a wide variety of minerals from rocks and mineral deposits within the earth. The water absorbs these minerals via leaching, is heated up and then forced back to the surface."

This geothermal heat is a clean-energy, renewable resource, and Peninsula Hot Springs runs it in pipes under their buildings to heat them. Known as hydronic heating, it reduces the need for non-renewable heat sources such as electricity, gas or oil.

While balneotherapy can involve hot or cold water, seawater and even mud, it usually refers to geothermal mineral springs. A hot spring is defined as a place where the waters emerge from the earth with a temperature in excess of the core human body temperature of 37°C (98.6°F), although warm pools also have healing benefits.

Many of these natural water sources are rich in particular minerals, such as magnesium, silica, sulphur, selenium and radium, which can be absorbed via the skin as well as, in some cases, taken internally. Different hot springs have different minerals, or combinations of minerals – Banff, for example, is high in sulphate, calcium, bicarbonate, magnesium and sodium – and are acclaimed for curing, or at least easing, different conditions.

Some are magnesium springs, which can be good for skin disorders, aching muscles, stress and converting blood sugar to energy; others are high in potassium, which is recommended for treating high blood pressure, eliminating toxins and purifying skin; and others have bicarbonate-rich waters, which improve circulation and open peripheral blood vessels. Some are rich in boron, which is believed to strengthen bones and muscles; chlorides, used to ease arthritis and rheumatic conditions and settle nerves; iron, used to treat anaemia, calm nerves, restore energy, maintain metabolism and support the immune system; or arsenic, which is not recommended for drinking but can be used as a footbath or hand soak to cure athlete's foot and other fungal infections, and was used in the past to treat syphilis and other venereal diseases.

Some springs have high concentrations of silica, good for cardiovascular health, bone formation, hair, skin and nail health and boosting the effects of other minerals; others are rich in sulphur, good for liver disorders, respiratory conditions, chronic skin disorders, rheumatism and urinary tract conditions; or radon, which can be used as a bath to ease gout, rheumatism, diabetes, arthritis, bronchial asthma, gallstones and fatigue.

Different springs have different methods of healing too – for some it's suggested that you drink the water, in others you should only bathe in it, and in some you simply breathe in the vapour of the steaming water and its minerals. The water from some springs works best when it's absorbed through the skin, and is especially helpful for easing skin disorders such as psoriasis, dermatitis and fungal infections, and for wound healing. Others are best ingested, allowing trace elements of minerals such as calcium, magnesium and lithium to be absorbed by the internal organs, normalising gland and hormone function, enhancing the immune system, calming the endocrine system and soothing the body.

Hot springs benefit people in two ways – from the minerals in the water and also from the temperature. Soaking in a hot spring, with or without a high mineral count, gradually increases the body's temperature, killing harmful germs and bacteria, with some springs being particularly effective at this. Regular hot spring bathing can also help reduce stress and improve body function and immune activity, increase hydrostatic pressure on the body, boost blood circulation and cell oxygenation, and help dissolve and eliminate toxins. It increases metabolism, aids digestion and stimulates the liver, and the waters also contain negative ions, which promote wellbeing, positivity and joy.

It is always best to consult a doctor before beginning a treatment program of hot spring baths, as there are certain conditions that are contra-indicated. Caution should be exercised if you have a disease involving fever, severe hypertension, some cancers, had a recent stroke, are pregnant or suffer from high blood pressure or diabetes. You should never bathe alone in a hot spring, in case you become faint and slip underwater, and should avoid overheating and overbathing – small doses are most effective. Also drink plain cool water, not the hot spring water, in order to remain hydrated, as some waters are good for soaking in but not ingesting.

Common spa prescriptions are for a program of three immersions a day for fifteen to twenty minutes at a time, immersed up to your neck. Putting your head under is not always advised, as too much of the minerals can be absorbed through your nose and mouth. Temperatures do vary though – in Japan there are some very hot springs, more than 52°C (125°F), which you should only stay in for three minutes at a time. Drinking small, carefully prescribed amounts of the waters several times a day is sometimes prescribed by spa doctors too, but not all mineral spring waters are suitable for drinking (and some taste yukky!). Even those that are can be very powerful even in small doses, and too much can cause an upset tummy, so be conscious of the effect the water has on you.

Japan, located on the Pacific Ocean's Ring of Fire, is a volcanically active land, and as a result it has thousands of hot springs. The country is renowned for these therapeutic mineral springs, which have been a part of their culture for thousands of years, as they believe that regular immersion will heal aches and pains as well as disorders including joint pain, chronic skin diseases, diabetes, constipation and menstrual disorders, and also act as a preventative health measure to ward off illness. These therapeutic hot springs are known as onsens, although the word can also refer to the bathing and accommodation facilities around the spring.

Traditionally they are outdoor springs, made up of natural rock pools fed by geothermal waters forced upwards from within the earth, and set in dramatic landscapes in the mountains, often ringed with snow in sharp contrast to the steaming waters. Today some indoor onsens have been developed, in cities or to protect from the elements, although only those that use naturally hot water from geothermally heated springs are deemed onsens – there are also indoor public bathhouses called sentos, where the baths are filled with heated tap water rather than mineral water.

Traditionally men and women would bathe together at the local onsen, but today, to cater to western tourists, many are now single sex, particularly in the cities. Onsens have strict etiquette rules regarding cleanliness – dirt is unacceptable, as is soap that remains on the skin – and many require bathers to be naked, as towels or swimsuits are considered unclean. Some very traditional onsens don't allow anyone with tattoos either, a hangover from the days when they were a symbol of gang or crime affiliation.

One of the most beautiful is at Kamuiwakka Falls, which means water of the gods, a natural hot spring in Shriretoko National Park. Despite its remoteness, it's a popular tourist destination. The area with the highest concentration of springs is Beppu, a pretty town on the southern island of Kyushu, located between the ocean and the mountains. It has the second largest volume of hot spring water in the world (after Yellowstone Park, USA), and thousands of sacred onsens. They each feature public baths and accommodation, and a wide variety of bathing experiences, from the usual hot water baths to sand baths, steam baths and mud baths.

There are also nine major geothermal hot spots referred to as the nine hells of Beppu, which are more suitable for viewing than bathing in. These include Umi Jigoku, the sea hell of hot blue water; Chinoike Jigoku, the blood pond hell of hot red water; Oniishibozu Jigoku, the mud hell named for the mud bubbles that emerge from boiling mud pools; Shiraike Jigoku, the white hell of hot and milky white water; Tatsumaki, the spout hell with a boiling hot geyser that erupts every half an hour; Yama Jigoku, the mountain hell made up of small ponds of steaming hot water; Kamado Jigoku, the cooking pot hell comprised of several boiling ponds; Oniyama Jigoku, the monster mountain hell; and Kinryu Jigoku, the golden dragon hell that boasts a greenhouse heated by the hot spring.

The Big Island is the only Hawaiian island still volcanically active, and it has several hot thermal springs. They're located in the Puna region, southeast of Hilo and downhill from the still-active Kilauea Volcano, and their creation, as a forerunner to man-made hot tubs, is credited to the goddess Pele. The most accessible is Ahalanui Hot Spring in the beach park of the same name, which even has a lifeguard during the day. It's a large, natural rock swimming pool, almost three metres deep at one end and wadeable at the other, separated from the ocean by a natural rock wall. It's a mixture of fresh ground water that was heated as it was forced upwards through magma-hot rocks on its way to the surface, with a dash of fresh seawater. The temperature and depth of the pool depends on the tides – it's cooled slightly when seawater pours in over the rocks and through a narrow outlet to the ocean, but goes no lower than 32°C (90°F), and is often 37°C (98.6°F) or above.

It's too warm to swim in for long, but it's wonderful to float on the surface and soak up the minerals, and do a few leisurely underwater laps so your whole body is covered. There are often carers holding people up in the water so they can absorb the healing minerals and the warmth of the spring water as a treatment for a range of illnesses. It's a beautiful pool, and the water is crystal clear – which means you can see the cute little fish that swim alongside you and occasionally nibble on your toes!

A mile further along the coast is Isaac Hale Beach Park, on the eastern edge of Pohoiki Bay, which has a boat ramp, waves for surfers and, a short walk along a lush green tree-lined path, a really awesome thermal spring, known as Pohoiki Hot Spring or simply Warm Pond. It's surrounded by vines and tropical jungle, a nice contrast to the desolate lava fields that make up much of the island, and is even hotter than Ahanalui, since it's far enough back from the ocean to have no seawater to cool it. It's really beautiful, and would only fit about six people at once, making it much more intimate and private than Ahanalui.

Saratoga Springs in New York state has long been lauded for its healing powers. Native American peoples were aware of the medicinal effects of this super hot – 55°C (131°F) – naturally carbonated water, which is forced to the surface through cracks and fissures along the Saratoga fault line. They believed they were a gift from the Great Spirit, and legends tell of them taking white settlers there to soak in the springs to recuperate when they were injured during battles. In the eighteenth century George Washington visited, and some of his colleagues followed, seeking cures for rheumatism, skin diseases and inflammation of the eyes, amongst other ailments. There are several springs and wells here, with different mineral compositions – including the only seltzer spring in the country, which was marketed as a natural form of antacid.

Companies began bottling the water in 1823, and over the next decade many doctors visited to explore the therapeutic use of the waters in medical treatments and disease prevention. People began flocking to the springs from around America, where it was known as "the Queen of Spas", and the new bathhouses, based on the European spas, became a popular destination for the wealthy.

Gas companies also began extracting the carbon dioxide from the waters for soda fountains and refrigeration, and by the early twentieth century, commercial overuse had begun to deplete the spring waters. In 1908 an injunction was issued against the gas companies, but they ignored it. A year later a bill was passed to make the area a state reservation, which authorised "the selection, location and appropriation of certain lands in the town of Saratoga Springs for a state reservation, for the purpose of the preservation of the natural mineral springs therein located." By 1930, when a laboratory was set up to investigate the treatment of chronic illnesses, particularly heart disease, with the spring water, the flow and mineral composition had returned to normal.

The springs and the beautiful land surrounding them became a state park in 1962, and it was also listed as a National Historic

Landmark in 1987. Success in treating respiratory illnesses, digestive problems, arthritis and malnutrition in children was noted, and a hospital for veterans was constructed there during World War II to treat wounded soldiers with the waters.

Although many of the original pavilions and bathhouses are gone, there are still a few places where you can bathe in this naturally carbonated, effervescent and mineral-rich spring water. The famous Roosevelt Baths & Spa, where the hot mineral water is pumped from the spring to individual bathtubs in private rooms, is now part of Gideon Putnam Resort. The Crystal Spa and Lincoln Bath House also offer traditional-style soaks, and you can view the geothermal activity, including small bubbling springs and the only active spouting geyser east of the Mississippi River, throughout the park.

> "Caxambu my dear land, you have in your air the beauty
> of the skies! You have in your water the Fountain of Life,
> you are the Eden of the Honeymooners!"
> *Antonio Mauricio Ferreira, Brasilian poet*

The small town of Caxambu, in southern Minas Gerais, Brasil, is a thermal resort famous for its springs, which are located in the Parque das Aguas that the town has been built around. It is unique in that there are twelve different springs which all have different minerals in them, some carbonated, some not, and all of varying temperatures. They are each capped with a beautiful oriental-style pavilion, with a tap to access the mineral waters, and they all have a different mineral composition (and different taste!), which are recommended for the treatment of various different ailments.

Several are named for the nineteenth century Brasilian royal family that visited often to take the waters – the Dona Leopoldina magnesium fountain, recommended for liver complaints, digestive disorders and aching muscles, the Teresa Cristina sulphur fountain, named for the empress and used for skin disorders, the naturally carbonated Dom Pedro fountain, recommended for stomach upsets and bottled for sale around the world, the Duque de Saxe fountain that was used to treat syphilis, and the Dona Isabel fountain, rich in iron and suggested to ease anaemia and aid fertility.

It was this latter spring that brought fame to Caxambu, when Princess Isabel, daughter of Brasil's last emperor, claimed that a month of daily drinking and baths helped cure her of infertility – her subsequent three sons seemed to prove its effectiveness. There are other fountains in the park renowned for helping treat conditions ranging from kidney stones and stomach ailments to eye problems, sterility, high blood pressure, arteriosclerosis and depression, along with the Viotti fountain, named for the doctor who recognised the healing power of these springs and formed the Caxambu Water Company in 1886, bottling it for sale.

This one contains traces of radon, which makes the water slightly radioactive, and is said to treat muscle and joint diseases, eliminate uric acid and stimulate sexual glands, among other things. Today there is debate about whether long-term use of such waters can be dangerous, and they're banned in the US, but in European spas they are still used, and in Caxambu it was claimed, citing the work of French physicist and engineer Jean-Bertrand Leon Foucault, that you could live to a hundred and fifty years old by drinking this radioactive, highly stimulating and diuretic mineral water.

The springs had been used by locals for some time before they were tapped in 1870, which allowed the healing powers of the waters to be easily accessed and discovered. From 1886, when Dr Viotti began bottling the water, it became popular around Brasil, and water from these springs is still bottled and sold throughout the world, winning many awards for its taste and nutrient density. Brasilians consume more than two billion litres of mineral water a year, most of it from their own natural mineral springs, which have been voted in top ten lists worldwide.

The beautiful water park also has a Turkish bathhouse where you can bathe in the waters or have a sauna or massage, and it's all situated around a pretty lake people sail on in small swan-shaped boats. Caxambu, named from the indigenous word catambu, meaning bubbling water, is part of a cluster of small Brasilian spa towns known as the Circuito das Aguas (Circuit of the Waters) that also includes Lambari, upmarket Sao Lourenco, with seven different fountains, and the smallest, Cambuquira, which boasts six varieties of mineral springs. Each town is based around a parque hidromineral, a water park constructed around the springs, which incorporates bathhouses to bathe in the waters, and fountains to drink from. Each spring is rich in a different kind of mineral, and thus is recommended to remedy different kinds of illnesses and conditions.

Caldas Novas in Goias, Brasil, boasts one of the biggest hydrothermal resorts in the world, which capitalises on the extensive hot springs in the area – springs that are famous because their huge volume ensures constant renewal of all the water in the pools. Situated on the banks of the Caldas River, these springs have long been used by people searching for a cure to various illnesses. Today there are eighty-six active wells, with the temperatures varying between 34°C and 57°C (93°F/135°F).

In this case it is not volcanic activity that keeps the thermal springs in the region hot, but warming via heat from deep within the earth, a natural phenomenon called geothermal energy. At the Rio Quente Resort there are eighteen existing springs and thirteen natural pools, while other places in the area also have several. There are also seven hotels and a water park, making a visit to bathe in the waters easily accessible.

At the base of Machu Picchu in Peru is the small village of Aguas Calientes, which translates as hot waters in Spanish, named for the natural underground mineral springs that bubble forth from deep within the mountains. Shallow pools have been built over the springs, and the healing power of the warm mineral water works on both physical and emotional levels. It was immersed in a similar hot spring that Shirley MacLaine had many of her most profound spiritual revelations, detailed in her classic book and movie *Out On a Limb*, and it was also where I spent several hours soaking as I assimilated the experiences of three days at Machu Picchu, luxuriating in the warm water and feeling the tension drain from my muscles as the bubbles danced against my skin and the warmth seeped soothingly into my body and, it seemed, my mind. It is also a popular place to recuperate for those who have hiked the Inka Trail through the mountains to Machu Picchu. Ranging from 38°C to 46°C (100°F to 115°F), these baths are renowned for their therapeutic properties, with claims that the waters are helpful in the treatment of rheumatism, joint pain and kidney disorders, amongst other things. There are a few different pools, all quite shallow with ledges around the side to sit on, with different minerals in some of them, and one of them filled with ice-cold mountain water. In addition to their healing powers they are pure bliss to soak in, an indulgent reward to soothe body and soul.

In England, the only naturally occurring hot springs are the three in the town of Bath – the King's Spring, Cross Spring and Hetling Spring. More than a million litres of mineral-rich water gushes up from within the earth every day, at a temperature of 47°C (117°F). The water fell as rain six thousand years ago, and soaked down through the limestone to a depth of two kilometres, where it's heated by geothermal rocks before rising to the surface under the natural force of artesian pressure to emerge at the source.

People have been soaking in these hot springs for at least ten thousand years. The water is rich in bicarbonate and sulphate, with additional traces of calcium, magnesium, potassium, iron, lead, strontium, sulphur and bismuth, and is slightly radioactive. It has been used to relieve ailments such as rheumatic and muscular disorders, skin problems, respiratory issues, infertility, gout, palsy from lead poisoning, scabies, psoriasis and polio. People with rheumatic issues were advised to soak in the waters, while drinking them was recommended for internal ailments.

Legend claims that in the ninth century BCE, a local prince contracted leprosy and was banished from his father's court. He got a job tending pigs, and noticed that they were healed of cuts and scabs when they rolled in the mud near where a hot spring bubbled to the surface. He followed suit and was cured, and eventually became king of Britain, constructing bathhouses around the springs in gratitude.

There is evidence of shrines built by the pagan Celts, who would have been aware of the healing properties of the springs, as well as their mystical powers as an entrance to the Otherworld. They utilised the waters and left offerings for Sulis, a mother goddess they worshipped as the guardian spirit of these springs.

When the Romans invaded Britain in the first century CE they named the town Aquae Sulis, the Waters of Sulis. Renowned for their love of bathing rituals, they built a beautiful bathing complex at the springs as well as a temple dedicated to Sulis Minerva, incorporating the local goddess with Minerva, their own deity of the waters, wisdom and medicine. For three hundred years the town, and its baths, were an important part of the empire, and the springs were incorporated into the grounds of an early monastery and cathedral. But after the Romans withdrew from Britain in the fifth century, these elaborate baths fell into disuse and disrepair.

The town and its baths have been revived at various times. In the early twelfth century a new cathedral with two baths in the grounds was built, followed by the Cross Bath and the Hot Bath over the springs. In 1613 King James's wife Anne visited, seeking a cure for dropsy, followed in 1624 by Sir Francis Stonor, and in 1687 by King James II's wife Mary, who claimed the waters cured her infertility (although it is claimed by some that it was Saint Winefride's Well that helped her). This royal approval made Bath a popular destination for the aristocracy. Gentlemen would take the waters to sweat out the excesses of rich food and alcohol, and treat conditions such as gout and rheumatism, while society ladies would plot marriages as they soaked in the baths. More recently, injured servicemen from both World Wars were sent to Bath to recuperate, and between 1948 and 1976 water treatments at the spring were prescribed and paid for by the National Health Service, which ended when the Spa was closed in 1978 and the water deemed not fit for consumption or bathing.

Today the original Roman Baths complex is a historical site incorporating the Sacred Spring, the Roman Temple, the Roman Bathhouse and a museum, and the water is too toxic to soak in, although you can drink the warm spring water from the refurbished neo-classical Pump Room salon. Nearby too, utilising the ancient waters through a series of recently drilled boreholes, the modern Thermae Bath Spa allows visitors to soak in the warm, mineral-rich waters of these powerful hot springs in the way of old.

The town of Droitwich Spa in northern Worcestershire, England, was also acclaimed for its thermal spring, although here the water – so salty it's almost saturated brine (ten times stronger than seawater and only rivalled by the Dead Sea) – is floated in rather than drunk. The baths were closed a few years ago, after years of providing relief for joint and muscle pain, arthritis and more, although the Droitwich Spa Lido, a large open-air saltwater swimming pool filled with diluted spring water, now operates.

The small town of Lisdoonvarna, in County Clare, Ireland, is famous as the location of Europe's largest annual matchmaking event, and for its Spa Wells Health Centre, the only active spa in Ireland. It became well known in the eighteenth century, when a surgeon discovered the healing effects of the town's mineral springs. The sulphur-rich Gowlaun spring, which also has a little lithium in it, is recommended for rheumatism and arthritis; while the iron-rich Rathbaun spring, which has some manganese in it too, is suited for a host of other conditions, and is wonderful to relax in. You can still visit the traditional Pump Room to drink the waters (sulphur spring water has a unique taste!), and luxuriate in one of the big old-fashioned tubs, which are pumped full of the hot spring water so you can soak up the minerals externally.

Iceland's famous Blue Lagoon geothermal spa is one of the most beautiful and intriguing of all the hot springs. Located in a lava field, the huge pool of water is an incredible frosted fluorescent blue, and steam billows atmospherically from the water's surface as it meets the chill in the air. It holds six million litres of geothermal seawater, which is renewed every forty hours.

The waters are around 40°C (104°F), hot enough that bacteria is not present, so no chlorine is required to keep it clean. The water originates two kilometres below the earth's surface, where it is heated by magma to 240°C (464°F). The water is rich in silica and sulphur, and is renowned for helping skin conditions including psoriasis and eczema, as well as for its general restorative powers. People rub the silica mud from the bottom of the lagoon on their face as they bathe in the waters. There's also a blue green algae in the water, which gives it its unique colour and plays a part in the healing process. There's a research and development facility studying the water and trying to find cures, and a range of Blue Lagoon skincare products have been formulated from the mineral-rich waters, including a Silica Mud Mask, Mineral Bath Salts, Algae & Mineral Body Scrub and various night creams and serums.

You can bathe in the huge public lagoon, and there are also lava caves for privacy, a waterfall that massages muscles, and in-water spa treatments and massages that are available as part of spa packages. It's been voted the world's best medical spa and won environmental awards. Oddly enough, in a country dotted with natural hot water springs, this one is actually man-made. The seawater that's heated by lava flows deep within the earth was originally tapped into for the nearby geothermal power plant, which provides all the electricity for the city of Reykjavik. The water then passes through a heat exchanger that heats the water for the surrounding area, before filling the huge lagoon where people swim and bathe, still perfectly clean and full of minerals. It's a wonderful consequence of using renewable energy for electricity, making it a win-win experience.

In New Zealand, a volcanically active and earthquake prone island country situated on the Ring of Fire, the Hanmer Springs Thermal Pools & Spa facility is set in a breathtaking natural landscape, surrounded by mountains and forests, its hot waters providing a wonderful contrast with the snow that surrounds them for much of the year. The thermal waters contain a wide variety of minerals including sulphur, sodium chloride, calcium, carbonates, magnesium and potassium, and are reported to offer great relief to those suffering from arthritis and similar ailments.

There are twelve open-air sodium chloride thermal springs, which also have trace amounts of boron, calcium and carbonate and vary from 28°C to 42°C (82°F to 108°F). There are also three sulphur pools that range in temperature from 40°C to 42°C (104°F to 108°F), which are completely natural and untreated, and leave your skin feeling soft and silky. There are many other outdoor springs too, each varying in size and temperature, some with aquatherapy components such as waterfalls or spa jets to further relax you. There are also waterslides and a play area for kids, private indoor thermal pools, a sauna, steam rooms, massages and other spa treatments.

Located in the Hanmer Mountains near Christchurch on the South Island, the springs were created when water seeped into the fractured rock bed along the Hanmer fault, was heated by the hot magma deep within the earth, then forced upwards to the surface. The water emerges at around 52°C, then a little heat is extracted before the water enters the rock pools at a more comfortable temperature. This complex of hot springs is renowned not just for their power to help people relax and unwind, but has also had positive results for those suffering from rheumatic conditions, paraplegia, orthopaedic conditions such as bone fractures as well as soft tissue injuries and for soothing away aches and pains.

In New Zealand's North Island, the town of Rotorua is nicknamed Sulphur City because of the scent that fills the air from the area's hot springs. The unique volcanic landscape makes Rotorua a natural thermal spring centre, boasting bubbling mud pools, gurgling hot springs, steaming fumaroles and gushing geysers. In Te Whakarewarera Park is Pohutu Geyser, which goes off up to twenty times a day, shooting hot water and steam thirty metres in the air. Even the town's church is naturally heated by the fiery action that continues just below the surface of the earth here.

Hells Gate Waiora Spa has thermal springs and mud baths set in fifty acres of wilderness, and features Kakahi Falls, the largest hot waterfall in the southern hemisphere, as well as hot sulphur springs where warriors would traditionally bathe to heal their wounds after battle. There are also five separate (very) hot pools, ranging from 70°C to 110°C (158°F to 230°F), with depths varying from five metres to fifteen. A legend tells the tale of Ruamoko, the god of volcanic activity, who watches over the thermal park and ensures bad luck to any visitor who harms the landscape in any way.

At Polynesian Spa, geothermic acidic and alkaline waters from two hot mineral springs flow into their twenty-six thermal pools. Three feature alkaline water, while another three are filled with acidic water from the radium hot spring, well known for its therapeutic properties. A constant supply of fresh mineral water enters the pools throughout the day. Nearby Waikite Valley Thermal Pools is another natural mineral spring bathing complex, with water filling the pools from the boiling Te Manaroa Spring, the largest single source of pure boiling water in New Zealand. This water is soft and calcite laden, and ranges from 35°C to 40°C (95°F to 104°F).

In Australia, the pretty country towns of Daylesford and Hepburn Springs in Victoria, just ninety minutes northwest of Melbourne in the foothills of the Great Dividing Range, are renowned for their natural springs, which are rich in magnesium, calcium and silica, amongst other minerals. This was the first spa centre in Australia, after European settlers and gold prospectors in the early 1800s discovered the more than sixty mineral springs in the region, the largest concentration in Australia, and started bathing in them and drinking the waters to relieve a variety of ailments, from stomach disorders to acne and arthritis to weakened bones.

The springs were considered more valuable than gold, so when gold mining started affecting the springs, locals lobbied for them to be protected, leading to the creation of the Mineral Springs Reserve in 1865. Thirty years later the Hepburn Bathhouse was constructed, which has been remodelled a few times since then. Its new incarnation is as the luxurious Hepburn Bathhouse & Spa, which includes large communal pools of heated mineral waters, as well as private rooms and spa and relaxation pools, spa couches, an aroma steam room and a salt therapy pool. It's located in the thirty hectare Hepburn Mineral Springs Reserve, where you can wander through the park, check out several springs and sample the different tasting waters. There are also day spas in both towns that use the spring water.

The high concentration of mineral waters is due to the volcanic nature of the area – Hepburn Springs is located in the Wombat State Forest between the extinct volcanoes Mount Franklin and Wombat Hill. Some of the springs include Soda, Sulphur, Pavilion, Locarno, Wyuna and Lithia Springs, which have varying mineral compositions. Many have hand pumps so you can access the water for drinking, while others stream from continuously flowing pipes. The Hepburn Mineral Springs Company started bottling this mineral water in 1910, and it is still sold around the world.

The 1980 Ground Water Mineral Water Act defines mineral water as: "Ground water which in its natural state contains carbon dioxide and other soluble matter in sufficient concentration to cause effervescence and impart a distinctive taste." In contrast, sodas and soft drinks have been artificially carbonated with carbon dioxide, often extracted from mineral springs, to create the bubbles.

On Mornington Peninsula, just ninety minutes southeast of Melbourne, is Peninsula Hot Springs, with its incredible natural thermal baths. Drawing its inspiration and influence from the hot springs of Japan, it is a complete bathing and relaxation experience, with many of the pools outside in nature so you can soak up the healing waters in the great outdoors. The temperature of the hot mineral waters varies from pool to pool, ranging from 37°C to 43°C (98.6°F to 109.4°F). The water contains many naturally occurring minerals including sulphur, calcium and magnesium. There are public baths as well as a private massage day spa offering a variety of treatments and private mineral baths.

Charles's Water Magic

Charles Davidson formulated the idea for Peninsula Hot Springs, Australia's first natural hot springs and spa facility, after travelling around the world researching bathing rituals and the healing power of geothermal mineral springs. At his relaxing centre, natural hot mineral waters flow into the outdoor rock pools and private baths, and massage and spa treatments are also available. Find out more at www.peninsulahotsprings.com.

Bathing as an art has been around as long as warm waters have flowed to the surface from deep underground. Balneology is the scientific study of the therapeutic benefits of naturally occurring mineral waters. It's not very well known in Australia, but in Europe and Japan, hot springs therapy is very much part of routine medical care. Prescriptions are given by licensed doctors for the treatment of a wide range of conditions, and bathing in mineral waters as part of preventative medicine is widely recognised and encouraged.

I was inspired to develop something similar here during a stay in Japan twenty years ago. I was in the hot springs town of Kusatsu, in a beautiful mountain environment. Snow still lay on the ground, and the open-air hot water pools were surrounded by trees. Laying back in the heat of the pool, in the cold of winter, was sublime. I'd never felt so relaxed and at peace. It made me wonder why Australia didn't have this, and it was then that the hot springs flame was lit inside me. I've undertaken research trips to eighteen countries to explore the ways various cultures bring hot springs into their bathing, relaxation, health and wellbeing practices, and many of these are incorporated into our facilities, such as the Turkish bath, reflexology walk, watsu (water shiatsu) pool and hydrotherapy facility.

Our water has been deep within the earth for more than ten thousand years, and by the time it surfaces it's around 50°C (122°F). The different pools vary in temperature from 37°C to 43°C, and the water contains a range of naturally occurring minerals including sulphur, magnesium, potassium, calcium and many others. The water is classified as a sodium chloride bicarbonate spring, and according to the Japanese Health Authority, the therapeutic benefits of this type of hot spring include the alleviation of neuralgia, bruising, articular rheumatism, stiffness of the shoulders, skin diseases, infertility, fatigue and muscular complaints.

An analysis of our water was conducted by the Institute of Geological & Nuclear Sciences in New Zealand and the University of Idaho in the US. The results were sent to the Mineral Water Association in Moscow and the Hot Spring Research Institute in Tokyo, which confirmed it's ideal for healthy bathing and relaxation.

The heat in the water helps in inducing blood flow and sweating, which releases toxins in the system and assists the body to heal itself. Hydrostatic pressure in the body increases, which results in increased blood circulation and cell oxygenation. The elimination systems of the body are thus stimulated, improving the body's capacity to detoxify, and metabolism increases, resulting in improved digestion.

A program of three to four weeks of regular thermal bathing assists the automatic nervous system and normalises the endocrine glands, and mineral water spas combined with massage are increasingly being used to treat work-related diseases such as back problems, stress and tinosinavitus, and are also proving effective for rehabilitation after accidents and for rheumatism and arthritis.

The earliest bathing in Australia was at Hepburn Springs in the 1800s, and it's still a mineral spring facility. The main difference between our water and theirs is that ours are naturally hot, and theirs have to be heated. The natural warmth of our waters means we can have open-air pools so you're out in nature surrounded by trees, birds, rocks and, in the evening, stars. That sense of connection and feeling at one with the environment is a core difference. Additionally our water is not re-circulated – fresh thermal waters are always flowing into the pools, so we have no need to heat, re-circulate or chlorinate the water in the way Hepburn Springs does, which means no red eyes and no chlorine smell!

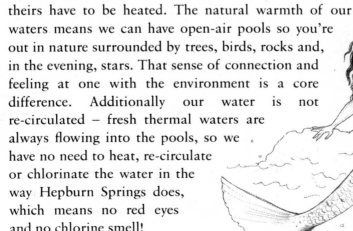

Divine Dolphins

"Pushing through green waters,
Symbol of joy.
You leap from the depths,
To touch the sky.
Scattering spray,
Like handfuls of jewels..."
Horace Dobbs, British dolphin researcher

A Mermaid's Best Friend

Dolphins have long been linked with magic, spirituality, humanity, healing – and mermaids. Many cultures have worshipped them, from the long-ago Minoan civilisation and many Australian Aboriginal groups to Ancient Greece, where a temple at Delphi was dedicated to a dolphin god, and killing one was punishable by death. These beautiful sea creatures have been associated with gods and goddesses, including Poseidon, Dionysus and Aphrodite, their image adorned the Queen's Palace at Knossos in Crete, and there are many myths that incorporate humans that turn into dolphins, and vice versa, who have bridged the gap between the species.

The northern hemisphere constellation Delphinus, Latin for dolphin, is named for them, several cultures thought dolphins carried the souls of the dead to the next world, and even today there are those who believe that dolphins are a higher life form, sent to shepherd us through a time of transition. There's also been much research into the incredible healing powers they are said to have, and many people have been transformed by being in their presence.

Dolphins breathe, like us, live in social groups and crave contact, like we do, and have a brain size comparable to our own. They have been credited with saving human lives, from the twelfth century BCE report that Telemachus, son of Odysseus and Penelope, fell overboard but was retrieved by a dolphin, and the tale that famed Corinthian musician Arion, circa 600BCE, was saved by dolphins when the captain of the ship he was travelling on decided to throw him into the sea and steal his treasure, to long-ago legends of sailors being rescued from shipwrecks, and recent news stories of dolphins pushing drowning swimmers up for air and fending off sharks so vulnerable surfers can make their way to shore.

Professional surfer Dave Rastovich was protected from a shark by a dolphin while catching waves at Angourie, on the east coast of Australia, just days after setting up the dolphin conservation group Surfers For Cetaceans with his artist friend Howie Cooke.

"We went surfing at this reef, and we came over this wave and there was a tiger shark coming straight at us, just a few feet away. My mate said: 'Oh my God, that's a shark!', and instantly I went: 'Oh my God, but that's a dolphin!' And a dolphin came across and pushed the shark away. The dolphin saved our lives, undoubtedly saved our lives, as the shark was motoring down on us. It was really amazing. I really think they have incredible intelligence," Dave says.

"And it was related, in my opinion – I'd had this incredibly strong feeling to want to help these creatures, and then just after I set up Surfers For Cetaceans, just a couple of days later, then instantly one came and saved my life. I definitely feel closer to them now because of that experience, even more so than before."

A few years ago in California a group of dolphins surrounded a surfer who was being mauled by a shark and helped him get to shore. In New Zealand, four lifeguards were saved from a great white shark by a group of seven dolphins who herded the swimmers together and formed a protective circle around them, slapping the water with their tails to drive the shark off. The dolphins stayed with them for forty minutes, until they were able to make it safely back to the shore. The mammals swam in tight circles to create a defensive barrier as the great white lurked beneath the surface.

Dr Rochelle Constantine, from Auckland University's School of Biological Science, says that while this was a rare event, she's heard of similar things happening overseas. "From my understanding of the behaviour of these dolphins they certainly were acting in a way which indicated the shark posed a threat to something. Dolphins are known for helping helpless things. It is an altruistic response, and bottlenose dolphins in particular are known for it," she says.

In Italy, a dolphin known as Filippo saved a teenager from drowning after the non-swimmer fell out of his father's boat. The dolphin pushed the boy up out of the water so he could breathe, then got close enough to the boat so his father could pull him from the sea.

A man swimming with dolphins in the Red Sea was attacked by a shark, but three dolphins placed themselves between him and the predator, swimming in tight circles around him and smacking the water with their tails to fend off the shark until he could be rescued. Oz Goffman, of the Israel Marine Mammal Research and Assistance Center in Haifa, said such behaviour is known in cases where dolphins are protecting their young from predators, but he knew of no previous instance of dolphins defending humans against sharks.

But the dramatic rescue came as no surprise to dolphin expert Mark Simmonds, head of special projects at the Whale and Dolphin Conservation Society. He says the mammals, who would have sensed the danger from a distance, behaved quite naturally because they regard humans as their allies. "The shark is the dolphin's natural enemy," he explains. "Dolphins accept us as part of their tribe and so they protect us as they would their own, which is why it's common for them to support drowning humans.

"In this case it was a natural response to scare away the shark. They'd have rammed it with their beaks. Dolphins don't bite, but they have enormous strength with their mouths shut. It's a rare case, but not untypical of their behaviour towards us."

In another case, an injured scuba diver who was lost at sea for fifty hours before being rescued claimed that a group of dolphins watched over him the whole time. Mark says it's entirely possible that they understood he was in trouble, and helped him.

"Certainly dolphins – as intelligent, air-breathing mammals themselves – are well known for helping other wounded or dying members of their own schools get to the surface. And they seem able to extend this understanding to our own situation," he adds.

They also save fellow dolphins and other sea creatures. In New Zealand a group of pilot whales was stranded on the beach. Local people kept their skin wet and tried to get them back out to sea, but it was a pod of dolphins who came into the shallows and led them back out. And solitary dolphin Moko, also from New Zealand, rescued two whales that were stranded near the bay he called home.

Dolphins have been recorded helping fishermen by herding schools of fish into the nets, delight in catching waves with surfers, and often mimic people who come to swim with them or take photos, displaying a love of play which contributes to the joy they instil in people. They've been known to lie on the bottom of the ocean, using their pectoral fins like arms and resting in a human-like pose as they mimic a cameraman shooting pictures of them.

They are considered highly intelligent, and it was recently discovered that some dolphins teach their young complex behaviours not typical of the species, such as foraging with sea sponges to protect their beaks, coming to shore to get food from people or purposely beaching themselves to catch sea lions, behaviours that are passed down through generations in a specific area. They develop strong social bonds with members of their pod, which helps them survive, they help each other catch fish, and they look after members of their group like an extended family, staying with a sick or injured dolphin and helping it to the surface to breathe if necessary.

> "Diviner than the dolphin is nothing yet created..."
> *Oppian, Ancient Roman poet*

There is something so beautifully uplifting about these gentle marine mammals. Just watching them dance in the ocean, catching waves, leaping in amazing acrobatic feats and playing with each other with such a sense of fun and grace is incredibly moving, and immersing yourself in their world and swimming alongside them is even more powerful and magical.

Swimming with wild dolphins in their natural environment is a truly amazing, awe-inspiring experience. It's been described as akin to being played like a musical instrument, as their energy courses through you and reaches every cell, and it's been shown to transform and heal emotionally and physically, as their powerful sonar is believed to act as a form of vibrational medicine.

It can help you overcome fears, self-limiting thought patterns and depression. People often experience an intense emotional release after being in the water with these beautiful creatures, managing to let go of pain, grief, loneliness and anger. This helps you reconnect to your true self, attune to and increase your intuition, remember who you really are and realise your full potential. Dolphins are a catalyst for emotional change, physical healing and regeneration, and a reminder of the importance of play. They open your heart, fill you with an overwhelming feeling of love and leave you in a state of joy.

Often they will allow people to come very close to them, or they will approach an individual swimmer and interact on their own terms. They are known to be fond of pregnant women, who they recognise because their sonar acts like an x-ray and can see inside us, and those who are sick. In one case a dolphin kept bumping into a swimmer in the same spot – when the bruise was checked out, a tumour was detected beneath it.

Entering their underwater world is like visiting another planet – it's so beautifully strange, slowed down and dream-like. Time ceases to exist, gravity loses its power, and a surreal feeling of freedom and possibility descends. Communication becomes no longer about words but gestures, emotions and eye-to-soul gazing.

"Swimming with wild dolphins is always in lists of the top ten things people want to do, and I think it's because of the joy factor," says Andrew Parker, who organises off-shore swims in eastern Australia. "When I was seventeen I had an amazing encounter with dolphins while surfing, and I have no doubt that that pod of bottlenose dolphins did something to me. They're amazing, amazing creatures, and I'm very glad they're in my life.

"People really connect with dolphins, there's just something about them, the way they swim and jump and play, the way they've mastered their environment, their intelligence. There's something about dolphins that just switches us on – when we're with them we're happy. It's the joy factor. When we're joyous we connect – with each other, with the experience that we're having. It transcends blocks, both emotional and physical. And when we're joyous we can learn and absorb information better, and we tend to be more aware," he says.

Each time I've been in the water with them I've been awestruck by their grace and the love they exude, as well as their natural curiosity and their eagerness to play and communicate with us human folk. In Port Phillip Bay in Melbourne, Australia, I went on a dolphin swim with a small group of people, and a pod of bottlenose dolphins engaged with us, twisting and turning below us, peeking curiously up at us, then swimming alongside for a while. They jumped around and frolicked so joyously amongst us, arcing up through the air, diving down beneath the surface, swimming off to catch a fish then returning to where we were treading water, watching their every move through little face masks and giggling as waves of happiness washed over us. Dolphins really do epitomise joy, and it's hard to resist the laughter that usually accompanies any interaction with dolphins. Laughter, tears of joy or tears of release and healing – there's always a deep emotional reaction.

Off the coast of Kona on the Big Island of Hawaii, dozens and dozens of spinner dolphins, so named because they leap out of the air and spin around in graceful, acrobatic pirouettes, frolic year-round in the warm, clear waters. When my husband and I swam with them there we were greeted by a few spinning around the boat the moment we left the harbour, which was so sweet. When we got out into deeper water and saw a pod nearby, we jumped in to see if they wanted to come play with us. They swam over to check us out, hovering beneath us, sometimes gazing up at us, other times streaming past in a tumble of graceful bodies. There were so many of them, including a baby, and lots of them sailed below us in pairs, hugging each other with their little pectoral fins as we held hands on the surface, our hearts filled with love and joy as they seemed to match our actions (or were we reflecting theirs?).

This was only the second time my hubby had ever snorkelled, and his first in deep water, and he was more terrified than he let on. But he leaped in anyway, overcoming his fear and becoming strong and confident in the water. Dolphins have helped many people around the world overcome their fears, somehow offering emotional support to break through barriers and self-limiting thoughts.

We saw manta rays too – the harmless, toothless and stingerless cousins of the Aussie stingrays, which were very graceful and very cool – as well as a few humpback whales spouting water into the air then breaching, frolicking around in the calm, warm winter waters to mate and give birth before heading back to the cooler north.

Another time, swimming in a freezing Irish bay where solitary dolphin Fungie long ago took up residence, I got to experience the immense wonder and magic of such close contact. Twice I went out on a small boat and slipped into the icy waters with a couple of other people (a few had changed their minds about jumping in when they felt the water temperature!), and watched this beautiful creature swim around where we had spread out in the water, then come slowly towards me and stop right below, suspended in the green water, so big and gentle and full of grace.

I peered down and watched in awe as he hovered there under me, smiling upwards, and slowly, effortlessly, spun around and showed me his white tummy. He was so close I could have touched him, but I didn't, I just stared in wonder, respecting his space, marvelling at his proximity, and he gazed right back at me.

I felt a jolt, a shiver of total peace and acceptance, as he stared right at me, and right into the very depths of my being. We held each other's gaze for what could have been seconds, or hours, and I could feel love radiating out from him, right into my heart. It was so moving, so emotional. I felt really teary, but in a happy way, an overwhelmed-with-so-many-emotions-and-deeply-touched way.

This is the magic moment that so many people have had when interacting with dolphins but which none can describe, when time seems to stand still and you simply float, hovering between our world and theirs, reaching out for the bridge you can sense will connect you, and feeling in that golden moment that everything is well, everything is possible, and everything can be healed.

Staring into their eyes fills you with the most overwhelming sense of love, peace and acceptance imaginable. Many people cry, and others laugh almost hysterically, when a dolphin gazes at them. It feels as though they're looking deep within your soul, filling any emptiness with joy and replacing any pain with love.

It was a moment just like this that encouraged Law & Order: SVU star Mariska Hargitay to incorporate swimming with dolphins into a healing program for victims of sexual assault. Moved deeply by her television role as a detective investigating rape cases, and the cathartic effect the show has on so many victims of sexual assault, Mariska did a counselling course and became a certified rape crisis counsellor, as well as testifying before judiciary subcommittees in an effort to improve procedures for victims.

But it was when she swam with a group of wild dolphins in the sparkling, sun-drenched waters off the coast of Kona, on the Big Island of Hawaii, that she realised how she could best help.

One of the dolphins swam up to her and gazed deeply into her eyes. Although she had swum with dolphins before, this was the first time she had experienced the incredible outpouring of love and joy, the emotional jolt, that occurs when they stare into your soul. She was deeply moved, filled with exhilaration and joy, and she broke down in tears, overcome with emotion and a sense of release. It was at this moment that she realised that swimming with wild dolphins might be able to help victims of sexual assault to heal.

Inspired, she went home to New York and started The Joyful Heart Foundation (www.joyfulheartfoundation.org), a non-profit group that has raised more than five million dollars to help victims of sexual abuse and domestic violence. It offers non-traditional healing retreats, such as swimming with dolphins and surf camps, along with conventional therapy programs.

"A lot of autistic children work with dolphins, but nobody had ever paired victims of sexual assault with the dolphins. That was an idea I had because of my own experience, which was groundbreaking, euphoric and heart opening. I had never experienced anything like it," Mariska explains.

"Dolphins have healing powers with their sonar, and they can read the body and know exactly what is wrong emotionally and physically. My experience of swimming with the dolphins is that the light goes on, and the trust is there, and you feel so in communion with what felt to me like God, because it's so pure, it's so natural.

"You're with these huge beings that have no agenda with you, and victims of sexual assault are people that somebody had an agenda with, and were objectified. And now all of a sudden there's a safety, and it feels like the doors all open and a little light can get in to that soul that was traumatised. And once there's a little light, it can grow," she says.

Healing With the Dolphins

Dolphins have long been renowned for their abilities as healers and communicators, and generate an awesome feeling of wellbeing in everyone who encounters them. In the 1950s, American Dr John Lilly began his groundbreaking work on the neuroanatomy of dolphins, their communication methods and the relationship between them and us. He said: "I hope for a time when all killing of whales and dolphins will cease, not from a law being passed, but from each human understanding innately that these are ancient, sentient earth residents, with tremendous intelligence and enormous life force. Not someone to kill, but someone to learn from. I suspect that whales and dolphins quite naturally go in the directions we call spiritual, in that they get into meditative states quite easily."

Dr Lilly invented the isolation tank, published scientific studies on biophysics, neurophysiology and electronics, and wrote several books, including the classic *The Mind of the Dolphin*. His work with dolphins and whales changed society's perception of these creatures, and led to the enactment of the Marine Mammal Protection Act in 1972. In 1976 he established the Human Dolphin Foundation, and he later released the dolphins he had done his research with, insisting that with the new understanding he'd gained from them, cetaceans – dolphins, whales and porpoises – should be accorded the same rights as humans. He died in 2001, but is still acknowledged as the father of dolphin research.

In the 1970s, Dr David Nathanson began facilitating a form of dolphin-human therapy for children with down syndrome, cerebral palsy and autism at Ocean World in Florida, and noticed amazing results, such as increased speech and motor skills, in patients diagnosed with developmental, physical and/or emotional disabilities. Nearby, at Dolphins Plus in Key Largo, Florida, Dr Betsy Smith also found that neurologically impaired children, particularly those with autism, responded well to close contact with dolphins, although both were criticised for their use of captive dolphins, and doubt has been cast on their findings because they didn't operate within the double-blind trial methods accepted by science. Dr Smith now only works with dolphins in the wild.

At the same time in the UK, medical research scientist Dr Horace Dobbs became a pioneer in dolphin healing and communication after his own transformative experience swimming with a wild dolphin off the Isle of Man. Opposed to the use of captive dolphins, he's conducted all his research with wild dolphins in the open sea, ensuring it was their choice to participate. They were always free to swim away – and often did – yet he showed that it's possible to work with totally free wild dolphins who choose to associate with humans.

Horace's classic book *Dolphin Healing* explores some of the incredible healings he has facilitated, for people suffering from different forms of clinical depression, severe autism, anorexia and even cancer, and the amazing progress they made after swimming with wild dolphins, amongst them Fungie in Ireland, Simo in Wales and the wild dolphin pods who choose to interact with people in the Bahamas. In the 1980s he set up a long-term research project, Operation Sunflower, which continues to investigate and record the healing power of dolphins. His work has contributed significantly to the acceptance of dolphin-assisted therapy and dolphin healing, and he's written several books – including *The Magic of Dolphins* and the children's series *Dilo the Dolphin* – and made documentaries, always with the welfare of the dolphins uppermost in his mind.

"For over three decades I have been exploring the special relationship and communication dolphins have with humans. During this time I discovered that dolphins have healing powers, and investigated this. I have also researched the possibility of artificially recreating the effects of swimming with dolphins in the wild to help those for whom this is not a possibility," he explains.

Dolphin-assisted healings have been experienced by people suffering from autism, cerebral palsy, spinal cord injury, ADHD, depression, multiple sclerosis, down syndrome, stress, phobias, addiction, arthritis and even, in some cases, cancer.

Scientists and medical researchers around the world have been trying to understand and explain how this works. One theory is that when a dolphin scans a person's body with their sonar, it triggers the healing process by boosting the production of T-cells and endorphins. Their high frequency sonar is used to echolocate their prey, creating a three dimensional image within their brain of what is in front of them. They can scan a shark that is a kilometre away to discover whether it has an empty or full stomach, and thus whether it's a threat to them, and when they "look" at a human, they also see right through them. This explains why dolphins are drawn to pregnant or sick people, as their sonar works like an ultrasound that reveals a foetus in the womb or a tumour in the body.

"Some therapists believe a dolphin's sonar causes a phenomenon called 'cavitation' inside the soft body tissue of the human body, which precipitates a ripping apart of the molecules," says marine biologist Amanda Green. "Many hospitals already use an ultrasound machine that uses low frequency sound waves to break up kidney stones and gall stones. The physics of that machine are not very different from a dolphin's sonar."

Dr Horace Dobbs's research led to a similar conclusion, that a dolphin's sonar sprays a person's body with sound waves that have a therapeutic physiological effect. Scientist David Cole, of the former AquaThought Foundation, a private research organisation, also echoes this theory. "It's very possible that dolphins are causing cavitation – a ripping apart of molecules – inside soft tissue in the body," he says. "And if they did that with cellular membranes, which are the boundaries between cells, they could completely change biomolecules, stimulating the production of infection-fighting T-cells or the release of endorphins. The dolphins produce an intense amount of echolocation energy. It resonates in your bones. You can feel it pass through you and travel up your spine."

Recent studies also show that interacting with dolphins increases the production and uptake of neurotransmitters such as dopamine, serotonin and oxytocin, and triggers the production of neurochemicals. And researchers have found that the sounds made by dolphins, an awesome series of clicks and squeaks, modify human brain waves, which causes changes in the nervous system, promotes relaxation and strengthens the immune system, resonates against and heals the spine, skull and brain, and zaps infected cells or diseased parts of the body.

Dolphin expert and psychotherapist Olivia De Bergerac has been studying these creatures and their interactions with humans for fifteen years. She takes people on overnight boat trips to swim with dolphins on the east coast of Australia, and has recorded hundreds of cases of physical as well as spiritual and emotional breakthroughs. In addition to keeping detailed journals and conducting follow-up sessions with participants, she uses an electroencephalograph (EEG) machine to monitor the changes in people's brain activity before and after a dolphin encounter.

The human brain operates at different frequencies of electrical activity. Usually it's in the beta range, a higher frequency that helps you focus, concentrate and take action – but which can lead to anxiety and stress if not balanced by also spending time in a more relaxed state. These slower alpha frequencies are conducive to good health, and can be achieved through meditation and relaxation techniques. An even slower frequency, theta, occurs in the time between waking and sleeping or in deep meditation, and helps you access the subconscious, grasp elusive ideas and experience deep healing.

Olivia noticed a change in people's brains, from stress-related beta brainwaves to alpha or theta waves, after they swam with dolphins – which helps explain the sense of peace and wellbeing felt when interacting with them. And she found these states could be accessed again, long after leaving the water and returning to daily life, by simply recalling the dolphin encounter.

In her book *The Dolphin Within*, Olivia records many case studies, as well as detailing some of her own healings with dolphins, which is what inspired her to start facilitating this amazing process for other people. As a teenager she had a major heart operation, which she felt she had physically healed from – but years later, while swimming with the dolphins at Monkey Mia in Western Australia, she felt her heart operation being finished the dolphin way.

"I swam away from the beach with the dolphins, with a mother dolphin and her baby under my heart, swimming and sending sounds through my body with her sonar. Such sound therapy, such high-tech surgery, was absolutely revolutionary for me. Swimming with this pod of dolphins that were zapping me with their sonar system, I realised that I had a new heart," she explains.

A year later, after resigning from her job to spend more time on dolphin research, Olivia had a debilitating motorbike accident. She couldn't work, she could barely walk, and for the first time ever she felt depressed, desperate and fragile. So she devoted all her time to researching the healing power of dolphins, with herself as guinea pig.

"I spent a year doing full-time research, recovering from my accident and slowly starting to do more work as my health got better with more and more dolphin swims. Doctors said I should have had operations for my neck, knee and lower back, but the only treatment I received was dolphin-assisted therapy. A year later I wasn't a hundred per cent fit, but I was no longer in bed, and no longer depressed."

Olivia's Dolphin Magic

Olivia De Bergerac is a psychotherapist and dolphin researcher, and author of *The Dolphin Within*. French by birth but Australian by choice, Olivia works as a business trainer and lectures in marketing, is an environmentalist dedicated to protecting marine life and its ocean habitat, and founder of The Dolphin Society, which carries out dolphin-assisted therapy and research, including trips to swim with wild dolphins in Port Stephens on Australia's east coast. Find out more at www.dolphinsociety.org.au.

The Australian dolphins made contact with me in the winter of 1990. Early one morning I went down to the beach for my daily swim, and spotted some dolphins. I jumped into the water, feeling that they were waiting for some human contact, and soon I was surrounded by six dolphins who swam around me. I stayed with them for an hour, completely frozen but so happy and joyful! I was in shock for months after that – my experience with the dolphins had awakened something very deep in me. It was extraordinary. It gave me an inner peace that transcended all human experience.

A few years later I organised my first Dolphin Within trip, with a few friends from the school of psychotherapy, and while we were swimming with the wild dolphins I realised that this was my mission. My family background, my studies in psychology and business, my spiritual work and my move to Australia were part of a big plan to bring me to research dolphin-human encounters. For more than fifteen years we've been recording people's experiences with wild dolphins, as well as testing our brains and those of participants before and after their interaction. The brainwave pattern changes that occur are remarkable, and are linked to the self-transformation and healing processes people report.

I still run Dolphin Within trips each summer. It's a two-day program that involves an encounter with dolphins in the wild, and is a journey of discovery of your dolphin within. People experience that specific state of bliss that we get from the dolphins, and then learn to integrate it back into their daily life. The gift the dolphins give us is a state of bliss, of being in the "now", being in the "zone" and the "flow". Scientifically, interacting with dolphins creates a specific brainwave pattern in humans – the theta state, which is a healing state – and a specific heart rhythmic called coherence. This dolphin-assisted therapy has helped people with depression, alcohol and drug addictions, phobias, epilepsy, stress-related illnesses and many other physical and emotional health challenges.

I've also noticed the effects dolphins have on us through my daughter Lilou. While I was pregnant I swam several times with dolphins, and she was actually born in the water like a dolphin at the Royal Women's Hospital in Sydney. She had the privilege of living with dolphins since conception, and she is happy, joyful, full of life and very strong physically. She has no fear – she loves swimming and surfing, and she even learned scuba diving with her uncle on Easter Island last year, at five years old. She loves animals – dolphins, whales, fish, turtles, dogs, cats and her guinea pig – and she absolutely adores horse riding.

I think people today yearn to interact with dolphins because humans and dolphins are like cousins. They are very close genetically and are attracted to each other, and the attraction works both ways. Dolphins have saved humans from drowning and from shark attacks, and humans can see in dolphins what they could themselves become – free of fear and emotions, and living in love. The thing I love best about them is their "high state" of being. They are high on life, without external substances.

Environmentally, the best thing we can do to help dolphins is keep our streets and beaches clean, pick up plastic bottles, bags and cigarette butts, and use environmental products so our waterways stay clean. Years ago, we campaigned to clean up the water in Sydney Harbour so dolphins and whales would visit more frequently, and now they do. Our harbour is not just a beautiful view – it's an amazing world beneath, and a treasure that we need to learn to enjoy and look after.

At this point in time, conclusive studies into dolphin-assisted therapy that meet the strict criteria of accepted clinical trials have not been completed, because no one wants to subject dolphins to the rigorous confines that would entail. Indeed Olivia's Dolphin Society aims to use the assessments of the brain changes after a dolphin encounter to develop a new form of dolphin-assisted therapy – one that does not involve contact with dolphins, either captive or wild, but instead creates a simulated learning environment in which people receive, with the assistance of coaching, healing from within themselves.

Dr Horace Dobbs has also been working to find a way to duplicate the therapeutic effects of interactions with dolphins in a way that would not require actual contact with these beautiful creatures, and which could be available to people no matter where they live. The Dolphin Dome Project, run by Horace and the non-profit organisation International Dolphin Watch (www.idw.org), which he founded in 1978 for the conservation and study of dolphins and the education of people about them, aims to identify the essence of the benefits humans receive from dolphin interactions and then replicate it, creating an interactive, sensory environment inside a dome where images and sounds can be projected that simulate the physical and psychological effects experienced during human-dolphin interaction.

"My aim was to create an interactive sensory unit, incorporating different elements of dolphin healing. Dolphin images carry their own healing power, and art, science and technology could overlap in the creation of an artificial dolphin experience that would be very healing, especially for the severely disabled," he says.

The importance of this is huge, because there are grave concerns about the effects of human interaction on dolphins. Swimming in the ocean alongside wild dolphins who have chosen to come and play with you, and can leave at any time, is one thing, but the issue of captive dolphins is a massive concern. Some dolphin-assisted therapy centres rely on the use of captive dolphins, but this new technology avoids the need for that. It is also cheaper than flying to specialised locations, such as Florida, and enables severely disabled children who cannot be treated in water to receive the benefits. The Dolphin Dome Project has also produced a mini dome that has proved helpful for children with asperger syndrome, amongst other conditions.

Dr Dobbs also completed an extensive study on the healing effects of what he terms "a dolphin audio pill" – a meditation CD called Dolphin Dreamtime, comprised of a thirty-minute visualisation by Tara Andre and thirty minutes of gentle dolphin music by Australian Glenda Lum, which is believed to capture the therapeutic essence of dolphins. The study, at the UK's Cambridge University, found that listening to the CD daily accelerated the recovery times of patients who had undergone surgery. A further study at Swansea University found that more than seventy-five per cent of people suffering from mental stress benefited from listening to it, and Dolphin Dreamtime is now used extensively to relieve stress, insomnia and nerves, help alleviate pain in childbirth, and to calm hyperactive children and those suffering from autism and cerebral palsy. It is also used in hospitals and prisons, and by stress management consultants, students taking exams, women in labour and anyone who wants to relax. The CD is available through the website of International Dolphin Watch, alongside Horace's many books and a wealth of information.

In a similar vein, inspired by the world's indigenous tribes that share special bonds with the ocean, Canadian psychologist and dolphin lover Jason Cressey has created a guided visualisation, the Dolphin Vision Quest, that he offers around the world. It allows people to relax and explore their personal connection with dolphins and whales without physical contact. A variety of dolphin breathing exercises are followed by a visualisation including music, dolphin and whale sounds and a personal narrative. He doesn't claim that it's a cure for anything, instead it is a self-awareness exercise which can help you develop your own visualisation skills to continue your dolphin journey, enhance your personal connection with dolphins and whales, gain insight into personal issues, clarify your goals and life path and reduce stress.

"It's a way to connect with dolphins without physically interacting with them – using guided imagery and visualisation, dolphin and whale sound recordings, many of which I've made over the years, and, where possible, a darkened room illuminated with blue light," Jason explains. "It's about taking people into their own private delphinic world. Simply being able to deeply relax while listening to such hauntingly beautiful – yet at the same time totally alien – sounds seems to affect people in ways they don't anticipate, and perhaps even influences the body or the brain's electrical activity in ways that instil a sense of calm and wellbeing."

Jason teaches workshops about dolphins, facilitates trips to swim with them around the world, gives school presentations to increase environmental awareness, wrote the book *Deep Voices: The Wisdom of Whales and Dolphin Tales*, and is the founder of The POD (www.people-oceans-dolphins.com), which promotes awareness of, respect for and contact with whales, dolphins and porpoises.

He says there are many ways you can connect with these beautiful creatures without getting in the water with them.

"In places such as Queensland, Patagonia, western Vancouver Island, Hermanues in South Africa, Hawaii and western Ireland it's possible to stand on the shoreline and watch dolphins and whales cavort in the waves – no boat or snorkel required. We can also immerse ourselves in dolphin and whale visuals, videos and sound recordings through the internet or on CD, and there are a number of workshops and presentations that allow people even in landlocked countries such as Switzerland to get a taste of that special relationship humans share with cetaceans," he says.

"I think the reason so many people yearn to swim with dolphins has a lot to do with intelligence seeking intelligence, and recognising – or needing to know – that we're not so alone on this big blue planet. Apart from the feelings of joy at the playfulness of dolphins, or the sense of awe that being next to a large whale can inspire, cetaceans offer us a sense that there are big brained, highly sentient and social creatures that share this earth with us – and they're doing a pretty good job of looking after themselves and their environment, even if we're responsible for decades of untold horrors that have negatively impacted cetaceans and their ocean home. Perhaps in them we also see then a beacon of hope – of what we can aspire to."

Jason is grateful for the objective, scientific approach his doctorate in psychology gave him, and believes that dolphins and whales provide a wonderful combination of the mystical and the scientifically astonishing.

"These wonderful, graceful, gentle beings satisfy and stimulate both the left brain and right brain, and much more besides. Being with dolphins and whales elicits tremendous joy in people. Everyone needs a little magic in their lives, and if dolphins and whales instil that magic in a person – be it through video, the internet, meditation or a physical encounter – that's wonderful," he says.

"As humans we want happiness – the dolphins have found this. We want peace of mind – when we swim with wild dolphins, we find it with them. They have a twinkle in their eyes that says: 'Let's play!'"

Joan Ocean, Hawaiian dolphin researcher, psychologist and author

One of the most important gifts of the dolphins is to reawaken happiness within us, and remind people of the importance of play. As I swam with dolphins around the world, I felt very clearly a wash of emotion that made me warm and happy inside. And I could sense their child-like joy in just being alive – they are so playful, and their sense of freedom and high spirits are contagious. I laughed out loud, giggled as I swam alongside these happy, loving, peaceful mammals, and for days afterwards found myself grinning goofily as I thought about then.

Surfers have long enjoyed the company of these playful creatures, who have been known to catch waves alongside them, keep them from going in to shore so they can interact for longer, and even nudge them on to a good wave. My dad and my brother-in-law are often joined by a pod of dolphins when they surf off the coast of their home in the southwest of Australia, and surfers in Byron Bay, on the east coast, also share their waves with dolphins from time to time, who surf upside down alongside the board riders, mimicking their actions and using their dorsal fin like a surfboard fin.

Dolphins also remind us to be environmentally aware, to feel connected to the great web of life and responsible for the health of the planet, its oceans and all the creatures who live within it. The documentary *The Cove*, and the dedication of several conservation groups determined to protect these beautiful sea creatures, such as Sea Shepherd, Save Japan Dolphins and the Whale and Dolphin Conservation Society, have all increased awareness of the threats to cetaceans, and helped people who live inland or in cities far from the ocean feel a kinship with these intelligent beings.

And all around the world, local swimmers have forged loving relationships with the dolphins of their area, interacting with them daily, often calling them by name, and developing a way of communicating with them and learning from them.

Some of the dolphins have even approached these human friends for help when they've had fishing line wound around them, been tangled in plastic bags or had fish hooks embedded in their skin.

On the west coast of the Big Island of Hawaii, where author and environmentalist Doreen Virtue has moved so she can spend more time with the dolphins, there are frequent human interactions with the curious sea creatures, who frolic in the warm, shallow waters and initiate contact with the people who share their watery home.

"The wild spinner and bottlenose dolphins who are always near the Kona coastline are very healing," Doreen says. "I've been in the water with them many times, and these amazing beings are definitely teachers and healers. They're exquisitely psychic, and stay away from people who are chasing them. Dolphins help those who are sad or in need of healing, and love to be around people who have their hearts wide open with love."

One of her most profound experiences with dolphins was after she'd spent the morning cleaning up fishing line while scuba diving, which she calls underwater housekeeping. "After I got back on the boat, a pod of dolphins surfaced nearby. I jumped back in the water without my scuba gear, and had three dolphins with me, one on each side and one beneath me. They were thanking me for cleaning up the fishing line. We swam around and around for ages, then they escorted me to the stairs of the boat to climb back onboard."

In San Francisco bay, a humpback whale became entangled in crab traps and fishing lines, and was weighed down so heavily she was struggling to stay afloat. Rescue divers with knives worked for hours to free her – and when they had eventually cut her out, the divers reported that she swam in joyous circles, then came back and nudged each person, one at a time, pushing them gently around as if she was thanking them. Some said it was the most profound moment of their lives. The diver who cut the rope out of her mouth said she followed him with her eyes the whole time, and most of them said it was the most beautiful experience they'd ever had, and they would never be the same again.

Places to Swim With Wild Dolphins

Today, as more and more people seek to connect with these incredible creatures, there are many places, from Australia and Hawaii to the Egyptian coast, where dolphin swims are facilitated, allowing us to interact with dolphins in their watery ocean realm. In most countries it is highly regulated, in order to protect the dolphins and ensure that human contact does not adversely affect them.

It's also for our benefit – although they're usually gentle and calm, and appear friendly, there have been incidents where a mother dolphin, feeling her calf is threatened, has lashed out and caused injury. Ric O'Barry, who trained TV dolphin Flipper and now campaigns for their freedom, was hospitalised after an incident with a captive dolphin. New Zealand dolphin Moko once kept a swimmer out playing in the water for so long that she had to be rescued, and other solitary creatures have nipped at people and even broken bones when someone harasses them. That beautiful dolphin smile is more about a lack of facial muscles than the happiness we interpret it as, and studies have found that dolphins suffer from depression as well as physical illness when kept in captivity.

Whether you're on an organised swim or simply take a dip in the ocean and meet a dolphin who's sought you out for some human interaction, be very attentive to their safety and their needs. Swim with your arms by your sides, rather than using an overarm stroke, which they construe as aggressive, and don't touch them or chase after them – let them come to you if they want to. They are naturally curious creatures, and if you're having fun in the water they will usually come over to see what you're up to, often mimicking your actions or any sounds you're making, and sometimes touching you with their fin or their beak.

Determine whether they are alone or with their babies – if it's the latter, make sure you never come between them. If they open their mouth, snap their jaw, jerk their head around or slap their tail in the water, steer clear, as these are signs of aggression. And be careful to never touch a dolphin's blowhole – this is how they breathe. Make sure you aren't wearing any jewellery or carrying anything sharp, as it could damage a dolphin's delicate skin. Don't use sunscreen around them, especially if you're somewhere that you can feed them – it irritates their eyes, and will make their fish taste yukky. Unless it is supervised and allowed by rangers, don't ever feed them, as this can cause them to become dependent and struggle to survive in the wild, and is illegal in many countries. If they are feeding, move away and observe quietly. If you see fishing line in the water, plastic bags or other rubbish, take it home with you.

Don't swim with dolphins if you're sick, as it could be contagious – dolphins have to breathe, just like us, so passing on any respiratory problems to them can cause serious health issues for their whole pod.

If you are planning a wild dolphin swim expedition, ensure that the operator is legit and follows the guidelines and regulations set for interacting with marine mammals. And if the dolphins don't appear, accept it with good grace and let them be – never chase or harass them, or let anyone bribe them to come over with fish handouts.

Through their daily interactions with these beautiful sea creatures, those who run wild dolphin swims know where they're most likely to be at a certain time, so an encounter is likely – but the protection and wellbeing of the dolphins is always their main priority, so heed their instructions. They are wild animals, and all human-dolphin encounters must take place on their terms, with strict regulations enforced to protect the dolphins. Boats should never chase them – credible operators will let the dolphins come to them. Marine conservation and education is a part of each dolphin swim facilitator's way of operating, and many of them incorporate long-term research into how best to protect the dolphins, and ensuring their presence does not harm them or change their behaviour in any way.

Many dolphins and whales frolic in the sparkling waters off the west coast of Australia. My dad surfs with them in the deep, wild waters of the southwest as well as further north, and there are other places where big wave riders interact with pods of them quite far out to sea. There are also three places in Western Australia where non-surfers can interact with dolphins.

More than a hundred bottlenose dolphins live in the sparkling waters of Koombana Bay, in the regional centre of Bunbury, two hours south of Perth. These friendly creatures interact playfully with the people who go out to swim with them, and a handful of regulars come in to shore every day to interact with the people lining the beach to meet them and be fed by the volunteers at the Bunbury Dolphin Discovery Centre (www.dolphindiscovery.com.au).

If you want to get a glimpse into the world of the dolphins, you can swim and snorkel with them out in the bay, under the direction of the centre's marine biologist or environmental scientist. The dolphins are wild, so it is up to them just how much proximity they will allow on any given day. Swim tours operate daily, weather permitting, from October to May, and you can sit and watch them from the boat if you don't want to swim with them.

There is also a marked Interaction Zone on the beach, where you can stand up to your waist in the calm, shallow waters and watch the dolphins as they swim around your legs and take food from the staff, who ensure the dolphins don't feel threatened in any way. Being wild, they come and go as they please, so their presence can't be guaranteed, but they usually visit between 8am and midday, and stay for up to two hours. There are less dolphins in winter, as some head north and others follow the fish migration out of the bay, but there are seven regular beach visitors, who the staff have named and keep an eye out for.

The centre takes the welfare of the dolphins very seriously, working with the Department of Environment and Conservation to monitor the impact of human interaction, and there are strict guidelines in place. Research has found that unregulated and excessive feeding of wild dolphins alters their behaviour, leading to a "taming" of wild animals and difficulty for them to survive on their own, so it is prohibited for visitors to feed them. The staff feed the dolphins that come in to shore a very small and closely recorded amount of their daily requirement of fish – less than three hundred and fifty grams of the eight to fourteen kilos dolphins need each day – as they don't want them to become dependent, or to have any impact on their normal behaviour.

There's also no touching allowed, you must remain within the markers, ensure you have no sunscreen on your arms or legs, and stay calm, not splashing the water or clapping your hands to try to attract the attention of the dolphins.

As well as a place to experience the joy of dolphin interaction, the Dolphin Discovery Centre is involved in research and marine conservation, and has formed a partnership with Murdoch University to work on the South West Marine Research Program. It aims to educate the public about dolphins and the environment in which they live, increase awareness of the need to protect marine mammals, observe and study the dolphins of the area to better understand their complex lives, and monitor the impact of humans on the dolphins and the bay. Staff also assist the Department of Conservation and Land Management in the rescue and rehabilitation of stranded or injured dolphins and other marine life, and provide an opportunity for people to interact with wild dolphins in a supervised setting where no harm will come to the dolphins. You can also adopt one of the dolphins, which helps the centre continue its important research, conservation and education programs.

An hour or so north of Bunbury, surrounding the town of Rockingham, is the spectacular Shoalwater Islands Marine Park, which is home to around two hundred dolphins as well as sea lions, pelicans, turtles and the state's largest colony of little penguins. Rockingham Dolphins (www.dolphins.com.au) facilitates wild dolphin swims in the sheltered waters of the bay from September to May, as well as dolphin-watching tours, trips to Penguin Island to see the penguins and sea lions, and glass bottom boat cruises through the marine park sanctuary zone. Again, all dolphin encounters happen on the animals' terms, and the team prides itself on its care and respect for the dolphins.

Through their relationships with the local wildlife, the company has also become involved in ongoing research and conservation issues concerning marine animals. They developed the Keep Perth's Dolphins and Sea Lions Wild project, which aims to protect the area's wildlife and educate the public. A five-year study of the seventy dolphins living in Cockburn Sound between Fremantle and Rockingham, conducted by local marine biologists Rebecca Donaldson and Hugh Finn, found that a quarter of them were conditioned to accept food from humans, which has a range of harmful effects, such as a greater risk of incidental interactions with vessels and fishing activities, which leads to an increased rate of boat propeller strikes and fishing line entanglements that result in injuries and fin amputation, a breakdown of normal social behaviour, including breakdown of male bonds with other males which are critical for obtaining mates, and an increased likelihood of becoming solitary loners, thus increasing their risk of shark attack.

One dolphin calf whose behaviour had been modified through becoming conditioned to being fed by people was found with fishing line wrapped around his lower jaw and pectoral fin – he died after the line lacerated down to the bone and severed his tongue. Discarded fishing line is notorious for entangling dolphins and sea lions, which often results in strangulation and limb amputation, and plastic bags have been responsible for many marine animal deaths. Another dolphin was found with multiple fishing hooks embedded inside the mouth, which resulted in infection and severe loss of health – fortunately this dolphin recovered, but many are not so lucky, and swallowing plastic, fishing gear and other objects can be lethal.

The study revealed the same findings as others from around the world – that feeding wild dolphins modifies their behaviour, predisposing them to boat strikes and fishing line entanglement, and causing them to engage in risky behaviours during feeding interactions, which in one case led to a dolphin being attacked by a shark because it wasn't paying attention to its surroundings. It can also lead to the transmission of infectious human diseases that can be fatal to dolphins, and serious ill health due to misguided individuals feeding them inappropriate food items such as fried chicken and chips, beer, pretzels, lollies and hot dogs, when their diet should consist only of live fish that they catch themselves. Fishermen have also been reported feeding them dead fish, contaminated food and tainted bait, which is disastrous for them.

Dolphins are hunters, so turning them into beggars alters their societal bonds and natural feeding patterns, and can make them unable to fend for themselves in the wild. Studies have found that adult males are at the greatest risk of becoming beggars. Once they start eating handouts, they frequent populated areas more regularly to get more food, and so more people feed them, in a downward spiral of dependence and increased danger.

They found that young dolphins are also at particularly high risk, as they will not survive if their mothers compete with them for human handouts and don't teach them to forage for food and catch fish. It's also been found that calves that become dependent on begging for food are at a greater risk of fishing line entanglement resulting in death. Provisioning dolphins also leaves them vulnerable to deliberate harm from people – as unimaginable as it sounds, there have been several cases in Australia of dolphins being shot or speared to death when they have started to live closer to humans.

There is also a risk to humans when dolphins become dependent on them for food and conditioned to approach them. One recent case involved a teenage girl who was bitten by a wild dolphin when she tried to pat it. Although they might look cute if they're swimming close to boats or jetties and begging for food, they are wild, and will bite when they are angry, frustrated or afraid. Some will also get aggressive, pushy and threatening if they are denied the food they have come to expect.

"Dolphins have a reputation for being friendly to humans, but the reality is that they are powerful, wild animals that can be very aggressive if provoked. People need to respect these animals in their natural habitat and let them stay wild," says marine mammal biologist Trevor Spradlin.

"We understand that people find it tempting to feed and to interact with wild dolphins, especially when they appear to be begging for food. However, people need to realise that feeding wild dolphins is harmful and illegal. One of the best ways that people can help protect the health and welfare of wild dolphins is to observe the animals at a respectful distance of at least fifty metres, resist feeding them and avoid any activities that risk harassing dolphins, such as chasing or touching the animals."

Stacey Horstman, bottlenose dolphin conservation coordinator for America's National Oceanic and Atmospheric Administration (NOAA), adds: "Feeding wild dolphins triggers a domino effect of harmful behaviours as dolphins learn to associate people with food and free handouts. We are at the point where we honestly need to change our behaviour so we don't change theirs."

In Australia, feeding wild dolphins is illegal under the Wildlife and Conservation Act and can result in fines of up to ten thousand dollars. In the US, feeding and harassing wild marine mammals is illegal under the Marine Mammal Protection Act, and can result in fines of up to twenty thousand dollars and one year in jail for the most serious violations. There is concern in America that dolphins are being turned into aggressive panhandlers, and there have been several reports of people being injured by dolphins begging for food. They have also learned to take fish off the lines of commercial fishermen, increasing their risk of ingesting baited hooks. And some dolphins been found dead with hooks and fishing line in their throats or stomachs.

While feeding wild dolphins is illegal in many countries around the world, there are a few places where carefully regulated managed feeding is allowed. One of these places is Monkey Mia (www.sharkbay.org), on the Western Australian coast more than eight hundred kilometres north of Perth, where there is a community of wild dolphins that chooses to come in to shore and interact with human visitors. More than two thousand dolphins reside in the deep waters of Shark Bay around Monkey Mia, while a group of around two hundred live in the Monkey Mia region. Of these, the same five adult dolphins, sometimes with their calves in tow, swim in to Dolphin Beach each day to accept small amounts of fish and interact with human visitors.

Rangers from the Department of Environment and Conservation carefully supervise the process and it is strictly regulated – only small, controlled amounts of fish are provided to the dolphins so they don't become dependent. Swimming with the dolphins in this zone is prohibited, but a small number of visitors are chosen to assist with the feeding each morning, and anyone can stand in the shallows and watch them swimming around and being fed. These friendly creatures sometimes approach people in the swimming areas outside the dolphin interaction zone, choosing to connect with them. This is where Olivia De Bergerac had her first major dolphin healing, and the first place I saw them up close, as I stood in the shallow waters as a teenager and they swam around my legs.

A group of bottlenose dolphins first started visiting isolated Monkey Mia beach in the sixties, when local fishermen would share their catch with them. These dolphins passed this unusual behaviour down to their offspring, and the ones that visit today are the third generation to do so. Such a phenomenon of learned behaviour being passed down has contributed to the scientific viewpoint that dolphins are highly intelligent creatures, and since the early 1980s the complex social behaviour of the Monkey Mia dolphins has been carefully studied. It's the longest continuous study of bottlenose dolphins in the world – and has resulted in international changes to human-dolphin interaction, and much stricter guidelines to ensure dolphins are not adversely affected by humans. This is also the place where scientists discovered that some dolphins had learned to use a sea sponge to cover their beak while foraging, which protected them and also made foraging more successful, and had passed this new skill down to their calves – it's the only place in the world where wild dolphins have been observed using tools.

Another groundbreaking discovery was the revelation that male dolphins form complex, multi-layered alliances, similar to gangs, which are like those of human males but unlike those of any other animal. Monkey Mia is not only the world's most significant dolphin behavioural research site, it's also the world's most significant tiger shark and dugong research site, and a significant place for research into loggerhead and green sea turtles, sea snakes and stingrays.

As a result of the increasing information and knowledge gained by researchers here, in 1988 the Monkey Mia Reserve was created to conserve the area, and two years later the waters surrounding Monkey Mia were declared a marine park, further protecting the environment and its dolphins and other sea creatures. There is now a visitor centre that offers information about dolphins and other marine animals, as well as the reserve and the surrounding Shark Bay World Heritage Area.

While the dolphins of southern Western Australia are common bottlenose dolphins (Tursiops truncatus), which grow up to four metres long and weigh up to six hundred and fifty kilos, the ones at Monkey Mia are Indo Pacific bottlenose dolphins (Tursiops aduncas), which only grow to two and a half metres long and weigh up to two hundred and fifty kilos, and look more like the spotted and spinner dolphins common in tropical regions such as the ocean surrounding Hawaii. Both types are smaller than the pelagic (open ocean) dolphins that live offshore in the deeper parts of the sea, who shun human interaction and beach visits.

Along the southern coast of Australia, in the waters of Melbourne's Port Phillip Bay, a group of up to a hundred wild bottlenose dolphins has been living and playing for many years. They are paler and slightly smaller in size than their offshore counterparts, and reside in the southern region of the bay during the warmer months. This is also one of the few places in the world where common dolphins have taken up residence in sheltered waters, rather than living offshore in the open ocean where they are usually found in large pods – of a thousand or more animals – that migrate according to the fish stocks they eat. Since 2006, the Dolphin Research Institute, a marine conservation organisation based in the bay, has been documenting the presence of this pod of twenty common dolphins, who reside along the eastern coast of the bay during the cooler months. A second generation of calves was recently born into the pod, which marine scientist Jeff Weir, head of DRI, says is a wonderful indication of the health of the bay and the work of conservationists to keep the animals safe.

A recent incident where a jetskier drove too close to the dolphins as they frolicked with their babies sparked outrage, with wildlife officers investigating, and led to increased awareness of the regulations, such as boats needing to stay at least a hundred metres clear of dolphins and whales, and those on personal watercraft such as jet skis needing to maintain a distance of at least three hundred metres.

DRI is dedicated to finding out how to best assist in the management and conservation of these dolphin populations, ensuring that they continue to thrive in Port Phillip Bay, Western Port and around the Victorian coastline, monitoring fluctuations in dolphin numbers and identifying areas of importance to the dolphins and their health and wellbeing. They also monitor potential human impacts on both dolphins and the marine environment, measure the extent of these impacts and develop strategies to manage them. And they introduce and enforce new laws to protect dolphins, and raise awareness in the community to encourage more caring behaviour around the dolphins.

There are a few eco tourism companies that offer a chance to swim here with the wild bottlenose dolphins in their own environment. The swim season is usually from October to April, as the dolphins often move north during Australia's cooler months.

In Sorrento, on the beautiful Mornington Peninsula south east of Melbourne, Polperro Dolphin Swims (www.polperro.com.au) conducts amazing swims that emphasise conservation and care. While sailing out to sea the captain talks about the importance of marine conservation, and describes the local dolphins the crew has come to know, along with their particular traits and personalities. He is usually interrupted by a few of said dolphins approaching the boat and leaping around the bow. Polperro staff help swimmers of all levels feel confident in the water when it's time to slip into the ocean and gaze in awe at the beautiful dolphins who come to check out the humans and swim around them. The crew also runs the environmental organisation Earth Sirens, which concentrates on research, education and sustainability in this beautiful marine area.

Moonraker Dolphin Swims (www.moonrakercharters.com.au) also offers dolphin swims in the same area, and across the bay at Queenscliff, Sea All Dolphin Swims (www.dolphinswims.com.au) has beautiful cruises through the Port Phillip Heads Marine National Park, world renowned for its rich and unique marine life, as well as wild dolphin swims. All tours are conducted under strict regulations designed to minimise the impact on the dolphins, with small groups of swimmers accompanied by experienced guides.

In South Australia, the offshore waters near the capital city of Adelaide are home to more than a thousand common and bottlenose dolphins, and closer to the coast there is a smaller community that has been interacting with people for some time. Marine biologist and conservationist Dr Mike Bossley, managing director of the Whale and Dolphin Conservation Society in Australia, has been studying these dolphins since 1987, when he saw a photo of a horse and a dolphin swimming together in the Port River. This dolphin, Billie, inspired him to begin one of the longest studies of a dolphin population anywhere in the world, and much of what is understood about how dolphins live in the wild and how they socialise and interact is because of his passion and commitment. Mike's research has revealed that about thirty dolphins reside in the Port River estuary, another thirty visit regularly, and more than a hundred visit occasionally.

"I've identified about three hundred individual dolphins over the years. A lot of them I've known for around twenty years, since they were babies, and now they've grown up and had babies themselves. So they're pretty used to the sound of my boat and, I guess, to the sound of my voice," he says. "I record who I see, who's with who and where they are. I also have a good look to see if there are any problems, because unfortunately a lot of these dolphins get tangled up in fishing line and so forth. If they do have any entanglements on them then we organise to catch them so we can cut them off."

Sadly industrial pollution and human cruelty have been a grave threat to the health and wellbeing of these dolphins, and there have been a few cases where dolphins were shot or stabbed to death. Mike and other local environmentalists, including the Whale and

Dolphin Conservation Society and residents concerned about the safety of the dolphins and the quality of their environment, campaigned to protect these beautiful creatures.

As a result of their efforts, the state government established the Adelaide Dolphin Sanctuary (www.tinyurl.com/3sa76wk) in 2006, which covers the Port Adelaide River Estuary and Barker Inlet. It was set up to protect the dolphins and their habitat, and maintain, protect and restore key habitat features. Two rangers now patrol sanctuary land and water, and conduct community education to let people know the best ways to behave around dolphins. They also work to maintain healthy water quality, as in the past, industrial complexes, wastewater and sewage outflows and power generation plants have dumped toxic materials in the river, resulting in chemical and thermal pollution, introduced marine pests, litter and excess nutrients in the water, and leading to high levels of mercury and other toxins in the local dolphins.

Mike's research, which involves up to sixty hours a week observing the dolphins and recording data, uncovered a behaviour never seen in other wild dolphins – tail walking, where the dolphin pushes itself out of the water and walks backwards on its tail. For a long time Billie, who died in 2009, was the only dolphin to do it, and she only did it very occasionally. It was believed that she'd seen dolphins performing this trick when she spent a short time in captivity many years ago, and that she later tried it herself. Then a few years ago another adult female dolphin, Waves, started doing it too, and since then four more dolphins have taken up this new sport.

"Culture in the wider sense of the term, defined as 'learned behaviour characteristic of a community', is now frequently on show in the Port River, and this cultural behaviour is of great significance for dolphin conservation," Mike says. "Cultural behaviours in animals have been identified in several species, particularly chimpanzees. However, most if not all the cultural behaviours described to date have been of a utilitarian nature, mainly to do with obtaining food," he explains.

"The only dolphin example seen up to now is in Shark Bay, where a small group of dolphins habitually carry a sponge on the end of their jaw while fishing to protect them from fish spines. As far as we are aware, tail walking has no practical function and is performed just for fun – akin to human dancing or gymnastics.

As such, it represents an internationally important example of the behavioural similarities between humans and dolphins."

Like dolphins in other Australian states, these ones are protected from harassment and physical harm under provisions of the National Parks and Wildlife Act 1972 and the Whale and Dolphin Regulations 2000. There's also a dolphin-watching cruise, with the option of swimming with the beautiful creatures, which leaves from Glenelg, a seaside resort just fifteen minutes from the CBD.

They're run by Temptation Sailing (www.dolphinboat.com.au), which was the first South Australian operator to be granted a licence to swim with wild dolphins. Over many years, owner and operator Stephen Waites, his daughter Jade and the crew of the Temptation have developed a high level of trust with many of the local dolphins, and they come over to the boat to play with their human visitors, rather than having to be sought out. One in particular is a young dolphin they named Jade, who came into the marina where they're based a decade ago, and took to people in a way that is very rare in dolphins – only a handful around the world, including Fungie in Ireland and Moko in New Zealand, take to people and crave interaction with them in such a strong way.

Further west, operating off the coast of the Eyre Peninsula in the Great Australian Bight, is the Baird Bay Ocean Eco Experience (www.bairdbay.com), run by Alan and Patricia Payne. Over many years of patient interaction with the sea lions and dolphins of the area, they've developed a friendship with them, and a knowledge of their behaviour and desire for play and human interaction – always on the dolphin or sea lion's terms. Their hope is that everyone who swims with these beautiful marine creatures will leave with their heart lifted, and a resolution to help protect them.

"Our adventures with the marine mammals of Baird Bay started in late 1992 by chance, with the first approach being made by a young sea lion inquisitive about what we were and what we were doing while we were fishing," Patricia says. "With Alan's curiosity matching this little lion of the sea, he could not resist the temptation to slip quietly into the water to return the gaze of this young, wide-brown-eyed lion. Now, after many years of constant encounters we have learned a great deal from these wonderful creatures, their likes and dislikes, what upsets them and what pleases them, and one thing we have really learned is that they love human interaction, they love a game – but it must be of their choosing.

"Swimming with the dolphins of this bay started in much the same way – their game though is much different. They are cats of the sea, and like a cat they are aloof and possess what seems to be a magical quality," she says. Like all reputable dolphin swim operators, Alan and Patricia have never fed any of the sea creatures – they are totally free, totally wild, unfed and untrained – and all interaction occurs solely on the dolphins' terms.

There are also several dolphin interaction programs on the east coast of Australia. The beautiful waters of Port Stephens Marine Park, two and a half hours drive north of Sydney, are home to around a hundred and seventy bottlenose dolphins. You can often view them from the shore, and there are many dolphin and whale-watching cruises that depart daily from Nelson Bay, and an agreed operating code for all vessels to stay clear of the dolphins so they can swim unhindered.

As part of Dr Olivia de Bergerac's Dolphin Therapy Research Program, she spends a number of days each year swimming with the dolphins in these waters. Also in Port Stephens is Dolphin Swim Australia, run by dive master Andrew Parker and his wife Elise Bailey, the dolphin biologist who heads the research team and swim permit compliance side of things. Andrew spent four years developing the Aquatic Marine Viewing Experience, and it is the only licensed dolphin swim in the state.

Like many such dolphin interactions, swimmers are attached to tow ropes off the boat, and ride the bow waves alongside the dolphins. They can also be part of the long-term and ongoing research into the short-beaked common dolphins that live in this area – which aims to be the most comprehensive migratory and distribution study in the world. These dolphins grow up to two and a half metres long, and weigh between eighty and two hundred and forty kilos – although the upper weight range is rare. Andrew and Elise have been studying the behaviour of the dolphins for some time, and noting their actions with joy. Some have now begun to include the humans that swim with them in their games. "To me, this means so much. It is an example of two completely different species connecting in a way that touches both," Andrew says.

Andrew's Aquatic Magic

Australian Andrew Parker has facilitated dolphin-assisted therapy programs and studied dolphin behaviour around the world, all of which led him to create a new form of wild dolphin swim, the Aquatic Marine Viewing Experience, which takes place in beautiful Port Stephens Bay in New South Wales with wild deep-water dolphins. Find out more at www.dolphinswimaustralia.com.au.

The AMVE is an off-shore swim with a type of dolphin no one else in Australia is swimming with. Most dolphin interaction around the world is with in-bay bottlenose dolphins, the species we all know as Flipper, and the one that's most often exhibited in captive situations. But a decade ago I began interacting with the short-beaked Pacific common dolphin, which we know very little about because it's a pelagic – oceanic – dolphin. This happened out in deep open water on our fifty-foot catamaran. Several of these dolphins started to ride the bow wave of the vessel, interacting of their own choice. This is a very cheeky, excitable, fast and intelligent form of dolphin that seems to like interacting with humans.

I began studying the regulations for human-dolphin interaction, and knew this had the potential to be an experience that did not contravene any legislation. And as very little is known about these dolphins, we could also include a long-term research program. My wife Elise is a marine biologist who's been interacting with and studying dolphins even longer than I have, and she's heading up our population study. We're numbering and naming the dolphins in pods, and creating a fin identification study too, because the dorsal fin of a dolphin is absolutely unique. For whales it's the tail flukes, for dolphins it's the dorsal fins. So we'll get to know whether these dolphins live in the area, or return each year, or only come by once, which is really exciting.

We've noticed some dolphins from previous years coming back, and we've had several dolphins interact with us repeatedly. They've been playing with us, which we're absolutely over the moon about. When a dolphin brings a toy to you, a piece of grass or some seaweed, that's a form of communication. They pass those things around to each other and chase each other around to get it, it's one of the games they most enjoy. So to watch them drop a piece of seagrass, let you pick it up, then you drop it and they bring it back to you, that's phenomenal. That's "let's play!" The fact that they now embrace us awkward swimmers in their games lets me know they are accepting us. They're creating activities to engage us.

It's always totally their choice to come over to us – we toddle slowly along on the boat and they can come in, check us out, hang with us for a little while then go off and do whatever they want to do. These guys can travel thirty knots in bursts, and are masters of the disappearing act. If they don't want to be there, they can disappear in an instant, so we know they're there because they want to be. In our very rudimentary way we're attempting to communicate – and they're communicating back to us in the most basic ways. Elise has been studying inter-species communication and dolphin language with respected scientists around the world, and we are absolutely committed to working on that, to breaking that species barrier with language. I'd love to be able to talk dolphin. One day!

Dolphin conservation is an important part of our research, and our lives. We want to inspire people to protect the marine environment and everything in it. Because these are deep-water, off-shore dolphins, a lot of their injuries come from the fishing industry rather than boat strike. Dolphins work together to hunt – they herd fish into tight balls and take their turn coming into the ball and feeding, then backing away for a fellow pod member to have a turn. They're used as an indicator species for tuna, because if fishermen locate pods of these dolphins, they know there's tuna underneath. They trawl through these fish balls, and their fishing line is almost invisible and causes serious damage to dolphin dorsal fins – we've seen some that have been removed completely. Thousands more are part of by-catch, dragged through the nets and thrown overboard in agony or dead. So if you eat fish, at the very minimum make sure it's dolphin safe.

A little further north of Port Stephens, in the Great Lakes region, Dive Forster (www.diveforster.com.au) provides in-water dolphin interactions as well as diving courses. Three hundred resident inshore bottlenose dolphins – many of which swim over to the boat to check out the humans – live here, and only one person at a time is allowed in the water with them – this person holds on to a rope attached to the boat while the dolphins swim under, beside and around them, while further offshore there are common dolphins, which are among the fastest dolphins in the world, reaching speeds of forty kilometres an hour. Oceanic dolphins are also seen at times – they're larger than the others, and are famous for their aerial acrobatics and freakish speed – and it's not far from here that Lucy has been blessed to find herself sharing an ocean swim with a local wild dolphin or two.

Operator Ron Hunter established the first dive centre in Forster thirty years ago, and has been taking people out into the ocean, teaching diving courses and protecting the local wildlife ever since. And it's not just dolphins he cares about – in the late 1980s, noticing a decline in the population of the grey nurse sharks that inhabit the area, he and two friends campaigned to get their plight recognised. After years of effort, grey nurse sharks were finally declared "critically endangered" – one step away from extinction – and further campaigns convinced the government to put into place protection zones at some of the declared critical habitat areas.

As well as dolphin swims, Ron offers many other marine adventures, including whale-watching cruises and dive trips around the world, such as swimming with whales in Tonga, swimming with sea turtles, sharks and other marine creatures in the Galapagos Islands, and diving with rays and snorkelling around uninhabited coral cays and atolls in the Maldives.

Further up the eastern coast, in the regional city of Coffs Harbour, is Dolphin Marine Magic Marine Park (www.dolphinmarinemagic.com.au), which is also known as the Pet Porpoise Pool, where you can meet and interact with the animals that live there, including dolphins, seals, little penguins, turtles, fish, a pelican and some land-dwelling animals. They run educational presentations to increase awareness about these wonderful creatures, and there is also the opportunity to have a dolphin or seal encounter, where you can spend time in the pool with them. The park was developed in the late sixties as a rescue and rehabilitation facility for injured marine animals, and it remains so today. The founders also started the Coffs Harbour Animal Rescue Trust, a not-for-profit organisation that treats and rehabilitates marine wildlife, monitors emerging diseases and supports and participates in programs of conservation.

As part of their rescue work they've saved many dolphins, seals and other animals that were close to death – some with extensive shark bites, others stranded, sunburned and dehydrated, and still others wrapped in metres and metres of fishing line and other garbage – rehabilitating them back to health over a lengthy period. Many are returned to the wild after treatment and recovery, but for some, who were too badly injured to go back to the ocean, it was deemed to be in their best interests to remain at the pool, as they would have been unable to survive on their own, or were likely to put themselves back in the same danger that nearly killed them before.

Two of the dolphins in the park, Bucky and Calamity, fall into this category – the latter was rescued and rehabilitated for the second time after her tail was almost severed, so being released again would be fatal. There are also two dolphin calves that were born in captivity, who would be unlikely to survive on their own in the wild, as well as a group of rescued Australian sea lions – which are listed as endangered – that are part of a breeding program that aims to return as many as possible to the wild and help them get off the endangered list. The park has a strong educational aspect, and works with Make A Wish and the Starlight Foundation to enable sick or disabled children to spend time with the dolphins in a safe environment.

But as much as I have wanted to go and meet a dolphin, and give them a hug, here or in Sea World in Queensland or similar places around the world, I feel deeply conflicted and can't bring myself to do it. The keeping of captive dolphins is a controversial and often terrible thing. It feeds the killing frenzy in places like Taiji, Japan, where dolphins are shepherded into a small bay, the "prettiest" ones sold to Asian water parks for a hundred and fifty thousand dollars each, and the rest slaughtered and sold for meat.

A recent scandal erupted in Las Vegas when it was discovered that The Mirage hotel keeps dolphins in a small swimming pool for guests to look at – and when they die, which they frequently do, they are simply replaced with a new dolphin, destined to live out its short life in cramped conditions and chlorine drenched water next to a busy, polluted highway in the desert.

Ric O'Barry, who captured and trained wild dolphins in the sixties for the TV show *Flipper*, has dedicated his life since then to campaigning for the freedom of dolphins and the closure of all captive dolphin facilities, because as happy as the dolphins at places like Sea World look, he believes all captive situations are linked.

"It's really about supply and demand. If I'm wearing ivory, I'm the reason the elephant is becoming extinct. Not the guy in the jungle with the shotgun, me the consumer. So it is true with this dolphin captivity issue. It's the one thing we ask people: 'Don't buy a ticket to a dolphin show.' This worked in the United Kingdom. There are no more captive dolphins there. Even when there was, they had laws to say you can't capture dolphins because there's something wrong with it, so they would import them from Florida with a permit from the National Marine Fisheries Service," Ric explains.

"There are a lot of things wrong with captivity, and it starts with the capture. I captured over a hundred dolphins for the Miami Seaquarium, and I can tell you that all the captures are violent, it's kind of like rape. You chase them down to exhaustion. You separate mothers and babies. You take the young. Eighty per cent of the captures are young females taken away from their mothers, and how this affects the gene pool nobody will ever know. Then they're placed in a concrete chlorinated box, reduced to circus clowns and sold as educational to the public. It doesn't work. It's a failed experiment. Keeping dolphins and other whales in a concrete box doesn't work. It never worked. That's why I left the industry."

In the 1960s, when *Flipper* was being made, information about dolphins was scarce. Back then it was believed that a dolphin who smiled as it performed for people in amusement parks was happy.

"People need to go beneath a dolphin's smile, because dolphins will smile even if they're sick, dying or dead," confirms Dr Toni Frohoff, a marine biologist who specialises in dolphin research.

Ric soon discovered that the dolphin's smile is nature's greatest deception, which inspired his books *Behind the Dolphin Smile* and *To Save a Dolphin*. After *Flipper* went off the air, most of the dolphins were sold to travelling shows or amusement parks, although Kathy, the main dolphin who played Flipper, who Ric had

lived with, trained and bonded
with for seven years, remained
in her tank. One day he got a
call to say she was not doing
well, and when he went to
see her, she was floating on
top of the unshaded tank, blistered
and black with sunburn because she spent most
of her time on the surface of the water. Her fin was bent from
being above water too long. And he knew she was depressed.

"She swam into my arms, looked me right in the eye, took a
breath, and just held it. She committed suicide. Dolphins and
whales are not involuntary air breathers like we are. Every breath
they take is a conscious effort. They can end their life whenever
they want to, and that's what Kathy did. She chose to not take that
next breath, and you have to call that suicide. I let her go and she
sank straight down on her belly to the bottom of the tank," he says.

This happened six days before the first Earth Day, in April 1970,
and was the incident that inspired Ric's passionate crusade to let
everyone know about the ugly underbelly of the captive dolphin
industry. On the eve of Earth Day he flew to Bimini in the Bahamas
to set a captive dolphin free. Although it was a disaster – after Ric
finally got the enclosure open, the dolphin wouldn't leave, he nearly
drowned in the process, and was then arrested and jailed for a week
– it kicked off his forty-year campaign to free captive dolphins,
stop dolphin slaughter and make people aware of what is going on.

"I wanted people to realise it was wrong to own dolphins, and
even worse, if possible, to make them do silly tricks. With the death
of Kathy, the dolphin I most dearly loved, I was on a pilgrimage to
try to undo at least some of the mess I'd made of things," Ric says.

Dolphin lover Jason Cressey agrees that people's attendance at
dolphin shows contributes to the cruelty and the slaughter of these
amazing creatures. "Never, ever go to see dolphins or whales in
captivity, and encourage your friends and family never to go to
these sea circuses either," he says. "As long as there is demand, this
business will continue. As long as these businesses continue, the
mindset that we can 'capture' nature to be delivered on tap will
continue to contort and pervert our relationship with the natural
world and the way we treat it – including our precious oceans."

The Issues With Captivity

☹ The average life span of a dolphin is forty-five years, but half of all captive dolphins die within two years, from pneumonia, intestinal disease, shock, ulcers, chlorine poisoning or stress-related illnesses.

☹ Dolphins are sonic creatures with incredibly sharp hearing, so an aquarium filled with shouting crowds and barking trainers is stressful. The white of the walls also causes them pain.

☹ Dolphins are accustomed to swimming up to a hundred and sixty kilometres a day – in captivity they are limited to a small tank.

☹ Most tank water is full of chemicals such as chlorine, which causes many health problems including blindness.

☹ The water in their tanks or pools is often full of bacteria too, which leads to infections, and many dolphins are injected with vitamins and medicines to try to prevent this, which is not good.

☹ Dolphins born in captivity have very high infant mortality rates, and often births are not announced until they are sure the calves will survive. Neither could they survive if they are released.

☹ Many marine parks starve their dolphins, and feed them only as a reward for learning new tricks and performing for crowds.

☹ Their diet should consist of live fish they catch themselves – in the wild they spend half their time hunting for food, which provides exercise and mental stimulation, but in captivity they are fed dead fish which has been handled, so it may have harmful bacteria, and is often cheap and of low nutritious value and quality.

☹ Many captive dolphins swim in a repetitive circle pattern, silent and with their eyes closed, because they're bored and depressed.

☹ Some bang their heads against the wall or abuse themselves in a similar manner to provide some form of stimulus.

☹ Dolphins are social creatures that, in the wild, live in large pods, with the freedom to come and go as they please and interact with other groups of dolphins. Some captive males, lacking interaction, become aggressive and attack other dolphins or their trainers.

☹ Many dolphins in captivity are caught and transported to a shallow, chlorine-filled pool in the desert, suffering weather extremes from hot, dry summers to freezing cold winters, with no protection from the sun or the snow.

☹ As they breathe air like we do, when they are inland rather than out at sea, they inhale huge amounts of pollution and smog.

Captivity is not a totally black and white issue though. Scott Taylor from the Cetacean Studies Institute and Dolphin Embassy, an initiative to recognise the rights of cetaceans to life, clean oceans and quiet seas (www.dolphintale.com), argues that rehabilitation centres such as the one in Coffs Harbour can play an important part in helping dolphins. And he points to new research that reveals an alarming trend in the euthanasia of stranded dolphins.

As the campaign to ban the captivity of all cetaceans grows, the opportunity for a dolphin that strands and requires long-term care, due to circumstances that make it inhumane to return it to the sea, has nearly disappeared. According to Scott, the Pet Porpoise Pool is now one of only two facilities in Australia licensed to rehabilitate dolphins, after another seven were pressured to close down – which itself led to several dolphin deaths as these creatures could not survive when returned from their tanks to the wild.

"All too often, rangers working for government agencies appear at cetacean strandings with hypodermic syringes filled and ready. If a dolphin or small whale is thought unlikely to survive if returned to the water quickly, or might require long-term care if rescued, it is killed on the spot," Scott claims.

A few years ago a dolphin was found stranded in the Coffs Harbour estuary. Before local dolphin experts could get it onto a stretcher to be carried to the Pet Porpoise Pool for rehabilitation, a ranger from the National Parks and Wildlife Service arrived and injected it with a lethal dose of chemicals, killing it immediately.

"The necropsy carried out the next day showed absolutely no pathology. This stranded dolphin was killed for no reason. It had no identifiable illness, disease or parasites. And it was only metres away from one of the only rescue facilities capable of helping it. It could have been helped to recover, and would then have been taken to sea and released. Or, if she had not been able to live in the ocean due to the extent of her injuries, she could have been given a lifetime of excellent care, living among humans as an ambassador for her kind."

Ric O'Barry agrees there are occasional instances where dolphins need rehabilitation, but disputes the need for tanks. "There are some dolphins that become stranded and need to be in captivity long enough to be rehabilitated and released. But you don't need these tanks. You can rehabilitate a stranded dolphin in natural seawater in a lagoon. Because as long as there's a tank, once he's taken out of it something else will be put in there. That's the problem," he says. "When I say I'm an abolitionist I mean abolish the tank, and abolish the dolphins performing for our amusement."

Dr Horace Dobbs, British scientist and dolphin researcher, says: "For me, dolphins in captivity is akin to that of human slavery. When slavery was rife we did not know, or care to accept, that all humans, regardless of their origins, have a right to freedom. The situation changed when William Wilberforce and others campaigned for the freedom of slaves because they felt the practice was immoral. Now that principle, of a right to freedom for all men, is accepted almost universally. A similar situation now exists with regard to dolphins in captivity. Many people, especially those who have worked closely with dolphins, feel that freedom is a right for these mammals that have been dubbed man's cousins in the seas."

Andrew Parker, who has worked with children with disabilities at the Pet Porpoise Pool in the past, also acknowledges the great work they do, but hopes that humanity can soon get to a level where we don't need to keep intelligent creatures in captivity.

"It started out with the best of intentions. I know Zip and Bucky and Calamity, I know little Bella, and they're beautiful, and the people who work with them are beautiful. And having a facility like that, you can work with kids and people who could never in a million years go out to sea and interact with a pod offshore," he says.

But Andrew adds that there's a big issue in that they are a family, and dolphins are sexual creatures. If there are no other dolphins around, as there would be in a large pod, they will have sex with each other. Bella will probably have to go to Sea World to avoid this happening – taken away from her family but not understanding why.

"Being in captivity in a concrete tank really does not allow the dolphins to exhibit their amazing sonic abilities either. Their language is dumbed down, they don't have the opportunity to talk to other dolphins, to understand what's happening outside," Andrew says. "Where it may work really well for us, those dolphins work very very hard, they're doing show after show after show, and swims and swims and swims, and meeting person after person after person. They can't go anywhere, they can't have a day off."

"The captivity question is a difficult one to answer," adds Melainah Yee of Hawaii's Sunlight On Water wild dolphin swim program. "In general we do not support captive dolphin programs, but there are a few excellent facilities, such as one that works with children with autism, and another that works with those with cancer and leukaemia, who have achieved some great results."

There are many issues and perspectives surrounding dolphin captivity, conservation and care, and the more information we have, the better we can make an informed decision about what we want to support and what we don't, and can begin to understand the consequences of our actions – from eating tuna to going to a dolphin show to campaigning for one cause over another.

Beautiful northern New South Wales is a great place for whale and dolphin-watching, with pods spotted from the shore at some Byron Bay beaches. To get up close, there's a kayaking tour (www.capebyronkayaks.com) that takes you out to spot dolphins, sea turtles and other creatures, learn more about them and discover how inquisitive they can be. Depending on the season, you'll also see humpback whales as they migrate north from Antarctica. No experience is needed, as the guides – local surfers and kayakers who know the area well – help you operate the kayak.

A few hours drive south of Sydney, in beautiful Jervis Bay Marine Park, there are around eighty local bottlenose dolphins, and more that visit occasionally. Dolphin and whale watching is popular, with many cruises available. Dolphin Watch Cruises (www.dolphinwatch.com.au) was one of the first dolphin and whale-watching companies in Australia, and they focus on protecting the bay's marine inhabitants and educating visitors about conservation as they show off the natural wonders of the area. Dolphin Wild Cruises (www.dolphinwildcruises.com.au) also offer dolphin-watching trips, in a special cruise vessel with unique underwater viewing windows, which allow passengers to view Jervis Bay and all its wildlife above, below and beyond.

Over the border in Queensland, home to the Great Barrier Reef and the beautiful – but endangered – Coral Sea, there are also many marine creatures. Across the bay from Brisbane is Moreton Island, an hour by ferry from the mainland. Once a whaling station, it is now the site of the Tangalooma Wild Dolphin Resort (www.tangalooma.com), which features supervised nightly feeding of the dolphins who choose to come in and interact with people. The rangers know them all by name, and introduce visitors to them while maintaining the safety of the dolphins.

Moreton Bay is home to around six hundred inshore bottlenose dolphins, but it is only eleven that come in to the shallow shores where rangers supervise guests as they hand feed them under strict guidelines. A dedicated Dolphin Care Team observes and records the behaviour of the dolphins each evening, monitoring growth, behaviour and interactions. The first dolphin, who they named Beauty, made herself known to staff in 1992, along with her calves Bobo and Tinkerbell (and later, a new baby, Shadow). Tinkerbell and Shadow are now mothers, and often bring their offspring with them. Over time more dolphins have arrived, including a young orphan who was adopted by the older female dolphins.

Like at Monkey Mia, these dolphins have passed down the learned behaviour of coming in to be fed. There are strict rules that govern interaction here too, starting with the washing off of any sunscreen, insect repellent or other lotion, and the golden rule – do not touch the dolphins. Although they choose to visit each night, these dolphins are still wild, and human contact can stress them out.

Three hours north of Brisbane is Barnacles Dolphin Centre (www.barnaclesdolphins.com.au), which offers a rare opportunity to interact with wild Indo-Pacific humpback dolphins. There is a supervised feeding progam, but swimming with them or touching them is prohibited, with penalties of up to eight thousand dollars.

There are also places to see and swim with dolphins around the world, in New Zealand, the British Isles, Japan, Hawaii, Indonesia and Bimini in the Bahamas, amongst other places.

In Hawaii, there are a few different dolphin swim facilitators who take people out into the deep water off the Kona coast to see if the numerous dolphins who live there want to come and play. There is strict self-regulation, and no operators feed the dolphins, chase them or harass them in any way – contact is always up to the dolphins, but there are so many of them in these warm, clear waters, and they so love to play, that it's very rare that they won't swim over to check out the humans.

In Panama City in northwest Florida, USA, Water Planet (www.waterplanetusa.com) offers wild dolphin encounters, including specific programs for children with special needs. They take people out on a boat into the Gulf of Mexico to observe and interact with the wild bottlenose dolphins who live in the warm waters of the Shell Island Nature Preserve. The swims include a cruise out into the bay, the dolphin swim itself, a marine ecology wet lab and dolphin and marine education.

At Lovina Beach, in northern Bali, fifty dolphins live just off shore, and as the sun rises each morning, they start to play. Visitors are taken out on the water in tiny outrigger canoes, which remain stationary, to simply watch the dolphins at play. It's truly magical to watch them leap up in the air and splash down into the fiery golden water, swimming teasingly close to visitors and seeming to revel in showing off their amazing acrobatic skills, and definitely worth getting up in the dark to experience this proximity to them.

In Malaysia, bottlenose dolphins and the rare Indo-Pacific humpback dolphins can sometimes be spotted in the waters surrounding the ninety-nine islands of Langkawi, in the Andaman Sea off northwest Malaysia, and in the Santubong River in Sarawak.

In Israel, on the shores of the Red Sea, there's a beach, the Dolphin Reef Eilat, where dolphins choose to interact with swimmers. They're never fed or otherwise induced to stay, and they come and go as they please, going out to sea to fish, then coming back to play.

Bimini, a chain of islands in the Bahamas, located eighty kilometres off the coast of Miami, Florida, is home to many wild dolphins, who regularly interact with swimmers in these warm, tropical waters. Dolphin researcher, psychologist and shaman Joan Ocean, the founder of Dolphin Connection International, takes groups down to Bimini each year so people can experience the joy of swimming with wild dolphins. It is also the place Horace Dobbs's UK foundation Operation Sunflower takes disabled children for their dolphin healing trips, the Cetacean Studies Institute of Australia organises trips there, and Dolphin Expeditions (www.dolphinexpeditions.com), the oldest wild dolphin swim in Bimini, offers one-week, live-aboard dolphin adventures, which include several swims with these majestic creatures out in the open water.

Solitary Dolphins Who Love Humans

Much of the human interaction with dolphins takes place with solitary dolphins, who, for reasons we don't understand, make their home at a certain beach, sometimes staying for years, and welcome human interaction. This is unusual behaviour for dolphins – most are highly social creatures who live in large pods, ranging across the oceans together, playing games together, co-operating to hunt fish, and looking after group members who become sick. Sometimes they'll spend time with a different pod or include humans in their games, but they usually lose interest quickly and swim off with their own group. Solitary dolphins, sometimes referred to as ambassador dolphins, forsake their pod and instead form human relationships.

In Ireland, Fungie, the world's second-most-famous dolphin (after Flipper), has lived in Dingle Bay for decades, interacting with humans who want to swim with him, playing games with people in boats and causing a little mischief. He so loves the interactions he has with humans, and the attention he receives, that he has driven off the occasional dolphins that have swum into his bay, preferring the company of people to others of his kind.

Fungie is a mature male bottlenose dolphin, four metres long and very heavy, who has been resident in Dingle since early 1984. He's become a tourist attraction, and is the longest-standing solitary dolphin in the world. Some people simply swim out into the bay in the hope that he will come and play with them, while others take a boat out to deeper waters to interact with him there.

He sometimes leaps right over small boats, or bobs up on one side then the other, or drenches boaters with water from a large jump. If he feels ignored he'll tug on a swimmer's flippers, or peck on their face mask with his beak, or swim up behind and nudge them. He also loves to play with kayakers and grab their paddles.

Fungie has given a few people bruises and even broken a few bones, although dolphin experts say this has never been intentional, he just doesn't always know his own strength. If a dolphin wanted to seriously harm a person it could and would, but this has barely ever happened, and only under extreme provocation. However they are wild creatures, and they should only ever be approached with respect, awareness and a little caution.

Not far from Fungie is another solitary Irish dolphin, a female known as Dusty. She spent time interacting with people in the waters off the small seaside village of Doolin, County Clare, in 2000, when she was very young. Later she moved about twenty kilometres north and settled near Fanore for four years, before moving south and taking up residence in the Green Island area, where she loves to interact with swimmers, divers, surfers and kayakers. She's been described as an extremely patient, playful and interactive dolphin, although she has been known to poke people with her beak if she doesn't want them to leave the water.

Much further north, off the coast of Donegal in the northwest of Ireland, a male dolphin christened Duggie has taken up residence in the freezing waters of Tory Island. He's often spotted in the harbour where ferries to the mainland arrive and depart, and he also likes investigating the small inlets around the coast. He seems to like swimming with people – although the cold water means he doesn't have a lot of companionship, so he's made friends with a labrador that lives at the island's hotel, and the two often swim together.

Another solitary dolphin, Dony, is famous for his unusual wanderings. He was first reported interacting with people in Dunquin Harbour and around the Blasket Islands in the Dingle Peninsula in 2001, but after a few months making friends there he set off on a journey, being spotted again along the French coast before moving north to the Channel Islands for the winter. A few months later he was seen in Weymouth, Dorset, on the southern English coast, where he stayed for a while, making short trips to Cornwall, before heading back to France. Then he moved along the Belgian coast before settling for a while off the coast of Brittany in western France. He would sometimes spend time with Jean-Floc'h, another solo dolphin, or a pod, and on one occasion he travelled six hundred kilometres in three days to visit Biarritz on the Spanish border. While he seemed settled along the French coastline, in 2007 he went back to England for a while before returning again to Brittany. He's been described as a fearless and curious dolphin, who investigates every person and every vessel he comes into contact with. Unlike many solo dolphins, who only let long-time swimming companions touch them, Dony is unafraid of physical contact, constantly inviting it and even seeking it out.

In the Turks and Caicos Islands (a British Overseas Territory in the West Indies), a unique friendship exists between California-born Dean Bernal and solitary dolphin JoJo, who has become the symbol of the marine conservation movement in the region. Dean, a free diver, writer and wildlife advocate, first met JoJo when he visited the islands in 1984. The curious young bottlenose dolphin would follow Dean as he swam around the reefs a mile off shore. At first he kept his distance, but each day the dolphin came a little closer, until he was leading Dean around, showing him his special spots and allowing Dean to help if he was injured. They developed a unique bond, and Dean moved to the islands based on the friendship that had developed between them – which proved lucky for JoJo. In 1987, after people complained that the dolphin was a hazard, the threat of life in captivity loomed.

"Although JoJo was very young, he had a reputation as a dangerous dolphin. People were saying that JoJo was attacking them, when in reality it was the people who were harassing the dolphin," Dean says. "Many would attempt to touch him if he was near shore, and to a dolphin this is an aggressive act that will provoke a wild animal, and he would defend himself with a bite to the offending hand."

Dean began a campaign and petitioned the government to declare JoJo a National Treasure. In 1989, he was appointed JoJo's official Marine Mammal Warden, and he was able to provide both legal and medical protection for the dolphin. Today he is still JoJo's caretaker, as well as director of the Marine Wildlife Foundation (www.MarineWildlife.org), dedicated to research and preservation of dolphins and all wildlife, educating the public and sharing information with universities and other research bodies. And JoJo remains protected, guarded by a policy that states that the dolphin will come to the beaches or boats when he wants company, and no one should seek him out for commercial interest or intrusion.

New Zealand has also had a few highly publicised solitary dolphins. The first was Pelorus Jack, a Risso's dolphin who, between 1888 and 1912, guided ships through a dangerous stretch of water in Cook Strait, between the North Island and the South Island, which was notorious for shipwrecks. According to reports, there were no accidents when this dolphin swam alongside a ship and escorted them through, and boats would often wait for the dolphin to show up before they set sail. Risso's dolphins are very rare in New Zealand waters, and many believe this one interacted with the ships because he was lonely.

In 1904 someone aboard the inter-island ferry steamer SS Penguin tried to shoot the dolphin. They missed, but the incident led to new legislation being introduced, and on September twenty-six that year Pelorus Jack became protected under the Sea Fisheries Act – the first individual sea creature protected by law in any country. Legend has it that he continued to guide boats through the treacherous waters – all except the SS Penguin, which shipwrecked in 1909. Pelorus Jack disappeared in 1912, but as his description at the time indicated he was quite old, it was assumed that he died of natural causes.

In 1955, a bottlenose dolphin called Opo became famous for playing with the children in Hokianga Harbour, near the small town of Opononi in the North Island. She would follow fishing boats, play with objects such as beach balls – as many solitary dolphins will – and allowed children to swim with her and even touch her. As her fame increased, locals campaigned for official protection for her, and on March eight, 1956, this was signed into law. Sadly she was found dead the next day – it was ruled an accidental death due to fishermen who were fishing with gelignite. Opo was buried with full Maori honours, a statue of her was erected in town, and two songs, a book and a few documentaries have been inspired by her. Several other solitary dolphins have been recorded interacting with humans in New Zealand, including Rampal in the Whitianga River estuary in the 1980s, Aihe at Onekaka in Golden Bay, and Maui, a solo female dolphin at Kaikoura.

When I began writing this chapter there was a much-loved male bottlenose dolphin on the east coast of the North Island of New Zealand, known as Moko, who welcomed human interaction. He had many close friends in the area, who regularly swam with him and photographed him, and many more who came to visit from all over the world. In March 2008 he rescued two whales who had become stranded at Mahia Beach. Human rescuers had been trying to refloat them, but they kept re-stranding, and Department of Conservation workers, devastated by their distress, were contemplating putting them down to avoid a slow, painful death. Then Moko came speeding into the bay, apparently alerted by the distress signals the whales were emitting. He guided them parallel with the beach for two hundred metres, to the end of the sandbar, then turned through the narrow channel and escorted them out to sea.

"What the communication was, I do not know. I was not aware dolphins could communicate with pygmy sperm whales, but something happened that allowed Moko to guide those two whales to safety," says a department representative. Moko returned to the beach soon after and began playing his games with the swimmers.

On the flipside, one winter afternoon he kept a swimmer out in the water with him for hours, refusing to let her go back in when she got tired. In the end, cold and exhausted, she had to scream for help and be rescued – although she insisted that the dolphin hadn't meant any harm, he just wanted to keep playing with her because in winter, with less visitors, he was often bored.

Sadly Moko died in July 2010, at the age of four, but the tributes from around the world showed the amazing impact he had on all those who met him. One person who spent a lot of time with this dolphin is New Zealand oceanographer and anthropologist Wade Doak, who's been researching cetaceans for more than four decades. He is the author of many books, including *Encounters with Whales and Dolphins* and *Ocean Planet*, and has made several marine life documentaries. With his wife Jan he founded Project Interlock in 1975, a global network that records encounters between humans and cetaceans and aims to develop an approach based on mutual respect and admiration for creatures he considers to be our closest brain neighbours. (Find out more at www.WadeDoak.com.)

"Our research began following an unusual underwater encounter with bottlenose dolphins, during which the dolphins appeared to demonstrate complex manoeuvres to the divers and respond positively when the divers imitated those patterns. From many sessions a pattern emerged that suggests non-captive dolphins avoid repetitious situations such as experimental routines, and respond to novelty," he says. Such games included playing with a ball, an oar, pieces of seaweed, a bottle, and riding the wake of the boats, and he's seen dolphins playing with dogs and horses. Wade observed Moko and shared stories of his behaviour with other dolphin experts, and met South Australian solitary dolphin Jock. He also spent a long time exchanging complex sounds with solo dolphin

Rampal, which led to a new avenue of research, documented in his book *Friends In the Sea: Solo Dolphins in New Zealand and Australia*.

The behaviour of solitary dolphins changes from day to day, and like humans and other social animals, they crave tactile stimulation. They also get bored, as evidenced by some incidents with Moko, as well as from a British solitary dolphin, Donald, who stayed for some time in a sea port in Wales, interacting with locals.

One Christmas, when everyone was keeping warm in the pub rather than paying attention to him in the cold ocean, Donald took the anchors of several yachts and tangled them together, creating chaos – and lots of attention. A barge and crane were required to raise them all, and when a diver got in the water to help, Donald pushed him aside. "Donald has also left bruises on young girls' legs, and caused minor lacerations," Wade says. "But he also located my friend's lost underwater camera for him, and has guided divers back to their boat through murky water."

Wade, as well as New Zealand's DOCs and other dolphin experts, disagree with those who advise that people stay away from solitary dolphins, knowing that these creatures interact with humans because they crave social contact, and it is only boredom that makes them a little too playful for our liking.

"During the course of our studies we became aware of a special category of human-cetacean encounter – the situation where a lone dolphin spends an extended period of time around human settlements. Its normal social intercourse seems to have been replaced by intensive interaction with people, although many solo dolphins eventually tire of humans and withdraw. Maui at Kaikoura now avoids people and has raised several young elsewhere," he says.

"Obviously such episodes offer little knowledge of the dolphin's normal social life, but they do complement dolphin pod observations, and provide unique insights into the flexibility and complexity of dolphins' relationships with an alien bipedal species that does not share much of their acoustic reality. Such episodes appear to have increased in recent years, perhaps facilitated by the change in attitude towards dolphins – an account from last century culminated in the dolphin's capture and display on a handcart! From very early times there have been tales of lone dolphins straying from their pods and seeking human company, but only recently have we learned to respond to these creatures with care and friendship," Wade says.

Melainah's Hawaiian Magic

Melainah Yee and her husband Michael operate Sunlight On Water on the Big Island of Hawaii, facilitating wild dolphin swims, night-time manta ray swims and whale-watching cruises, with the sanctity and safety of the animals their highest priority. Melainah also conducts retreats on Hawaiian spirituality and the ancient land of Lemuria and co-ordinates spiritual events. Michael, the son of Hawaiian kahuna Lanakila Brandt, is a surfer, boat captain and diver. Visit them at www.SunlightOnWater.com.

Dolphins are magical beings, and most people understand there is something very special about them, even if they have never seen one for themselves. Dolphins are all about love and joy, and they meet you in your heart centre. It is very hard not to smile when you see dolphins. They touch something very deeply in most people.

From them we gain awareness that we share this planet with other beings who are intelligent, who live together in pod consciousness in unity and co-operation – lessons that would serve humans very well. It is our hope that in introducing people to our ocean family, they will gain an awareness of how special they are, an appreciation of them and their environment, and the knowledge that it is up to us to be good stewards of the earth's treasures, which will ultimately help protect them and their environment.

I have a very strong connection to the ocean, which creates appreciation for all sentient life, and the awareness that everything that exists on our planet has consciousness, including the ocean, wind and sun. We all have the ability to connect at a deeper level with everything we have been given to enjoy, and through that connection and awareness we have the opportunity to connect to a deeper part of ourselves and to understand fully that there is a greater power that exists. One of the things we have been taught by our Hawaiian kumu and kahunas is that everything is here because we are here. All of it is a gift to be treasured, but for many it is still taken for granted.

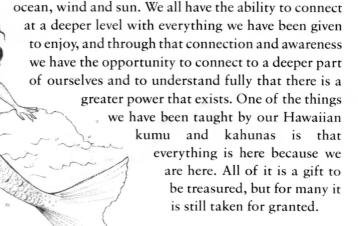

We need to keep our oceans clean, and stop toxic wastes from being dumped into them. We must also support efforts to convince other world governments to ban the killing of dolphins and whales, because thousands are slaughtered around the world each year, and support efforts to hold the US Navy accountable for their sonar testing, which explodes blood vessels in the heads and eyes of cetaceans.

The captivity question is a difficult one to answer. In general we do not support captive dolphin programs, but there are a few excellent facilities, such as one that works with children with autism, and another that works with those with cancer and leukaemia, who have achieved some great results.

Currently in the US there aren't regulations that dolphin swim facilitators must follow, like there are in Australia, but NOAA is attempting to impose regulations and restrictions for dolphin swims. And there are protocols that have been established by those of us who have been swimming with them for years, which we self-police, because dolphins are our passion. If you go swimming with wild dolphins, you want to be sure you go with someone who is respectful and knowledgeable about the dolphins and their habits, and that you are well informed before you enter the ocean.

Hawaii is also where the humpback whales from Alaska come to breed and give birth, so it is with special love and pride that we consider them to be Hawaiian humpback whales. They are protected here under the Endangered Species Act, so after being almost wiped out, their numbers are now stable and increasing. Seeing a whale up close, you absolutely know that you are in the presence of grace. They are one of the most powerful energies embodied on our planet. They are gentle giants, and we consider them to be the Ancient Ones. Dolphins and whales are the angels of the sea. And I believe mermaids have existed, and still do in other dimensional worlds.

Wonderful Whales

"Our clients are the whales, sharks, seals, fish, whatever.
We don't give a damn what you think. Find me one whale that
disagrees with what we do and maybe we might reconsider, but until
then we're going to do what we do... Our business is to sail into
harm's way to defend the defenceless from the remorseless."
Paul Watson, founder of Sea Shepherd

Most Majestic of the Sea Creatures

Whereas dolphins have been worshipped throughout history and
are known for saving people's lives, humanity has had a different
relationship with whales. Over the past few centuries they've been
hunted for meat and other uses – so much so that several species
have been pushed to the brink of extinction. In prehistoric times
many coastal communities relied on whales for food and oil,
hunting them in small numbers and harvesting beached whales to
survive, which placed little pressure on whale stocks.

But in the 1700s industrial whaling began, and it increased
dramatically over the following centuries. Their meat was used for
food, while the blubber was reduced to oil which was used to make
margarine, soap, cosmetics, perfumes and candles, in leatherworking
and other industries, and as fuel for lamps and heating. Whalebone
was used in corsetry, skirt hoops, parasols and other items where
flexibility and strength was required, such as horsewhips and
weapon bows. Other whale-derived products included incense,
food flavourings, aphrodisiacs, medications and a lubricant for
machinery in clothes manufacturing, linoleum production and in

the building industry. And while whale oil was pretty much replaced by the advent of petroleum drilling in the late 1800s (which has its own environmental issues), whaling continued to boom.

By the twentieth century, demand had become so high, and methods of hunting so efficient, that whale numbers began to plummet, and it was realised that many whale species were on the verge of extinction. In 1937 many countries signed the International Agreement for the Regulation of Whaling. In 1946 its successor, the International Convention for the Regulation of Whaling (ICRW) was signed in Washington DC, which aimed to "provide for the proper conservation of whale stocks and thus make possible the orderly development of the whaling industry". This international agreement governs the commercial, scientific and aboriginal subsistence whaling practices of member nations – including Australia, the US, the UK, China, Japan, India, New Zealand, Denmark, Norway and South Africa. It aims to protect whales from overhunting and regulate the whaling industry through the establishment of the International Whaling Commission (IWC).

In 1979 the IWC established the Indian Ocean Whale Sanctuary, which banned all commercial whaling in this region. It extends from Western Australia to Africa and north to Asia, and protects the warm water calving grounds and migratory routes of many whales. In 1982 the IWC placed a moratorium on commercial whaling from 1986 onwards, so stocks could recover, but a pro-whaling faction led by Japan continues to campaign for the end of the moratorium and a return to annual quotas, while an anti-whaling faction, which includes Australia, is pushing for the indefinite continuation of the moratorium and the creation of more whale sanctuaries.

In 1994 the IWC created the Southern Ocean Whale Sanctuary, an area of fifty million square kilometres surrounding Antarctica, which covers the waters where eighty per cent of the world's whales live. Japan opposed its conception, and continues to ignore it, claiming it is "illegal". Japan also continues to hunt whales there – they've killed more than twenty four thousand under the guise of "scientific research", which, due to a loophole in IWC legislation, no one can stop. Norway and Iceland also continue whaling under objection to the moratorium, with the latter also carrying out so-called "scientific research" hunts. Scientific research is the claim that they need to kill whales in order to learn about them – which is ridiculed by actual scientists as completely untrue. New knowledge about them and their conservation can only be gained by studying whales that are alive and in their natural habitat.

According to the World Wide Fund For Nature (WWF): "Whales are currently under threat from a wide range of human activities, despite there being a moratorium in place against commercial whaling for over twenty years. More than fifteen hundred whales have been hunted each year since commercial whaling was banned in 1986. Whaling is taking place right now and increasing yearly."

Sadly the IWC is a voluntary organisation, and member nations can simply leave if they disagree, or lodge a formal objection to a specific regulation, as Japan did, and ignore it. Today it seems that activists such as Sea Shepherd have more chance of shutting down whaling than any government. And the more that Japanese whalers – for it is only a small group, not the whole country – flout the ban, the stronger the worldwide outrage becomes, and the more powerful and effective conservation groups become.

On February 16, 2011, Captain Paul Watson of Sea Shepherd sent a message to supporters, titled The Whalers Have Been Shut Down!, which outlined the success of the seventh annual campaign he and his crew have mounted to stop Japanese whalers illegally killing whales in the Southern Ocean Whale Sanctuary.

"The Japanese Fisheries Agency is saying that the whale hunt has been suspended due to the interventions of the Sea Shepherd Conservation Society. I think it is premature to see this as a victory for the whales yet. There has been no mention of how long this suspension will be. It could be permanent, for this season only, or it could be for a matter of weeks or even days.

"What we do know is that the whalers will not be killing any whales for the next few weeks. Not because of any suspension, but because it is physically impossible for them to do so. This is not a voluntary suspension. Sea Shepherd interventions have forced a closure to their illegal poaching activities."

Fellow marine conservationist Ric O'Barry sent a message a few days later to supporters of his Save Japan Dolphins. "It's official. The Japanese government has recalled its whale-killing fleet from Antarctica, citing interference from activists from Sea Shepherd. The withdrawal is a resounding victory for whales and all the organisations working to stop Japan's killing of whales and dolphins.

"It has also sent shock waves through the notorious and politically powerful Japanese Fisheries Agency. Even Japan's mafia, the Yakuza, has used the whaling issue to vilify foreigners and the influence of environmentalists. Many of our allies in Japan have been regularly intimidated by the combined power of the government and the extreme nationalist groups. But while the Japanese Fisheries Agency has maintained that it would never stop its Antarctic whale killing, it has now done just that. The impacts on the entire whaling and dolphin-killing policies of Japan are in flux."

Not that this success means the end of the need for Sea Shepherd and other environmental groups, or the growing outrage of so many over the continuing threats to our beautiful planet.

"We must be prepared to return to the Southern Ocean next season – we do not know if the whalers will resume hunting but we will be prepared to intercept them if they do," Paul Watson says. "In the meantime, we have bluefin tuna to save in the Mediterranean, pilot whales to save in the Danish Faroe Islands, and poachers to intercept in the Galapagos. From plankton to the great whales, there are many threats and challenges to marine wildlife and we must address what we can, where we can, and as best we can with the resources we have available to us."

> "We owe it to our children to be better stewards of the environment. The alternative? A world without whales. It's too terrible to imagine."
> *Pierce Brosnan, Irish actor and environmentalist*

Whaling was one of Australia's oldest industries – some of the ships that brought convicts from Europe were whalers that dropped off their human cargo then filled up with the spoils of their whaling in the Southern Ocean on the way back. As the Southern Ocean is home to the highest number of whales in the world, whalers came from America and Europe to hunt the majestic creatures, and in the early 1800s whales were so common in some coastal estuaries that they were a hazard to small boats. According to Stuart Macintyre's *A Concise History of Australia*: "Sealing and whaling contributed more to the colonial economy than land produce until the 1830s."

In 1826 the first settlement in the west of the country was established in Albany, in the Great Australian Bight, followed by one three years later in Perth. Albany soon became a thriving whaling port, with many of the settlers taking up a harpoon and chasing whales too. By the mid 1800s there were more than three hundred whaling ships plying the waters south of Australia, and many whaling stations had been set up along the coast to extract the oil from them.

It was a dangerous but lucrative occupation, until petroleum was discovered in America's Pennsylvania in 1859 and a new industry was born. The Australian gold rush of the 1850s also saw workers abandon whaling for the gold fields, and most of the whaling stations closed down. Yet a few companies did continue. A whaling station operated at Tangalooma, Queensland, between 1952 and 1962, which was finally forced to close after drastically reducing the humpback whale population on Australia's east coast – it harvested and processed more than six thousand whales in a decade. And in Albany, whaling continued until 1978.

The seventies saw the beginning of the global anti-whaling movement, and the first Greenpeace campaign in Australia was a reaction to its ongoing whaling. Canadian Bob Hunter, who founded Greenpeace with Paul Watson, travelled to Albany in August 1977 to organise a direct action campaign against the three whale chaser ships still operating from the Cheynes Beach Whaling Company. He and Aussie members of the Whale and Dolphin Coalition went fifty kilometres out to sea in tiny rubber boats called zodiacs to place themselves between the harpoons and the whales, a practice Paul Watson's Sea Shepherd continues today. Several of the environmentalists who took part then started Greenpeace Australia.

The following year, influenced by the growing environmental movement and their campaigns, the Australian government appointed Sir Sydney Frost to conduct an inquiry. His report, *Whales and Whaling: Report of the Independent Inquiry*, recommended banning whaling in Australia. The Cheynes Beach Whaling Company finally closed down, and since then, to varying degrees, the country has remained a global anti-whaling advocate, openly critical of Japan's whaling in the Antarctic Ocean, and with a total ban on commercial whaling and the export of any whale product.

Today in Albany, a museum and tourist attraction called Whale World is situated on the site of the old Cheynes Beach Whaling Station, which conserves the history of the place as well as celebrating the beauty of whales. Visitors can tour one of the company's old whale chaser boats to experience what whalers went through to hunt them, do a gruesome sounding tour of the old whaling station to learn how it was done, see the Giants of the Sea skeleton exhibit, and watch films in former whale oil storage tanks that have been converted into theatres. There's also information about whales and a whale-watching guide, and the town that once hunted whales now has a thriving whale-watching industry.

An increasing number of marine parks are also being legislated to protect the ocean and its inhabitants, and conservationists continue to fight to increase the number of them and the size of the areas covered. These parks provide a safe haven for commercial fish stocks as well as for endangered species, and offer alternative sources of income such as tourism.

Albany is now part of the Great Australian Bight Marine Park and whale sanctuary, which was established in 1995 to provide a haven for southern right whales (named because they were the "right" prey for whalers) that come to Australian waters between May and October each year to mate, socialise and give birth to their calves, spending the rest of their time in the Southern Ocean between Australia and Antarctica. Only twelve thousand of these majestic creatures remain worldwide – a fraction of the hundred thousand that roamed the oceans before whaling began. Thanks to increased awareness and sanctuaries like this their numbers are slowly increasing, but they are still vulnerable to extinction, which makes the ongoing Japanese whaling in Antarctic waters such a concern.

"Thoughts flowed through my mind of the deadly harpoon gun we had filmed in the local museum. Old photos of whalers posing with a stash of giant ribs. Huge, swollen carcasses being stripped of blubber," says Wade Doak, oceanographer and underwater photographer.

"It all seemed so unbelievable that now, a century later, a cameraman is approaching two whales, a tiny land creature out in all that watery vastness, his mission totally benign: eyepiece for a global audience that now regards whales with awe and delight, that were once made into candlesticks and corsetry."

Another previous whaling nation has also transformed from hunting to whale watching. In the early 1800s, many whaling boats stopped off in Hawaii to replenish supplies on their way south, and many locals, adept in the ocean and expert boatsmen, joined them to take advantage of the lucrative new enterprise. Today the Hawaiian Island chain is one of the world's most important habitats for the endangered North Pacific humpback whale – it's the only place in the US where they mate, breed and nurse their young. Two thirds of this whale's worldwide population travels to spend their winters in the warm Hawaiian waters, making it one of the best places to see them, either from the shore or from one of the boats that carefully sail among them. The Hawaiian Islands Humpback Whale National Marine Sanctuary, created in 1992 to protect these whales and their habitat, surrounds the main Hawaiian Islands, and is one of the world's most important humpback whale habitats.

When I was in high school in Margaret River, a pod of a hundred and fourteen false killer whales beached themselves near Augusta, fifty kilometres south of us, on the edge of the Southern Ocean. It was the middle of winter, but there was such an overwhelming number of people who raced down there to help, and stayed around the clock for two days and two nights, that it made the international news, and is still cited in stories about more recent strandings.

Dad was up north surfing at the time, and when he heard about it on the news he assumed a few local fishermen would go and help. He had no idea that Mum, my sister and I had each squeezed into one of his wetsuits – lucky he has lots! – and headed down there after school, staying all that night and the next day doing what we could to encourage them back out to sea. (The principal was pretty cool about us missing school too ☺) People came from all over the southwest region, driving for hours to help. One guy even piloted a helicopter down from Perth. Even more came down with hot tea and snacks to keep those in the water as warm as possible.

It was well coordinated by conservation department staff, with some volunteers comforting the whales still on the sand and keeping them wet until they could be pushed back into the water, and others in the icy water holding the animals up in the shallows so they could regain their strength, and making sure no more headed for the shore. We were encouraged to come out of the water every few hours, swapping places so we could thaw out, then going back in.

It was really beautiful to be a small part of such an incredible show of human altruism and outpouring of love for a fellow creature. Ninety-six of them survived and were returned safely back to the ocean, in what apparently still remains the world's largest and most successful whale rescue.

False killer whales (pseudorca crassidens) are the third-largest members of the oceanic dolphin family. They're sometimes displayed alongside bottlenose dolphins in water parks such as Florida's SeaWorld, and look more like dolphins than the massive blue whales we picture. They're dark grey with a lighter grey chest and neck, narrow, short and pointed flippers, and a dorsal fin that is sickle-shaped. Males grow up to six metres long, and can weigh up to two tonnes. They are hunted in small numbers in parts of Asia, including Japan, and studies show that the Hawaiian population has declined dramatically in the last two decades.

Unfortunately it's not uncommon for false killer whales to strand, and not all strandings end well. Between 1984 and 2005 there were twenty-one mass strandings of whales and dolphins along the West Australian coast, mostly between Busselton and Augusta, and it happens around the world too. In 1988, another large pod stranded near Augusta. Thirty-two were returned to sea, but in a separate beaching nearby, sixteen of the twenty-four had to be euthanised. In a South African beaching in 2009, fifty-five whales were discovered on a sandy beach, but despite the best efforts of all the volunteers, by the afternoon the decision was made to euthanase them all by shooting the whales – forty-four were killed.

A 2005 stranding in Busselton had a better outcome. Hundreds of volunteers rushed to help, and only one of the seventy-five whales died, with the rest being successfully returned to the sea. The fact that so many people want to help them reflects the growing awareness of these beautiful creatures, and humanity's desire to save whales, rather than hunting them.

"This is an amazing reflection of the depth of feeling people in Western Australia have for our marine life, especially whales," said then environment minister Judy Edwards. "While governments can attempt to persuade Japan to drop its whaling operations under the pretence of 'science' at a political level, the people involved in this rescue have sent an even more potent message. This was a clear message to the world – Japan, stop the slaughter."

Yvonne's Whale Magic

Yvonne Miles is a biologist, and the managing director of Scanning Ocean Sectors, which trains marine mammal observers as well as navy personnel, and advocates for whales and dolphins. She teaches in the UK and Australia, and works with Blue Dolphin Marine Tours in Hervey Bay, where she's become known as the Whale Whisperer. Yvonne is a reiki practitioner and a PADI rescue diver, and merges her scientific qualifications with her love of the ocean and its beautiful creatures. Visit www.bluedolphintours.com.au.

My first connection with marine life was on a family holiday in Malta. We went to an aquarium, and my jaw ached from my beaming smile. We were taught about dolphin physiology and hand signals, then were allowed in the water with them. They came to us individually, very close without touching, then we got to feed them and stroke them. It was the highlight of the holiday, the year, the decade! After university I spent months tracking George, a solitary bottlenose dolphin, around the south coast of the UK, recording the interactions he had with people swimming, diving, kayaking and boating. He put me on the road to a lifetime of working with marine mammals. There was not a force on earth that could stop people rushing into the sea to get close to him, touch him and feel his energy. He was the ocean's magnetic force to humans! People who could not swim went rushing in, they couldn't help themselves, his energy just oozed out of the ocean at you.

The work I do now on the whale-watching boats in Queensland has brought me very close to the energies of whales. People's faces light up, they look ten years younger, and those who are very controlled lose it when they see them! Once two elderly ladies who'd recently lost their husbands came whale watching. Two humpbacks spyhopped out of the water and hovered at the stern until the ladies had eyes full of tears. Everyone on the boat was stunned; they had come so close and had stayed so still and so far out of the water

so the ladies could not miss them. They had both said a prayer and asked for their husbands to be with them on their trip, and in unison they turned to me and said those two whales were sent by their husbands, and judging by the joy in their eyes and the tears running down the faces of most of the visitors, we all felt it.

When the humpback whales are hard to find and people are getting restless, I move to the stern and send reiki healing and love into the water, and a message of thanks to the whales. I ask them to come and show their love to us by joining us at the boat, and within minutes they come. My boss noticed me going to the stern, and the whales turning up, and started calling me the Whale Whisperer! So whenever the whales aren't around he'll say: "Yvonne, get to the back and do your stuff." And we're always blessed with a visit.

I believe the ocean has its own healing force. How many of us go to the beach to watch the ocean, to feel the energy, to feel invigorated and cleansed? Walking on the beach helps the thinking process, as salt in the air helps synaptic transmissions within the brain, helping you think faster and more clearly. When I feel troubled I go to the ocean and sit and ask for help. The ocean helps with communication and healing – it transfers healing as quick as we can send it. We just need to connect with the ocean's energies and wait for the magic to happen and the energy to flow.

I do believe in mermaids. And I've been called a mermaid, which is so beautiful, one of the best compliments I've had! They are the ocean's equivalent of the unicorn – they are mystical, magical and always there to take us to a place we need to find in times of trouble. The mermaids and the humpback whales both sing a sweet, enticing song. And both have been attracting humans for a long time.

Delightful Dugongs and Manatees

"Dugongs use their flippers like hands. They can hold you when
you dive with them – they sometimes wrap their flippers around us.
And they love to be patted. They are very intelligent. We still don't
know that much about them. We're learning as we go."
Amy Wilkes, Australian aquarist

The Original Mermaids

Then there are the dugongs, the big, lumbering yet graceful sea
creatures scientists believe are the basis of the mermaid myth. "It's
nice to think that dugongs, huge graceful animals with soft smiling
faces, could be mistaken for mermaids," says Welsh marine biologist
Dr Vicki Howe. "Sailors on long journeys at sea, working hard with
poor diets and plenty of grog, may have resorted to wishful thinking."

Dugongs and manatees are marine mammals from the order
Sirenia (the sirens of the sea!). Although they seem kin to cetaceans,
they are related to elephants. There are now only four remaining
Sirenia species – the West Indian manatee, the West African
manatee, the Amazonian manatee and the Indo-Pacific dugong.

Their main diet is seagrass, which they graze on in shallow sea
meadows, a habitat that's led to the unflattering moniker sea cow.
They're the only plant-eating mammals that are entirely marine, and
because they have no blubber and a slow metabolism, they don't
generate much body heat – to keep themselves warm they must eat at
least a tenth of their body weight every day, the equivalent of more
than two hundred lettuce! Despite their fat-free diet though, they
weigh up to five hundred kilograms and grow up to three metres

long. Pig and Wuru, the two dugongs at Sydney Aquarium, are fed cos lettuce – up to forty kilos of leaves a day – which is the closest substitute for the seagrass dugongs consume in the wild. They also eat a little English spinach, bok choy, endive and chum soy.

Dugongs live for up to seventy years, and spend half their time sleeping. They breathe through their nose, and must surface for air every twenty minutes while resting, and much more frequently when active. Their nostrils have special flaps that close tightly when they dive, to prevent water getting in. They usually swim at around five to eight kilometres an hour, but can increase to thirty kilometres an hour if they feel threatened and are fleeing danger.

They have a large, bulky and streamlined body with no hind fins, making them among the most aquatically adapted of all mammals, but unable to survive on land as their body weight would crush their internal organs. Instead they have a powerful tail fluke that looks like a whale – or mermaid – tail and acts as a rudder, and powerful front limbs, fore flippers, that they use to hold their food and to steer as they swim. Like dolphins, they never fall completely asleep, rather they rest their brains by dozing, floating in one place and letting their eyelids droop a little, fluttering open and closed.

The word dugong derives from the Malay word duyung, meaning "lady of the sea". They are generally solitary creatures, who pair up to mate then go back to their own lives. There's a strong bond between cow and calf though, and babies remain with their mothers, nursing for the first two years, then staying close for a while to learn how to feed and stay safe from predators. They are tactile, so touching is important to them. Although rare, there have been instances where researchers have built up enough trust to be allowed to swim with them and pat them, and have found themselves embraced in a watery, whiskery hug.

Dugongs don't like the cold, so they are native to the shallow tropical and subtropical waters of northern Australia and along the coasts of eastern Africa, India and Asia. Australia is known as the dugong capital of the world – around seventy thousand inhabit our waters, of only a hundred thousand worldwide. Sadly a James Cook University study found that dugong numbers in Queensland fell by ninety seven per cent between 1960 and 2000, which has renewed calls for the dugong to be added to the critically endangered list. They are listed as vulnerable to extinction by the International

Union for Conservation of Nature and the Queensland Nature Conservation Act 1992, and one of the reasons the Great Barrier Reef was nominated as a World Heritage Area in 1981 was its importance as a feeding ground for dugongs.

Hundreds of dugongs were slaughtered in the nineteenth century after an Australian company offered money for dugong oil, many were killed and eaten during World War II, and in more recent times they have been hunted almost to extinction in the South Pacific Islands. Today industrialised man is their greatest threat, and numbers have plummeted around the world. They are frequently hit by boats, because they must surface regularly to breathe, and are also victim to habitat destruction, coastal development, chemical run-off from farmland into the ocean, which kills off their seagrass food supply, entanglement and injury caused by fishing nets, fishing lines and the accidental consumption of plastic and other rubbish, as well as indigenous hunting and natural predators that include sharks, killer whales and crocodiles.

In 1959, a five-thousand-year-old wall painting of a dugong was discovered in Tambun Cave in Perak, Malaysia, which indicates their importance to Neolithic peoples. Today though they have disappeared altogether from some of their old stomping grounds, including Mauritius, western Sri Lanka, the Maldives, much of the Philippines and parts of Cambodia and Vietnam. As one of the few developed nations that is still home to these creatures, Australia has a responsibility to protect them from disappearing for good.

There's also a small group of dugongs off the Okinawa coast of Japan, and they've been listed as critically endangered in the Japanese Environment Ministry's Red List. Killing them has been banned in Japan, although they still die in boat collisions and from consuming plastics and being caught in fishing nets. As dugongs only give birth every five to seven years, after a thirteen-month pregnancy, increasing their population is a long and difficult process.

Very little is known about dugongs, partly because they are shy and flee from human contact, partly because there are only small numbers of them left, partly because they aren't perceived as being as cute or pretty as dolphins, and partly because their habitat ranges across fairly isolated ocean areas. Monkey Mia in Western Australia is the world's most significant dugong behavioural research site, and two dugongs that were rescued as orphaned calves now make their home at Sydney Aquarium. Eleven-year-old male Pig and five-year-old female Wuru are beautiful to watch, and are raising the profile of this graceful creature and its need for protection. They were rescued several years ago after being found stranded and malnourished off the coast of Queensland. Despite repeated attempts to release them, they were considered unable to survive in the wild, so a home was found for them at the aquarium.

"There are a lot of human pressures on dugongs in the wild," Amy Wilkes says. "But these two are doing really well, they're very popular. It's a great opportunity for people to fall in love with them."

Manatees are a little better known thanks to their proximity to Florida in the USA and the waters of the Caribbean, and the marine programs there. Manatees look very similar to dugongs but have a different tail, being rounded and paddle-shaped rather than fluked, and a shorter snout. They breed every three to five years, rather than the seven of dugongs. They are also listed as vulnerable to extinction, the victims of watercraft strikes as well as the cold. Manatees prefer warm, shallow waters, and can get sick – and even die – if the water temperature falls below 21°C (70°F). For this reason they seek warmer waters in winter – the Florida manatees head to the natural warm springs of the coastal rivers, and they've also been known to spend time at places where electric power plants discharge warm water. Many of the warm springs they visit in winter are protected sanctuaries, and it's illegal in the United States to disturb manatees or harass them in any way, as they are protected under federal law by the Marine Mammal Protection Act and the Endangered Species Act. These make it illegal to harass, hunt, capture or kill any marine mammal. They are also protected by the Florida Manatee Sanctuary Act. Violations can result in civil or criminal convictions and fines and/or jail. The Florida Manatee Recovery Plan is coordinated by the US Fish & Wildlife Service, and aims to recover manatees from their endangered status. Scientists are studying manatees to better understand them and their needs, increasing public awareness and education, sponsoring research, rescue, rehabilitation and release efforts, and advocating for boat speed zones and sanctuaries.

To the Maya people of Guatemala, manatees were believed to possess supernatural powers, and the ear bones were worn as talismans around the neck to ward off evil. Today they are thought to represent grace and gentleness, and remind women of their connection to the universe and Spirit, acting as divine messengers.

But to the sailors of old, and the scientists of today, dugongs and manatees are the inspiration for the idea of the mermaid. Explorer Christopher Columbus, on his journey to the Americas in 1493, also mistook manatees for these women of the sea, writing in his log: "The three mermaids raised their bodies above the surface of the water and, although they were not as beautiful as they appear in pictures, their round faces were definitely human."

Sirenias often feed standing upright in the water, balanced on their tails with their head out of the water to chew, and their flippers held out before them like arms or used to put seagrass in their mouth. When the females hold their calves in these flippers, it is said, they look like women nursing a baby. They also prefer to graze at night, and seeing them by moonlight no doubt added to the effect they had on the lonely sailors who'd been months at sea and thought these sweet-natured, shy creatures were half-woman, half-fish.

In the 1930s, fishermen in Mozambique caught a dugong in their nets, and thought it was a white porpoise. A foreign blacksmith bought the creature, embalmed it and took it to Johannesburg, where he sold tickets to see "the only genuine mermaid – half-fish, half-human". Then in 1955, a dugong was speared by locals in the Palau Islands northwest of Indonesia. A scientist who was there collecting marine samples, Stanford University ichthyologist Dr Robert Rees Harry, bought the animal, tended the wounds and then flew it – bathing it in salt water every half hour so it wouldn't dry out – to a San Francisco aquarium to go on public display. Sadly though the dugong, named Eugenie until it was discovered to be Eugene, died from pneumonia six weeks later.

Changing with the times, a few years ago the Dubai Municipality was presented with an embalmed dugong as a gift from a businessman, which they display in their office to inspire people to protect the oceans and preserve these beautiful creatures.

Caryn's Dugong and Manatee Magic

American professor Caryn Self-Sullivan became fascinated with aquatic mammals and how they use sound while studying marine science at university. For her graduate program she studied manatees in Belize, and she fell in love as soon as she saw them. The Sirenias – manatees and dugongs – are the least studied of the marine mammals, yet to Caryn they are the most fascinating. She founded Sirenian International to promote conservation of manatee and dugong populations and their habitats around the world. Find out more – and adopt a mermaid ambassador – at www.sirenian.org.

Christopher Columbus wrote that he'd found the source of the mermaid legend when he first saw manatees in the Caribbean. And there are several behavioural characteristics that make them a good source for the legends – they are elusive, they are slow moving, they are curious, they use their hands to manipulate objects, including their young, and they're often seen with long leaves of seagrass hanging out of their mouths, which could be confused with long hair trailing from their heads. They also have only two distinct teats where their young nurse, one under each forelimb, which is similar to the location of human mammary glands.

For people who haven't seen one, I'd say to imagine a cross between a very large seal and a very large dolphin. They have a rotund yet elongated body that narrows and then widens into a tail – either a large flat paddle on manatees or a whale-like fluke on dugongs – which they use for propulsion. Adults are three to four metres long and weigh up to six hundred kilos, although one animal in Florida weighed more than sixteen hundred kilos! They have elongated forelimbs that are much more useful than those of seals or dolphins, and they can manipulate objects as well as human toddlers wearing mittens can, as they have five individual fingers webbed together by the skin covering their hands. They use these forelimbs and "hands" to walk on the bottom of the sea, to manipulate vegetation into their mouths, to play with objects such as nautical lines, and to hold their young calves. They have vibrissae, whiskers, on their faces like a walrus, and a prehensile upper lip they use to manipulate objects and kiss other manatees.

Sirenians are the most docile mammals in the world. All mammals make a choice between "fight" or "flight", but these ones always choose to flee. Even if they have a calf with them, a mother will simply move away and call to the calf to follow. And when several males are in a mating herd in pursuit of a female, they jockey for position rather than fighting over the female. Basically, they show no aggressive behaviour towards any animals, including humans.

They are extremely elusive, but also quite curious. Some are wanderlusts, travelling long distances for no apparently essential reason. They all have individual personalities. And they are unique – they are the only herbivorous aquatic mammals to survive extinction, and there are only four Sirenian species extant – three manatees and one dugong. All the rest are now extinct, although more than fifty species have been identified in the fossil record.

While many people know of the Florida manatee, very few know they're also found throughout the Caribbean, Central and South America and West Africa, or have heard of the dugong, which is found from Mozambique to Japan. I think a good movie would go a long way to redressing this. Think about what *Free Willy* did for the recognition of orcas. Perhaps *Free Manny*, about the manatee calf stolen from its mother to be sold on the black market!

Most work on Sirenians has been done on manatees in Florida and dugongs in Australia. I study the behaviour and ecology of the populations outside these areas, in developing nations where most of the animals are located but little funding is available. I work with a population in Belize in Central America, and I advise on studies in Ghana, Cameroon and the Dominican Republic. I also mentor and advise scientists and students around the world through Sirenian International. All my work is done in situ, in the field (well, water!) in their natural habitats. I try to learn more

about their habitat needs and behaviours in an effort to assist locals develop better conservation strategies to protect them.

Today there are three major threats to Sirenians – illegal and incidental catching and hunting in developing nations; destruction of habitat from agricultural and mining pollution, and the loss of seagrass beds caused by dredging and sedimentation; and accidental mortality from watercraft strike and fishing gear.

For the first, people can help by supporting conservation and education-oriented projects in the developing world, such as through Sirenian International. For the second, people must lobby for preservation of coastal habitats and vote for politicians who deem environmental health more important than immediate economic gain, especially as, in the long term, environmental health is *essential* for economic gain. And to prevent the third, people in watercraft can slow down in prime manatee and dugong habitats, wear polarised sunglasses to better spot them, participate in local marine mammal stranding networks, and support sustainable tourism and agencies that develop and enforce regulations to reduce negative encounters between humans and marine animals.

Sirenians are unique, gentle – and threatened with extinction. They are considered endangered almost everywhere they're found. We need to help them survive because they give us pleasure, and because, as the only large aquatic herbivores remaining, they help maintain a healthy riverine and coastal ecosystem. They do us no harm, ever! They're curious, have individual personalities, perceive danger, feel pain, and females nurture their young for two years. All these characteristics reveal them to be sentient, and that's why we introduced our Adopt a Mermaid Ambassador program – the word mermaid tends to get folks' attention and enhance the idea that these gentle creatures are ambassadors for our coastal zone.

Sweet Sea Turtles

"They're not freaky, they're graceful,
almost mesmerising to watch glide through the water.
They look old and wise,
And patient, like seasoned survivors.
But time may be running out for sea turtles."
Alexa, ten years old, founder of Oceans4Ever.com

The Oldest Surviving Creatures on Earth

When I was in Hawaii I fell in love with the green sea turtles there, who I swam with in the warm shallow waters of the Big Island. The first time was in the early evening, as the sun was setting on the horizon. I was awestruck when a huge turtle swam right below me, gracefully making its way to shore to eat the algae on the rocks. I was also a bit panicked for a second, because you have to stay a respectful distance from them, and I hadn't meant to get close to one – I didn't even know he was there until I saw him below me.

They're so beautiful in the water, diving and ducking and poking their little heads up for air, and they can reach good speeds when they're out in the open ocean – more than thirty kilometres an hour. On land though, and as they try to slurp algae off the rocks, they are far more clumsy. Every wave batters them against the rocks, pushing them away from their feeding spot, and there's often a flipper waving in the air as they try to regain their balance.

One morning a turtle nudged me on the back of my ankle as I was getting out of the water, which was very cute. While they're protected by law and people aren't allowed to touch them, I guess they're allowed to touch us! Another day as I was leaving the beach, I saw a turtle basking on the rocks in the sun, and went over to watch him for a while – he's been named Rocky by the local ReefTeach volunteers, because he basks on the rocks every day at the same time, the only one of the turtle community at this beach to do that. He was so sweet, and so ancient looking. When he started to lumber back to the water it looked so uncomfortable, so awkward and laborious, and they are very vulnerable on land – which could explain why most male sea turtles (except Rocky!) never set foot on shore after they hatch, and females only return to lay their eggs. I can't believe they haven't evolved an easier way to live and get around, especially as sea turtles are one of the oldest creatures on earth. The seven species that have survived have been around for more than a hundred and twenty million years!

They are clever in other ways though. Green sea turtles can stay underwater for up to five hours, although a feeding dive is usually only for five minutes or less. Their heart rate slows so they can conserve oxygen – they can go nine minutes between heartbeats. Their lungs are adapted for rapid exchange of oxygen, which reduces the amount of time they need to spend at the surface, and means no gases will be trapped internally during deep dives. They see better underwater than they do on land, which also adds to their comfort in the sea.

They undertake long migrations, some swimming more than two thousand kilometres between their feeding grounds and the beach where they nest. Sea turtles are philopatric, meaning they return to the place they were born to lay their eggs, no matter how far they've roamed by then. It is believed that they use the earth's magnetic forces to navigate through the oceans and find their way.

Adult males are identified by their long tails and slightly larger bodies, although until maturity both genders are very similar. It is not until they are between twenty and forty years old that they are considered adult. Females retain the sperm from numerous matings inside them, and release it over time to fertilise several clutches of eggs, which helps to keep the gene pool wide enough for survival.

The females lay eggs every two to four years once they've reached maturity, and make from one to eight nests per season, which could be why they take a year or two off inbetween! When she's ready to lay her eggs she comes ashore and excavates a nest, usually at night, and lays the soft-shell eggs in it – between fifty and two hundred and fifty each time, depending on the species – before filling it with sand and covering it back up so it's almost undetectable. Then she leaves them to make their own way in the world.

Incubation takes around two months, and the gender of each turtle depends on the temperature of the sand of its nest. This is another reason why climate change is such a worry for sea turtles, because if the temperature of the beach sand rises too much – above 31.5°C (90°F) – only female turtles will be born.

Once they're ready to hatch, the babies tear open the shell with their caruncle, a temporary egg tooth, and dig their way out of the sand nest. Then they have to quickly make their way to the safety of the sea, before predators catch them or they become dehydrated.

It can take a couple of days for a batch to dig their way out, especially if the sand above them has been compacted by four-wheel drives, while others do it in the first night. If they hatch by day, most of the babies will be eaten by seagulls, raccoons, dogs, birds and other predators before they can reach the ocean. If they do make it to the water, they still have to avoid sharks and large fish that want to eat them. Of a hundred eggs that are laid, sometimes only a few turtles will grow to adulthood ☹

Sea turtles need fresh water to survive, yet they live in the ocean – a quandary they deal with by having developed skin and a shell that is highly resistant to water diffusion, as well as the ability to drink seawater. They have special glands near their eyes, in the nostrils or on the tongue, depending on the species, that excrete the excess salt – people sometimes think they're crying, but it's simply their body allowing them to drink from the ocean and convert it to fresh water by filtering out the salt.

They have large upper eyelids that provide protection for their eyes, from the sun and any irritants, and internal ears with no external ear opening. They have an excellent sense of smell, but no teeth – instead they have serrated bony plates which they use to grind and chew their food, and their jaws have modified into a range of beaks to suit their particular diet.

They have a large bony shell which protects them from predators and from scrapes and abrasions. The top part is called a carapace, which ranges in shape from oval to heart-shaped, and the bottom of the shell is the plastron. In all species except the leatherback, the carapace is covered in scutes, bony plates or scales, and the number, pattern and shape of them helps scientists to identify the species.

Sea turtles have evolved into an aquatic creature after once living on land. Their front flippers evolved from land limbs to help them swim, and are long and paddle-like, while their back flippers help them with propulsion and steering, stabilising and directing them, and are used by females to dig a nest to lay her eggs.

Another clever sea turtle adaptation is that they are immune to the sting of the deadly box jellyfish, and are even able to eat them, which helps keep the beaches safe for other species, including humans. They also help the marine ecosystem by munching on seagrass, which needs to be kept short to help it grow and spread, vital because these seagrass beds provide breeding and developmental grounds for numerous marine life, including dugongs.

Sea turtles are air-breathing marine reptiles, and inhabit all of the world's oceans except the Arctic. They are usually quite solitary, and primarily interact with each other for courting and mating, then go their separate ways. Their shell is streamlined for swimming through the water – they are characterised by their large, sleek shell as well as their non-retractable head and limbs. Land turtles can retract their head and legs back into their shell when they feel threatened, but sea turtles can't as it is part of their body.

They can live for up to eighty years, and were here before the dinosaurs. Sadly they may soon go the way of the dinosaurs though, as all the sea turtle species are on the IUCN World Conservation Union Red List, which means they face a high risk of global extinction. Scientists fear that leatherbacks in particular could be extinct within the next decade.

In the legends of the Americas, sea turtles were highly revered. On the islands off the east coast of Nicaragua, the creator was believed to be the Turtle Mother. Further north, one creation myth speaks of the earth once having been all water, with nowhere for the animals to live, until a giant turtle arose from the seas and offered its shell as a home, and thus North America was born, an island perched on a turtle's back. Others claim the name refers to the shape of North America being like a turtle. All these stories and legends encourage respect for the earth and the oceans, and all the marine creatures.

Millions of sea turtles once swam peacefully through the planet's oceans, but today all the remaining species are considered incredibly endangered. They are hunted in some regions for food, accidentally caught then killed as by-catch in the modern fishing industry, and the victims of habitat destruction, oil spills and pollution. Several species have been described as "the most endangered of all", which points to the threat to all of them.

Green sea turtles (chelonia mydas) are the largest of all the hard-shelled sea turtles. They are so named not because of the colour of their shell, which is a golden brown, but because their flesh is green – and sadly it's still considered a delicacy in some nations, which is one more threat to its survival. This is the only sea turtle that is herbivorous – although as a youngster it eats some protein, it stops this at maturity, which is at around twenty years old, and from then on feeds on seagrasses and algae. The other sea turtles are carnivores and have a diet of jellyfish, sea squirts, sponges, soft corals, crabs, squids and fish. Green sea turtles are listed as endangered, which means they'll soon be extinct if the threats to their survival continue.

Leatherback sea turtles (dermochelys coriacea) are the largest of all the sea turtles, and the only species with a soft leathery shell, which has a texture like hard rubber. Adult leatherbacks can reach two metres in length (more than six feet), and weigh more than nine hundred kilos (two thousand pounds), and are most notable for their deep diving ability. They feed mostly on jellyfish, and they range wider than other sea turtle species, partly because they are able to stand colder water thanks to the thick, oily layer of fat under their skin, which keeps them warm, and their ability to turn off blood flow from their cold extremities. They are listed as critically endangered, the highest risk category assigned, which means numbers have decreased, or will decrease, by eighty per cent or more within three generations – if they're not already extinct. It takes some time to quantify that a species has become extinct, and those in danger, like the leatherbacks, may already have gone.

Kemp's ridley sea turtles (lepidochelys kempii) are the smallest of them all, weighing between thirty and fifty kilos and growing to around seventy-five centimetres (thirty inches) in length. They live almost exclusively on the Atlantic coast of Mexico, and feed mainly on crabs. They change colour as they grow up – the hatchlings are grey-black all over, while adults have a lighter grey-olive carapace but are creamy-white or yellowish underneath. When they are mature, their shell is as round as it is wide. They are also listed as critically endangered, and some scientists believe it is already too late to save this species.

Olive ridley sea turtles (lepidochelys olivacea) are named for the colour of their heart-shaped shells. They're also known as Pacific ridleys. Like their cousin the Kemp's ridley, they are smaller than other species. The hatchlings are dark grey, but they appear all black when wet, and they darken as they mature. Traditionally they have been hunted for food – particularly the eggs – as well as bait, oil, leather and fertiliser. They are listed as endangered.

Hawksbill sea turtles (eretmochelys imbricata) are named for their pointed, beak-like mouths, which they use to forage in rocky crevices for sea sponges. Unfortunately their shell is so beautiful that it's often hunted for that alone. Yep, tortoiseshell jewellery and artefacts traditionally came from real turtles, and some still do. There is a black-market demand for authentic tortoiseshell, which is used for decoration as well as for its supposed health benefits. They lay up to two hundred and fifty eggs at a time, but survival rates are low and they too are listed as critically endangered.

Loggerhead sea turtles (caretta caretta) are named for their large heads. Western Australia is the location of the two major breeding sites, at Turtle Bay on Dirk Hartog Island in the Shark Bay World Heritage Area and the Muiron Islands near Ningaloo Marine Park. There are also large populations of green, hawksbill, olive ridley, leatherback and flatback turtles in these waters, and the Department of Environment and Conservation's Western Australian Marine Turtle Project centred around Shark Bay is a vital research area. They're also found in warm temperate waters around the world, and migrate hundreds of kilometres between nesting and feeding grounds, with some known to travel from Japan all the way to Mexico to lay eggs. They are listed as threatened, although some consider them the most endangered sea turtle species in the world – they are *all* on the edge of extinction, and need to be protected.

Flatback sea turtles (natator depressa) are native to Australia and Indonesia, and are the only sea turtle species that breeds and nests exclusively there. Their name comes from their shell being flat (funnily enough!). They primarily eat sea cucumbers and crustaceans – and saltwater crocodiles eat them, actively hunting for nesting turtles. Hatchlings are light tannish-grey with black outlines along the carapace, while mature flatbacks have a yellow-grey or green-grey oval shell. It was once believed to be related to the green sea turtle, but it is not, and it now has its own genus. Their conservation status is not confirmed due to lack of data, but their restriction to Australian shores adds to their danger of extinction.

The main threats to sea turtles are pollution and changes to their natural habitats, such as coral reefs, seagrass beds, mangrove forests and nesting beaches, all of which are caused by humans. They are also vulnerable to over-harvesting of turtles and eggs, the predation of eggs and hatchlings by foxes, feral pigs, dogs and goannas, boat strikes, drowning after being trapped in fishing nets and fishing gear, four-wheel driving on nesting beaches, industrial development and disturbance from artificial lights, which can throw off their breeding patterns and be fatal to hatchlings.

If you live near a turtle nesting beach, turn off outdoor lights or at least shield or lower them. In some beachside areas all the streetlights are a special kind of glowing orange, so the turtles don't get confused and think a streetlight is the moon. At night they use the lunar light and its reflection to find their way to the water. Artificial lighting also discourages females from coming ashore and laying eggs, which has a huge effect on turtle numbers and their ability to increase their population. It also confuses the hatchlings and messes with their sense of direction, causing them to head inland instead of out to sea, where they could be run over or harmed in many ways. Also be aware of when they are nesting and hatching, and keep out of their way.

Another major threat to sea turtles is the black-market trade in eggs and meat, particularly in the Philippines, India, Indonesia, Mexico and Nicaragua. A few years ago in the Philippines, Chinese poachers were apprehended with more than a hundred sea turtles and ten thousand sea turtle eggs.

Injured sea turtles are sometimes rescued and rehabilitated by organisations such as the Mote Marine Laboratory in Sarasota, Florida; the Marine Mammal Center in Northern California; the Clearwater Marine Aquarium in Clearwater, Florida; Sea Turtle Inc on South Padre Island, Texas; Chelonia Wildlife Rehabilitation & Release Centre in Broome, Western Australia; and Projeto TAMAR in Brasil, which has been protecting sea turtles for three decades, while also educating and transforming local turtle hunters into turtle protectors and creating alternative employment for them so they no longer have to catch sea turtles to survive.

This is where I first saw sea turtles, in large pools constructed along a beach in Bahia, Salvador, where they have developed a very successful breeding program, and also rehabilitate injured creatures. The conservation workers build small structures around each beach nest to protect the hatchlings from being trampled by people or animals, or the sand becoming compacted over them so they can't get out of the nest. By 2008 TAMAR, an abbreviation of Tartarugas Marinhas, Portuguese for sea turtles, had released more than eight million turtles into the sea. The project has now grown to include many sea creatures, including sharks, as they are all part of the delicate marine ecosystem on which the sea turtles rely.

In the Nicholas Sparks book (and Miley Cyrus movie) *The Last Song*, the young heroine learns a lot about life, and herself, by looking after a turtle nest on the beach near her dad's house, and preventing people and predators from harming it, either purposely or accidentally, through lack of awareness. We can all learn from these beautiful creatures, and all of nature, and be inspired to help them survive – which is all part of the greater web of life, and will help us to survive too.

Lesley's Sea Turtle Magic

Wildlife rehabilitator Lesley Baird created the Chelonia Wildlife Rehabilitation & Release Centre in Broome, Western Australia, to help sick and injured sea turtles. It's the only dedicated rehabilitation centre for sea turtles in the state, and is fully voluntary. She takes in around seven hundred animals a year, and has saved dozens of hawksbill, loggerhead, flatback and green sea turtles, along with many birds and reptiles. To find out more visit www.chelonia.org.au.

I came out of the womb loving animals. I lived across the road from my primary school, but I was constantly picking up animals I wanted to keep just in that short walk home. My mother had to send me back to return them. My first memories are of kissing my beloved fox terrier Inky, and for the first seven years of my life I pretty much lived in the chook yard – the girls were my friends, I read stories to them and played games such as doctors and nurses. Now my family are my animals – I have two dingoes, two dogs and a number of cats. I could not live without animal companionship.

Before I started Chelonia I worked as a bird carer with another group, and started rehabilitating turtles. The group had a committee and human egos and other frailties that made it hard to work there, so I broke away and established Chelonia. I named it that because the group of reptiles that sea turtles belong to are chelonids.

Bip was the inspiration for me to start this work. She was a juvenile green sea turtle who came in suffering from floating syndrome. I didn't even know what that was at the time, and I didn't have any facilities for keeping sea turtles, so she started off in the bath. Over time I learned more, although I didn't get much help from other sea turtle people, because a mentality of "knowledge is power" seems to exist, so I had to learn most of what I know from my own experience.

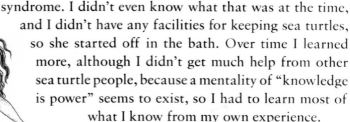

Bip recovered and survived to be released, more by luck than my good management I am sure, but she did and I was inspired to keep going. Maybe if she had died I wouldn't have pushed on with sea turtles. But she lived, and now I have saved many of them. They are the ancient gentle sentinels of the sea.

Sea turtles are by no means the Rhodes scholars of the ocean, but they each have their own little personality. I had a very special relationship with a large male flatback some years ago – if he had been human I think it would have gone further. His name was Hercules and he used to flirt with me. When we released him he swam out to the open ocean, and when he was at the swell line, where with a few more strokes he would have been out of the line of sight, he raised his right flipper out of the water, looked back and waved, then was gone. There wasn't a dry eye amongst the small group who'd helped me carry him down to the water.

The sea turtles all learn to come to you when you approach the tank, most love to have a scratch on the back, some are very affectionate, and others bear a grudge at being in captivity and fight you at every turn. But I respect and love those characters too, they are the fighters. The average stay in rehab is three months for a sea turtle – a small number are out quicker, and quite a few stay much longer. And after all the hard work there is nothing like the reward of seeing a rehabilitated sea turtle sprint out from the shore and swim strongly back to the freedom of the ocean. The fact that they are all endangered adds a special reward and sense of achievement.

To help sea turtles, people should be acutely aware of discarding rubbish, and of not using chemicals and poisons outside as they wash their cars and tend to their gardens. Everything that hits the ground near the sea has a very good chance of ending up in it – pollution caused by toxins washed into the sea settles on the turtles' food and gets mistakenly eaten, which can kill them, as well as rubbish such as cigarette butts, ring-pulls, bits of twine, discarded fish hooks and fishing line, plastics – the list goes on and on.

People should also not drive on the beach, and should exercise respect if they encounter a nesting turtle, keeping their distance, because interference can disrupt the egg-laying process. Every nest, every egg, every hatchling is precious and is worth its weight in gold.

Marine Conservation

"How inappropriate to call this planet Earth,
when clearly it is Ocean."
Arthur C Clark, British author and inventor

Cleaning Up Our Oceans and Savings its Creatures

The seas, rivers and lakes of the world cover more than seventy per cent of the planet's surface – with ninety-seven per cent of this water comprised of ocean alone. These waters provide us with drinking water (oceanic evaporation is the source of most rainfall), generate most of the oxygen we inhale, supply the major source of protein for half the world's population, and regulate our climate, which is affected to a large degree by the temperature of the ocean.

Yet we continue to pollute our rivers, dry up lakes and trash the ocean. We pump sewage and chemicals into them. We carelessly discard rubbish that is killing marine life. Our guzzling of petrol means companies are searching for ever more pristine locations to find the crude oil required – which places the ocean and its creatures at risk of major oil spills that take years to clean up, and impact on the health of the environment immediately as well as far into the future. A year after America's 2010 Gulf Oil Spill, hundreds of decomposing dolphins were still washing ashore, and the death toll of sea turtles, birds and other marine animals continues to climb.

Mining and agriculture leach toxic chemicals into the soil, which end up back in our waterways. Australia's 2011 Queensland floods sent cascades of contaminants into the ocean that are damaging not just the marine creatures who live in it, but also the

Great Barrier Reef – a vital ecosystem on which many plants, corals, aquatic animals as well as people depend.

In Japan (and other nations), dangerous levels of mercury have made their way into the oceanic food chain via high carbon emitting industries, and are having a devastating effect on everything from the tiniest sea creatures to apex predators like sharks, dolphins, marlin and tuna – and on the humans who eat them. Mercury is the world's most toxic non-radioactive element, and high levels can destroy the brain and nervous system and lead to death.

When Louie Psihoyos, head of the Oceanic Preservation Society, was in Japan filming environmental documentary *The Cove*, he was alarmed at the high levels of mercury found in the dolphins slaughtered there, which contained up to five thousand times the safe limit prescribed by the Japanese government. He was further shocked while having lunch with the doctors he was interviewing – when he asked why he was the only one eating the sushi, they said they hadn't eaten any fish since they started testing those at the top of the food chain for mercury poisoning. Louie eats no meat, but in America he consumes lots of fish. He got tested, and had forty parts per million (ppm) of mercury in his blood – one ppm is considered high. He had to stop eating fish altogether to get his levels down.

"Dolphin flesh is essentially a toxic waste dump for all the mercury we pump into the atmosphere in the emissions from coal-fired power stations and cars," Louie says. "Dolphins and whales are polluted mainly because of the dumping in the ocean of toxins from man's activities. The burning of fossil fuels, particularly coal, contributes to most of the build-up of mercury in the environment, so getting us off coal is important in saving the oceans."

His point reinforces the interconnectedness of our planet. Dust and sand from the Sahara Desert ends up in Florida. Coal plants in India or China pollute the whole world, not just one nation. (Equally, one country curbing their emissions will have a positive impact on the whole world's atmosphere.) Rubbish thrown off one coastline will contaminate marine life in every ocean. Nickel, lead or arsenic particles swallowed by a tiny river fish in the southern hemisphere could one day, through the extensive oceanic food chain, end up on a dinner plate in the north. Toxic whale and dolphin meat that's crushed to make fertiliser can affect rice products bought anywhere. Industrial pollutants from inland gold or copper mining can travel down river and into the global ocean. A decision in Australia to buy a reusable stainless steel water bottle rather than multiple single use plastic ones could save the life of a Hawaiian sea turtle. Even normal urban runoff can send nitrogen, phosphorus and other nutrients into lakes, rivers, oceans and water supplies, causing unhealthy outbreaks of algae that pollute the water and kill off vital phytoplankton. The pond across the road from me has a warning that the water is not safe for drinking or even touching, for humans or pets, because of such an outbreak.

We Need to Change Climate Change!

Climate change is another serious concern – it's raising ocean temperatures and increasing the amount of carbon dioxide in the atmosphere. Surprisingly it's not just trees that absorb carbon dioxide from the air – oceans and coastal ecosystems also play an important role in the global carbon cycle, acting as a natural carbon sink that accumulates and stores carbon-containing chemical compounds. (Landfills and carbon capture facilities are artificial forms of these sinks.) Scarily though, the increasing amount of carbon dioxide in the atmosphere is turning the ocean acidic, which impedes its ability to absorb this compound, impacting on marine life and fish distribution, and thus fishing economies and food sources. Corals are already being affected, and given that they are an important part of many marine ecosystems, this will ultimately impact on all of the animals and people of our planet. Sea levels are also rising, and some small islands are already feeling the effects as the waters slowly lap at their shores, threatening to one day swallow them entirely.

A recent study led by oceanographer Samar Khatiwala of Columbia University's Lamont-Doherty Earth Observatory confirmed that the ocean plays a key role in regulating climate, absorbing more than a quarter of the anthropogenic (human-created) carbon dioxide that's created through emissions from fossil-fuel use and deforestation, and concluded that the oceans are struggling to keep up with rising emission levels. "The ocean plays a crucial role in mitigating the effects of this perturbation to the climate system, sequestering twenty to thirty-five per cent of anthropogenic CO_2 emissions," Samar wrote. "But the more carbon dioxide you put in, the more acidic the ocean becomes, reducing its ability to hold CO_2. Because of this chemical effect, over time the ocean is expected to become a less efficient sink of man-made carbon."

A study by National Oceanic and Atmospheric Administration scientists also found that large amounts of acidified water are upwelling close to the Pacific continental shelf off North America – a vital area where much marine life lives and breeds – which could have serious consequences for fish stocks and ocean health.

So regardless of whether climate change is caused by man or not (an ongoing debate that's a favourite delaying tactic of politicians in order to distract from the real issue), we need to do something. And while it should certainly be an international, government- and industry-led change, we can all do little things to reduce our carbon footprint. Imagine if every person on earth made just a tiny change!

One of the most obvious and easiest to change threats to the ocean is the way some people treat our waterways like a tip. Marine debris is human rubbish such as plastic bags, the plastic six-pack rings around drink cans and discarded fishing line, which floats on the ocean or is suspended within it. It's incredibly lethal to bird and aquatic life, and is pushing many species to the brink of extinction. Flimsy plastic shopping bags are particularly dangerous to sea turtles, who think they are moon jellyfish and eat them. When the bags break down into smaller pieces, jellyfish and other small creatures start to consume them, so they enter the food chain in a new way and end up inside various larger animals too. When swallowed by a marine creature, such plastic debris can lodge inside their stomach and block up their digestive system, causing infections that can kill them or forcing them to slowly starve to death. Others end up fatally injured through entanglement, or suffocated by the rubbish. Many dead birds and fish have been found with a stomach full of plastic debris such as bottle caps, discarded machine parts, plastic containers and other bits and pieces. Albatross and other large sea birds are particularly susceptible to this because floating debris often becomes coated with seaweed, algae, crustacean eggs or other marine life, so that it looks like food and they eat it.

Discarded or broken fishing nets are also a huge issue – dubbed ghost nets, they trap thousands of sea creatures who either drown because they can't surface to breathe, such as dolphins and sea birds, or are strangled and suffocated in the net.

Eighty per cent of marine debris is plastic, which takes years and years to biodegrade, if it will at all. Even when it does start to disintegrate, the smaller pieces become a danger to a new group of aquatic animals, and later the miniscule invisible molecules that remain are poisonous to sea life for years. A new phenomenon, called the Great Pacific Garbage Patch, has formed between the USA and Japan. This huge patch of litter – believed to be at least twice the size of Texas – is the result of converging ocean currents, which pick up litter originating from other coastlines and force it to this location. Made up of plastics and other debris, along with chemical sludge, effluent and all the poisonous, toxic chemicals that arise as plastic breaks down, this Pacific Trash Vortex is especially bad news for the Hawaiian Island chain, which is located in the middle of the Pacific Ocean.

One beach in particular, Kamilo on the Big Island, is now famous for its accumulation of plastic marine debris that washes ashore from the Great Pacific Garbage Patch, and the danger it presents to all marine life, including endangered sea turtles who use the beach to lay their eggs. Before a recent clean-up, the debris was three metres high. One year, volunteers removed four hundred huge garbage bags of debris along with ten tonnes of fishing nets, and a year later four million more pieces of plastic were collected.

It's not just objects thrown directly into the sea that pollute the oceans. Cigarette butts dropped on city streets are swept into drains, harsh chemicals used to wash clothes make their way to the sea, litter blown out of car windows or dropped in the bush can travel much further than you'd imagine. Some of the millions of plastic water bottles discarded every day can travel for miles on ocean currents and wash ashore in a faraway place. And then there's all the pollution that can't be seen – poisonous chemicals, toxic minerals, even, up until the 1960s, radioactive waste that was poured into the ocean because it was believed that it would dilute enough to do no harm.

There's also the sound pollution from ships, oil rigs, naval sonar and jet skis, amongst other things, that affect marine creatures. In Taiji in Japan, fishermen shepherd the dolphins into the killing bay by banging steel poles on the side of their boats – as sound is the primary sense of cetaceans, loud noises confuse and terrify them, and send them off course. According to oceanographer Sylvia Earle: "Undersea noise pollution is like the death of a thousand cuts. Each sound in itself may not be a matter of critical concern, but taken all together, the noise from shipping, seismic surveys and military activity is creating a totally different environment than existed even fifty years ago. That high level of noise is bound to have a hard, sweeping impact on life in the sea."

Make Your Own Difference, However Small

There are lots of small ways we can help protect the marine ecosystem, and the more we do, the bigger the overall impact.

✶ Pick up rubbish along the beach. Dispose of your own rubbish considerately, and try to cut down on the disposable packaging you use, from takeaway containers to beauty product wrapping.

✶ Switch to stainless steel drinking bottles instead of buying lots and lots of small plastic ones, which will save you money and save the environment. The amount of landfill these take up is horrifying, as is the energy used to make them – let alone what they do when they find their way to the ocean. My drink bottle is covered in affirmations, which according to Dr Masaru Emoto changes the structure of the water inside, charging it with positive energy and emotion, and making it more healing to drink.

✶ If you must buy bottles of water, look for ones that give profits to a water charity – there are still millions of people worldwide who don't have access to clean water, or have to walk miles to get it – and reuse it for as long as you can. Australian company Water For Water (www.waterforwater.com.au) raises money to provide safe drinking water for some of the more than three million people, mostly children, who die every year from water-related diseases.

✶ Be aware of your water usage, and recycle it when you can, such as catching shower water for your garden. According to the organisers of the annual World Water Day, each year fifteen hundred cubic kilometres of wastewater is produced globally. While this can be reused productively for energy and irrigation, it usually is not.

✳ Instead of just throwing up your arms in horror because a petrol company wants to explore for natural gas, consider your usage. The oil has to come from somewhere because we demand it for our cars. Boycotting BP, or any other company, will just make them cut costs further, impacting on safety measures and increasing the danger to the marine environment. There have been many oil spills in the last hundred years, by many companies.

✳ Be aware of your power – and your responsibility – as a consumer. You don't have to stop driving, or flying, or eating certain foods, you just need to become responsible for your choices and aware of the consequences of them. If you must eat fish, ensure it is "dolphin safe". Put pressure on companies to fish ethically. When travelling, request that hotel towels and sheets are not changed every day.

✳ Learn more about marine conservation and encourage further education. Pro surfer and environmentalist Dave Rastovich wants surf schools to include information on cetaceans, and it's a great idea – all of us who love the ocean, whether we spend time in it or not, need to become more connected to it, and more a part of the solution.

✳ Support the creation of more marine parks, and let politicians know how important they are. Overfishing also threatens the delicate balance of our ecosystems, and is starting to impact on human food sources as well as the upper food chain predators, like dolphins, who are running out of things to eat. (One of Japan's excuses for slaughtering dolphins is that they eat too many fish!)

Campaign For More Marine Parks

Other sea creatures also need protection, and environmental groups are pushing for at least half of the world's oceans to be declared no-take areas or marine sanctuaries, so fish stocks can increase, endangered animals can be protected, and other marine life can survive and start to thrive again. The WWF reports that three hundred thousand whales, dolphins and porpoises are killed each year as by-catch – where unplanned marine creatures are swept up in fishing dragnets along with the targeted species. Cetaceans, who breathe air like us, get trapped in these nets and are unable to surface for air, so they drown. Those that survive to make it to the deck of the boats are killed and discarded once the haul of tuna, for example, has been picked out. By-catch is one of the greatest threats facing cetaceans around the world. Lots of marine animals also get trapped and die in shark nets, including sea turtles, dolphins and sharks.

Marine sanctuaries are created to protect habitats and ecosystems, improve commercial and recreational fisheries by protecting breeding grounds, protect threatened species, support research and education, manage introduced marine pests, reduce the risk of pollution by excluding oil and gas developments and improve ecotourism opportunities while conserving cultural heritage. There are currently five thousand marine protected areas around the world, which doesn't even encompass one per cent of the ocean's surface. Recently the island nation of Palau dedicated most of its waters as a marine park, and also created the world's first shark sanctuary.

The Great Barrier Reef Marine Park on the east coast of Australia was until recently the largest in the world. It's the biggest natural feature on earth, stretching more than two thousand kilometres, and the largest coral reef system. It also has seagrass, mangrove, sand, algae and sponge garden habitats, amongst others. It protects many threatened species, including dugongs and sea turtles, and is home to six hundred species of echinoderm (starfish and sea urchins), fifteen hundred species of fish, three hundred and sixty species of hard coral and five hundred species of marine algae – with many relying on each other for food, habitat control and survival.

Australia has fifteen Marine Protected Areas, including the beautifully named Mermaid Reef Marine National Nature Reserve near Broome, and the federal government has committed to creating more. America has fourteen National Marine Sanctuaries, including the largest, the Papahanaumokuakea Marine National Monument surrounding the Northwestern Hawaiian Islands, which was created in 2006, and countries including New Zealand, France, Sweden and Greece all now have at least some areas in which aquatic species can successfully breed, recover and live, and many nations develop their protected areas in consultation with others in their region.

There are various different zonings and levels of protection, which restrict human activity in certain ways in order to protect resources – anything from limiting building development and policing what fishing gear can be used to restricting fishing seasons, putting limits on catch loads and even implementing complete bans on removing marine life of any kind.

Marine Conservation : Eco Warriors

"I have been honoured to serve the whales, dolphins, seals and
all the other creatures on this earth. Their beauty, intelligence,
strength and spirit have inspired me. These beings have spoken to me,
touched me, and I have been rewarded by friendship with many
members of different species. If the whales survive and flourish,
if the seals continue to live and give birth, and if I can contribute
to ensuring their future prosperity, I will be forever happy."
Captain Paul Watson, animal rights and environmental activist

Inspiring Environmental Groups and Causes

There are many, many wonderful organisations dedicated to
protecting the oceans and waterways of the world, as well as the
diverse life forms that make their home in the aquatic environment.
They all rely on supporters donating their time, passion and money,
and all do incredible work. We're not suggesting any are more
worthy than others or more deserving of your support, and nor is
this a complete list. But we do encourage you to contribute to a
cause that inspires you, be it with a donation of money or time, a
fundraising effort to support a cause close to your heart, or an email
campaign to lobby governments to do more for the oceans, such as
zoning more areas as marine parks or pressuring international
governments to follow whaling regulations. If you have a favourite
charity or cause we haven't mentioned, email us the info, at
MermaidMagics-Book@yahoo.com.au, and we'll add it to our website.

Sea Shepherd

In an informal poll of friends, Sea Shepherd was voted the favourite marine protection group. Controversial and inspirational, the Sea Shepherd Conservation Society is dedicated to research, investigation and enforcement of laws, treaties, resolutions and regulations established to protect marine wildlife worldwide. It's led by Captain Paul Watson, who is loved and loathed in equal measure, but is so passionate about his cause that he puts his life on the line to protect the animals he loves so much. Whatever you think of his methods, it is very moving to understand the depths of his commitment.

Their mission statement explains: "Established in 1977, Sea Shepherd Conservation Society is an international, non-profit marine wildlife conservation organisation. Our mission is to end the destruction of habitat and slaughter of wildlife in the world's oceans in order to conserve and protect ecosystems and species. Sea Shepherd uses innovative direct-action tactics to investigate, document and take action when necessary to expose and confront illegal activities on the high seas. By safeguarding the biodiversity of our delicately-balanced ocean ecosystems, Sea Shepherd works to ensure their survival for future generations."

Paul is described as a modern-day pirate – a compliment from some, an insult from others. Whaling nations, seal hunters and illegal shark poachers claim he's a terrorist, but Paul insists his actions fall within international law, in particular the right to enforce regulations against illegal whalers and sealers, and Sea Shepherd has never harmed a person in the pursuit of its mission to stop illegal whaling, drift-netting, dolphin slaughter and sealing. What many critics forget is that the group is enforcing existing laws against those who are flouting them in defiance of the wishes of governments and people. And he is supported by many peace-lovers, including the Dalai Lama, who says: "I am happy to lend my support to those who, like the volunteers of the Sea Shepherd, seek to protect our oceans and our fellow creatures like the whales who live in them."

Paul has always cared about animals. As a kid in Canada, he'd find and destroy beaver traps, disrupt deer hunters and prevent other boys shooting birds. In 1969, aged eighteen, he started Greenpeace with friends, and he was one of the founding members and directors (his official membership number was and continues to be 007, which seems fitting!). In 1975, he and Robert Hunter were the first to put their lives on the line to protect whales – placing their tiny inflatable boat between a Russian harpoon vessel and a pod of these majestic sea creatures. And it was this moment that set Paul on his life path.

A giant harpooned whale in its death throes loomed over them. "I thought, this is it, it's all over, he's going to slam down on the boat," he says. "But instead he pulled back. I saw his muscles pull back. It was as if he knew we were trying to save them. As he slid back into the water, drowning in his own blood, I looked into his eye and I saw recognition. Empathy. What I saw in his eye would change my life forever. He saved my life and I would return the favour."

In 1977, Greenpeace became opposed to direct action campaigns. Paul left because he felt their original goals were being compromised, and formed Sea Shepherd. Best known for their missions to stop Japanese whalers in Antarctic waters, they also negotiated an end to the dolphin slaughter of Iki Island, Japan, have sent crews to Taiji and to the Solomon Islands, and are working with the National Marine Park service in the Galapagos Islands of Ecuador on anti-poaching enforcement and conservation programs. They've been fighting sealers since they began, and continue to do so, saving hundreds of thousands of seals from slaughter using many different and creative methods, and they are also waging a battle to save sharks from decimation. Visit www.seashepherd.org.

Paul's top tip to save the oceans? "Stop eating the ocean. Don't eat anything out of the ocean – there is no such thing as a sustainable fishery. If you eat meat, make sure it's organic and isn't contributing to the destruction of the ocean, because forty per cent of all the fish caught is fed to livestock – chickens on factory farms eat fishmeal."

Oceanic Preservation Society

This is a non-profit organisation that creates movies, photos and other media to raise awareness and inspire people to save the ocean. Founded in 2005 by photographer and avid diver Louie Psihoyos, their first film *The Cove* won dozens of awards, including the Oscar for Best Documentary, and inspired more than a million people to action. This exposure of the horrifying slaughter of dolphins in Japan led to greater awareness, international pressure and an end to school children being fed toxic dolphin meat. They also had an LA eatery shut down after their undercover filming exposed the fact that they were serving endangered whale meat in their sushi.

OPS provides valuable information about the issues facing the world today, including the toxic levels of mercury in fish, underwater noise pollution and marine mammals in captivity, and how to make more responsible choices as a consumer, how to be an advocate and many ways to volunteer to help the cause, including helping Global Vision International (www.gvi.co.uk, www.gviusa.com) on one of their conservation initiatives and community projects that run for anywhere from one week to two years. Visit www.opsociety.org.

Save Japan Dolphins

This group was formed by Ric O'Barry to put an end to the Japanese slaughter of dolphins and the capture and live trade to zoos and aquariums around the world. Ric inspired *The Cove*, which documents his work to halt the senseless slaughter of dolphins in Japan each year. He forced worldwide pressure, gathered petitions with more than two million signatures from a hundred and fifty countries, and continues investigating and monitoring the killing cove in Taiji and exposing the mercury in Japanese dolphins.

Ric spent the 1960s capturing and training dolphins, including the five females who played the role of *Flipper* in the popular US TV series. When one of these dolphins died suddenly in his arms – committing suicide, he insists, because of the horror of living in captivity – Ric realised that taking dolphins out of their natural habitat and training them to perform tricks is wrong, particularly when they are starved to force them to do so, and he has dedicated the past forty years to fighting the dolphin captivity industry. The group's website lists many ways you can help, including petitions to sign, letters to send and pledges to commit to.

Although the situation in Japan is the major focus of Ric's work, he is also a leading voice in the fight to end brutal dolphin hunts wherever they occur, including the Solomon and Faroe Islands, and close down the captive dolphin trade worldwide. He has rescued and released more than twenty-five captive dolphins in Haiti, Colombia, Nicaragua, Brasil, the Bahamas and the US, and works tirelessly as a voice for the dolphins at international government meetings, in the media and on the ground (and beaches). The image of him standing with a video screen strapped to his chest for days on end in a busy mall in Japan to raise awareness about Taiji moved me deeply, and his passion and commitment is breathtaking. He's the Marine

Mammal Specialist for Earth Island Institute, Huffington Post's 2010 Most Influential Green Game Changer, on O magazine's Power List of Men We Admire for his "Power of Passion" and author of the inspiring books *Behind the Dolphin Smile* and *To Free A Dolphin*.

Ric stars in his own Animal Planet series *Blood Dolphins*, with his son Lincoln, who is the creator and producer. It picks up where *The Cove* left off, following the father and son team to Indonesia, Egypt and the Solomon Islands, where, after four hundred and fifty years of killing dolphins, villagers agreed to stop. He's also mobilised the celebrity world, knowing that getting Robin Williams, Sting, Jennifer Aniston, Ben Stiller, Mariska Hargitay and other stars on board is a sure-fire way to get publicity and bring this important issue to the world. Visit www.savejapandolphins.org.

Earth Island Institute

This is an umbrella organisation involved with more than sixty projects that work for the conservation, preservation and restoration of the earth, including Save Japan Dolphins. It has a long and active history in dolphin-related causes. In 1986, through the International Marine Mammal Project, they pressured US tuna companies to end the intentional chasing and netting of dolphins with purse seine nets, and to adopt "Dolphin Safe" fishing practices. They used consumer pressure, litigation and revisions of the Marine Mammal Protection Act, and in 1990 the first companies pledged to become dolphin safe. Today one hundred per cent of US tuna is verifiably dolphin safe, and EII regularly inspects tuna companies to ensure it remains that way.

Since 1982, the Earth Island Institute has been a hub for grassroots campaigns dedicated to conserving, preserving and restoring the ecosystems on which our civilisation depends, acting as an incubator for start-up environmental projects, giving crucial assistance to groups and individuals with new ideas for promoting ecological sustainability, and providing fiscal sponsorship to more than a hundred projects around the globe. They also inform and inspire people to take action through their quarterly magazine *Earth Island Journal*, and their New Leaders and Restoration initiatives, which highlight the amazing accomplishments of young people working for sustainability, provide emerging leaders with mentoring resources, and fund community-based coastal protection and wetland restoration efforts. Visit www.earthisland.org.

Surfers For Cetaceans

An Australian-based volunteer group that mobilises surfers and ocean crew worldwide against the harassment, capture and killing of cetaceans and other marine mammals, and for coastal and marine conservation, it seeks to be a human voice for and defender of cetaceans worldwide, and is committed to activating ocean-minded people everywhere to support the conservation and protection of whales, dolphins and all marine life.

It was founded by pro surfer Dave Rastovich and artist and activist Howie Cooke in 2004, to educate surfers on environmental issues and help create sanctuaries for dolphins, whales and porpoises that are caught in driftnets and slaughtered. They joined with OPS for a front-line expose of Japan's annual dolphin drives, and in 2007 they held two peaceful ceremonies in the killing cove in Taiji, the first when no dolphins were being killed, the second in the blood-stained waters as the fishermen slaughtered a pod of twenty-four. With international media present, the group of surfers and celebrities managed to slow the kills and expose the brutal reality to millions of people worldwide. They also held protests outside Japanese embassies in Australia and educated children through school visits.

S4C co-created the Humpback Whale Icon Project with IFAW and The Oceania Project, in which towns along the Australian coast adopt one of the whales that pass by twice a year. The acknowledgment of individual whales, identified by their unique body markings, raised awareness, increased education and celebrated whale migration, an important step in saving them. They also oganised TransparentSea, in which Dave and a group of surfers went on a thirty-six-day, eight-hundred-kilometre kayaking odyssey following whales down Australia's east coast, to highlight their plight when they get to the Southern Ocean and are at the mercy of the Japanese whaling fleet. In conjunction with Surfrider and Tangaroa Blue, they also participated in beach clean-ups along the route and highlighted other areas of environmental concern.

S4C focuses on cetacean issues due to the human-cetacean relationship surfers have – they both ride waves for the sheer joy, so their love for dolphins and whales is born of interaction in the ocean, which creates compassion and kinship. Visit www.s4cglobal.org.

International Fund for Animal Welfare

IFAW began four decades ago in response to the horrific slaughter of harp seals in Canada. They drew international attention to the plight of seal pups and successfully rallied worldwide condemnation of the hunt – thanks to their continued vigilance, it is now illegal to hunt whitecoat seal pups for commercial purposes on the ice floes off Canada's east coast. The fight is not over yet though, and they continue to document and expose abuses of other commercial hunt laws. They've also expanded to fight for all animals and against all cruelty, from seals, dolphins and whales to bears, elephants and primates, as well as helping pets through dog and cat rescues and the deliverance of free or low-cost spay and neuter services, and providing education to prevent animal cruelty. Visit www.ifaw.org.

Greenpeace

Despite criticism for not being confrontational enough, Greenpeace continues its important environmental work. It addresses key threats such as overfishing, by-catch, pollution and industrial and pirate fishing through campaigns to put whaling on trial, protect dolphins, improve fishing processes, amongst many others. They encourage supporters to lobby governments and big business, protest and get educated about the issues. While they also campaign to save forests, address climate change and find alternatives to nuclear energy, the health of the oceans and its inhabitants remains a priority, and they've had victories in diverse areas, from pressuring chemical giant Clorox – which uses a mermaid in their ads – to phase out the use and transport of dangerous chlorine gas to forcing seafood suppliers Gorton's, Sealord and parent company Nissui to withdraw their active support for Japanese whaling. Visit www.greenpeace.org.

Environmentalist, mermaid and Sea Shepherd collaborator Daryl Hannah's tip? "If Greenpeace would join forces with Sea Shepherd they would shut down the whaling industry right away."

International Bird Rescue

In 1971, two oil tankers collided beneath San Francisco's Golden Gate Bridge, spilling more than three million litres of crude oil into the bay. Despite the attempts of hundreds of volunteers, only three hundred birds survived from the seven thousand collected, as little was known then about oiled bird care. A small group of these volunteers started International Bird Rescue, with the aim of developing cleaning and rehabilitation techniques, promoting ongoing research and providing response capabilities. Since then they have responded to an increasing number of oil spills, cared for more than a hundred and forty species of birds, mammals, reptiles and amphibians, and become California's primary bird response group.

They operate wildlife hospitals, develop better treatments for aquatic birds, and run education programs in oil spill response for volunteers, the petroleum industry, government fish and wildlife agencies, wildlife rehabilitators and researchers, and have helped manage the rehabilitation efforts in more than two hundred oil spills, including the 1989 Exxon Valdez spill in Alaska and the 2010 Deepwater Horizon spill, during which Lucy and I adopted a pelican and a duck through their program, as did many friends.

On World Oceans Day 2010, IBR's executive director Jay Holcomb was named Oceana's Ocean Hero for leading the bird rescue effort in the Gulf of Mexico. "It is poignant that I won this award in the midst of the greatest oil spill in US history," Jay says. "I've always approached my work as trying to change the world one bird at a time. I hope this award reminds people that whatever we can do personally to protect our ocean does make a difference, no matter how overwhelming the task may seem." Visit www.bird-rescue.org.

Protect Our Coral Sea

The Coral Sea is a tropical marine jewel located east of the Great Barrier Reef Marine Park, which extends to Australia's maritime borders with Papua New Guinea, the Solomon Islands and New Caledonia. It features spectacular coral reefs, remote islands, towering underwater mountains and deep-sea canyons, and is home to whales, dolphins, sea turtles, sharks, rays and seabirds – yet less than one per cent is protected, and many fishermen now operate boats there as overfishing closer to home pushes them further afield.

Global icon of marine conservation Dr Sylvia Earle is patron of the Coral Sea Campaign, which urges the government to declare it the largest marine heritage park on earth, a no-take zone that would be like a Kakadu on the water, and become a "hope spot" for the oceans. "The Coral Sea is a rare thing – a place where majestic ocean-going fish can still be found in great numbers. In the last fifty years, the world has lost ninety per cent of these large ocean creatures due to overfishing. We need to do all we can to protect one of the world's last remaining refuges," she says.

Acclaimed author and environmentally aware surfer Tim Winton also urges action. "Marine parks are needed because our oceans are fragile and in trouble. We still have the notion that the ocean is inexhaustible, irrepressible and indestructible, that it can go on forever, survive anything you drag out of it and everything you tip into it. Well, most coastal people's experience and the overwhelming science shows that's just not true," he says. "The Coral Sea is one of the last places on earth where the greats of the ocean deep, like tuna, sharks and marlin, swim wild in healthy numbers. This is a once-in-a-lifetime opportunity to protect them."

Other ambassadors include Australian actress and dolphin campaigner Isabel Lucas, tennis star Pat Rafter, fashion designer Akira Isogawa and Netscape founder and executive producer of *The Cove* Jim Clark. The Wilderness Society, Whale and Dolphin Conservation Society and International Fund for Animal Welfare also support the campaign. Visit www.protectourcoralsea.org.au.

Oceana

Founded in 2001, this is the largest group focused solely on ocean conservation. They believe science is vital to identifying solutions, and their scientists work with economists, lawyers and advocates to achieve tangible results, aiming to return the world to a place where dolphin sightings are common, marlins and tuna are abundant, whales and sea turtles thrive, and fish are a safe, growing and plentiful food source. They conduct research around the world, and the resulting photo and video documentation of rare species, as well as illegal fishing, provides evidence to protect vulnerable species and habitats. They also work to reduce overfishing and destructive fishing practices, to combat climate change and its effects on the ocean, and advocate for clean energy. They propose new marine protected areas and lobby for them to be legislated, and work towards oceans free of mercury and other toxins. They have a newsletter, info on global campaigns, material on marine creatures and their endangered status, locations that need protection, articles on ocean science, a safe seafood guide, a plastics pledge you can make, and more. Doreen Virtue commits a percentage of her salary to them because of the important work they do to save our oceans. Visit www.oceana.org.

Project Save Our Surf

This Southern California group advocates for clean beaches and oceans and to protect surf breaks. It brings together influential people of means in order to make positive change. Founded by actress and surfer Tanna Frederick to raise funds for and awareness of clean water issues, they run fundraising events to support environmental groups such as Surfrider Foundation and Heal the Bay. Their Surf 24 charity event featured surfing, mural painting, arts and education projects, volleyball, yoga and eco-friendly food, as well as actors including *True Blood*'s Sam Trammell and *24*'s Eric Balfour taking to the waves in a comp against pro surfers. They have also joined the Save The Waves Coalition in support of the Malibu World Surfing Reserve. Visit www.projectsaveoursurf.org.

Australian Marine Wildlife Research & Rescue Organisation

Project Dolphin Safe began in 1998 in response to the brutal killing of six dolphins in Adelaide's Port River Estuary. Three were shot, two were stabbed with spear guns and the sixth died from starvation as her mother was murdered. The group patrolled the waters so the dolphins could swim freely, and began restoration of sensitive habitats, educational talks, community clean-up days and rescue responses if dolphins were injured or seabirds entangled in fishing tackle. After a presentation by Australian Seabird Rescue, the members of Project Dolphin Safe started a local Seabird Rescue group, and now the two groups have merged into the Australian Marine Wildlife Research & Rescue Organisation, which provides marine wildlife services to South Australian ocean and estuary waters.

They recently rescued two green turtles who were "floaters" – animals that are unable to dive to any depth to feed due to gases that have developed under their shell due to gut impaction, a result of eating plastic and other man-dropped rubbish. These two turtles were nursed back to health, then flown to Queensland for release. AMWRRO is the only organisation in South Australia licensed by the Department for Environment and Heritage to actively rescue and rehabilitate marine life. They also raise awareness through school and community education programs about the importance of maintaining a contaminate-free environment. Visit www.amwrro.org.au.

International Dolphin Watch

Headed by Dr Horace Dobbs, International Dolphin Watch is a non-profit organisation for the study and conservation of dolphins, and a global family of dolphin lovers. Education, for children and adults, is a large part of what they do, and they also carry out research into wild (not captive) dolphins in order to know how to better protect them. They study the effects of dolphin healing too, investigate ways in which the benefits of swimming with wild dolphins can be recreated artificially, and support Operation Sunshine, which offers kids with severe mental disadvantages the opportunity to swim with dolphins (www.operationsunshine.org).

Their aim is to ensure the seas and rivers are clean, healthy and productive for the benefit of both humans and dolphins, to encourage respect for the rights of dolphins to a free life in their natural environment, and to recognise that dolphins have long had an affinity with humans, and allow this to evolve. They lobby governments, press for laws to be upheld when they're infringed, and urge changes in legislation that will help save dolphins and protect the oceans. They also work with like-minded organisations on the rescue and treatment of stranded and injured marine mammals, and forge links with indigenous peoples to find ways to apply their ancient wisdom of the natural world to help solve our ecological crisis.

IDW has saved the lives of countless dolphins, enabled thousands of people to swim with wild ones, and formulated guidelines on how to behave in the presence of dolphins for swimmers and boat users (listed on their website). Members receive newsletters about wild dolphins around the world and places to see them, updates on campaigns against captive situations, information on their other dolphin projects, and the chance to participate in the joy of dolphins at whatever level you wish with others from around the world.

Their non-profit Virtual Dolphin Project explores the uplifting experience of interacting with cetaceans and finds new and creative ways of bringing this joy to ill or disabled children who can't meet dolphins in the wild. They do this by replicating the experience using modern technology. Captive dolphins are never used. The work they do brings joy to very sick children, and donations to further this work are always welcome. Dr Horace Dobbs has written several wonderful books about dolphins, for children and adults, and they have a great online shop. Visit www.idw.org.

Whale and Dolphin Conservation Society

Established in 1987, this is dedicated to the welfare of cetaceans and their habitats. They provide a world voice, creating pressure to bring about change, and aim to reduce then eliminate the continuing threats to whales and dolphins, including hunting, captivity, chemical and noise pollution, ship strikes and entanglement in fishing nets. They fund campaigns and projects across the globe, and encourage supporters to get involved in their ongoing work, such as campaigns to stop Icelandic whaling, to create twelve new Marine Protected Areas for whales and dolphins by 2012 and to protect the dolphins of Scotland's Moray Firth as well as river dolphins in developing countries, as they are amongst the most endangered in the world.

Their website contains cetacean news from around the world, both happy and sad, info on current campaigns and petitions to sign, guides to different species, a kids' zone to educate children and more. The WDCS is an international organisation with offices in the UK, USA, Germany, Argentina and Australia, which all contribute to international issues, as well as including campaigns tailored to each region. The head office in Australia is in Adelaide, with a key focus on the welfare of the Port River dolphins by marine biologist Dr Mike Bossley. His twenty years of work with the local dolphins is one of the most detailed studies in the world. Visit www.wdcs.org.

The Oceania Project

Australia's Oceania Project, established in Byron Bay in 1988, is a not-for-profit research and information organisation dedicated to raising awareness about cetaceans and the ocean environment. They have been studying, photographing, filming and recording the humpback whales that visit Hervey Bay, Queensland, each year, which provides new insights into the behaviour and social organisation of the species and how they are using the area. You can participate in their annual whale research expedition, and there is a youth project for teens to take part in whale and dolphin expeditions. The website includes news about cetaceans, protection and conservation, and the shop offers photos, documentaries, songs, sounds and more. They offer research cruises to observe humpback whales around Hervey Bay, and a wide range of information about cetaceans, with excellent links. Visit www.oceania.org.au.

The Marine Mammal Commission

This US body is the governmental watchdog organisation responsible for monitoring the status of marine mammals. It was created under the Marine Mammal Protection Act of 1972 to protect and conserve marine mammals. Their website provides information on the activities, programs and publications of the commission and its committee of scientific advisors, and conveys other relevant information on the conservation and protection of marine mammals and their ecosystems. Visit www.mmc.gov.

World Society for the Protection of Animals

WSPA's vision is of a world where animal welfare matters, and animal cruelty ends. They've been promoting animal welfare for three decades, working on issues including whaling, live exports, factory farming, disaster management, captive bears, commercial exploitation of wildlife, responsible pet ownership, humane stray management and animal cruelty matters. With consultative status at the UN and Council of Europe, WSPA is the world's largest alliance of animal welfare societies. They lobby governments and key decision makers to change practices and introduce new laws to protect or improve the welfare of animals, help people set up new animal welfare groups and, knowing that human ignorance is a major factor in the continuation of animal cruelty, their education programs facilitate a positive change in people's attitudes towards animals. Visit www.wspa.org.au and www.wspa-international.org.

Australian Conservation Foundation

This group promotes a wide range of environmental issues, including land management, climate change, nuclear issues, forests, oceans, environmental law reform, water preservation and ecologically sustainable development. It focuses on advocacy, policy research and community education rather than hands-on projects, protecting and sustaining the environment by educating people to make changes. You can read up on all manner of topics, support them financially or use the website to educate yourself and make a difference. Their EarthKids section encourages children to get involved in saving the planet, with information, practical solutions and fun activities, and you can sign up for the Green Home Challenge and learn how to tread more lightly on the earth. Visit www.acfonline.org.au.

Sea Watch Foundation

Founded in 1991 by Dr Peter Evans, Sea Watch is a UK marine conservation research charity dedicated to protecting cetaceans. Its work contributes to international understanding of marine mammals and their environment, and the development of biodiversity action plans. Sea Watch scientists monitor and study whale and dolphin populations, gaining knowledge of their status, numbers and distribution as well as the condition of their marine habitats, so they can alert government, industry and eco organisations to problems, and prompt practical measures to protect them from existing and impending threats. They also provide a list of places to watch whales and dolphins in the UK, information on how to watch, and encourage the public to be part of their monitoring programs. Sea Watch has contributed to the legislating of protected areas and to an Agreement for the Conservation of Small Cetaceans in the Baltic and North Seas. They also run an Adopt a Dolphin scheme to protect the dolphins of Cardigan Bay, Wales. Visit www.seawatchfoundation.org.uk.

Save Our Seas Foundation

This group is committed to protecting our oceans by funding research, education, awareness and conservation projects focusing on the major threats to the marine environment. They have become a major player in the fight to save the world's oceans and the wealth of marine life they contain, and have provided financial and, equally important, practical assistance to more than a hundred and fifty marine research and conservation projects in locations spread around the world, in the vital areas of research, education, awareness and conservation. Visit www.saveourseas.com.

Sea Turtle Foundation

Sea turtles have existed for more than a hundred million years, but the oceans are now so dangerous for them, and human impacts have depleted their populations so badly, that we are in danger of losing them forever. This group works to protect and conserve marine turtles through research, education, awareness and action. Based in Townsville in Queensland, their mission is to safeguard sea turtle populations, migration routes and habitats, and support a range of activities that will help increase sea turtle numbers worldwide. Visit www.seaturtlefoundation.org.

Surfrider Foundation

This group focuses on clean water, beach access and preservation and protecting special places. It's a non-profit grassroots organisation dedicated to the protection and enjoyment of oceans, waves and beaches. Founded in 1984 by a group of surfers in Malibu, California, they now have more than fifty thousand members and ninety chapters worldwide, with each group focusing on local issues as well as worldwide concerns. Their achievements include winning the second-largest Clean Water Act lawsuit in American history, brought against two pulp mills that were charged with more than forty thousand violations of the law, blocking a marina which would have destroyed historic natural wetlands as well as vast areas of sandy coast, preventing breakwaters that would have degraded water quality, eliminated surf and destroyed kilometres of pristine coastline, protesting against a dioxin dump off the coast and restoring natural sand dune habitats.

In Australia, Surfrider is the peak coastal group, dedicated to the protection and enjoyment of the country's oceans, waves and beaches through conservation, advocacy, research and education. They advocate for sustainable management and use of the coastal zone, including coastal river catchments and offshore activities, were involved with S4C's TransparentSea vision, and work to increase awareness of the issues impacting enjoyment of the coast to ensure our children have similar opportunities to enjoy its clean water, biodiversity and spectacular landforms. Visit www.surfrider.org.

Project Aware Foundation

This diving group conserves underwater environments through education, advocacy and action. Their annual Splash for Trash Day is a huge underwater clean-up, and calls on all divers, snorkellers and water enthusiasts to help reverse the ocean debris issue by getting into the water to pick up rubbish. It also spearheads global underwater clean-ups year round to address the devastating impact of marine debris. It empowers dive centres and individuals to clean the world's oceans, lakes and rivers, and collects data that is vital for change. In 2007, more than three hundred and fifty thousand volunteer divers helped clean fifty thousand kilometres of coastline and remove three million kilos of rubbish. Visit www.projectaware.org.

Remove Shark Nets

This group campaigns to have the shark nets removed from beaches on the east coast of Australia, and to expose the truth about these popular safety precautions – that there is very little, if any, benefit to humans. They aim to educate people to abandon their fears about sharks and to understand their importance in the ocean ecosystem. For more than seventy years shark nets have been trapping sharks, as well as dolphins, whales, stingrays, turtles and dugongs, many of which die as a result. Their website explains the negative impacts of shark nets on marine creatures, and they hope to garner support to help this innocent yet greatly feared marine species which has no voice. Shark numbers around the world are declining – and Australia's shark control program is one of the things adding to the problem. The use of shark nets in Australia began in the 1930s, but it's since been found that they are an ineffective and unsustainable strategy. The website has a petition you can sign and lots of information, and you can volunteer time to educate people about sharks and dispel the scary myths, or be part of their events and community. Visit www.removesharknets.com.

Shark Savers

Another shark protection group is Shark Savers. Shark conservation is an enormous challenge because sharks are being fished out of the water by the millions each month and cannot reproduce fast enough to ensure their survival. In addition, they are not as sweet and friendly looking as dolphins or whales, so they struggle to get support. Yet the thing we should fear most about sharks is their looming extinction. Each year, up to seventy-three million sharks are killed, and a third of shark species are gravely threatened. In addition to the threats facing all marine creatures, sharks are relentlessly overfished to feed the demand for their valuable fins, the ingredient in the popular Chinese shark fin soup. Fishermen catch the sharks, cut off their fins then throw them back in the water. These sharks either die from suffocation or are eaten as they can no longer swim. Like them or not, we need sharks – as apex predators they're vital to the ocean and its fragile balance. Recent studies indicate that regional elimination of sharks can cause disastrous effects further down the food chain, including the collapse of fisheries and the death of coral reefs. Visit www.sharksavers.org.

Australian Seabird Rescue

This is a NSW conservation group known for their work in rescuing pelicans, and over the years their expertise has expanded to include all manner of seabirds, sea turtles and marine mammals. They travel around Australia providing seabird conservation and protection workshops to volunteers and government wildlife agencies. Members also undertake regular clean-up campaigns, removing tonnes of marine rubbish and domestic waste from our precious waterways. They are researching marine debris and its interactions with wildlife, and their work has already forced a change in legislation, with the introduction of a ban on the mass release of helium balloons in NSW. Australian Seabird Rescue has now gained an international reputation as a provider of not only seabird rescue services but also many associated activities. Visit www.seabirdrescue.org.

ORRCA

ORRCA is an Australian whale rescue organisation developing more effective ways to rescue whales and other marine mammals. They work with government agencies, and train people in marine mammal rescue. They also protect seals, sea lions, dolphins and dugongs, and their input is sought when legislative bodies are amending existing laws or introducing new ones. They assist with, monitor and give advice on marine animal entanglements, and are the only wildlife carers group in New South Wales licensed to be involved with marine mammal rescue, rehabilitation and release. Visit www.orrca.org.au.

Tangaroa Blue Ocean Care Society

Founded in 2004 to create awareness in the community of ocean conservation issues and proactively participate in and organise marine projects, this group is Australia-based, but also works in Hawaii and New Zealand, and on global issues. With the support of volunteers, community groups, industry and government agencies, they created the South West Marine Debris Project to target deadly marine rubbish along beaches around the world. It is estimated that in every square mile of ocean, forty-six thousand pieces of plastic are floating, and seventy-seven Australian species, twenty of which are already listed as endangered, are seriously impacted by this dangerous trash. Since the group started, more than half a million pieces of rubbish have been removed from beaches around Australia.

Data is also collected on items found, which is used to trace the most common objects back to their source, which can lead to changes being made in design or use to prevent the litter in the first place. Tangaroa is the Polynesian god of the sea and all that lives within its depths (including mermaids). The name highlights the importance of protecting our oceans and creating projects to help communities keep their local coast clean and healthy. Visit www.oceancare.org.au.

Australian Marine Conservation Society

AMCS is a voice for Australia's oceans, working to protect marine wildlife, create large marine national parks, make fisheries sustainable and protect and recover threatened ocean wildlife. They also work to protect fragile coasts from inappropriate development and human-created climate change. AMCS is a committed group of passionate scientists, educators and advocates who have defended the ocean for more than forty years. Their first achievement was to successfully contest and defeat a proposal to mine limestone on the Great Barrier Reef in the 1960s, which led to the campaign that secured the Great Barrier Reef as a marine park and later recognised it as a World Heritage Area. AMCS and its allies protected WA's Ningaloo Reef from an inappropriate marina development then secured a third of the Ningaloo Marine Park as a green zone, and also ensured shark finning at sea is now illegal in Australia. Visit www.amcs.org.au.

Worldwide Fund for Nature

This group works on many issues, including climate change, oceans, forests, species and industry. They invite people to take part by donating money, adopting an animal or volunteering time or skills. They support many animals, including panda bears and elephants, as well as whales, dolphins and sea turtles. In northern Australia, their marine debris tracking program, in partnership with Aboriginal communities, addresses the entanglement of marine wildlife in nets and other debris in the Arafura Sea. On WA's Ningaloo Coast, which is home to endangered sea turtles, WWF is part of the Ningaloo Community Turtle Monitoring Program. They also campaign for more marine sanctuaries, and have joined Save Our Marine Life (www.saveourmarinelife.org.au), a collaboration of global, national and state environmental organisations working to secure the future of Australia's southwest marine environment. Visit www.wwf.org.

About the Authors

Born under the sign of water, Lucy Cavendish is a witch who adores the ocean. She works magic every single day of her life, embracing it as a creed for personal and planetary fulfilment and happiness, and as a belief system that sees us all as part of nature, and thus gives us all the motivation to respect and revere and delight in our unique experience here on planet earth.

She is the author of *Oracle of the Shapeshifters*, *Oracle of Shadows & Light*, *The Book of Faery Magic*, *The Lost Lands*, *Wild Wisdom of the Faery Oracle*, *Oracle of the Dragonfae* and *White Magic*, and creator of the CDs *As Above So Below*, *Return to Avalon* and *The Seven Gifts of Faery*. She created *Witchcraft* magazine in 1992 and is a feature writer for *Spellcraft*, *Mermaids & Mythology* and *FAE*.

Lucy is a founding member of the Goddess Association in Australia, and an active member of the international Order of Bards, Ovates & Druids. She lives in Sydney with her pixie-like daughter and their plant allies and animal companions. She swims, surfs and walks the beach as often as possible. Join her on Facebook or visit her at www.LucyCavendish.com.

Serene Conneeley grew up by the ocean, and still loves connecting with water physically as well as magically. She is a writer and reconnective healer, and has studied magical and medicinal herbalism as well as politics and journalism. She's the editor of several children's magazines, and has written for *Cosmo*, *Dolly*, *New Idea*, *Woman's Day*, *The West Australian*, *Hot Metal*, *Spheres* and *Spellcraft*, and contributed to international books on witchcraft, psychic development and personal transformation.

Serene is the author of *Seven Sacred Sites: Magical Journeys That Will Change Your Life*, *The Book of Faery Magic* and *A Magical Journey: Your Diary of Inspiration, Adventure and Transformation*, and creator of the CD *Sacred Journey: A Meditation to Connect You to the Magic of the Earth*, which helps create a connection with the power of the elements and balances the masculine and feminine energies of your heart and soul.

She lives in Sydney with her sweet husband in their magical little purple realm, and loves swimming, snorkelling, sea turtles, hiking, reading, drinking tea and celebrating the energy of the moon, the tides of the ocean and the magic of the earth. She loves travelling, and the myth and mystery of ancient sacred places, but she's also discovered the wonder of finding true happiness and peace at home. Visit her at www.SereneConneeley.com.

CPSIA information can be obtained at www.ICGtesting.com
Printed in the USA
LVOW11s0415221214

419898LV00002B/468/P